Keeping the Promise of Social Security in Latin America

Keeping the Promise of Social Security in Latin America

Indermit S. Gill, Truman Packard, and Juan Yermo

With the assistance of Todd Pugatch

A COPUBLICATION OF STANFORD ECONOMICS AND FINANCE,
AN IMPRINT OF STANFORD UNIVERSITY PRESS, AND THE WORLD BANK

Stanford University Press   The World Bank
1450 Page Mill Road   1818 H Street, NW
Palo Alto, Calif. 94304   Washington, DC 20433

ISBN 0-8213-5817-0   (World Rights except North America)
ISBN 0-8047-5181-1 (hardcover)   (North America)
ISBN 0-8047-5238-9 (softcover)   (North America)

Library of Congress Cataloging-in-Publication Data

Gill, Indermit Singh, 1961-
Keeping the promise of social security in Latin America / by Indermit S. Gill, Truman
Packard, and Juan Yermo.
    p. cm. — (Latin American development forum)
    Includes bibliographical references (p.) and index.
    ISBN 0-8213-5817-0
    1. Social security—Latin America. I. Packard, Truman. II. Yermo, Juan, 1972- III.
Title. IV. Series.

    HD7130.5.G55 20004
    368.4'0098—dc22

                                  2004050929

Latin American Development Forum Series

This series was created in 2003 to promote, debate, and disseminate information and analysis, and convey the excitement and complexity of the most topical issues in economic and social development in Latin America and the Caribbean. It is sponsored by the Inter-American Development Bank, the United Nations Economic Commission for Latin America and the Caribbean, and the World Bank. The manuscripts chosen for publication represent the highest quality in each institution's research and activity output, and have been selected for their relevance to the academic community, policymakers, researchers, and interested readers.

Advisory Committee Members

Inés Bustillo, Director, Washington Office, Economic Commission for Latin America and the Caribbean, United Nations

Guillermo Calvo, Chief Economist, Inter-American Development Bank

José Luis Guasch, Regional Adviser, Latin America and the Caribbean Region, World Bank

Steven Haber, A. A. and Jeanne Welch Milligan Professor, Department of Political Science, Stanford University; Peter and Helen Bing Senior Fellow, the Hoover Institution

Eduardo Lora, Principal Adviser, Research Department, Inter-American Development Bank

José Luis Machinea, Executive Secretary, Economic Commission for Latin America and the Caribbean, United Nations

Guillermo E. Perry, Chief Economist, Latin America and the Caribbean Region, World Bank

Luis Servén, Lead Economist, Latin America and the Caribbean Region, World Bank

About the Contributors

Indermit S. Gill is an economic adviser in the Poverty Reduction and Economic Management Network at the World Bank. He received a Ph.D. in economics from the University of Chicago, and has extensive experience in the areas of labor policy and social insurance in Latin America, including service as lead economist for the World Bank's work on pension reform in Brazil. Before joining the Bank staff in 1993, he taught economics at the State University of New York at Buffalo.

Truman Packard is a senior economist in the Latin America and the Caribbean department of the World Bank. He began work on pensions in 1995, when he worked with Bank staff in Mexico to develop adjustment operations needed to support pension reform. Since then he has participated in analytical and lending assistance to support both pension reform and broader efforts to strengthen social insurance. His research focuses on how pensions and social insurance affect the efficiency of labor markets and incentives to save. He holds a Ph.D. in economics from the University of Oxford.

Juan Yermo is an administrator at the Organisation for Economic Co-Operation and Development in Paris, where he directs private pensions projects in the financial affairs division. He is currently secretary of the OECD Working Party on Private Pensions, which hosts biannual meetings where policymakers and representatives from the private sectors of 30 member countries survey pensions and advise members on policy issues. He manages a broad research program on the operation, regulation, and supervision of pension plans and funds, and has consulted for the World Bank Group on pension reform in Latin America. He holds master's degrees in economics from Cambridge and Oxford universities.

Todd Pugatch is a junior professional associate in the Poverty Reduction and Economic Management Network at the World Bank. Prior to joining the Bank he studied economics as a Morehead Scholar at the University of North Carolina at Chapel Hill, and as a Rotary Ambassadorial Scholar at the Universidad Nacional de Costa Rica. In 2005 he will begin a doctoral program in economics.

Contents

Foreword   xvii

Acknowledgments   xix

1 RETHINKING SOCIAL SECURITY PRIORITIES IN LATIN AMERICA   1

PART I. RETROSPECTIVE: FISCAL, FINANCIAL, AND
SOCIAL BENEFITS FROM PENSION REFORM   17

2 STRUCTURAL REFORMS TO SOCIAL SECURITY IN
LATIN AMERICA   19

3 THE FISCAL SUSTAINABILITY OF PUBLIC PENSION
PROMISES IN LATIN AMERICA   39

4 THE FINANCIAL BENEFITS OF PENSION REFORM   57

5 SOCIAL GAINS FROM PENSION REFORMS IN LATIN AMERICA   89

PART II. ANALYTICAL: HOW GOVERNMENTS
CAN HELP INDIVIDUALS DEAL WITH RETIREMENT   107

6 HOW INDIVIDUALS VIEW SOCIAL SECURITY   109

7 HOW WELL HAS THE "SAVINGS" COMPONENT
PERFORMED FROM THE INDIVIDUAL'S PERSPECTIVE?   125

8 THE PREFERENCES THAT INDIVIDUALS REVEAL   165

PART III. PROSPECTIVE: THE FUTURE OF SOCIAL SECURITY
IN LATIN AMERICA   197

9 PREVENTING POVERTY IN OLD AGE: IMPROVING
   THE POOLING COMPONENT   199

10 FACILITATING CONSUMPTION SMOOTHING: IMPROVING
   THE SAVINGS COMPONENT   227

11 THE WAY FORWARD   267

   Technical Annex. Assumptions of PROST Simulations   283

   Appendix. Background Papers for *Keeping the Promise*   291

   Bibliography   293

   Index   321

BOXES
1.1   Three Central Dilemmas of Pension Privatization   3
3.1   Bolivia's Pension Reform: A Transition
       Considerably More Costly Than Expected   45
3.2   Virtuous and Vicious Fiscal Circles: The Cases of
       Chile and Argentina   47
4.1   The Importance of Concomitant Reforms in the
       Financial System   64
4.2   Inflation-Indexed Securities in Latin America   74
5.1   Defining the Coverage Problem: What Is It and
       Why Do We Care?   95
5.2   Was Increasing Coverage an Objective of
       Pension Reform?   97
6.1   The Welfare State as a Piggy Bank to Reduce
       Old-Age Income Insecurity   110
6.2   A Theory of "Comprehensive Insurance"   113
7.1   The Four Fundamental Risks in Retirement
       Income Security Systems   127
7.2   Comparing Notional Defined Contribution Systems
       and Pension Funds Invested in Inflation- and
       Wage-Indexed Government Bonds   128
7.3   Argentina's System in Crisis: Do Private Accounts
       Protect Workers from Policy Risk?   133
7.4   Points to Keep in Mind When Comparing
       Risks in Pension Fund Portfolios in
       Latin America   137

8.1   PRIESO: Social Risk Management Surveys in
        Chile and Peru   176
8.2   Peru's Reformed Pension System: Multipillar in
        Name Only   179
9.1   The *Cuota Social*: Preventing Poverty among
        Elderly Men and Women in Mexico   208
9.2   BONOSOL: Bolivia's Universal Pension Program   210
10.1   The Big-Bang Approach to Voluntary Pension
        Savings Reform in Chile   248
10.2   The Role of the Financial System in Brazil's
        Voluntary Pension Savings Plans   250
11.1   The Role of the Second Pillar   278

FIGURES
1.1   Pension Systems Cover between 10 and 60 Percent
        of the Economically Active Population in
        Latin American Countries   6
1.2   Between One-Tenth and Two-Thirds of the
        Aged Populations Receive Pensions in
        Latin American Countries   7
2.1   Rising Life Expectancy Increases the Share of
        Elderly People in the Population and Upsets
        the Balance of Pure PAYG Pension Systems   20
2.2   Destination of Mandatory Pension Contributions   29
3.1   Simulated Implicit Pension Debts (IPDs) with
        and without Structural Reforms   40
3.2   Total Pension Debt (Explicit) Accumulated
        after 2001, with and without Structural Reforms   43
3B.1   Cash Flow Gap in Bolivia   45
3B.2a   Chile Was Fiscally Strong prior to Reform;
        Argentina Was Not   47
3B.2b   Pension System Deficits Contributed Significantly to
        Deteriorating Fiscal Balance in Argentina   48
3.3   There Is No Indication That Pension Reform
        Increased Mexico's Country Risk   52
4.1   Pension Funds Are Major Investors in
        Government Debt   63
4.2   Interest Rate Spreads Have Declined in Peru and
        Bolivia Since the Reforms (1993–2002)   79
4.3   Stock Market Turnover Ratios in Selected
        Latin American Countries (1990–2001)   81
5.1   Structural Reforms Are Likely to Improve Equity by
        Lowering Regressive Transfers and Returns   91

5.2   Structural Reforms Make the New Systems More
        Gender Neutral, but Women's Average Benefits
        Can Be Significantly Lowered by the Use of
        Gender-Specific Mortality Tables   92
5.3   Pension Income Increases Inequity Relative
        to Earned Income from Labor   94
5.4   Has Participation Increased? There Is No Clear
        Pattern in Data on Contribution to National
        Pension Systems   100
7.1   Pension Funds Invest Mainly in Government
        Bonds and Instruments Issued by Financial
        Institutions   132
7.2   The Standard Trade-Off between Risk and
        Return Has Not Materialized in Latin America
        (Returns from Inception to December 2000)   136
7.3   In Chile Intercohort Differences in Returns
        Have Been Large   139
7.4   Returns on Deposits in Chile Have Been Lower
        but More Stable Than Pension Fund Returns   140
7.5   Brady Bonds Would Have Been a Better Investment
        Than Domestic Equities for Peruvian Pension Funds   141
7.6   Variable Commission Rates Have Risen as a Result of
        Declines in Contribution Rates in Argentina and Peru   147
7.7   Half of the Pension Contributions of the
        Average Chilean Worker Who Retired in
        2000 Went to Fees   148
7.8   Participation in the Second Pillar Is Costlier for
        Poorer Workers in Chile   149
7.9   Annuities Have Yielded Varying Levels of
        Retirement Benefits in Chile   154
7.10   Chile's Pension Funds Did Not Do a Good Job of
        Educating Participants: *Fondo 2* Had Few
        Takers Despite Earning Higher Returns   156
7.11   Chilean Workers' Choices in the New Multifund
        System Largely Correspond with the Default Options   158
7.12   Choices Are Similar for Different Income Groups
        in Chile If Controlling for Age   159
8.1   Chile: Reported Contribution Density   180
8.2   There Is No Difference in Risk Preferences between
        Employees and Self-Employed Workers Who
        Responded to the PRIESO Survey in Chile   182
8.3   Self-Employed Workers Who Contribute to the AFP
        System in Chile Have a Greater Tolerance for Risk   183

8.4   Peru: Reported Contribution Density   184
8.5   There Is No Difference in Risk Preferences between
        Employees and Self-Employed Workers in Peru   187
8.6   Self-Employed People in the AFP System in Peru
        Are More Risk Averse   188
9.1   Rising Life Expectancy Increases the Share of
        Elderly People in the Population and Upsets the
        Balance of Pure Pooling Pension Systems   200
9.2   Accumulated Wealth Increases with Age and
        Is Greatest among Old People   204
9.3   Relative Generosity and Cost of Alternative
        Public Poverty Pension Arrangements in
        Selected Countries   212
9.4   Average Noncontributory Pensions Are between
        30 Percent and 60 Percent of Average Contributory
        Pensions   217
10.1   In Peru, Fees Remain Persistently High, Despite
        Increasing Returns and Declining
        Administrative Costs   234
10.2   Savings Products Offered by Insurers Are More
        Popular Than the AFPs' Liquid *Cuenta 2*   249
10.3   Mutual Funds Have Grown Significantly Only
        in Brazil, Where Pension Funds Are Voluntary   252
10.4   Fees for Equity Mutual Funds in Chile Have
        Remained Stubbornly High   255
10.5   Economies of Scale in Fund Management Kick in
        at Low Asset Levels   256
10.6   Insurance Company Bankruptcy Is a Threat to
        Policyholders   258
11.1   Coverage Can Vary at Similar Stages of Economic
        Development   274

TABLES
1.1   Instruments of Old-Age Income Security   10
2.1   Principal Features of Structural Reforms to Social
        Security Systems (Old-Age Disability and Death)
        in Latin America during the 1980s and 1990s   23
2.2   Principal Features of Structural Reforms to Social
        Security Systems (Old-Age Disability and Death)
        in Latin America during the 1990s and 2000s   26
2.3   Contribution Rates and Earnings Ceilings in
        the Mandatory Funded Systems   32
2.4   Voluntary Funded Pillars in Latin America   35

3.1   Current Pension Deficits (Benefit Expenditures Less
      Contribution Revenue) Financed by
      Government Transfers   42
4.1   Portfolio Ceilings by Main Asset Classes
      (December 2002)   61
4.2   Portfolio Floors by Country   62
4.3   Assets Held by Pension Funds Have Doubled as a
      Percentage of GDP (December 1998–December 2002)   62
4.4   Pension Funds Invest Mainly in Debt of Governments
      and Financial Institutions (December 2002)   67
4.5   For the Average Latin American Country, the Two
      Largest Institutions Control Two-Thirds of the
      Pension Funds (December 2002)   68
5.1   There Is Evidence That Pension Reforms
      Positively Affect Incentives   102
5.2   Participation Rates and Incidence of Benefits
      Show a Regressive Pattern of Coverage by
      Formal Pension Systems   104
6.1   Justifying a Government-Imposed Mandate to
      Save for Old Age—Microeconomic Reasons   117
6.2   Justifying a Government-Imposed Mandate to
      Save for Old-Age—Macroeconomic Reasons   120
7.1   Gross, Real Returns to Pension Funds Have
      Been High   130
7.2   Asset Allocation and Portfolio Limits   142
7.3   Workers Still Pay High Commissions in
      Some Countries (December 2002)   145
7.4   The Form of Benefits Is Usually Inconsistent
      with an Assumption of Retiree Irrationality with
      Respect to Saving   151
7.5   The Five New Funds in Chile Vary by Proportion
      of Equity Investment   157
8.1   Probability That Workers Contribute to Social
      Security Is Determined by Individual, Household, and
      Labor Market Factors   171
8.2   Reformed Pension Systems in Chile and Peru Are
      Similar, but There Are Important Differences   178
9.1   Poverty among Elderly People Is as Frequent as
      among Other Age Groups When Measured by
      Current Income   202
9.2   Expenditure on Noncontributory Pension Programs   215
9.3   Noncontributory, Poverty Prevention Pensions Cover a
      Significant Portion of Pension Recipients   216

9.4   As a Share of Average Wages, Minimum Wages
        Are Relatively High in Chile, Colombia, and
        Some Other Latin American Countries   218
9.5   Cost of Providing and Guaranteeing a Public
        Pension Equal to the Minimum Wage   220
10.1   Reform Options to Reduce the Operational
        Expenses of the New Private Second Pillar   235
10.2   Reform Options to Ensure That Savings Are
        Passed on to Affiliates as Lower Commissions   240
10.3   Reform Options to Improve Investment and
        Longevity Risk Management   243
TA.1   Assumptions Common to All Country Cases   283
TA.2   Country-Specific Details, Assumptions, and
        Sources of Data   284
TA.3   Assumed Profiles of Representative Affiliated
        Men and Women   289

Foreword

AT PRESENT, NATIONS AROUND THE WORLD (both large and small, rich and poor) are engaged in debate over how to reform their social security systems and care for the aged. For many countries this debate requires speculation on hypothetical scenarios, but in Latin America a rich body of experience on social security reform has been accumulating for more than a decade (for Chile, more than two decades). *Keeping the Promise of Social Security in Latin America* takes stock of those reforms, evaluates their successes and failures, and considers the lessons that can be drawn for the future of pension policy in the region. The authors draw on a series of background papers and surveys commissioned specifically for this inquiry, as well as existing research conducted by themselves and other pension experts. The report was also enriched by discussions with policymakers, pension fund industry managers, and academics at a regional conference held in Bogotá, Colombia, on June 22–23, 2004.

The task of assessing reforms that are still in progress must be undertaken with both caution and humility. But the stakes are high, and it would not be advisable to wait until the reforms have run their course. This study is intended to inform an ongoing debate, not to end it.

The authors find that structural reforms undertaken in Latin America in the last two decades mark a major improvement in many dimensions with respect to the earlier pay-as-you-go systems. In particular, reforms reduced fiscal liabilities, contributed to financial sector development, and improved the equity of pension systems, although there is still much to be done in these areas. Most importantly, the shift to individual accounts was a major structural improvement to the income-smoothing objective of pension systems for most current contributors. But there have also been significant disappointments, chief among them the failure to extend access to social security to a broader segment of society.

More than just an empirical assessment of reforms, this volume is also an attempt to rethink the priorities of social security systems in the region. The authors argue that the main priority of any publicly established pension system should be to prevent poverty in old age. If preventing poverty among old men and women is the most important policy priority, then the extent of coverage must be the most important criterion by which to judge any formal social insurance system. Detractors of social security reform in Latin America have rightly criticized the failure of reforms to increase coverage, despite any positive effects reforms may have had on fiscal balance sheets or financial sector development. This report meets the detractors in that arena, by analyzing why coverage has not adequately increased following reform and discussing the range of appropriate policy responses.

The authors argue, thus, for increased attention to the poverty prevention function of social security and a less prominent role for mandated savings. They claim that Latin America has not paid enough attention to pillars "zero" or "one"—those pillars whose main purpose is precisely to avoid the risk of falling into poverty in old age. They also argue that excessive attention has been paid to "pillar two" (mandated individual savings accounts) and not enough to the "third pillar" (voluntary savings). They do *not*, however, propose a "corner solution" composed of just pillars one (or zero) and three in all cases. The authors recognize the need to strike a balance between people's improvidence in planning for old age, on the one hand, and a government mandate to save, on the other—both of which can cause damage. Finding a suitable equilibrium between these tensions is a delicate task and one on which even experts can disagree. The appropriate final balance will depend, among other things, on the degree of development of financial systems, institutional capabilities, and past history of pension systems. The proper design of pillars "zero" and "one" is also difficult, as bad designs may encourage moral hazard and provide additional disincentives to participate in the formal labor market. Furthermore, the transition toward the desired system is not easy. Developing a strong zero or first pillar will be demanding in fiscal terms, requiring many countries to first finalize the "first generation" reforms in order to reduce the large fiscal liabilities that still exist today in favor of highly privileged middle- and high-income individuals. Meanwhile, developing a zero pillar must be weighted against the priorities of other poverty prevention programs.

Some of the ideas presented in this book may strike some readers as radical. However, in the debate on pension reform there is no orthodoxy, as reflected in major differences of opinion among leading experts in this area of policy. Despite more than a decade of experience with pension reform in Latin America, although undoubtedly a major step forward, reforms are still works in progress. No magic formula for success exists. We hope that this report will further enrich an already vibrant policy dialogue that is of crucial importance to the future of the region.

Guillermo Perry
Chief Economist, Latin America and the Caribbean Region
World Bank Group
July 2004

Acknowledgments

THIS BOOK HAS BEEN PREPARED BY A TEAM led jointly by Indermit S. Gill (Senior Economic Adviser to the Poverty Reduction and Economic Management Network Vice President, World Bank) and Truman G. Packard (Senior Economist, Social Protection, World Bank), consisting of Juan Yermo (Economist, Private Pensions and Insurance Unit, Organisation for Economic Co-operation and Development), Todd Pugatch (Junior Professional Associate, Poverty Reduction and Economic Management Network, World Bank), Asta Zviniene (Social Protection Specialist, World Bank), Norbert Fiess (Economist, Office of the Chief Economist, Latin America and the Caribbean Region), Salvador Valdés-Prieto (Consultant, Catholic University, Santiago de Chile), Rafael Rofman (Senior Economist, Latin America and the Caribbean Region), Abigail Barr (Consultant, Oxford University), Oliver Azuara (Consultant, World Bank), and Federico Escobar (Consultant, World Bank).

This volume was prepared under the overall guidance of Guillermo Perry (Chief Economist, Latin America and the Caribbean Region). Luis Servén (Regional Studies Coordinator) and Xavier Coll and Ana-Maria Arriagada (Sector Directors, Human Development during 2000–02) ensured generous funding. The team also acknowledges the financial support and technical guidance of the World Bank's Research Support Budget. Chris Chamberlin (Sector Manager, Social Protection, Latin America and the Caribbean Region) provided encouragement, general guidance, and technical comment in the final stages of preparation, and Augusto de la Torre (Senior Adviser, Office of the Chief Economist, Latin America and the Caribbean Region), Hermann Von Gersdorff (Lead Economist), Anita Schwarz (Senior Human Resources Economist), Robert Holzmann (Sector Director, Social Protection, Human Development Network), Michal Rutkowski (Sector Manager, Social Protection, Eastern Europe and Central Asia Region), Robert Palacios (Senior Pensions Economist), Jean-Jacques Dethier (Lead Economist, Development Economics Research

Group), Roberto Rocha (Lead Economist, Financial Sector Operations and Policies), Fernando Montes-Negret (Sector Manager, Finance Cluster, Latin America and the Caribbean Region), David Lindeman (Principal Pensions Analyst, Organisation for Economic Co-operation and Development), Andras Uthoff (Coordinator, Special Studies Unit, Economic Commission for Latin America and the Caribbean, United Nations), Maureen Lewis (Interim Chief Economist, Human Development Network), Marcelo Giugale (Country Director, Bolivia, Peru, Ecuador, and Venezuela), and William Maloney (Lead Economist, Office of the Chief Economist, Latin America and the Caribbean Region) provided valuable feedback and comment on the concept paper and earlier drafts of the book. Neither these individuals nor the World Bank are, however, responsible for its contents.

This book synthesizes 16 background papers specially commissioned for the book. Simulation analysis conducted by Asta Zviniene with the World Bank's *Pension Reform Options Simulation Toolkit* (PROST) is cited throughout the book. The background papers were written by Oliver Azuara, Abigail Barr, Federico Escobar, Norbert Fiess, Truman Packard, Rafael Rofman, Salvador Valdés-Prieto, Juan Yermo, and Asta Zviniene. The background papers are listed in the appendix at the back of this volume and are available online at the Web site of the Office of the Chief Economist, Latin America and the Caribbean Region: www.worldbank.org/keepingthepromise.

Naoko Shinkai, Ricardo Fuentes, Enrique Mezanotte, Elizabeth Dahan, and Mauricio Cifuentes provided invaluable assistance in conducting research and analysis.

This book has also benefited immensely from the comments of peer reviewers inside and outside the World Bank. The peer reviewers for this task were Anita Schwarz, Dimitri Vittas (Senior Adviser, Financial Sector Development, World Bank), Dean Baker (Center for Economic and Policy Research), and Olivia Mitchell (University of Pennsylvania–Wharton Business School), who provided detailed comments, and to whom the team owes a debt of gratitude. Again, these individuals are not responsible for the contents and messages of this book.

The book was also greatly enriched by the presentations and comments of participants in a regional conference on pension reform, hosted by the World Bank and FEDESARROLLO, held June 22–23, 2004, in Bogotá, Colombia. Of particular value were discussions with Luis Fernando Alarcón (Private Funds Association, Colombia), Mariano Paz Soldán (Profuturo AFP, Peru), Bernhard Lotterer (Integra AFP, Peru), Fernando Muñoz-Najar Perea (AFP Association, Peru), Ligia Borrero (Banking Superintendency of Colombia), Kristhian García Aranda (Finance and Public Credit Ministry, Nicaragua), Francisco Perez (FEDESARROLLO, Colombia), Carmelo Mesa-Lago (University of Pittsburgh), Fabio Bertranou (International Labour Organization), Guillermo Larrain (Superintendency of Pension Fund Administrators, Chile), Augusto Iglesias (PrimAmerica Consultants, Chile), and Amparo Ballivian (World Bank).

Finally, the authors would like to thank the social security and pensions supervisory authorities in Argentina, Bolivia, Brazil, Chile, Colombia, El Salvador, Mexico, Peru, and Uruguay for providing much of the data used in this analysis.

1

Rethinking Social Security Priorities in Latin America

TWO DECADES AGO CHILE'S GOVERNMENT radically altered its approach to old-age income security. Simply put, it changed the basis of public pensions from collective to individual: instead of the widely used system that pooled the risk of being unable to earn while aged, the Chileans adopted a system that relied on mandatory individual savings accounts. The shift was seen by its detractors as a retreat from "solidarity," and by its supporters as a move toward greater "personal responsibility." Neither characterization is entirely correct, but a debate has raged ever since on the shift's main effect: has the change left Chileans better or worse off?

An important event in this debate was the World Bank's 1994 publication of *Averting the Old Age Crisis*. The report explained that the existing approach to ensuring income support for elderly people was unsustainable, it neatly characterized the institutions involved using a novel terminology, and it prescribed a new doctrine for better addressing the challenges in this difficult area of public policy.

Using the terminology suggested in *Averting the Old Age Crisis*, the new approach has come to be called the "multipillar" model of old-age income security.[1] Although this approach has been used by reformers worldwide, it can be safely asserted that no region has taken it more seriously than has Latin America. In addition to Chile, governments in 11 countries—Peru (1992), Colombia (1993), Argentina (1994), Uruguay (1996), Mexico and El Salvador (1997), Bolivia (1998), Costa Rica and Nicaragua (2000), Ecuador (2001), and the Dominican Republic (2003)—representing about half of all Latin Americans, have adopted or are in the process of adopting various forms of the multipillar model as suggested by the World Bank. These changes have been seen by policymakers as necessary, but many of their citizens see in them a relinquishing of responsibility by government. The debate rages on: Will these changes make Argentines and Mexicans and Colombians and the citizens in these other countries better or worse off?

The Benefits of Hindsight

In this book, using both the experience of these countries and simple analytical principles, we try to shed light on this question. Thus, as in *Averting the Old Age Crisis*, we analyze public policy toward pensions over the last two decades, but especially since the early 1990s. But there are differences between that volume and this one, principally because of the developments in the last decade. We have benefited from advances in thinking that *Averting the Old Age Crisis* substantially stimulated. What is perhaps more important is that we have the benefit of more experience so we can replace informed conjecture based on the reforms in one country (Chile) with empirical evaluation of the reform experience of more than two decades in Chile; about a decade's worth of experience in Colombia, Peru, and Argentina; and somewhat shorter but still informative experience with reforms in several other countries, especially Bolivia and Mexico.

Latin America is not alone in its experience with structural pension reform. Eight countries in Eastern Europe also have undertaken multipillar reforms in their transition to market economies. Although these countries also offer important lessons, their institutional and demographic context (adapting formerly socialist systems to meet the needs of a population with an older age profile) is sufficiently different from that of Latin America to present a distinct set of issues that lie beyond the scope of this book. Furthermore, a much larger set of countries, in Latin America and elsewhere, have engaged in "parameter tinkering"—adjusting the size and scope of their single-pillar social security systems. Our purpose here, however, is to focus on multipillar pension reform in Latin America and present policy implications appropriate for the region, not to offer a global study.

This book is based both on specially commissioned background papers and on other work done at the World Bank and elsewhere. Some of the background papers address general questions such as the need to mandate participation in pension schemes (e.g., Packard 2002 and Valdés-Prieto 2002b). Some papers focus on more specific issues such the fiscal, labor market, and capital market effects of social security reforms (e.g., Fiess 2003; Zviniene and Packard 2002; Packard, Shinkai, and Fuentes 2002; Packard 2001, 2002, Yermo 2002a) and more country-specific experiences (e.g., Rofman 2002 for Argentina; Escobar 2003 for Bolivia; Valdés-Prieto 2002c and Yermo 2002c for Chile; Azuara 2003 for Mexico). Other papers assess how workers fared under the new pension system (Yermo 2002b) and their reactions to the reformed systems using data collected in purpose-built household surveys (e.g., Barr and Packard 2002 and Packard 2002 for Chile; Barr and Packard 2003, for Peru). We also take advantage of efforts at the World Bank and elsewhere to collect quantitative information and to refine actuarial techniques, again inspired by the debates initiated in good measure by *Averting the Old Age Crisis.*[2]

There are some differences in our approach as well, principally because of differences in the circumstances that have prompted this inquiry. Whereas a primary (although not exclusive) objective of prior efforts has been to improve the public pension system's fiscal health or to help governments better administer and regulate the systems, the principal objective of this inquiry is to try to determine whether *participants* (not just the administrators or providers) in pension systems are better or worse off since the reforms. That is, we evaluate reforms from the viewpoints of individuals (and their households) and of the policymakers who represent them.

A payoff to emphasizing the perspective of individuals is that this enables us to exploit well-accepted insights provided by the economics of insurance to answer the critical questions raised in the debate on social security, even some of those raised in *Averting the Old Age Crisis* (see box 1.1). Matching insights gained from applying an analytical framework to the problem of old-age income security with the experiences of countries that have reformed their social security systems can help point the correct way forward.

It is reasonable to ask, however, whether enough time has passed to expect tangible results, and whether we are too quick to assert that some fresh thinking is required. We think the time is right. Although most countries that have implemented the multipillar reform model improved incentives for workers to participate in the system, the main concern among policymakers is that the degree of coverage—measured as the number of workers participating in formal pension arrangements—is now stagnant at levels less than half of the labor force. Covering the largest possible number of citizens

---

Box 1.1 Three Central Dilemmas of Pension Privatization

1. *If mandatory schemes are needed because of shortsighted workers, how can these same workers be counted on to make wise investment decisions?* That is, if workers are myopic (which is the primary justification for the mandated private pillar) how can they be trusted to make good investment decisions?

2. *If governments have mismanaged their centrally administered pension plans, how can they be counted on to regulate private funds effectively?* That is, if governments mismanage pay-as-you-go (PAYG) systems, how can they be trusted to properly regulate mandated private pillars?

3. *If government regulates and guarantees the plans, won't it eventually end up controlling these funds?* That is, does it really make a difference whether the funds are privately or publicly managed?

Source: World Bank (1994), p. 203.

against the risks associated with aging is among the objectives of policy-makers in every country of the region. We intend to persuade the reader that our approach, with its focus on the individual—and the role of government emerging from individual welfare maximization—provides useful pointers for policymakers who wish to increase the reach of pension systems. We provide analytical and empirical evidence to show that the reforms have been in the right direction. But we do not stop here. We go on to consider how this progress can be continued by meeting the many detractors of pension reforms where they have somewhat cynically taken the debate (i.e., the concern for low coverage) and examine the problems raised from the per-spective of the participants in the new multipillar pension systems.

Significant Progress, but Stalled Coverage

Latin America is the right place to study pension reform. The longest and most varied experience with the multipillar approach is in Latin America. Starting with Chile in 1981, 12 countries in the region have adopted mul-tipillar arrangements, best distinguished from earlier systems by the prominence of a mandatory funded component administered by purpose-built and dedicated private providers. But often overlooked are the con-siderable differences in the systems adopted, most notably in the degree of choice allowed to workers between the old pay-as-you-go (PAYG) system and the new multipillar arrangement, and the level of benefits in the PAYG component. Costa Rica and Uruguay, for example, have kept a large earnings-related and defined-benefit (DB) system, whereas Argentina, Colombia, and Peru offer workers a choice between a reformed defined-benefit PAYG and the new defined contribution (DC) funded component to finance the bulk of their retirement income.

In Mexico, on the other hand, workers rely fully on the funded system but have a guarantee of benefit levels equal to what they would have re-ceived under the old system. Chile and El Salvador also rely largely on the funded pillar, and the government has limited the PAYG component to providing a basic pension or "topping-up" to ensure a minimum level of retirement income. What is common, however, is the "individualization" of social security (see also Lindbeck and Persson 2003).

When judged against the objectives of the reform, the multipillar approach can be credited with considerable success. The fiscal burden of pensions has been reduced: the most illustrative example is that total pen-sion debt-to-GDP (gross domestic product) ratios have fallen in most of these countries, as a result of both reduced benefits in the reformed PAYG component and a lower rate of accumulation of new liabilities (see Holz-mann, Palacios, and Zviniene 2001; Zviniene and Packard 2002). The re-forms appear to have improved the incentives to contribute to the formal system: recent analysis indicates that the introduction of individual accounts (in which benefits are closely linked to contributions) lowers labor market distortions and improves incentives for workers to participate in formal pension arrangements (Packard 2001). The reforms have also increased equity: internal rates of return have become less regressive (Zviniene and Packard 2002). There also has been an increase in the depth of capital markets, at least in part attributable to pension reform (Yermo 2002a). These successes warrant that future reforms should build upon the new systems.

In each of these areas, the experience has revealed shortcomings as well. In Argentina, Colombia, and Peru, the option given to new workers to choose between the old and new systems creates uncertainty regarding the fiscal liability of government. In Colombia, where workers can change their choice every three years, the disequilibrium between benefits and contributions in the old defined-benefit PAYG system is particularly acute and severely weakens the reformed system. Chile is increasingly concerned about the rising costs of the minimum pension guarantee, driven in part by falling numbers of active contributors in the labor force. And pensions of government workers continue to exercise a serious fiscal burden in countries such as Argentina, Mexico, and Peru, although these constitute a greater burden even in countries, such as Brazil, that have not adopted the multipillar approach. These and other shortcomings, if not a failure of the reform *model*, are indeed failings of the *actual* reforms undertaken in the region.

The ability of the multipillar model to isolate the pension system from abuse by governments may also have been oversold by reformers. It is now clear that unsustainable fiscal and monetary policies can jeopardize even well-implemented funded schemes. Whereas this was highlighted most dramatically in Argentina during the economic crisis in 2001 when the government made the administrators of second-pillar pension funds increase their holdings of increasingly risky government bonds and eventually even confiscated their deposits in banks, similar threats to the viability of funded pension schemes can emerge in other countries of the region. In Bolivia, for example, there have been attempts to force a swap of dollar-denominated government debt held by pension funds for less attractive bonds denominated in the local currency (Escobar 2003).

After rising modestly as a result of the reforms, coverage ratios have stalled at levels of about half of the labor force in those countries where workers' participation is highest. In most countries the ratios are much lower (see figures 1.1 and 1.2). Although many factors other than pension reforms (e.g., changes in labor and social legislation[3]) can affect participation, stagnant coverage ratios are indicative of skepticism of the new system, despite its virtues. In Chile, for example, special survey data indicate that workers may perceive AFP (*administradora de fondos de pensiones;* pension fund administrator) accounts as a relatively risky retirement investment (see Barr and Packard 2002 and Packard 2002); this is confirmed by the low number of workers who use AFP accounts as instruments for long-term saving despite their tax advantages. These same data show that many workers cease to contribute to the pension system after completing the minimum contribution requirement, preferring other long-term savings instruments to those offered by dedicated pension providers, and even more importantly revealing a preference for government schemes for pooling resources to insure against old-age poverty, compared with government-mandated saving instruments (Packard 2002). Preliminary indications are that these may be more widespread phenomena: analysis of the contribution behavior of a sample of Peruvian affiliates suggests that the longer workers have contributed to the reformed pension system, the less likely they are to continue contributing, and that where workers are free to choose how to save, many prefer to invest in housing and in their children.

Figure 1.1 Pension Systems Cover between 10 and 60 Percent of the Economically Active Population in Latin American Countries

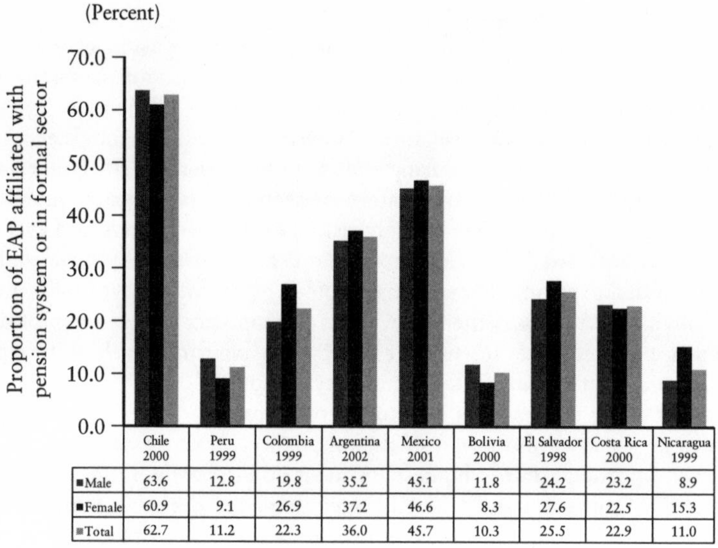

(Percent)

	Chile 2000	Peru 1999	Colombia 1999	Argentina 2002	Mexico 2001	Bolivia 2000	El Salvador 1998	Costa Rica 2000	Nicaragua 1999
■Male	63.6	12.8	19.8	35.2	45.1	11.8	24.2	23.2	8.9
■Female	60.9	9.1	26.9	37.2	46.6	8.3	27.6	22.5	15.3
■Total	62.7	11.2	22.3	36.0	45.7	10.3	25.5	22.9	11.0

EAP Economically active population.

Source: Household surveys between 1997 and 2002, analyzed by Todd Pugatch.

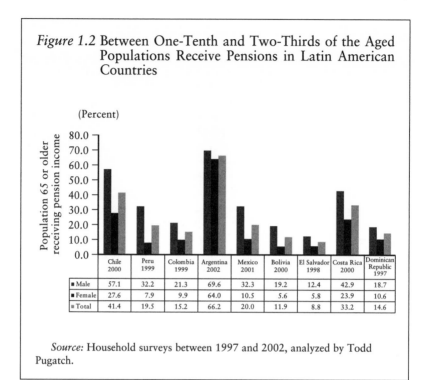

Figure 1.2 Between One-Tenth and Two-Thirds of the Aged Populations Receive Pensions in Latin American Countries

(Percent)

Population 65 or older receiving pension income

	Chile 2000	Peru 1999	Colombia 1999	Argentina 2002	Mexico 2001	Bolivia 2000	El Salvador 1998	Costa Rica 2000	Dominican Republic 1997
■ Male	57.1	32.2	21.3	69.6	32.3	19.2	12.4	42.9	18.7
■ Female	27.6	7.9	9.9	64.0	10.5	5.6	5.8	23.9	10.6
■ Total	41.4	19.5	15.2	66.2	20.0	11.9	8.8	33.2	14.6

Source: Household surveys between 1997 and 2002, analyzed by Todd Pugatch.

The coverage ratios shown in figures 1.1 and 1.2 are the best illustrations for why further thought has to be given to how to close the coverage gap, beyond the simple multipillar recipe of reforms. Although ensuring fiscal stability was the primary impetus behind the region's pension reforms, advocates of multipillar reform, including the World Bank, saw the potential for increased coverage as an additional motivation (see box 5.2). But there are other reasons as well. Although the precarious fiscal positions of governments in the region have resulted in high gross returns on the portfolios of dedicated pension providers (through high interest rates on government debt issues), several factors provide cause for concern.

The first factor is how long these high returns can be maintained as fiscal adjustment lowers the spreads on government debt. The second factor (where fiscal adjustment is slow) is that a good part of these high returns reflects the risk of default, as the experience in Argentina illustrates. The solution is greater diversification into domestic nongovernment and foreign assets, and while these changes are difficult to engineer during times of fiscal stress, they should be introduced gradually as conditions improve. The third factor is that in some countries management fees have remained relatively stable, while the operational costs of the pension fund industry have fallen. This indicates deficiencies in regulation that should be corrected, but also the impact of weak overall fiscal positions of governments in the region.

In Chile and a few other countries, commission rates are slowly coming down to reasonable levels (less than 20 percent of contributions or 1 percent of assets). This raises questions of intergenerational fairness: the first generations of workers pay higher commissions in order to cover the start-up costs of the new industry of dedicated providers. The fee structures in Chile and elsewhere also result in within-generation inequity as poorer workers end up paying a larger share of their contributions as commissions (Yermo 2002b).[4] But most worrisome are findings that point to difficulties in regulating the firms that manage mandatory pension funds. In Peru, for example, management fees have remained steady even though the ratio of operating costs to fees fell by almost half between 1998 and 2002 (Lasaga and Pollner 2003). Whereas these high management fees would be troubling if discovered for voluntary pension funds, such diversions from worker contributions that are mandated by governments should be cause for concern. Only Bolivia acknowledged the natural oligopolistic nature of the industry and from the start decided to minimize administrative costs within this constraint. The bidding contest used led to the lowest commissions in Latin America, although since then the fees charged in other countries have approached the Bolivian level.

Governments also face a dilemma as they aim to make their funded systems more flexible by permitting workers to choose among a range of investments. In most countries, mandatory pension savings are backed by minimum pension guarantees (or even more generous guarantees) that expose the state to a contingent liability that depends on the investment performance of the pension funds. The ensuing incentive to take unwarranted risks (what is commonly referred to as a moral hazard) is a reality in Chile, where workers can choose among five funds with different allocations to equities. The tension between benefit guarantees and individual choice is evidence of the inherent weakness of pension systems that rely exclusively on mandatory contributions to funded accounts.[5]

In summary, it is safe to conclude that these reforms have been a major step forward. As part I (chapters 2 through 5) of this book shows, the reforms have led to lower fiscal burdens, a slower rate of growth of pension-related public liabilities, financial deepening and less regressive pension expenditures, although there is still much to do in these areas. As we reason in part II (chapters 6 through 8), the shift from defined benefit to defined contribution schemes as the mainstay of old-age income security accords well with the basic principles of the economics of insurance. But it may also be reasonable to question the effectiveness of the currrent multipillar systems in creating an attractive instrument for retirement savings. Concerns over stalled coverage indicators and the vulnerability of all the multipillar components to macroeconomic instability—a fact of life in Latin America—reflect weaknesses that merit reexamination of the multipillar parameters. In part III (chapters 9 through 11) we argue that fiscal, coverage-related, equity, and financial indicators over the last decade show that a return to single-pillar, defined-benefit PAYG systems as the mainstay for old-age income security is not the answer, although in some countries in the region even this alternative is being considered.[6]

But the way forward is far less obvious. Using a blend of theory and empirical analysis, in part III of this volume we examine the options for the future and propose a rationale for continuing, redirecting, or strengthening various aspects of the reforms initiated during the last two decades.

Distinctions That Matter—Pooling vs. Saving, and Mandatory vs. Voluntary

In this volume we categorize the components of a multipillar pension system by their objective, rather than by whom they are administered (the public or private sector), how benefits are structured (final-salary benefit formula or defined contributions), or their financing mechanism (PAYG or full funding). Thus we use the term "first pillar" or "pillar one" to refer to the part of a pension system intended to keep elderly people out of poverty,[7] "second pillar" to refer to the mandated part intended to help individuals smooth consumption over their life cycle (i.e., to prevent a dramatic fall in income at the time of retirement), and "third pillar" to identify the instruments and institutions available on a voluntary basis for workers to increase their income in retirement. A simple way to characterize the main differences among these pillars is the differing role of government: in the case of the first pillar government defines benefits, in the second it defines contributions,[8] and in the third it defines incentives for retirement savings. Table 1.1 summarizes the main features of instruments for old-age income security that together constitute the multipillar system.

In general the issue of interest is not whether a country should have three pillars (or tiers) or just one. It can be shown without much difficulty that individuals are better off diversifying the risks to adequate income in old age and thus that a country does better for its elderly population by instituting more than one of these components (see Lindbeck and Persson 2003). The critical question is: What should be the relative importance of the three pillars—that is, their "weights" in the system? That is one of the questions this volume addresses. In doing so it exploits two fundamental dichotomies:

1. The nature of the instrument: *pooling*, where there is by definition a transfer in every period from the more to the less fortunate; and *saving*, where there is by definition a transfer of one's income from one period to another but no redistribution between individuals.[9]

2. The role of government or the main reason for participation by the individual: *mandatory*, where the government mandates participation and

Table 1.1 Instruments of Old-Age Income Security

Nature of instrument	Mainstay: Pooling	Mainstay: Saving[a]	
	Mandatory	Mandatory	Voluntary
Common name	First pillar	Second pillar	Third pillar
Main function	Insure against poverty in old age, lower income inequality	Smooth consumption over life cycle	Smooth consumption over life cycle
Main role of government	Defines benefits	Defines contributions	Defines incentives
Principal risk-bearer	Government	Worker	Worker
Financial instrument	Unfunded PAYG	Funded: individual accounts	Funded: tax-preferred individual accounts

[a] See chapter 6 for an important qualification: the use of annuities in the saving components implies that the risks associated with unexpected longevity are pooled.

defines the rules of the game; and *voluntary*, where the rules are made clear but people have the choice to participate or not.

Exploiting the first dichotomy enables the use of well-developed insights from the economics of insurance to answer the question of relative weights of the first pillar on the one hand, and the second and third on the other. The first pillar is pooling-based whereas the second and third are primarily savings-based, although there is an important role for pooling in the form of annuities and survivors and disability insurance. Throughout this book we refer to the first pillar as the pooling component and the second and third pillars as the savings component of a pension system. Combined with insights from the study of household behavior and financial institutions, the second dichotomy helps in deciding the relative weights of the second and third pillars. Together these can help determine the unfinished reform agenda needed in countries that have already adopted the multipillar approach, and the options that should be considered in those that are seriously contemplating pension reform. It may even persuade obstinate nonreformers to reexamine their strategies to help elderly people achieve income security.

A Summary of the Main Findings

This volume approaches the problem of old-age income security principally from the viewpoint of individuals, rather than that of governments alone. Although previous analyses have certainly not ignored the individual's perspective, an explicit focus on the individual has been employed too infrequently in the literature in our view. Consistent with the advice of Barr (2001), who pointed out that analysis of pensions requires an understanding of macroeconomics, microeconomics, financial economics, and the theory of social insurance, this book examines pensions in Latin America using all four of these lenses. Taking this perspective, we find that the successes of pension reform are not where commonly believed: the successes of the reform are not in the much-touted shift to "pre-funding," but in the switch from pooling to saving as the mainstay of old-age income security. Put another way, the merit of the reform is not in the privatization of schemes for old-age income support but in their "individualization." And contrary to the claims of proponents of reforms, the strength is not in arriving at a durable and permanent system, but in breaking with a past of approaches that demographic and economic changes have made defunct.

It should therefore be emphasized once again that future reforms should build upon the efforts that countries have undertaken. The objective of future efforts should be to improve the functioning of all components—first, second, and third pillars—in countries that have adopted the multipillar approach, within the fiscal and administrative constraints they face.

In summary, this volume uses available evidence, including that presented in background papers and surveys commissioned specifically for our inquiry, to draw several important lessons from the Latin American experience with pension reform.

First, and most important, the *poverty prevention* pillar should get a lot more attention than it has in Latin America during the last decade. This poverty prevention role of government only *increases* in importance with economic development—as the likelihood of poverty in old age declines, the fundamentals of insurance make pooling of this risk across individuals more, not less, appropriate. A government mandate is necessary for such a defined benefit system because private insurance markets are unlikely to provide such coverage. Systems of this type are also best financed and managed separately from the savings component, which is not the case in countries such as Chile, El Salvador or Mexico. The defined benefit formulas of such programs call for conservative investment strategies that can clash with the need for individual portfolio choice in the savings pillar.

Second, it should be emphasized that although such poverty prevention tiers will provide a minimum pension to those people who are unfortunate or unwise, saving should be the mainstay for *earnings replacement* during old age (i.e., mechanisms to cover the loss of earnings capacity while living). Retirement programs on top of the poverty prevention pillar should closely link benefits to contributions and do so in a similar way for most workers. The individual capitalization schemes that have been introduced in

Latin America are fully consistent with this objective. In particular, rising life expectancy does not affect the link between benefits and contributions in these new schemes. On the other hand, countries that still have large earnings-related defined-benefit PAYG pillars (e.g., Colombia, Costa Rica, and Peru) will see benefits grow out disproportionately relative to contributions as life expectancy increases. These countries may therefore consider adjusting their benefit formulas to replicate a savings system (through notional individual accounts) or may provide more space to the funded system by closing down the earnings-related PAYG pillar to new entrants to the labor force.

Third, incentive compatibility between the poverty prevention and individual savings pillars is key. Excessively generous or badly designed poverty prevention pillars may create further incentives to informalization of employment and reduce contributions to the mandatory and voluntary savings pillars.

Fourth, more attention should be paid to the size of the mandatory savings pillar. High contribution rates and maximum taxable earnings can discourage worker participation, especially by young and poor populations with other urgent, competing demands on their disposable income. Large second-pillar pensions may be a useful instrument for effecting a transition from overly generous defined-benefit PAYG systems. They may also provide an initial boost to capital and insurance markets. However, these are needs that become less important over time, calling for a reduced mandate. Mandatory savings plans may not even be necessary in countries such as Brazil, which have overcome many political hurdles to social security reform and already have the foundations for thriving capital and insurance markets. Careful consideration of country circumstances, backed by solid country-specific analytical work, is necessary to determine the appropriate size of the second pillar.

Fifth, for countries that do have mandatory savings plans, the priority should be to lower costs to affiliates and improve risk management. Further reductions in commissions would also improve the attractiveness of the funded pillar, and there are various options for achieving this goal. At one extreme there is the centralized management model. At the other extreme there is a fully contestable market where different providers compete by offering diverse products. Latin American countries will need to assess which is the best solution for them, and we do not propose country-specific solutions in this volume. The choice will depend largely on the extent to which other financial institutions are appropriately regulated and supervised and the population's ability to make difficult choices. With respect to risk management, more consideration should be given to the value of international diversification of pension fund portfolios, the pros and cons of worker choice, and improving benefit options at retirement.

Countries with high fiscal net liabilities (and thus regressive transfers) may need to eliminate those net liabilities to make the "fiscal space" needed to fund a poverty reduction pillar.

A Roadmap to this Volume

This volume consists of three parts. In part 1, following a brief description of the reforms in the region in chapter 2, in the next three chapters we provide evidence on the performance of countries that have adopted the multipillar approach in three dimensions: fiscal, financial, and social. The numbers show that countries in Latin America that have adopted the multipillar approach have done well in terms of the objectives of reforms. This finding should form the basis of future reform efforts.

Part 2 makes the point that these countries have made progress in another (much less widely acknowledged) aspect: they have made or begun the transition to a more sustainable and meaningful social contract. The main reason for judging the changes with optimism is the switch to savings from pooling as the basis or mainstay of old-age income security. One can reasonably make the case that the shift from unsustainable defined-benefit PAYG to sustainable old-age income security systems had to go through this stage for reasons of political economy. So it would be a mistake to go back to the unsustainable structures that existed prior to the institution of the multipillar systems. But it would also be a mistake to think of this stage as the "final structure." In fact, the report argues that the 1990s could be seen as a transition in reforming Latin American countries to structures that are sustainable at their levels of institutional sophistication. Chapter 6 asks and answers the question, how do we know what is the appropriate structure? The main proposals stem from well-accepted principles in the economics of insurance that argue for saving as the mainstay of a comprehensive insurance strategy against a frequent loss—of being without earning capacity while living—and pooling as an auxiliary instrument for a risk that is now smaller—that of poverty in old age.

Chapter 7 continues to address the issue using this relatively simple analytical framework. It examines how well the mandatory and voluntary savings components have done from the individual worker/contributor's perspective. High contribution rates may have discouraged young and poor workers from participating in the formal pension system. Most countries also have very high earnings ceilings for calculating mandatory contributions and some have no ceiling at all. High contribution rates and earnings ceilings may explain why few workers have found it worth making voluntary contributions to their individual accounts in most countries, even when they are relatively liquid and offer attractive tax benefits. In addition, the operation of the savings component (both the mandatory and voluntary parts) presents some weaknesses arising primarily from high commissions, lack of international diversification, and inadequate risk management over the life cycle.

Chapter 8 provides some evidence on what may be wrong with seeing the multipillar structure with its heavy reliance on mandated saving as a final structure. Using survey data from Chile and Peru, the two countries with the longest experience with mandated private savings, we provide evidence that supports worker rationality and reveals their preference for government provision of instruments to *insure against old-age poverty* over those that *enable individual saving*. Although the evidence is not definitive given the small size of the samples, it is more than merely suggestive. In view of this rationality (evidence of the ability to distinguish between risky and less risky instruments of old-age income security, and preferences for alternative long-term savings and investments) and in light of governments' difficulties in providing either PAYG pensions or efficient savings instruments, we propose here that the size of the mandate to save in the form of a rigidly defined and not-so-easily regulated instrument deserves to be reassessed.

Part 3 of the book proposes that the time is right to reflect on the government mandate to save for old age. Chapter 9 discusses how best to insure against the risk of poverty in old age, and chapter 10 treats the equally important issue of facilitating saving for retirement—the mainstay of old-age income security. The volume proposes continuing the move toward a system that consists of a sustainable first pillar to address the risk of poverty and a vibrant, competitive savings pillar to address the need for consumption smoothing over the life cycle. Chapter 9 proposes what may be seen by some as a radical increase in attention of Latin American governments to the poverty prevention function of public pensions. In contrast, chapter 10 proposes a gradual reform of plans to encourage saving for old age. But the principle that guides all the recommendations is that these changes be welfare-improving, institutionally feasible, and fiscally sustainable.

In chapter 11 we look back and ask whether the decade or so of reform has been a success. The answer is that in many respects, it has. But if the new structures are viewed as a final design, the efforts may well be assessed harshly because scores of people are left uncovered just as they were under the old systems, there are still some adverse equity effects and fiscal liabilities, and the cost and risk management features of the savings pillar are somewhat deficient. On the other hand, if the current structures are viewed as a transitory stage, social security reforms should be viewed as successful because the movements have been in the right direction. This is true in all countries surveyed in this book. In countries such as Brazil this is also true, even though the country has eschewed a mandated private savings pillar in favor of efforts to strengthen the third pillar.[10] Even in Argentina, where the second pillar is in the midst of a crisis, we believe that the current social security system is superior to the one it replaced; the reforms of the 1990s have to be built upon, not abrogated. The greatest dangers to all that the reforms have achieved lie not in countries where the new approach to ensuring income support for the aged is being scrutinized and altered, but in countries where large mandated saving is viewed as a solution for the ages.

Notes

1. Barr (2001) correctly points out that "tier" is a better characterization than "pillar" because it "is linguistically more apt: pillars can only be effective if they are all in place and all, broadly of the same size . . ." (p. 133). Because the relative size of these components is a central concern of this book, Barr's point is especially pertinent.

2. All 16 background papers for the book are available online at the Web site of the World Bank's Chief Economist for Latin America and the Caribbean region, www.worldbank.org/keepingthepromise.

3. We discuss the range of factors influencing the decision to participate in public pension systems more extensively in chapters 5 and 8.

4. In addition to the high costs borne by younger workers, a comprehensive generational accounting framework would necessarily account for many other factors to estimate the net intercohort impact of reforms. Such a framework is beyond the scope of this book, however.

5. Even in Chile, a country with one of the highest participation rates, the government considers that low participation in the private pension system will keep effective replacement rates low and thus put mounting pressures on the minimum-income plan for retirees.

6. In Argentina, for example, a draft law that would allow workers to switch between the public and the private branches of the pension system was passed in 2002 in the Lower House with only one vote against and one abstention. In Peru in late 2002 some articles proposed during the rewriting of the constitution would have allowed affiliates to the funded system to return to the public PAYG system and to lower the retirement age from 65 to 60 years. These articles were only narrowly defeated. In Chile in early 2002 civil servants started demonstrations demanding to be allowed to switch back to the pre-reform PAYG regime as a result of disappointing projected replacement rates from individual accounts.

7. We discuss the emerging distinction between "pillar one" and "pillar zero" poverty prevention pensions in chapter 9.

8. Although the second pillar can be implemented as a defined benefit scheme, its predominant association with defined contribution plans in both theory and practice overwhelms this distinction in our view.

9. Because the Ehrlich-Becker "comprehensive insurance" framework underlying our approach (and presented in chapter 6) would use the term "insurance" in reference to both the consumption-smoothing ("self-insurance") and poverty prevention ("market insurance") functions of social security, we use the more contemporary terms "pooling" and "saving" in order to avoid confusion.

10. The recent decision to raise the maximum taxable salary, however, will reduce the clientele in the third pillar substantially.

I

Retrospective: Fiscal, Financial, and Social Benefits from Pension Reform

2

Structural Reforms to Social Security in Latin America

AMONG DEVELOPING REGIONS, LATIN AMERICA has a relatively long tradition of formally institutionalized social security. Governments at various levels, unions, and trade associations have been administering retirement, disability, survivor insurance, and in many cases unemployment insurance since the early 1900s. National public pension systems were first established in Chile in 1924 and then in Uruguay in 1928. In the past 20 years, however, a slow but dramatic shift has occurred across the region in the approach taken by governments to providing social security, primarily in retirement pensions.[1]

Demographic Changes in Latin America

As in other regions, Latin America's population is aging. Advances in technology and health care have increased average life spans dramatically in the last 50 years. Although the pace of the region's demographic transition varies widely, from relatively "younger" countries like El Salvador to relatively "older" countries like Uruguay, falling fertility rates combined with lengthening life expectancy are increasing the portion of the population in old age and lowering the number of new entrants into the workforce (see figure 2.1).

This demographic change has been accompanied by economic liberalization and greater integration with the world economy. Structural adjustment after the debt crisis in the 1980s and the need for greater efficiency as countries opened their economies to competition from abroad in the 1990s forced a steady reallocation of the labor pool. Changes in the relative size of different branches of the economy show a clear increase in the number of workers employed in small firms, temporarily employed, and self-employed and a fall in the number of people working in large private firms and in the public sector.

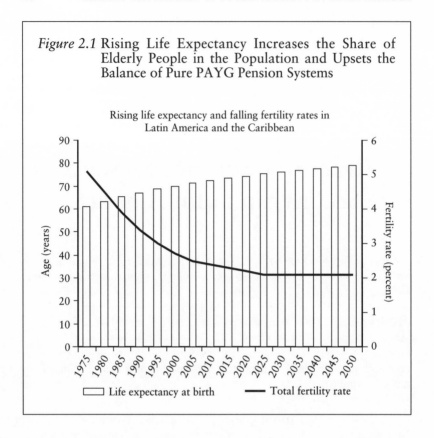

Figure 2.1 Rising Life Expectancy Increases the Share of Elderly People in the Population and Upsets the Balance of Pure PAYG Pension Systems

Rising life expectancy and falling fertility rates in Latin America and the Caribbean

☐ Life expectancy at birth   ━━ Total fertility rate

Growth in the share of elderly people and the push for competitiveness have forced policymakers in the region to reexamine labor market institutions—primarily public pension systems—to accommodate these trends. Latin America, however, is still a relatively young region. The fiscal deficits and mounting contingent liabilities of overly generous public pension systems plagued by mismanagement and fraud have often proven a more immediate impetus for structural reforms.

Taxonomy of Social Security Reform in Latin America[2]

Structural reforms to social security in the region were initiated by Chile in 1981 and continued in the 1990s by Peru, Colombia, Argentina, Uruguay, Mexico, Bolivia, and El Salvador. Costa Rica, Nicaragua, the Dominican Republic, and Ecuador enacted reforms between 2000 and 2001.[3] Each reform involved a transition from purely public pension sys-

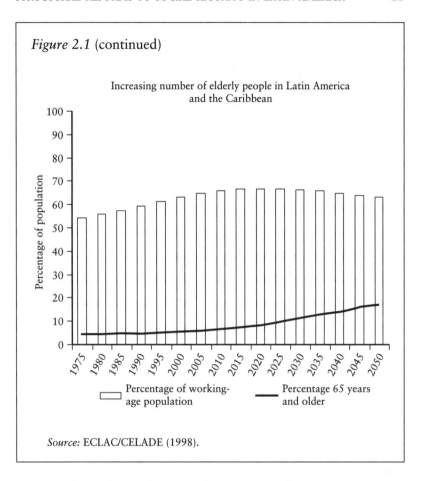

Figure 2.1 (continued)

Increasing number of elderly people in Latin America and the Caribbean

Source: ECLAC/CELADE (1998).

tems (similar to those administered in Europe and the United States) to systems with explicitly defined "multiple pillars" administered and/or mandated by government.

Although reforms have varied widely, most countries have retained or restructured a publicly mandated and administered first pillar operated on a PAYG, *defined benefit* basis with a redistributive safety-net function. To that pillar they have added a publicly mandated but privately administered second pillar of individual retirement savings accounts funded with *defined contributions* and managed by a new industry of dedicated pension fund managers. Finally, reformers have tried to increase savings for retirement by *defining incentives* through regulation of a third pillar of voluntary retirement saving and pension plans arranged privately between employers and their workers.

Although the function (and sometimes the form) of formal pension institutions that existed prior to these reforms could also be categorized in three pillars,[4] the multipillar model has come to be distinguished in Latin America by the prominence of mandated private savings, relative to mandatory public social insurance and voluntary forms of savings and insurance.

Most multipillar systems are designed so that the bulk of workers' retirement income is financed from mandated private savings in individual accounts. These funds are invested in bonds and equities by dedicated private pension fund managers. Although the activities of these fund managers and other financial service providers in the voluntary pillar are strictly regulated, the direct role of the state in the new model is reduced to enforcing the mandate to save, regulating the new fund management industry, and guaranteeing a minimum threshold income to keep individuals from falling into poverty in old age.

What should be emphasized is that the general character of social security reforms in the region has been similar. Despite claims to the contrary made by several opponents of reforms, however, there is no single, cookie-cutter "Latin American" reform model. There are important differences that mark the introduction of the new pension systems from one country to the next. Tables 2.1 and 2.2 show some of the principal characteristics and differences between (structurally) reformed pension systems in the region.[5]

In Bolivia, Chile, El Salvador, and Mexico, mandated individual retirement accounts replaced public defined-benefit PAYG institutions as the state's primary intervention to provide retirement income. In addition, in Chile there is a (broadly defined) first pillar that consists of guaranteed minimum contributory benefits, subsidies, and other social assistance to the elderly indigent population, financed through general taxes.[6] In El Salvador the state also guarantees a contributory minimum pension but there is no social assistance program for elderly people who do not meet contribution requirements. In Mexico workers who contributed to the old system have a guarantee of benefits equal to their accrued benefits under the old system. As in El Salvador, there is no social assistance program for elderly men and women. Bolivia offers a basic pension to all Bolivians 65 and older who were at least 21 at the end of 1995.

In contrast, in Argentina, Costa Rica, Ecuador (if and when the reform is implemented) and Uruguay, a PAYG-financed, contributory first pillar underpins pensions financed with accumulated individual savings. This first pillar provides a basic flat-rate pension in Argentina and earnings-related pensions (backed by minimum pension guarantees) in Costa Rica, Ecuador, and Uruguay. Benefits are conditional on a certain minimum number of years of contribution.[7] Rather than pillars, in Ecuador and Uruguay the new systems are best characterized as "tiers." Participation in the new tier of private individual accounts is only mandatory for workers whose salary is above a certain level. In Uruguay only 10 percent of all contributors earn above the threshold level of approximately six minimum

Table 2.1 Principal Features of Structural Reforms to Social Security Systems (Old-Age Disability and Death) in Latin America during the 1980s and 1990s

	Chile	Peru	Colombia	Argentina	Uruguay	Mexico	Bolivia	El Salvador
Year of reform	1981	1992/1993	1994	1994	1996	1997	1997	1998
Contribution-related PAYG system?	Closed	Remains	Remains	Remains	Remains	Closed	Closed	Closed
Total payroll tax rate, pre-reform (%)	33.0	18.0	17.8	42.0	40.0	20.0	19.0	11.8
Total payroll tax rate, post-reform (%)	20.0	20.5/22.0[a]	33.8	46.0[b]	40.0	26.0	24.0	13.5
Participation of new workers?	Mandatory	Voluntary	Voluntary	Voluntary[c]	Voluntary[d]	Mandatory	Mandatory	Mandatory
Participation of self-employed workers?	Voluntary	Voluntary	Voluntary	Mandatory	Mandatory	Voluntary	Voluntary	Voluntary
Remaining separate system for civil servants?	No	No[e]	Yes	No[e]	No	Yes	No	No
Dedicated fund managers	AFP	AFP	AFP	AFJP	AFAP	AFORE	AFP	AFP
Contribution to IRA (%)[f]	10.00	8.00	10.00	7.72	12.27	12.07	10.00	10.00
Fees and insurance premiums (% of wage)	2.31	3.73	3.49	3.28	2.68	4.48	2.50	3.00

(Table continues on the following page.)

Table 2.1 (continued)

	Chile	Peru	Colombia	Argentina	Uruguay	Mexico	Bolivia	El Salvador
Switching between fund managers?	2 times annually	1 time annually	2 times annually	2 times annually	2 times annually	1 time annually	1 time annually	2 times annually
Payout options	Annuity or scheduled withdrawal	Annuity or scheduled withdrawal	Annuity or scheduled withdrawal	Annuity or scheduled withdrawal	Annuity only	Annuity or scheduled withdrawal	Annuity only	Annuity or scheduled withdrawal
Minimum return on investment?	Relative to average	Relative to average	Relative to average	Relative to average	Relative to average	Unregulated	Unregulated[g]	Relative to average
Minimum contributory pension?	Yes	Yes (only for affiliates born before 1945)	Yes	Yes	Yes	Yes	No	Yes
Social assistance pension?	Yes	No	No	Yes	Yes	No	Yes (only affiliates born before 1974)	No

Notes: AFAP pension fund administrators (*administradoras de fondos de ahorro previsional* [Uruguay]); AFJP retirement and pension fund administrators (*administradoras de fondos de jubilaciónes y de pensiones* [Argentina]); AFORE retirement fund administrators (*administradoras de fondos para el retiro* [Mexico]); IRA individual retirement account.

a. 20.5 for private pension system, 22.0 for national system. Maximum taxable earning for disability and survivorship insurance: S/6130.88 or US$1,751.

b. Maximum allowed by law. The effective tax rate has been falling since the reform, and it varies by sector and region. The current rate is less than 30 percent.

c. Although new affiliates can choose, up to 80 percent of them in each year fail to make an explicit choice. The private second pillar is the default option.

d. Participation in individual accounts in Uruguay is determined by income level. Workers below a threshold level choose to split contributions between PAYG and individual retirement accounts.

e. Exceptions exist for some subnational systems.

f. At time of publication.

g. Guarantees required from the fund managers.

Source: Adapted from Cerda and Grandolini 1998; Queisser 1998a; Devesa-Carpio and Vidal-Meliá 2002; AIOS 2002; FIAP 2002; and country pension supervisors. The authors wish to thank Ximena Quintanilla (Chile), Elio Sanchez (Peru), Carlos Grushka (Argentina), Maria Nela Seijas (Uruguay), and Francisco Sorto Rivas (El Salvador) for their assistance in compiling table 2.1. The authors take sole responsibility for factual errors in the table.

Table 2.2 Principal Features of Structural Reforms to Social Security Systems (Old-Age Disability and Death) in Latin America during the 1990s and 2000s

	Costa Rica	Nicaragua	Ecuador	Dominican Republic
Year of reform	1995/2000ᵃ	2000, as yet not implemented	2001, as yet not implemented	2001ᵇ
Contribution-related public PAYG system?	Remains	Closed	Remains	Closed
Total payroll tax rate, pre-reform (%)	22.00	17.00	—	9.25
Total payroll tax rate, post-reform (%)	26.0	21.5	Varies, but no more than 20.0	20.0
Participation of new workers?	Mandatory	Mandatory	Mandatory	Mandatory
Participation of self-employed workers?	Voluntary	Voluntary	Mandatory	Mandatory
Remaining separate system for civil servants?	—	No	—	Yes
Dedicated fund managers	OPC	AFP	EDAP	AFP
Contribution to IRA (%)	4.25	7.50	8.33	10.00
Fees and insurance premiums (% of wage)	c	2.5	4.0	2.0
Switching between fund managers?	1 time annually	1 time annually	—	1 time annually
Payout options	Annuity or scheduled withdrawal	Annuity or scheduled withdrawal	—	Annuity or scheduled withdrawal
Minimum return on investment?	Unregulated	Unregulated	Relative to average	Relative to average
Minimum contributory pension?	Yes	Yes	—	Yes
Social assistance pension?	Yes	Yes	Yes	Yes

Notes: EDAP future savings depository entities (*entidades depositarias de aborro previsional* [Ecuador]); IRA individual retirement account; OPC complementary pension fund operators (*operadoras de pensiones complementarias* [Costa Rica]); —not available.

a. Costa Rica introduced voluntary retirement accounts in 1996 but made private individual retirement saving mandatory as a complement to the defined benefit system in 2000.

b. Implemented in 2003.

c. Fees are charged as a percentage of returns from investment and capped at a maximum of 8 percent of returns or 4 percent of contributions.

Source: Adapted from Cerda and Grandolini 1998; Queisser 1998a; Devesa-Carpio and Vidal-Meliá 2002; AIOS 2002; FIAP 2002; and country pension supervisors. The authors wish to thank Tomás Soley (Costa Rica) for assistance in compiling table 2.2. The authors take sole responsibility for factual errors in the table.

wages. Workers with lower salaries can if they wish deposit up to one-half of their mandatory contributions in the funded plan.

In Argentina, Peru, and Colombia each new generation that joins the labor force (and that takes up formal employment) is allowed to choose between a significantly downsized, earnings-related PAYG pillar and individual retirement accounts as the primary financing mechanism for their pensions. Irrespective of their choice, Colombian workers are covered by the same first-pillar arrangements (i.e., minimum guarantees and basic poverty prevention pension).[8] In Peru, as in Argentina's second pillar, new workers who choose the public pillar are always allowed to move to the private system at a later date. However, workers who choose private accounts cannot choose to move back to the PAYG pillar. As a political concession to pass the reform, workers in Colombia were given the option to switch back and forth between systems every three years. Largely in reaction against a policy of assigning all undecided workers to private individual accounts by default, draft legislation to allow similar switching was considered in Argentina (Rofman 2002). Similar attempts by the legislature to allow affiliates to return to the public system were recently defeated in Peru.

Reforms in Latin America, therefore, differ significantly in the extent of private provision of formal retirement income. There is not yet a consensus on how to measure the extent of "privatization" of what were once purely public national pension systems. Some authors present the mandatory contribution rate earmarked for private individual accounts as a portion of total mandated contributions for retirement income security (as in Palacios and Pallares-Miralles 2000), or contributions to individual retirement accounts as a share of total payroll taxes for social insurance (as in Packard 2001). Others propose the projected portion of future pension benefits that will come from the new private pillars (as in Brooks and James 2001) as a proxy for the degree of privatization.

From the perspective of new entrants to the labor force, the reformed Latin American pension systems can be divided into four main groups (see figure 2.2):

1. Countries where the funded component is the only source of earnings-related contributory pensions available for new workers: Bolivia, Chile, the Dominican Republic, El Salvador, and Mexico.

2. Countries where new workers must choose between the funded and the PAYG system for their earnings-related pension: Colombia and Peru. In Colombia workers may switch between the two systems every three years. In Peru the default option is the funded system.

3. Countries where new workers remain in a PAYG system providing a basic, flat-rate pension and choose between a complementary PAYG and a funded pillar for their earnings-related pension: Argentina. The default option is the funded system.

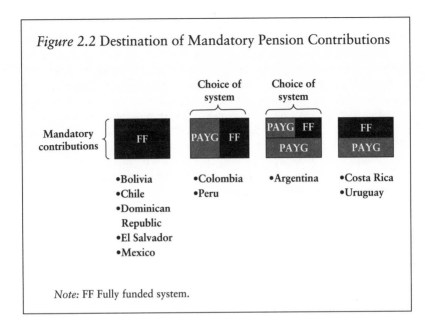

Figure 2.2 Destination of Mandatory Pension Contributions

Note: FF Fully funded system.

4. Countries where new workers remain in a reformed PAYG system that provides earnings-related defined benefit pensions that are lower but still generous, and make additional mandatory contributions to the funded plan: Costa Rica and Uruguay. In Uruguay the funded plan is optional for low- and middle-income workers. Although not yet implemented, structural reforms in Ecuador would introduce a system similar to that of Uruguay.

In most countries the reform did not equally affect private and public sector employees. Usually out of political considerations, reforming governments avoided making structural changes to the public pension systems benefiting the military and civil servants. After structural reforms to the social security systems for workers in the private sector, separate public pension systems remain for civil servants in Colombia, El Salvador, and Mexico. Although the plan is nominally closed to new entrants, organized groups of workers have continually tried to be covered by the generous PAYG parameters of Peru's pension regime for civil servants (the *cédula viva*), with mixed success. The retirement regimes for federal civil servants in Argentina were integrated into the reformed national system, but separate, relatively generous pension systems remain for civil servants in roughly half of Argentina's provinces. The military (and in many cases the police) retain separate, special retirement and other income security arrangements in all of the countries where reformed systems are now in place.

There also are important differences among countries, even within each of the four groups with respect to the transition arrangements put in place for private sector workers who were already participating in the formal pension system prior to reforms. In Bolivia and Mexico all workers were switched to the new system. In Chile workers were given a choice between staying in the old system and switching to the new one. In the Dominican Republic all workers under 45 years of age are required to contribute to the new plan. In El Salvador all workers under 36 years of age at the time of the reform were required to switch to the new system. Men between 36 and 55 and women between 36 and 50 were given one year to choose between the old and the new systems. The default option for these workers was the funded system. Older workers were left in the old system. In Uruguay, all workers over 40 were given the choice between the old and new systems, and those below that age were automatically transferred to the new plan. In Argentina, Colombia, and Peru all workers who were under the old PAYG system and did not express a wish to switch to the new privately funded pillar remained in the reformed PAYG system.

Past contributions to the old system for those who decided or were required to switch to the new system were acknowledged in most cases through recognition bonds. The main exceptions are Argentina and Uruguay, where a complementary benefit will be paid at retirement, and Mexico, where contributors in the old system at the moment of the reform were offered a guarantee that their retirement benefit would be no lower than that which would have been received in the old PAYG system.

Except in Chile where the system has been in place for more than two decades, Latin American workers retiring from the reformed pension systems over the next decades will receive most of their retirement income in the form of benefits that accrued under the old PAYG systems. Therefore, the analysis in this chapter on the performance of the funded pillar provides only a partial view of the performance of the overall mandatory retirement income security system. Over time, however, benefits accrued in the old PAYG systems will dwindle in relation to those accrued in the new funded pillars, except in Argentina, Colombia, and Peru, where the relative size of each pillar will depend on workers' choices, and in Costa Rica, which decided to retain a large PAYG system. Since the reform, however, new workers in Argentina and Peru have overwhelmingly chosen the funded pillar, signaling some degree of confidence in the new system.[9]

Structure and Implementation of the Mandatory Savings Component

In this section and the next we will specify in greater detail the structure of the "savings" pillars of multipillar reforms in Latin America, addressing first the mandatory and then the voluntary components. It should be noted that in some countries, such as Argentina, Colombia, and Peru, the mandatory component is not mandatory in one sense of the term—workers can choose between a downsized earnings-related PAYG plan and the funded individual accounts. But it is mandatory in that the worker *must* pick one of these alternatives.

The accumulation stage (of both the mandatory and the voluntary savings components) is based on a defined contribution formula whereby contributions are saved in pension fund accounts managed by dedicated pension fund administrators.[10] A portion of workers' contributions to the private pillar pays for the services provided by the fund managers and covers the cost of premiums for group disability and life insurance policies they are required to provide to contributing workers.[11] Workers are allowed to choose their fund manager from among the limited number in the closed industry, and workers who have been with a fund manager for some minimum period of time are allowed to switch to another manager.

The minimum mandatory contribution is based on the minimum salary in all countries except Uruguay, where contributions to the pension fund system are mandatory only on the portion of the salary above approximately six minimum wages for workers who earn above this level. Workers who earn less may direct up to half of their mandatory contributions to the pension fund of their choice. The contribution rates that are channeled into the individual's capitalization account (net of commissions or insurance premiums) and the maximum monthly earnings subject to the mandate to save are shown in table 2.3. Contribution rates for the individual account vary over time in four countries—Argentina, El Salvador, Mexico, and Uruguay—because commissions and insurance premiums are paid from the total contribution. In the remaining countries that have undertaken reforms, on the other hand, the contribution for the individual account is fixed as a percentage of the worker's salary. In Mexico workers make an additional mandatory contribution to the housing fund managed by a state body, INFONAVIT.

Contributions and investment income are tax-exempt, but retirement income is taxed. In Mexico workers who participate in the funded system also get a public subsidy equivalent to 5.5 percent of the minimum wage in January 1997, indexed to the consumer price index (CPI; see box 9.1). Self-employed workers who contribute to the new mandatory funded system in the Dominican Republic will also receive a public subsidy, but its value is still to be determined. In Colombia another form of account subsidy has been introduced in a solidarity tax on affiliates with higher incomes.

Contribution collection and record keeping are managed by the pension fund administrators in all countries except Argentina, the Dominican Republic, and Mexico, where this function has been centralized. In Argentina the internal revenue tax authority is responsible for collecting income taxes and all

Table 2.3 Contribution Rates and Earnings Ceilings in the Mandatory Funded Systems

(December 2002)
(Percent of wages)

Country	Contribution into fund/individual's salary	Maximum contributable earnings/average national earnings
Argentina	2.75	5.80
Bolivia	10.00	12.50
Chile	10.00	3.10
Colombia	10.00	10.00
Costa Rica	4.25	No ceiling
Dominican Republic	10.00	10.30
El Salvador	11.02	14.40
Mexico	6.27	6.40
Peru	8.00	No ceiling
Uruguay	12.27	5.70

Notes: The total contribution rate (for capitalization, insurance, and commission) was cut to 5 percent in Argentina in December 2001. The contribution that is channeled into the individual's account therefore dropped dramatically between 2001 and 2002. During 2003 the total contribution rate was gradually raised back to its original value (11 percent). The contribution rate in the Dominican Republic is rising gradually until it reaches 10 percent in 2008. Similarly, the contribution rate in Costa Rica is being increased gradually from 1.5 percent to 4.5 percent. In Uruguay poorer workers can split their 15 percent mandatory contribution equally between the PAYG and the funded system. The figures reported assume that the total contribution is made to the funded system. Figures for Chile are based on the average earnings for workers who contributed to the system in December 2002. (This average is higher than the national one because of the informal and self-employed workers.)

Sources: Devesa-Carpio and Vidal-Meliá (2002) and Whitehouse (2001).

payroll contributions for social insurance programs, including the pension system. In contrast, Mexico established a centralized record-keeping and collection system with the sole purpose of handling the flows of information and funds in the new pension system. Another important difference is that the Mexican agency is owned by the new dedicated pension fund management industry and set up as a nonprofit company. In the Dominican Republic a nonprofit, private foundation is also responsible for record keeping. The Treasury monitors this institution and is ultimately responsible for sanctions and for ensuring that funds are correctly allocated to each of the individual programs within the social security system.

The pension fund administrators charge a fee or commission in remuneration for their services. All countries except the Dominican Republic and Mexico permit only charges on contribution flows. In the Dominican Republic a performance-related fee is allowed, whereas in Mexico there is complete freedom in the type of charge that the administrators may set. Two countries, El Salvador and the Dominican Republic, have set caps on charges. In El Salvador the total charge for commissions including insurance was limited by law to 3 percent of wages. In the Dominican Republic the charge for commissions is set at 0.5 percentage points out of the total contribution of 10 percent.

Each pension fund administrator can manage only one fund, except in Chile, where each administrator offers five funds with different risk–return characteristics. In Mexico the pension legislation contemplates multiple funds, but as yet only one is permitted. Legislation passed in March 2003 but not yet implemented will allow the fund managers in Peru to offer multiple funds.

All countries restrict the frequency of switching between providers. In Argentina, Colombia, El Salvador, and Uruguay two annual switches are permitted. Mexico permits only one switch annually. Chile and Peru have not established legal restrictions, but the switching procedure actually allows at most one per year. In Bolivia switching between the two fund managers is currently not permitted.

The balance in affiliates' individual retirement accounts reflects changes in the market value of the financial assets in which the new funds are invested.[12] Hence, during the fund accumulation stage (i.e., before retirement) both investment and longevity risk are borne fully by the individual.[13] Moreover, the asset allocation of pension funds is constrained by quantitative investment limits, and in some countries (Argentina, Chile, Colombia, El Salvador, Peru, and Uruguay) the performance of each fund cannot stray too far from industry averages. As a result, the funds offer similar risk–return trade-offs.

The retirement income that workers obtain from the mandatory funded pension pillar is protected by a minimum pension guarantee in those countries where the PAYG pension is being phased out (Bolivia, Chile, Dominican Republic, El Salvador, Mexico, and Nicaragua). The minimum pension guarantee is set at a level close to that of the minimum wage. In Mexico contributors in the old system at the moment of the reform were offered an additional guarantee that their retirement benefit from the new system would be no lower than that which would have been received in the old PAYG system. Workers in Colombia are also protected by a minimum pension guarantee, regardless of whether they choose the PAYG plan or individual accounts. In Argentina, Costa Rica, and Uruguay there is no minimum pension guarantee in the funded pillar, but workers' benefits are underpinned by an explicit PAYG minimum benefit. Affiliates who choose the PAYG option in Peru are guaranteed a minimum benefit, but those who choose individual accounts are not guaranteed any minimum pension.[14]

Structure and Implementation of the Voluntary Savings Component

As mentioned previously, the new funded pillars usually have both a mandatory and a voluntary component. Conceptually, the new pillars can combine both second- and third-pillar features. As shown in table 2.4, workers may make additional, voluntary contributions to the individual accounts managed by the pension fund administrators. The voluntary component of the new funded pillars has a similarly restrictive design to the mandatory component in all countries (except in Chile since early 2002; see below).

In some countries, such as El Salvador, these voluntary contributions must be deposited in the same fund as the mandatory contributions; in others, such as Colombia and Mexico, there is a separate fund for voluntary contributions that is subject to a more flexible regulatory regime. In Colombia fiduciary societies are also able to manage these voluntary retirement savings. In October 2002 Chile became the first Latin American country to liberalize the market for tax-preferred voluntary retirement savings, by permitting other financial companies to act as pension plan providers and to offer products that could substitute for individual retirement accounts.

In order to benefit from tax incentives on voluntary savings, deposits must normally be left in the individual account until retirement. There are two exceptions to this restriction: in Colombia and Mexico funds deposited on a voluntary basis can be cashed out at any time with six months' notice. Chile also recently modified pension legislation permitting distributions at any time, although they are subject to a tax penalty.

In addition to voluntary contributions to the funded system, workers in Latin American countries can save in a variety of financial instruments. In some Latin American countries employers can also set up pension plans for their employees. With the exception of occupational plans in Costa Rica, all these instruments are subject to a much less advantageous tax treatment than is the voluntary funded system.

Conclusion

Proponents of the multipillar reform model claim that the new systems distribute and diversify the risks to retirement income more efficiently than do pure PAYG systems (World Bank 1994). Instead of government primarily bearing the risk as in a single-pillar system, the multipillar approach's mix of government guarantees, mandated individual savings, and voluntary pension arrangements—including those between employers and their workers—spread the demographic (longevity), macroeconomic

Table 2.4 Voluntary Funded Pillars in Latin America

Country	Voluntary tax-favored savings vehicle
Argentina	Individuals and their employers can make voluntary contributions to their individual pension fund accounts that cannot be cashed out until retirement. The tax treatment for these voluntary savings is the same as for mandatory savings.
Bolivia	Individuals and their employers can make voluntary contributions to their individual pension fund accounts that cannot be cashed out until retirement. The tax treatment for these voluntary savings is the same as for mandatory savings.
Chile	Until October 2002 individuals and their employers could make tax-favored (same treatment as mandatory) voluntary contributions to their individual pension fund accounts that could not be cashed out until retirement (*Cuenta 1*). After October 2002 these contributions could be deposited in any registered pension plan offered by AFPs, banks, or insurance companies. The funds can now be cashed out at any time but are subject to a 10 percent tax penalty.
	In addition, individuals can make voluntary deposits to the so-called voluntary savings accounts (*Cuenta de Ahorro Voluntario* [CAV], also known as *Cuenta 2*) that are also managed by the pension fund administrators. Individuals can withdraw funds from these accounts up to four times a year. There are some tax incentives but fewer than for the *Cuenta 1*. The CAVs have not been affected by the reform that took place in 2001.
Colombia	Individuals and their employers can make voluntary contributions to their individual pension fund accounts up to 30 percent of their salary. The tax treatment for these voluntary savings is the same as for mandatory savings. The funds can be cashed out after five years at any time with at least a six-month notice. The voluntary pension funds can be administered by life insurance companies and bank trusts as well as by the pension fund administrators.
Costa Rica	Individuals and their employers can make voluntary contributions to their individual pension fund accounts. Employer and employee contributions are tax deductible and are not subject to social charges of up to 10 percent of the employee's salary. Tax penalties apply if the accumulated balance is cashed out before retirement. Partial withdrawal cannot be more than 50 percent of the fund. Total withdrawal is only permitted after 66 months of contributions and payment of tax.

(Table continues on the following page.)

Table 2.4 (continued)

Country	Voluntary tax-favored savings vehicle
El Salvador	Individuals and their employers can make voluntary contributions to their individual pension fund accounts that cannot be cashed out until retirement. The tax treatment for these voluntary savings is the same as for mandatory savings. Contributions are only tax deductible up to 10 percent of salary.
Mexico	Individuals and their employers can make voluntary contributions to their individual pension fund accounts. The tax treatment for these voluntary savings is the same as for mandatory savings. The funds can be cashed out at any time with at least a six-month notice.
Peru	Individuals and their employers can make voluntary contributions to their individual pension fund accounts that cannot be cashed out until retirement. The tax treatment for these voluntary savings is the same as for mandatory savings. Individuals who have been affiliated with a plan for more than five years (or are older than 50) and their employers can also deposit additional voluntary contributions into their individual pension fund accounts that can be cashed out before retirement.
Uruguay	Individuals and their employers can make voluntary contributions to their individual pension fund accounts that cannot be cashed out until retirement. The tax treatment for these voluntary savings is the same as for mandatory savings.

Source: Relevant pension legislation for each country.

(inflation and recessions), and investment (low or negative returns) risks to retirement income. Although not yet optimal, the diversification of risk in these multipillar systems is widely regarded as an improvement over that which prevailed under the single-pillar, defined-benefit PAYG systems.

The new multipillar approach to providing retirement income security was expected to have both direct and secondary benefits. The downsized public pillar would provide a more fiscally sustainable form of basic income protection against poverty in old age and would correct regressive transfers that prevailed under the single-pillar defined-benefit PAYG systems, whereas the introduction of explicitly defined mandatory and voluntary private pillars would have positive medium-term effects on the labor market (a more efficient allocation of labor and a greater coverage of formal income security) and the development of the financial sector.

Combined, the multipillar approach was presented as a new package of social security policy that would protect old people through a better distribution of risks to retirement income and the promotion of economic growth (World Bank 1994). In the chapters that follow we take stock of developments in each of these areas—fiscal sustainability of public pension promises, development of capital markets and the financial sector, and improved equity and efficiency in the labor market leading to an extension of coverage. We examine each of these promises to the extent that is possible, keeping in mind that a definitive evaluation cannot be made of what are still relatively young reformed pension systems, but exploiting all the tools available to provide guidance to policymakers that some may find valuable. Our focus is on the countries presented in table 2.1, which have instituted reforms; we pay less attention to those in table 2.2, whose reforms are very recent or have yet to be implemented.

Notes

1. Along with old-age pension benefits, structural reforms to social security systems in the last 20 years in Latin America have dramatically affected the provision of disability and life insurance and, in some cases, workplace injury insurance.
2. This section summarizes only the most salient aspects of the reformed pension systems in countries where the new systems have been fully implemented. It is not intended as an exhaustive description of the multipillar model in each country. We have made every attempt to keep up to date with developments, but new reform legislation is being debated and has even been passed in several countries in the region. For excellent, detailed reviews of each of the reformed systems, see Queisser (1998a) and Devesa-Carpio and Vidal-Meliá (2002).
3. These reforms, although passed into law, have yet to be implemented in Ecuador and Nicaragua. Several articles in Ecuador's reform are disputed as unconstitutional.
4. In this volume we categorize "pillars" by their objective rather than by whom they are administered (the public or private sector), by how benefits are structured (final salary benefit formula or defined contributions), or by their financing mechanism (PAYG or full funding). Thus we use the term "first pillar" or "pillar one" to refer to the part of a pension system intended to keep elderly people out of poverty; the term "second pillar" or "pillar two" to refer to the part intended to help individuals smooth consumption over their life cycle (i.e., to prevent a dramatic fall in income at the time of retirement); and the term "third pillar" or "pillar three" to refer to the institutions available on a voluntary basis for workers to increase their retirement income. We discuss the emerging distinction between pillar one and "pillar zero" in chapter 9.
5. Although Brazil introduced significant reforms to its retirement security regime for workers in the private sector, its reform does not qualify as "structural" among pension specialists because it did not introduce a system of mandated private saving. Brazil's reform is referred to as "parametric" because reformers adjusted contribution and benefit parameters within a PAYG financing framework (although it required changes to the country's constitution).
6. We take up the discussion of pension programs designed to prevent poverty and the emerging distinction between the contributory pillar one and the noncontributory pillar zero in chapter 9.
7. In these four countries some sort of noncontributory benefit targeted to the elderly poor population also exists. The issue is taken up again in chapter 9.

8. Peru is exceptional in the region for not providing a poverty prevention pension to the majority of workers who affiliated with the new system of private accounts. Although a first pillar minimum pension guarantee still exists for workers affiliated with the reformed PAYG system, and a guarantee similar to that in Chile was put in place in July 2002 for older affiliates of the private system, the majority of workers covered by a formal retirement security system are not covered against poverty in old age.

9. The high rate of affiliation with the funded system is partly because workers who do not express a choice are assigned automatically to the funded system.

10. *Administradoras de fondos de pensiones* or AFPs in Chile, Peru, Colombia, Bolivia, and El Salvador; otherwise named in the remainder of countries that mandate private savings for retirement.

11. In Mexico and Costa Rica disability pensions are still paid by the public pillar.

12. Market valuation is not always possible because most securities, especially those issued by the private sector, are thinly traded. Regulators have developed mechanisms to proxy the value of less liquid securities. Argentina allows pension funds to value part of their government bond portfolio at book prices. Since 1998 a maximum of 30 percent of the total pension fund portfolio can be valued in this way.

13. It is interesting that while workers are fully exposed to investment and longevity risks over the accumulation stage, they are fully insured against the risks of disability and death. The premiums for these policies are paid by the pension fund administrators to private insurance companies, except in Mexico, where the Social Security Institute has retained the monopoly on these services.

14. The poverty prevention pillar, which can take several different institutional forms, including those described briefly here, is discussed at length in chapter 9.

3

The Fiscal Sustainability of Public Pension Promises in Latin America

PENSION DEBT SERVICE IS OFTEN one of the largest items in government budgets. Governments' inability to meet growing pension liabilities—implied in the benefit promises of single-pillar PAYG systems, and often unaccounted for on public sector balance sheets—can be a source of policy risk to old-age income security and is usually the driving force (and a political selling point) of structural reforms (Holzmann, Palacios, and Zviniene 2001; Holzmann 1998). Just as with the pure PAYG institutions that were replaced, the fiscal sustainability of public pension promises after the introduction of the multipillar model with a large funded component can determine the credibility of the reformed pension system. The question therefore is this: have structural reforms made governments' remaining public pension promises more fiscally sustainable?

This chapter presents the results of simulation analysis of the likely medium- and long-term fiscal outcomes of structural reforms to retirement security systems in Latin America (as explained in Zviniene and Packard 2002). Although several studies conducted both prior to and since reforms have presented the simulated fiscal impact of the shift to multipillar systems with individual accounts, rarely do existing studies extend beyond a single country case. Zviniene and Packard evaluated the likely fiscal impact of very different reforms in a group of diverse countries, using a uniform set of indicators and applying a single generic simulation model, the World Bank's *Pension Reform Options Simulation Toolkit* (PROST).[1]

The results of PROST simulations are followed by a note of caution on just what simulations can and cannot show and how the simulated cost of reforms can diverge dramatically from actual transition costs. Moving beyond the fiscal impact of reform, we discuss the potential links between structural reform and economic growth. Furthermore, we present a discussion of wider macroeconomic risks that arise with structural reforms, and how these can determine the sustainability of long-term pension promises, presented in Fiess (2003).

We find that although remaining public pension promises are fiscally more sustainable after structural reforms, the broader macroeconomic impact of making a portion of implicit pension liabilities explicit with the transition to private individual accounts is uncertain.

Simulated Fiscal Impact of Structural Reforms

Figure 3.1 shows the value of governments' implicit pension promises in each of the countries that undertook structural reforms to their retirement security systems. The figure also shows one relevant counterfactual—the value of this indicator had there been no reforms.[2]

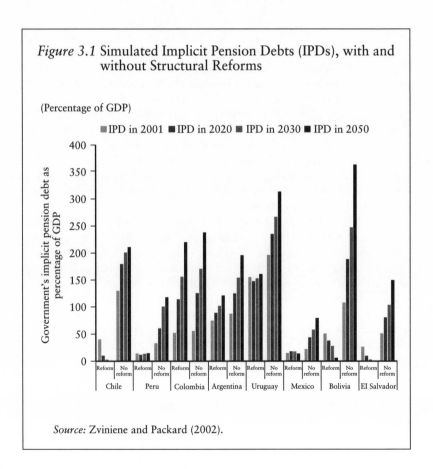

Figure 3.1 Simulated Implicit Pension Debts (IPDs), with and without Structural Reforms

(Percentage of GDP)

Source: Zviniene and Packard (2002).

The value of pension promises is referred to as *implicit pension debt* (IPD) and is defined as the present value of the stream of future benefits that a public pension system will have to pay current participants (contributors, beneficiaries, and their survivors), according to the defined parameters of the system, to recognize their contributions up to the particular year in question. There are several different concepts and methods for calculating the IPD. The simulations presented here employ a "practical termination liability approach," described in detail in Holzmann, Palacios, and Zviniene (2001) and proposed as the best method of calculating the IPD for cross-country comparisons.

It comes as little surprise that where reforms phased out earnings-related pensions from the public PAYG pillar—Chile, Mexico, Bolivia, and El Salvador—the simulated cost of governments' pension promises (as a percentage of GDP) falls rapidly (figure 3.1). However, even in countries where an earnings-related PAYG pillar was retained—Argentina, Colombia, and Peru—and where explicitly defined first-pillar benefits underpin pensions from a private second pillar—as in Argentina and Uruguay—reforms are likely to slow the growth of public pension liabilities, as measured by IPD.

A decrease in governments' implicit pension promises is to be expected from reforms that partially privatize public pension systems. The simulated implicit pension debt falls in the wake of reforms as a portion of these obligations is converted into explicit debt or paid with transfers from the general budget.

Thus, although changes in the implicit pension debt reveal the extent of reform and how countries chose to spread the costs of transition from one regime to the next, a better measure of fiscal sustainability is the rate at which the total public debt for pensions is accumulating after reforms, compared with the rate of total debt accumulation had there been no reforms. The total pension debt shown in table 3.1 and figure 3.2 is that financed by government borrowing, and includes (a) the current deficits of remaining PAYG systems (the difference between pension payments and contribution revenues), (b) payments to cover the minimum guaranteed pensions for workers contributing to private individual retirement accounts where such guarantees exist, (c) government contributions to either a PAYG regime or individual accounts in countries where these are made explicit in the law, and (d) payment of recognition bonds to honor workers' contributions to pre-reform systems.

Even an analysis of governments' simulated total pension debts accumulated after 2001 and the rate of accumulation (figure 3.2) on the whole show a dramatic improvement in fiscal sustainability brought about by reforms. The simulations show substantial savings from the introduction of individual accounts and accompanying reforms. These savings are most apparent in Bolivia, Chile, El Salvador, Peru, and, Uruguay.

Table 3.1 Current Pension Deficits (Benefit Expenditure Less Contribution Revenue) Financed by Government Transfers

(Percent)

	Uruguay		Argentina		Mexico		Bolivia		Colombia		Chile		El Salvador		Peru	
	Reform	No reform	Reform	No reform	Reform	No reform	Reform	No reform	Reform	No reform	Reform	No reform	Reform	No reform	Reform	No reform
2001	(4.0)	(3.4)	(2.5)	(0.1)	(0.5)	0.2	(3.5)	0.8	1.6	(0)	(7.2)	(0.1)	(1.4)	(0.8)	(0.7)	0.7
2010	(2.6)	(2.2)	(2.2)	0.1	(0.6)	0	(2.2)	0	1.5	(0.4)	(4.6)	0.2	(2.2)	(1.0)	(0.9)	0.7
2020	(2.1)	(2.2)	(2.3)	(0.3)	(0.7)	(0.3)	(2.1)	(1.1)	1.0	(1.5)	(3.4)	(1.0)	(3.2)	(1.4)	(0.9)	0.4
2030	(2.2)	(3.4)	(2.8)	(1.3)	(0.7)	(0.8)	(2.1)	(3.0)	(0.7)	(3.3)	(1.5)	(2.7)	(2.9)	(2.1)	(0.9)	(0.1)
2040	(2.5)	(5.0)	(3.6)	(2.8)	(0.7)	(1.5)	(1.7)	(5.3)	(3.4)	(5.5)	(0.5)	(3.9)	(2.6)	(3.1)	(0.8)	(1.2)
2050	(2.8)	(6.6)	(4.4)	(4.3)	(0.6)	(2.3)	(0.9)	(8.5)	(5.4)	(7.6)	(0.8)	(4.0)	(0.5)	(4.1)	(1.0)	(2.3)

Source: PROST simulations in Zviniene and Packard (2002).

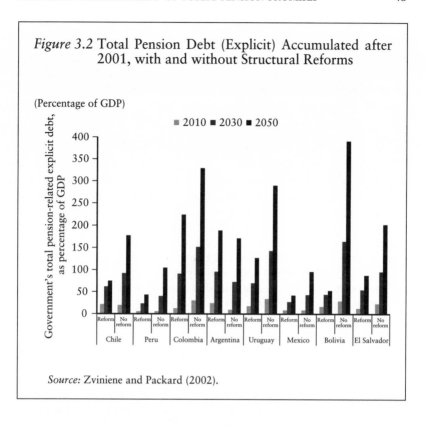

Figure 3.2 Total Pension Debt (Explicit) Accumulated after 2001, with and without Structural Reforms

(Percentage of GDP)

Source: Zviniene and Packard (2002).

In Argentina, however, the simulations summarized here show a considerable increase in the federal government's total expenditure on pensions in the reform scenario.[3] In addition to capturing the loss of contribution revenue from workers who switched to individual accounts, these projections capture the increase in PAYG deficits that arose from a policy of lowering employer contributions to the public pillar—a policy introduced after the 1994 reform in an attempt to increase compliance with the mandate for employers and workers to participate in the system.[4]

Another critical factor that caused Argentina's total spending on pensions to balloon since the reform in 1994 was the federal government's policy of accepting the liabilities of overly generous pension plans for civil servants at the provincial level. Provincial governments that agreed to close their pension regimes to new entrants and to force contributing civil servants to join the national system along with private sector workers (either the publicly administered, earnings-related PAYG branch or mandated private individual accounts) transferred the obligation of paying the relatively generous benefits of retired provincial civil servants to the federal system. The sudden increase in total pension liabilities combined with revenue reductions to the retirement security system stemming from lower contribution rates, widespread evasion, and a long recession aggravated the fiscal stance of Argentina's multipillar pension system. However, our simulations show only the effect of lower contribution rates.

What Simulations Can and Cannot Show

The results of our simulations presented in the previous section show that, with some notable exceptions, structural reforms with more modest public pension promises in Latin America are likely to have a beneficial impact on the fiscal sustainability of pension systems. As stressed by Holzmann, Palacios, and Zviniene (2001), however, the sort of cross-country simulation analysis presented here has to be interpreted very carefully, and cannot replace careful country-specific analysis of reforms.

The indicators of fiscal sustainability presented above are simulations of the fiscal impact of reform laws and, thus (somewhat optimistically), they assume that reforms were implemented correctly and that the new systems are adequately administered. The simulations cannot capture probable administrative difficulties that could cause fiscal costs of reform to balloon unexpectedly. In background papers for this book Escobar (2003) and Fiess (2003) showed how the case of Bolivia is instructive in this regard: the transition proved more costly than initially anticipated. When the Bolivian reform was designed and implemented, insufficient attention was paid to the institutions that were to govern the transition from the old to the new system. Although a regulatory body was set up to govern the new private pension funds, the system transition itself was insufficiently regulated and thus invited fraudulent claims and a lax interpretation of the rules for the transition. This has contributed to higher than expected transition costs (see box 3.1). Similarly, Mesa-Lago (2000) pointed out that the initial projections of the transition costs of reform in Chile understated the true fiscal costs by more than half.

Finally, the simulation results in this chapter are used solely to evaluate whether the sustainability of public pension promises has been improved by structural reforms in the region. This is to say that we are concerned with the reduction of "policy risks" to retirement income. Therefore our analysis is solely focused on whether the reductions of what were unsustainable PAYG pension promises are likely to reduce the risk of governments having to default on workers' public pension rights. The simulations cannot address wider macroeconomic concerns and possible risks that arise when governments convert implicit pension debts into explicit debts with structural reforms to the pension system (box 3.2).

Box 3.1 Bolivia's Pension Reform: A Transition
Considerably More Costly Than Expected

In 1996 Bolivia's pure PAYG retirement security system was insolvent
and illiquid. A structural pension reform was implemented that termi-
nated the old defined benefit system and introduced a new system based
on defined contributions paid by the employee and, to a lesser extent, by
the employer. As elsewhere in Latin America, the new system is administered by private fund managers, under supervision of a government regulatory body.

At the time of the reform it was estimated that the transition costs
would decline steadily and disappear completely some time after 2037
(Von Gersdorff 1997), but with the benefit of hindsight observers agree
that this projection was far too optimistic. In fact, the transition-related
cash-flow gap has been steadily increasing from 4 percent of GDP in 1998
to 5 percent of GDP in 2002 (see figure 3B.1 below).

The increase of Bolivia's pension-related deficit has been attributed to
a series of factors (Revilla 2002; IMF 2003). The government has
allowed the law to be loosely interpreted to permit a higher number of
early retirees. Some groups that were not initially covered have managed
to retire under the old system. The number of fraudulent claims has also
been on the rise; estimates indicate that payments equaling half a point
of GDP are fraudulent. Furthermore, the pension law introduced index-

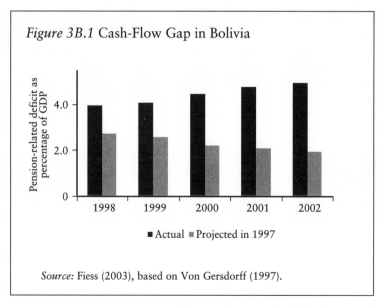

Figure 3B.1 Cash-Flow Gap in Bolivia

■ Actual ■ Projected in 1997

Source: Fiess (2003), based on Von Gersdorff (1997).

(Box continues on the following page.)

Box 3.1 (continued)

ation linked to the exchange rate, which has proved very costly. The indexation mechanism was recently reversed. Finally, following social unrest the government introduced a minimum pension of B$850 per month in 2001—nearly twice the minimum salary. In many cases the new minimum pension substantially exceeds original entitlements.

When the reform was designed and implemented, insufficient attention was paid to the institutions that were to govern the transition from the old to the new system. Although a regulatory body was set up to govern the new private pension funds, the system transition itself was insufficiently regulated, and that invited fraudulent claims, a lax interpretation of the rules for transition workers, and higher than expected transition costs.

Effects of Structural Pension Reform on Economic Growth

Several studies have gone beyond fiscal impacts to address the wider macroeconomic effects of structural pension reform. As Barrs (2000) noted, economic growth is central to the viability of any type of pension system because pensions represent claims on the level of future (rather than current) output. Theory suggests that pension reform can lead to increased economic growth through three principal channels: (1) stimulation of savings and investment; (2) labor markets, by raising employment and labor productivity; and (3) capital market development leading to more efficient resource allocation and enhanced total factor productivity. Yet there is much disagreement over whether pension reform does indeed increase growth, both in theory and practice. Although a complete treatment of the wider macroeconomic effects of pension reform is beyond the scope of this book, in this section we summarize the key issues.

Proponents of the view that structural pension reform increases economic growth argue that the effect occurs through various channels. First, mobilization of savings through second- and third-pillar contributions raises the aggregate savings rate, which leads to higher investment and output. Second, reductions in payroll taxes lead to increased employment and a shift of workers to the formal sector, raising both labor supply and labor productivity. Third, the savings channeled into pension funds through the second and third pillars stimulates capital market development and financial innovation, which leads to more efficient resource allocation and increased total factor productivity.

*Averting the Old Age Crisis: Policies to Protect the Old **and** Promote Growth* (World Bank 1994) [emphasis in original] typifies this perspective,

Box 3.2 Virtuous and Vicious Fiscal Circles: The Cases of Chile and Argentina

The often-touted fiscal effects of structural pension reforms can depend in large measure on whether a country embarks on reform from a position of relative fiscal strength or weakness. Although any well-designed reform will yield fiscal benefits in the long term, countries that undertake reforms in a position of fiscal strength are better able to absorb short-term transition costs. Furthermore, because financial markets can react negatively to the conversion of implicit pension debt to explicit debt, a country's initial fiscal position plays a major role in determining whether structural reforms generate a virtuous or vicious circle of fiscal adjustment. The cases of Chile and Argentina provide contrasting examples of the impact of pension reform in Latin America.

In Chile, "authorities deliberately strengthened the fiscal stance for some years before beginning the pension reform" (Holzmann 1997, p. 173). Fiscal surpluses averaged more than 5 percent of GDP in the two years prior to the 1981 reform (figure 3B.2a), and contributed to ensuring that Chile's post-reform fiscal deficits were relatively mild and short-lived.

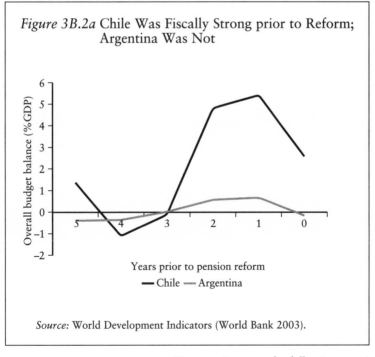

Figure 3B.2a Chile Was Fiscally Strong prior to Reform; Argentina Was Not

Years prior to pension reform

— Chile — Argentina

Source: World Development Indicators (World Bank 2003).

(Box continues on the following page.)

Box 3.2 (continued)

In contrast, Argentina did not substantially bolster its fiscal situation prior to the 1994 reform, despite enjoying several years of strong economic growth. The conversion of implicit debt to explicit debt that accompanied structural reform in Argentina revealed that the pre-reform fiscal stance "had been worse than shown by the published figures" (Perry and Servén 2003, p. 38). Further payroll tax deductions reduced revenues and worsened pension system deficits (Rofman 2000), contributing to growing fiscal deficits (see figure 3B.2b). To be fair, not all of the growing pension deficit was a result of the reform (Perry and Servén 2003), but Argentina's failure to take advantage of strong growth prior to the reform contributed to its post-reform fiscal deterioration.

The cases of Chile and Argentina demonstrate why governments should develop a relatively strong fiscal position prior to undertaking structural reforms and they underscore the importance of reducing the implicit debt of unfunded PAYG systems prior to making the debt explicit by shifting to a funded second pillar (Holzmann 1998).

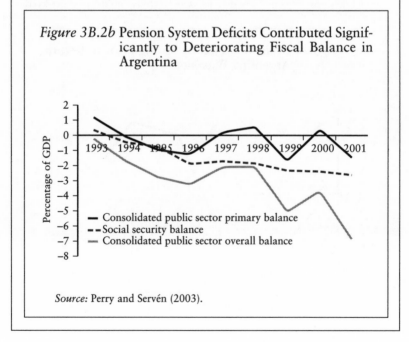

Figure 3B.2b Pension System Deficits Contributed Significantly to Deteriorating Fiscal Balance in Argentina

— Consolidated public sector primary balance
- - Social security balance
— Consolidated public sector overall balance

Source: Perry and Servén (2003).

particularly with respect to the expected growth benefits of the second pillar: "A mandatory multipillar arrangement for old age security helps countries to . . . increase long-term saving, capital market deepening, and growth through the use of full funding and decentralized control in the second pillar" (pp. 22–23).

Do these growth benefits materialize in practice? The most recent and comprehensive attempt to quantify the effect of structural pension reform on growth is a study of Chile by Corbo and Schmidt-Hebbel (2003). Controlling for other reforms, the authors used time-series regressions for the period 1981–2001 to estimate separately the impact of pension reform on the capital stock, labor supply, and total factor productivity. They then substituted these estimates in a Cobb-Douglas production function to estimate the overall impact of pension reform on economic growth.

Corbo and Schmidt-Hebbel found that pension reform's impact on savings and investment, labor markets, and total factor productivity led to average annual economic growth of 0.49 percent, or almost one-tenth of Chile's average annualized growth of 4.63 percent over the period 1981–2001. The authors noted, however, that although they controlled for other reforms to the Chilean economy over the period, their estimate may capture some of the interactive effects of pension reform with other structural changes. They also noted that the effect of pension reform on growth is likely to decrease to zero over the long term as the system matures and the economy approaches steady-state growth.

Although the Corbo and Schmidt-Hebbel study is econometrically sound, it is emblematic of an approach that relies on assumptions about the nature of pension reform and economic growth that are far from certain. Regarding the effect of pension reform on savings, Barr (2000) argued, "There are not one, but three links in the argument that future output will be higher . . . : [that] funding leads to a higher rate of saving than PAYG; that higher saving is translated into more and better investment; and that investment leads to an increase in output. None of the three links *necessarily* holds." Similarly, Easterly (2001) pointed out that economists have not yet shaken off their adherence to Harrod-Domar growth models, which posit formulaic savings-investment-output relationships that fail to materialize in practice.

With respect to labor market efficiency, establishing a link between pension benefits and contributions does appear to improve the incentives to join the formal sector, as we will argue in chapter 5. But as we also argue there, these improved incentives are likely to have little impact on worker behavior in the absence of complementary labor market reforms and other favorable conditions, as the stagnant social security coverage rates in Latin America demonstrate.

Finally, the evidence that pension reform contributes to capital market development is tenuous, as we explore in detail in the next chapter. The assumption of increased total factor productivity through pension funds' more efficient resource allocation is even more dubious, given the restrictions imposed on pension fund investment in equities in many countries and their heavy investment in sovereign debt.

None of these reservations mean to say that structural pension reform cannot or does not contribute to economic growth—indeed it can, and country-specific analysis may find that it does. The link between pension reform and growth is not automatic, however, but rather is dependent on a number of associated linkages that may or may not materialize. And without denying the fundamental importance of growth, policymakers should remember that the function of a social security system is not to stimulate growth but to prevent poverty and smooth consumption in old age.

Broader Risks and Macroeconomic Concerns Raised by Structural Reforms[5]

Several authors have argued that standard debt sustainability indicators should be enriched with a measure of implicit pension liabilities to provide better performance indicators for fiscal sustainability and solvency (Holzmann, Palacios, and Zviniene 2001). Whereas previous studies (Feldstein and Seligman 1981; Moody's 1998) showed that markets and rating agencies take unfunded pension liabilities of corporations into account when determining share prices and ratings, Truglia (2000, 2002) argued that the situation is entirely different for the impact of unfunded public pension liabilities on sovereign credit risk.

Truglia (2000, 2002) stated that to date, net-present-value estimates of implicit pension liabilities have not influenced Moody's sovereign credit risk ratings.[6] There are two reasons for this. First, net-present-value calculations are highly susceptible to sizable swings depending on relatively small changes in a number of parameters. Second, and more important, although net-present-value calculations of future pension liabilities provide a projection of a given scenario, they do not assign a probability that the projection will come true. Assessing fiscal solvency on the grounds of projected implicit pension liabilities alone does not account for the fact that policymakers tend to change the parameters of the present pension system and hence the level of implicit pension liabilities before financing concerns become too pressing.

Although a public pension promise is similar to a government bond in the sense that it represents a claim on future income, society treats both claims quite differently. Public pension promises are changed in ways that debt instruments would never be altered. Truglia (2002) pointed out that although no industrial country has defaulted on its debt since World War II, almost every industrial country has adjusted its pension system in ways that changed the original contract, that is, by increasing the retirement age, changing the benefit formula, or both. The fact that pension reform is generally not referred to as "pension default" illustrates that society differentiates between changes in contractual terms of public pension and debt claims.

However, the fact that risk-rating agencies do not account for implicit pension liabilities in their country risk ratings does not mean that pension reforms (and in particular the financing of the transition deficit) have no impact on country risk premiums. It is often argued that during the transition period, when implicit debt is made explicit, the market perception of sovereign risk might rise as the observable debt burden increases. To our knowledge no empirical study has analyzed the impact of pension reforms on country risk. In an attempt to better understand potential links between pension reforms and country risk in Latin America, Fiess (2003) drew from the literature on country risk to develop some guidelines for future research.

The literature suggests a number of determinants for country risk, including measures of liquidity and solvency, macroeconomic fundamentals, and external shocks (see Edwards 1986; Haque et al. 1996; Barnes and Cline 1997; Eichengreen and Mody 1998; Kamin and von Kleist 1999; Min and Park 2000; Fiess 2003).

Within this framework there are two main channels through which pension reforms might affect country risk. First, pension reform can change the level of implicit and explicit liabilities and, as such, potentially affect the *perception* of solvency. In most cases perception is reality. Second, it is argued (although not generally accepted) that pension reform positively affects economic growth. As we discussed in the previous section, the relationship between pension reform and growth stems from an assumed direct effect that reforms may have on growth through savings and capital accumulation, and via an indirect growth effect through the development of capital markets.

If establishing a clear empirical link between pension reform and economic growth is hard, proving a relationship between implicit and explicit pension liabilities and country risk seems equally difficult. To do so one would have to disentangle at least two simultaneous effects that are not directly observable and are likely to affect country risk in opposite directions: (1) an implicit-to-explicit debt conversion is likely to increase country risk if financial markets are myopic or suffer from fiscal illusion[7] and if governments are liquidity constrained; and (2) if financial markets value implicit pension liabilities, a structural pension reform that manages to reduce the level of implicit pension liabilities is likely to be rewarded with a discount on country risk as long-term solvency is improved.

Figure 3.3 shows the Emerging Market Bond Index spread, a series of idiosyncratic country risks (Fiess 2003), the Institutional Investor's Country Credit Rating Index, and the debt-to-GDP ratio of Mexico from 1994 to 2000. Mexico's pension reform was fully implemented in July 1997.

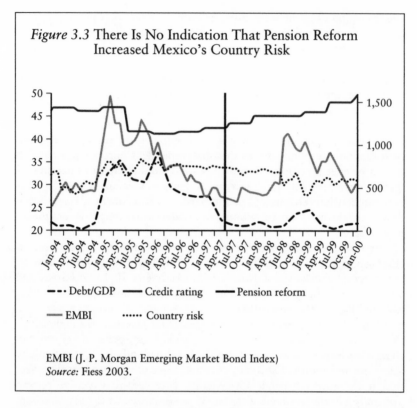

Figure 3.3 There Is No Indication That Pension Reform Increased Mexico's Country Risk

EMBI (J. P. Morgan Emerging Market Bond Index)
Source: Fiess 2003.

Casual observation of the information provided in figure 3.3 suggests that Mexico's pension reform had no direct impact on country risk.

However, little visible impact on the indicators in figure 3.3 does not imply that pension reform has no impact on country risk at all. Mexico had one of the lowest implicit pension debts (IPDs) in Latin America before its reform (less than 30 percent of GDP), and the reform only reduced it marginally. As a result, the impact of the reform on country risk may have been less significant than in a country such as El Salvador, which drastically cut its IPD. In Argentina, where both explicit pension debt and (by many measures) implicit pension debt indicators worsened after the reform, country risk deteriorated to the point where the government was forced to default on its debt. More generally, it is likely that a pension reform will affect country risk through multiple and highly complex dynamics, which might even cancel each other out. Understanding these changes is important for countries contemplating multipillar reforms.

The first issue concerns financing the transition.[8] In theory a government could pay off its total implicit debt by issuing checks to all transition workers and pensioners who have accrued rights under the old system. This would make all implicit debt immediately explicit at the time of the reform. For budgetary reasons, reforming countries generally did not choose this option (James 1999) but rather adopted a mixture of instruments to finance the transition deficit to spread the fiscal costs of transition over time.[9]

As a second issue, reforms can introduce new implicit liabilities. Measuring implicit pension liabilities is a difficult task, and comparing implicit pension liabilities pre- and post-reform is not straightforward because counterfactual measures are not observable. Several reforming countries have introduced new implicit liabilities, such as minimum pension guarantees, that could even have raised the level of implicit pension liabilities. In the case of Chile, Schmidt-Hebbel (1999) and Schreiber (2001) found that the costs of minimum pension guarantees are not negligible. Mexico's new pension system offers a "life-switch option" instead of recognition bonds to transition workers—that is, it allows transition workers to choose at the time they retire from the system the option (old or new) that will give them the highest level of benefits (Rodriguez 1999). The costs of this life-switch option are likely to be high if market returns are below expectations.

As a third issue, investment rules can create captive finance for government debt. How private pension funds are regulated can also affect country risk. In Latin America most pension funds' investment strategies are affected by quantitative regulations that limit the extent of investment in specific kinds of assets. These restrictions are more severe for equities and foreign securities than for fixed-income securities. Portfolio limits for pension funds can produce a guaranteed market for government bonds and thus help smooth a debt-financed transition.[10] Yermo (2002b) pointed out that although pension fund administrators in Latin America have been relatively efficient as financial risk managers, the new private second pillars have not been effectively insulated from political interference. Pension funds are effectively used by the governments as captive sources of finance. Government meddling in fund portfolios, as in Argentina in 2001 (see Rofman 2002) and in Bolivia in 2003 (see Escobar 2003), underscores this point.

The fourth issue is that one must be able to account for idiosyncratic country risk. Researchers have to disentangle global risk from idiosyncratic risk because only the latter is relevant when evaluating the impact of pension reform on country risk. Sovereign bond spreads are often used as a measure of country risk. Bond spreads, however, are affected by both idiosyncratic and global factors. Global factors were primarily responsible for increasing country risk during the Asian (1997) and Russian (1998) crises. Because the crises coincided with the implementation of many pension reforms in Latin America,[11] attempts to isolate the impact of pension reform on country risk should be undertaken with some care.

As a final issue, the impact of pension reform would have to be isolated from other structural reforms. Pension reforms generally were not carried out in isolation. Corbo and Schmidt-Hebbel (2003) pointed out that the 1981 pension reform in Chile was part of a wider structural reform effort that included fiscal adjustment, labor market reform, financial liberalization, and capital market reforms. The complementarities of these reforms make it extremely difficult to properly isolate the impact of a specific reform. It is likely that the combined impact on growth or capital market development was larger than the individual impact of any given reform.

Conclusion

Although the simulations presented in Zviniene and Packard (2002) showed that structural reforms in Latin America are likely to deliver substantial reductions in public pension liabilities, fiscal sustainability is far from certain. Because of the different contractual nature of pension liabilities, a positive impact of pension reform on solvency perceptions is not as obvious as theoretical models claim. Furthermore, pension reforms can create new implicit and explicit liabilities. Although the benefits to economic growth from pension reform are important, the theoretical links between structural reforms and growth are not straightforward, and empirical evidence is still scarce. Finally, empirical evidence shows that pension reforms can produce severe cash-flow problems in excess of initially projected transition costs and hence seriously constrain public sector liquidity.

Notes

1. Even where the multipillar reform models chosen by policymakers in different countries are very similar, circumstances directly and indirectly related to formal retirement security differ widely, causing difficulties for any attempt at cross-country comparisons. Thus the results of the simulations cannot be used to determine whether Chile's reform was fiscally "more successful" than Peru's or Mexico's, or whether the impact of reforms on equity in Argentina were "greater" than in Colombia. Furthermore, the authors pointed out that because a number of the assumptions imposed are likely to vary from one study to the next, the results can be used only as indicators of the order of magnitude of various statistics and can facilitate only rough comparisons among countries. So the sort of cross-country simulation analysis presented in this chapter (and elsewhere; see Holzmann, Palacios, and Zviniene 2001) has to be interpreted very carefully and cannot replace country-specific analysis of reforms using tailor-made simulation models.

2. To project a "no-reform scenario"—a counterfactual to structural reforms—the current number of beneficiaries, wage distribution of contributors, and the like were used, and the parameters of the old single-pillar PAYG system were applied.

3. Readers should note that our data and assumptions for Argentina were taken prior to the 2001–02 crisis and the devaluation of the peso. An account of the crisis and its impact on the reformed pension system can be found in the Rofman (2002) (see appendix at the end of this volume).

4. The policy of lowering employer contributions was pursued to increase compliance. However, regulations in the product and factor markets that have little to do with the social security system keep the cost of compliance and formalization in Argentina very high. Thus, lowering employer contributions to the public pension system had no substantial impact on lowering evasion and has only served to deepen pension deficits (Rofman 2002).

5. The remainder of this chapter is drawn directly from a background paper prepared by Norbert Fiess in the Office of the Chief Economist for Latin America and the Caribbean Region. The principal authors are grateful for this contribution. Readers can find a more detailed discussion of the issues raised here in the background paper.

6. This does not imply that such will not be the case in the future (Fiess 2003).

7. If financial markets do not suffer from fiscal illusion, a trade-off between implicit and explicit pension liabilities should be of little consequence.

8. A more detailed discussion of transition cost financing can be found in Holzmann (1998), "Financing the Transition to Multipillar," available at http://www.worldbank.org/pensions.

9. There are many different ways to finance transition costs, and countries usually apply a mixture of instruments (James 1999). For example, transition costs can be financed (1) through a reduction of the value of IPD (e.g., by downsizing the old system through reducing benefits and increasing retirement age, or by retaining a public PAYG pillar in the new system), or (2) through special revenue sources (e.g., privatization revenues from public enterprises) or use of general taxation or borrowing (through fiscal adjustment or debt financing).

10. In the longer term, however, portfolio limits can undermine any benefits associated with a fully funded pension system for aggregate savings, economic growth, and capital market development (Srinivas, Whitehouse, and Yermo 2000).

11. That is, when Costa Rica (1996), Uruguay (1996), Bolivia (1997), Mexico (1997), and El Salvador (1998) were conducting reforms.

4

The Financial Benefits of Pension Reform

AN IMPORTANT JUSTIFICATION FOR PENSION reform in Latin America has been its expected benefits for capital markets. The growth of pension funds and other institutional investors can help make capital markets more resilient and dynamic. In turn, the development of capital markets can improve the efficiency of resource mobilization and investment in the economy. Deep and liquid domestic capital markets can also help curtail dependency on foreign capital and thus reduce the economy's vulnerability to external shocks. Levine and Zervos (1998), and Beck and Levine (2001) have found that capital market development has a positive impact on economic growth.

The Latin American pension reforms have led to marked changes in the financial sectors of Latin American countries that have introduced mandatory individual accounts. Foremost among these changes has been the appearance of a new market player—the special-purpose pension fund administrators who have captured all mandatory (second-pillar) and the bulk of tax-advantaged (third-pillar) pension savings.

The Regulation of Mandatory Pension Funds

The introduction of privately managed individual accounts created the need to establish regulations governing fund managers and the investments they can make.

Regulation of Pension Fund Managers

Latin American pension fund administrators (AFPs) are independent legal entities whose exclusive purpose is the management of pension funds.[1] The governance of pension fund administrators is subject to a variety of regulations that aim to protect the members from conflicts of interest.

Such regulations include a prohibition on transactions between the administrator and its employees and the pension fund. Pension fund administrators are also banned from purchasing on their own behalf stocks that may be acquired by the fund. In Chile the pension fund administrators must have some independent directors whose duty is to guard the interest of affiliates. Chilean regulations also set forth a high principle of fiduciary responsibility: AFPs should ensure the adequate profitability and safety of the investment of the funds they manage. They are obliged to reimburse the pension fund for any direct damages they may cause, whether by omission or commission.

Regulations also cover the role of pension fund administrators in corporate governance. Chilean pension fund administrators are required to attend the shareholder meetings of those companies in which they have acquired stocks for the pension fund, and they must vote in all agreements, including the election of board members. The AFPs cannot vote for board candidates who are related to the majority shareholders or to those who control the company. They are also typically required by the supervisory authority to file reports regarding events or transactions by security issuers that may harm pension fund investments.

There are also some regulations that actually limit the extent of collusion in collective action by pension fund administrators. In Chile the supervisory authority has ruled that "it is entirely contrary to the spirit of the law (D.L. 3.500) for one or more funds to form an association or act in a block in order to exercise their shareholders' rights" (Iglesias 2000, p. 117). Nonetheless, an explicit authorization can be granted to AFPs to act jointly at board elections. In Chile there is also a prohibition against participating in "or having any bearing on the management of a company," which essentially restricts the influence of AFPs to their participation in shareholder meetings (Iglesias 2000).[2] In Peru pension fund administrators are not required to attend or vote in shareholders' meetings, and they face the same prohibition as in Chile with respect to their involvement in the administration of the companies in which they invest.

Rules governing disclosure to plan members, external audit, and reporting to the supervisory authority are also applied widely and effectively in Latin American countries. The supervisors oversee the operations of both the administrators and the pension funds they manage. Potential administrators wishing to enter the market must apply for a license from the supervisory authority. The companies must comply with the minimum capital requirements established in the legislation.

Pension fund managers in some countries (such as Argentina, Chile, Colombia, El Salvador, and Uruguay) must also guarantee a certain minimum return on the pension fund (usually relative to the industry average) and must maintain a capital reserve to meet any shortfalls in the fund's rate of return relative to the minimum. This reserve must be invested in the same way as the pension fund.

Some countries have imposed limits on the share of the market that pension fund administrators may have. In Mexico, for example, the retirement fund administrators cannot control more than 17 percent of the pension fund market until 2002. Since that date they have been allowed to have up to 20 percent of the market. The law, however, does not specify whether the market share measure is assets under management or number of affiliates.

Restrictions on Pension Fund Investment

The investment of pension funds is subject to a comprehensive prudential regulatory framework. In each country that has reformed, all liquid financial assets bought by pension funds must be traded in secondary markets and valued at market prices.[3] For the less-liquid assets the supervisory authorities of some countries, such as Mexico, set a valuation mechanism based on historical prices and the valuation of related securities.[4]

All countries that permit investment in securities issued by private sector companies and traded in regulated, secondary markets have also introduced new systems for risk rating (Colombia is the only exception). Investment limits also include limits by issuer and ownership concentration. For example, a Chilean pension fund cannot own more than 7 percent or invest more than 5 percent of fund assets in any given company's stock. Other countries also impose limits on the percentage of a company stock that pension funds can hold (5 percent in Argentina and El Salvador, 10 percent in Colombia and Uruguay, and 15 percent in Peru).

Possible conflicts of interest between pension fund managers and related entities arising from the investment of pension funds are also strongly regulated. All countries set low limits on investment in securities of issuers related to the pension fund managers. In Chile and Mexico the limit is set at 5 percent of the pension fund assets. Pension funds may not be invested in assets issued or guaranteed by members (or relatives) of the governing body of the pension fund administrator, or by managers or owners of authorized entities.

As shown in table 4.1, there are also limits by asset class. These limits are less justifiable from a prudential perspective except for the fact that capital markets may not be adequately regulated. Governments may also wish to avoid high-risk portfolios to the extent that they offer minimum pension guarantees.[5] In Argentina, Bolivia, Colombia, Costa Rica, and Uruguay the regulatory framework does not distinguish between domestic securities issued in local and in foreign currencies. In Chile the limit on foreign securities applies also to foreign currency–denominated securities issued by local entities. In Peru the limits on private sector securities apply equally to local and foreign currency–denominated assets. Pension funds were only allowed to invest in dollar-denominated government bonds (Brady bonds) in July 1998. In Mexico until December 2001, pension funds could invest up to 10 percent of their assets in dollar-, euro-, and yen-denominated federal government and Central Bank securities. Since then, private securities have also become eligible.

Portfolio limits have been relaxed in some countries, such as Chile, as the respective regulatory and supervisory frameworks were established or reformed to ensure a proper functioning of the capital markets. Hence, for example, equities investment was permitted in Chile in 1985, five years after the passing of the securities law. Investment in foreign securities was first permitted five years later following legal reforms that, for example, permitted companies to issue American depository receipts (ADRs) for the first time.[6] Other countries are also gradually liberalizing their investment regimen. Peru first permitted investment overseas in 2001. At the beginning of 2002 the Bolivian supervisor set out the regulatory framework that permits foreign investment for the first time (the legislated limit was set at 50 percent at the time of the reform). Mexico recently eliminated a rule that required pension funds to invest at least 65 percent of their assets in financial instruments with a maturity of fewer than 182 days.

The investment floors present in some countries are a greater source of distortions (see table 4.2). In Bolivia and Uruguay the goal of investment floors on government bonds was to ease the fiscal cost of the transition to a funded pension system. In Mexico the requirement to invest in inflation-indexed securities can also be justified as a measure to ensure a stable real rate of return on the funds. Such conservative investment helps the government manage its contingent liability as a result of the retirement benefit guarantee offered to transition workers. In Costa Rica the floor is applied to mortgage securities, a decision that appears to be justified by the government's desire to promote housing finance while offering to pension funds an attractive long-term investment. Despite the positive objectives of some of these floors, governments must take into account possible distortions to the diversification and performance of pension funds.

In all countries, custody of pension assets must be carried out by entities independent of the pension fund administrator. In Chile, until 1994 all assets were safeguarded by the Central Bank. As a result of the Capital Markets Law of 1994 private companies offering security deposit services can also act as custodians of pension funds.

Rapid Growth in Pension Savings

Thanks to its privileged position, the new pensions industry is beginning to dominate the financial system. As shown in table 4.3, in Chile, the earliest reformer, pension assets directed by the pension fund managers were more than 50 percent of GDP. Asset growth in other countries that have

Table 4.1 Portfolio Ceilings by Main Asset Classes (December 2002)

(Percent)

	Government securities	Financial institutions	Stocks	Corporate bonds	Investment funds	Foreign securities[a]
Argentina	80	30	70	40	30	20
Bolivia[b]	100	30–50	20–40	30–45	5–15	10–50
Chile[b]	50	50	30	40	20	20
Colombia	80	42	30	30	5	10
Costa Rica	85[c]	100[d]	5	70[e]	10	0[f]
El Salvador	50	40	20	20	20	0
Mexico	100	10[a]	0	100[g]	0	0
Peru	30	40[h]	35	40[i]	15	9
Uruguay	60	30	25[j]	25[j]	25	0

[a] Maximum of 250,000 in local currency (Mexican pesos) and US$25,000 in foreign currency plus the required amount for currency matching. The limit on foreign investment applies to the total of all funds administered by an AFP.

[b] This information refers to Fund C (the one with the average allocation to equities).

[c] Declining to 50 percent in 2009.

[d] Maximum of 20 percent for public financial institutions.

[e] The 70 percent limit applies to AAA-rated bonds; 50 percent to AA-rated corporate bonds; 20 percent to A-rated corporate bonds.

[f] Foreign investment is currently not permitted by the supervisor, but the law set a ceiling of 25 percent, which can be increased to 50 percent if domestic returns are low.

[g] No limit (AAA-rated corporate bond); 35 percent (AA-rated corporate bonds); 5 percent (A-rated corporate bonds).

[h] Joint limit between deposits, bonds, and promissory notes.

[i] Corporate bonds of nonfinancial institutions.

[j] Joint limit.

Source: Pension fund supervisors in the countries described.

Table 4.2 Portfolio Floors by Country

Country	Description of regulations
Bolivia	The two pension funds together must invest a minimum of US$180 million annually between 1998 and 2013.
Costa Rica	At least 15 percent of the pension funds' assets must be invested in mortgage securities, with a minimum return no less than that of the mandatory complementary pension system.
Mexico	At least 51 percent of the pension funds' assets must be invested in inflation-indexed securities. Until December 2001 only federal government and central bank securities were eligible for investment under this rule. Since then, state and private securities that are indexed to inflation are also eligible.
Uruguay	Pension funds must invest between 40 percent and 60 percent of their assets in government securities.

Source: Pension fund supervisors in the countries described.

Table 4.3 Assets Held by Pension Funds Have Doubled as a Percentage of GDP (December 1998–December 2002)

(Percent)

Country	1998	1999	2000	2001	2002
Chile	40.3	53.3	59.8	55.0	55.8
Peru	2.5	4.1	5.4	6.6	8.1
Colombia	2.7	4.2	5.5	7.0	7.7
Argentina	3.3	5.9	7.1	7.4	11.3
Uruguay	1.3	2.8	3.9	6.1	9.3
Mexico	2.7	2.3	3.0	4.3	5.3
Bolivia	3.9	7.0	10.8	11.0	15.5
El Salvador	0.4	1.7	3.6	5.5	7.4
Costa Rica	0.0	0.0	0.0	0.1	0.9
Average	7.1	10.2	12.4	11.4	13.5

Note: Assets held by the Bolivian capitalization fund are not included.
Source: AIOS 2002, Colombian Banking Superintendency.

undergone pension reform has also been rapid. In Bolivia as in Chile the earnings-related PAYG pillar is being phased out and AFP-managed pension assets quadrupled as a share of GDP, from 3.9 percent in 1998 to 15.5 percent of GDP in 2002. In Latin America as a whole this ratio has doubled in just five years.

In addition, in their role as providers of disability, survivors', and longevity insurance in the new systems, insurance companies have accumulated a significant amount of pension assets. However, because most systems are still primarily in their accumulation stage, the importance of insurance companies as financial market players is dwarfed by that of the pension funds. By December 2002 the assets held by pension funds were more than three times those of insurance companies.

The dominance of pension funds in the domestic capital markets is demonstrated by the extent of capitalization of the various markets in which they invest. Throughout Latin America pension funds are becoming particularly important investors in government debt (see figure 4.1). Their presence in private sector securities markets is generally less significant, except in Chile and Peru. In Chile pension funds owned more than half of the total stock of mortgage and corporate bonds in December 2002. In Peru pension funds also owned more than half of the total stock of corporate bonds in circulation (see Yermo 2002a).

The growth of pension funds is turning these new institutional investors into key players in the financial system, underscoring the importance of

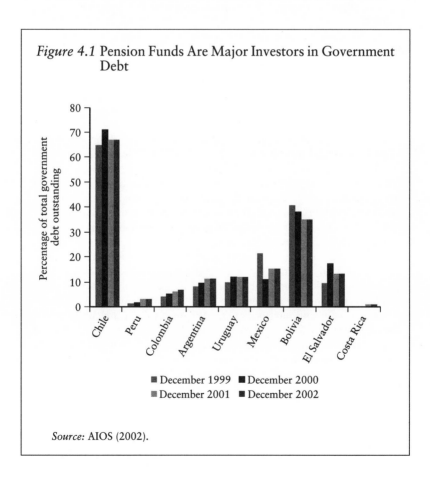

Figure 4.1 Pension Funds Are Major Investors in Government Debt

■ December 1999 ■ December 2000
▨ December 2001 ■ December 2002

Source: AIOS (2002).

Box 4.1 The Importance of Concomitant Reforms in the Financial System

In addition to laying the basis for the new pension fund industry, Latin American governments have been active in reforming other aspects of the financial system. Three main reforms can be identified, some of which have been at least partly driven by the need to ensure the smooth functioning of the private pension system.

Concomitant Reform 1: Modernization of Financial Market Infrastructure

Key elements of the financial infrastructure, such as risk-rating, custodial, and brokerage services, and trading and settlement systems should be modernized before the introduction of pension funds. Although such functions are essential for every sector of the financial system, the reform of the pension systems has brought home the need for improving many of them.

As mentioned above, the development of the risk-rating industry in Latin America is intrinsically related to the establishment of the pension fund industry. Risk rating has also been extended to all issuers of publicly traded instruments in Chile, not just those that receive investments from the pension funds. Another important pension reform–related improvement in the financial infrastructure is the modernization of trading systems in stock exchanges. Pension fund portfolios are valued daily in Latin American countries. This has necessitated a revamping of the technology used by financial institutions to value their assets. Some hindrances to market trading remain in several countries, however. In Mexico, for example, trades carried out through the electronic system cannot be executed from outside the exchange. In all Latin American countries, depository and custodian services must be provided by a financial institution independent of the pension fund administrator. This regulation has helped develop the custodial services industry.

Clearing and settlement systems are also still to be modernized in most Latin American countries. In Chile a public company was created in 1989 to deal with all clearing and settlement of securities transactions. The company is owned by the Santiago Stock Exchange and the main financial institutions and intermediaries. Settlement of instruments issued by financial institutions takes place the same day as the transaction, those of fixed income securities the day after, and stocks trading two days after the transaction. The system contrasts with that in place in Peru, where settlement is still concentrated in one medium-size bank, which could represent a significant systemic risk.

Concomitant Reform 2: Regulatory Reform Within the Financial Sector

The enforcement of financial contracts through regulations and effective supervision is a key institutional feature that enables the development of

Box 4.1 (continued)

financial markets. La Porta et al. (1998) argued that the efficiency of the financial system is based on the extent to which contracts are defined—and made more or less effective—by legal rights and enforcement mechanisms. Levine et al. (2000) provided evidence that the quality of legal rights in financial systems can explain economic growth, whereas the relative role of banks versus markets cannot.

Reforms in securities markets have often been engineered with the goal of improving the functioning of private pension systems. For example, the 1994 reform to capital markets in Chile had as its main objective increasing the flexibility of the investments by pension funds and life insurance companies. This reform also improved the regulation and supervision of conflicts of interest (including insider trading). The reforms to the Capital Markets Law proposed in Peru in 2001 (and now in the process of being approved) also contemplated significant changes, such as the introduction of clear fiduciary responsibilities for asset managers.

Some efforts have also been made to improve shareholders' rights. In a survey by La Porta et al., Chile got as high a score as Organisation for Economic Co-operation and Development member countries. Minority shareholder rights have been further strengthened in this country through the latest reform to the Capital Markets Law. In Peru amendments to that law and the law protecting the rights of minority shareholders were also proposed in 2001. Some of the measures proposed in Peru included permitting proxy voting by mail, stricter disclosure requirements for listed companies, and the promotion of independent directors.

A new code of best practices has been proposed recently by the Mexican Stock Exchange to address some deficiencies in corporate governance. Some weaknesses also exist in the Argentine Capital Markets Law. A project recently presented to the Argentine Congress is expected to improve corporate governance practices in accordance with international standards (including the introduction of a minimum number of independent directors).

Reforms are still needed to strengthen creditors' rights in all Latin American countries. La Porta et al. showed some deficiencies in this area, particularly in Colombia, Mexico, and Peru, which had the lowest score in the region. In Mexico enforcement of creditors' rights still suffers from several deficiencies, especially in bankruptcy and collateral laws that weaken creditors and undermine market discipline. A bankrupt business can enter into reorganization without requiring creditors' consent. Secured creditors are not necessarily paid first; the claims of various social constituencies precede them.

Some Latin American countries also have recently reformed the regulation and supervision of their insurance industries, but in general much

(Box continues on the following page.)

Box 4.1 (continued)

work remains to be done. These reforms are of paramount importance given the role of the insurance industry as providers of disability and survivor insurance and of retirement annuities. A starting point for many countries is to ensure compliance with international standards (in particular those established by the International Association of Insurance Supervisors).

Reforms to the banking system, although largely unrelated to the pension system per se, have also been enacted throughout Latin America since the debt crisis of the early 1980s. In Chile in 1986 a new banking law was approved that required significant diversification, closer asset–liability matching, and limits on related party transactions. Banks were also prohibited from holding equity, with a few exceptions. At the end of 1997 new amendments introduced to the banking law led to the adoption of the Basel recommendations on capital requirements and a new licensing process.

The mutual fund sector is the laggard in the financial system, handicapped by regulatory and supervisory deficiencies, such as insufficient control of conflicts of interest. In Mexico the establishment of the private pension industry has made more patent the deficiencies of the regulation and supervision of mutual funds. As a result, the government is coming to grips with the problem and is developing a new regulatory framework. This framework would include stricter disclosure rules and fiduciary standards in line with those applied to the pension fund administrators.

Concomitant Reform 3: Tax Reform

The tax treatments of different forms of savings and investment are key determinants of the evolution of any financial system. In many countries debt is preferable to equity as a source of financing because of its less onerous tax treatment. In Chile, where the benefits of pension reform are most pronounced, a significant tax reform also took place. In 1984 the tax rate for reinvested profits was reduced from 46 percent to 10 percent, and taxes for distributed profits of open corporations were reduced from 43.3 percent to 31.5 percent. Uthoff (1998) argued that the tax reform explains much of the increase in savings observed in Chile over the past two decades. The liberal Chilean tax reform contrasts with the Mexican tax structure. In Mexico capital gains tax must be paid on private sector securities but not on government securities. The difference in after-tax returns is sufficiently high to distort the investment strategies of pension funds and other institutional investors toward government securities.

Source: Yermo (2002a).

concomitant reforms in the financial system (box 4.1). Because of the high investment in government securities and the banking sector, however, direct pension fund financing to the private sector through bonds and equities is still relatively low compared with bank credit. Even in Chile total direct investment in the nonfinancial private sector represented less than 12 percent of GDP in December 2002. Bank credit to the private sector, on the other hand, was close to 67 percent of GDP at that time.

As shown in table 4.4, direct pension fund investment in the private sector is even lower in other Latin American countries (less than 20 percent of total pension fund assets), the only exception being Peru (46 percent of total assets). In Costa Rica, El Salvador, and Uruguay pension funds provide little direct financing to the nonfinancial private sector (less than 5 percent of total assets).

How the Pension Fund Industry Operates

To understand the role of pension funds in capital market development it is important to consider not just the size of their portfolios but also how these portfolios are managed. Pension fund administrators can also play an important role in regulatory reform and in financial innovation. In this section we take a closer look at the governance of the pension fund industry.

Table 4.4 Pension Funds Invest Mainly in Debt of Governments and Financial Institutions (December 2002)

(Percentage of portfolio shares)

Country	Government securities	Financial institutions	Corporate bonds	Equities	Investment funds	Foreign securities	Other
Argentina	76.7	2.6	1.1	6.5	1.8	8.9	2.4
Bolivia	69.1	14.7	13.4	0.0	0.0	1.3	1.5
Chile	30.0	34.2	7.2	9.9	2.5	16.2	0.1
Colombia	49.4	26.6	16.6	2.9	0.0	4.5	0.0
Costa Rica	90.1	5.3	4.6	0.0	0.0	0.0	0.0
El Salvador	84.7	14.4	0.5	0.5	0.0	0.0	0.0
Mexico	83.1	2.1	14.8	0.0	0.0	0.0	0.0
Peru	13.0	33.2	13.1	31.2	0.8	7.2	1.6
Uruguay	55.5	39.6	4.3	0.0	0.0	0.0	0.5

Note: Information for Colombia refers only to the mandatory pension fund system.
Source: AIOS 2002, FIAP 2002 (data for Colombia).

Decisionmaking in an Oligopolistic Industry

Latin American pension fund administrators do not have to meet any contingent liabilities on the funds they manage, other than ensuring that the funds' performance lies within the stipulated bands. Their investment objectives are therefore similar to those of mutual funds. In practice, however, there are important differences between the investment practices of pension funds and the practices of mutual funds. The main reasons for these differences are, first, investment regulations, which tend to be more strict for pension funds. Second, Latin American pension fund administrators have a captive market where individuals' contributions are retained until they retire. Third, the extent of switching between pension fund administrators is heavily regulated. Finally, in all countries except Chile individuals have no investment choice: under the guidance of regulators the administrators decide the asset allocation.

Some of these regulations (single fund, restrictions on switching, investment rules, lack of individual choice), combined with economies of scale and the size of markets have created the perfect conditions for a highly concentrated industry where the only pressure to perform comes from other regulations (performance rules, fees regulations). The most extreme case of concentration is in Bolivia, where two administrators were assigned regional monopolies in the market. Even in the other countries the extent of concentration is very high (see table 4.5).

The herding instinct among pension fund managers is particularly worrying in the context of an industry that is increasingly the dominant in-

Table 4.5 For the Average Latin American Country, the Two Largest Institutions Control Two-Thirds of the Pension Funds (December 2002)

Country	Number of administrators	Market concentration (two largest institutions)
Argentina	12	42.7
Bolivia	2	100.0
Chile	7	55.0
Colombia	6	49.8
Costa Rica	9	70.7
El Salvador	3	99.7
Mexico	11	45.0
Peru	4	59.2
Uruguay	4	74.7
Average	6	66.3

Note: Assets held by the Bolivian capitalization fund are not included. Information for Colombia refers only to the mandatory pension fund system.

Source: AIOS 2002, Colombian Banking Superintendency.

vestor in bond markets. To the extent that a few pension fund managers who invest in a similar way dominate capital markets, it is unlikely that market liquidity will grow to the levels observed in Organisation for Economic Co-operation and Development (OECD) member countries. The increasing process of concentration in the pension fund management industry, although efficient with respect to economies of scale in account management and record keeping, will only put investment decisions into even fewer hands.

Reform of capital markets, such as the 2001 reform in Chile that introduced member choice over five pension funds of different risk–return characteristics, may help reverse this trend. By promoting individual choice and competition among different providers in the huge pension savings market, the extent of homogeneity of portfolios and synchronization of trading decisions is likely to fall substantially. Liquidity, the key to vibrant capital markets, is likely to rise.

Dealing with the Transition Debt

The pension reforms undergone by Latin American countries were envisaged to end the fiscal imbalances that plagued their social security regimens. However, as discussed in chapter 3, the move from pure PAYG to funding raises in itself short-term fiscal pressures because pensions in payments and accrued rights must be financed from a lower level of mandatory contributions. In some countries, such as Bolivia, Chile, El Salvador, and Mexico, governments can no longer rely at all on the mandatory contributions because these are destined exclusively for individual funded accounts.

Despite the radical and pioneering nature of its pension reform, Chile has been by far the most successful in managing the pension debt. As discussed in box 3.2, the government ran fiscal primary surpluses on the order of 5.5 percent of GDP prior to the reform to soften the impact of transition costs on government finances.

No other Latin American country, however, has been able to effect such a huge fiscal contraction prior to reform. On the contrary, some countries, such as Argentina, embarked on reform with large fiscal imbalances and tensions on the exchange rate. The partial move to a funded system and the reduction in contribution rates only worsened further the finances of the social security system.

The Argentina experience demonstrates that against a backdrop of macroeconomic instability the private pension system is not free from political manipulation. By the end of 2001 nearly two thirds of its pension fund assets were invested in government securities either directly or indirectly (through bank trusts). The latter were not counted by the superintendency for purposes of meeting the ceiling on investment in government securities. This move, however, was not sufficient to soak up the debt created by the pension reform. The pension funds had accumulated assets worth only 7.4 percent of GDP by December 2001, slightly over half the debt created by the loss in revenue to the social security system.

The burden of the fiscal cost of the transition has forced many other governments in the region to impose quantitative investment restrictions that help channel pension funds toward government securities. Even in Chile pension funds were not allowed to invest in any asset class other than government bonds and banking instruments during the first four years of the system.[7] Bolivia, Mexico, and Uruguay have imposed floors on government bond investments. Even in the absence of quantitative restrictions, the instability created by a large transition debt is an obstacle to the deepening of financial markets. In the absence of a sustained fiscal effort, therefore, transition costs can severely curtail the positive impact of pension funds on capital markets.

Asset Management Practices, Financial Innovation, and Regulatory Reform

Pension funds have complete freedom in their investments as long as they stay within the regulatory ceilings established by the industry supervisor. We can therefore assess asset management practices in Latin American countries by taking into account the constraints that they face. Even in countries with more liberal investment regimens, such as Colombia, Chile, or Peru, pension funds' equity and corporate bond portfolios are concentrated in large companies. This is partly a consequence of the stage of development and small size of their economies, which result in a low number of firms whose securities are traded regularly in liquid markets. Regulations, however, also play a role because investments are restricted according to the risk rating of individual securities and their trading record in regulated markets. Performance regulations, which require pension funds to obtain a rate of return within a band set as a percentage of the industry average, may also explain the high degree of homogeneity in pension fund portfolios and the general conservatism in their investment strategies.

On the other hand, pension funds have played a role in the process of modernization of financial markets experienced by countries such as Argentina, Chile, and Peru. Lefort and Walker (2000a) mentioned the marked improvement in professionalism in the investment decisionmaking process and their involvement in bringing about a more dynamic legal framework. For example, pension fund managers in Chile added flexibility to foreign investment rules by obtaining permission to use currency forward contracts as hedging instruments. The pension fund administrators also played a central role in the 1989 establishment of the Electronic Stock Exchange, which competes directly with the Santiago Stock Exchange. The pension fund administrators had a strong interest in increasing competition in the market because they pay directly any transaction costs from investment activities. But the impact of pension funds on stock market development should not be overstated. Although pension funds in Latin America and the Caribbean can be large as a percentage of GDP, they are also small as equity holders, holding less than 10 percent of domestic equity in all Latin American and Caribbean countries for which data are available (Catalán 2003).

Role of Pension Funds in Corporate Governance

A captive market of mandatory pension contributions and a highly concentrated industry in which pension fund managers make all investment decisions may not be the ideal recipe for liquid capital markets. Pension funds cannot easily sell securities that are performing badly. If they do so they can turn prices against themselves, especially because other pension funds are likely to follow suit. On the other hand, pension funds can exert their power on capital markets indirectly by asking and voting for changes in corporate governance practices. This role, however, is not free of constraints. In all Latin American countries there are limits on the percentage of the capitalization of a certain issuer that can be held by a pension fund. These ceilings range from 5 to 15 percent of total capitalization.

It is largely because of these regulations that pension funds have only begun to play an active role as shareholders in Chile. The size of pension funds is such that they have become collectively the largest minority shareholder of many companies traded in the stock market.[8] Iglesias-Palau (2000) identified three main factors that explain increased shareholder activism by pension funds: (1) the counterproductive effects of exit strategies, (2) the high sensitivity of pension fund managers to the public's reaction to bad investments, and (3) the high concentration in ownership of Chilean corporations.

Some examples of the corporate governance role of pension fund administrators in Chile are their voting for independent directors (a regulatory requirement) and the pressure they exert to improve the transparency of company accounts. Independent directors have been particularly active in monitoring potential conflicts of interest between majority and minority shareholders. Iglesias-Palau (2000) also argued that independent directors have promoted the establishment of specialized committees, such as audit committees.

The pension fund administrators are also required by the supervisor to file reports regarding events or transactions by security issuers that may have negative effects on pension fund investments. This whistle-blowing role is played effectively by the Chilean Association of Pension Funds' informing the authorities and the public in general about corporate governance situations that are detrimental to pension fund performance. These regulations have led to better corporate governance despite the fact that pension funds are only minority shareholders. According to Lefort and Walker (2000a), other investors often explain their ownership plans to pension fund administrators and consider their opinion as influential shareholders.

Pension funds are helping create a new balance in the Chilean corporate ownership structure. Public firms in Chile, as in other Latin American countries, are dominated by one large group or conglomerate, which often has a single family owner at the top of the pyramid. Pension funds, together with ADR holders, are the largest minority shareholders of Chilean firms. Unlike ADR holders, who are a diversified and unconnected group, Chilean pension funds have similar objectives and follow practically identical investment strategies. Hence, they can present a united and powerful voice to defend minority shareholder rights. But given the small share of domestic equity in the hands of pension funds in the region, even in Chile, the impact of the funds on corporate governance should not be exaggerated (Catalán 2003).

Effects of Reforms on the Market for Government Debt

Except in Chile and Peru, more than half of pension fund investments are directed toward government securities. In this section we take a closer look at the role of pension funds in the development of this market.

Development of the Market for Public Sector Debt

Historically one of the key deficiencies of Latin American governments has been their inability to raise long-term financing domestically and their consequent dependency on volatile foreign capital. The weakness of domestic government debt markets is itself largely a reflection of a lack of fiscal rectitude that Latin American governments have only recently started to address. Chile stands out as having succeeded in the 1980s at avoiding the worst of the debt crisis and has since been hailed as a model of fiscal rectitude. El Salvador, Mexico, and Uruguay gained investment-grade ratings in the 1990s, and the prospects for government debt markets were promising. The collapse in liquidity in international markets in 2000–01, however, truncated the hopes of most Latin American governments. The Argentine crisis spread to Uruguay, which lost its investment-grade rating. International investors have stampeded from Colombia, which also lost investment-grade status.

Of all Latin American countries, Chile has been the most successful in limiting its sensitivity to portfolio flows and in lengthening the maturity of government debt. It may be tempting to link these developments to the role of pension funds, but there are other, more important factors at play. The practical elimination of the government's and Central Bank's foreign debt, a unique case in Latin America, was a public objective achieved thanks to two decades of fiscal surpluses. Meanwhile, short-term borrowing by the private sector and portfolio inflows have been discouraged through punitive reserve requirements. Fiscal frugality has also made possible the successful development of a long-term public sector bond market in Chile, together with two other factors: the development of an efficient indexation unit, the *unidad de fomento* (UF), and the government's and central bank's promotion of market liquidity through debt management.

The UF, an inflation-indexed unit of measure for all financial transactions, was first introduced in 1974 and was adopted widely as the reference index only in 1984. Currently the UF is used for pricing more than one-half of financial assets and practically all medium- and long-term fixed income securities and instruments of financial intermediation. Although other Latin American countries have introduced indexation mechanisms, none have been as successful as the UF (see box 4.2).

The Chilean government's and central bank's debt management strategies have also been beneficial to the health of the bond market. By promoting liquidity in the market the indexation unit was made a more acceptable currency unit and has ensured an adequate supply of securities for institutional investors. Markets have rewarded these policies with the lowest spreads in Latin America. Chilean public sector bonds also have the longest average duration in Latin America. The bonds have a maturity of between 90 days and 20 years.

Although mandatory indexation helped the Chilean bond market develop, it is certainly not a prerequisite for a healthy bond market. Other Latin American countries have recently succeeded in raising the maturity of their debt without requiring indexation of all fixed-income securities. In Colombia and Mexico the government is issuing inflation-indexed securities that are attractive to domestic investors, and the average duration of government bonds is increasing.

In Colombia the government started to issue inflation-indexed bonds in 1999. In 1997, 86 percent of government bonds had a maturity of less than five years. By March 2002, 22 percent of domestic treasury bonds were inflation-indexed. The share of government bonds with a maturity of between 5 and 10 years has also increased from 11.5 percent in 1997 to 46.7 percent in 2002.

The Mexican government recently also started issuing inflation-indexed securities. Only 14 percent of government bonds outstanding at the end of 2000 were inflation-indexed. Meanwhile, the maturity of the debt is beginning to creep up slowly, from its low level during the 1994–95 crisis. The average maturity of government debt increased from less than one year at the end of 1994 to more than two and a half years by December 2002. This trend is likely to progress because the government has stated its objective to lengthen the maturity of its debt. The government recently succeeded in introducing 10- and 20-year bonds. More than one-half of net public borrowing in 2001 was in fixed rate bonds with three- and five-year maturities.

Box 4.2 Inflation-Indexed Securities in Latin America

Chile was the second country in Latin America, after Brazil, to introduce widespread indexation of financial securities to a measure of the cost of living. Walker (1998) argued that indexation worked in Chile because (a) the unit has credibility, in the sense that it will not be manipulated by the authorities, and is based on the consumer price index that is computed by an independent entity, the National Institute of Statistics; (b) legislation requires that medium- and long-term credit be indexed to the *unidad de fomento* (UF), and calculation of assets and liabilities of insurance companies is in UF; (c) there exists a deep, liquid market for central bank indexed bonds, giving a risk-free rating used in other transactions; and (d) tax regulations are consistent with a generalized indexation of the economy. In addition, the UF was successfully adopted in Chile because it is updated on a daily basis, functioning as a quasi-perfect indexation mechanism.

Indexation in bank intermediation and government funding permitted the practical elimination of money illusion and hence created the conditions for macroeconomic stability. The inflation rate has been falling gradually since the early 1980s. In 2000 it was already below 4 percent. Indexation also permitted the stabilization of real interest rates and the targeting of the real exchange rate around what were deemed equilibrium values. These developments, coupled with the government's tight fiscal policy stance, created the conditions for a healthy government bond market. This market has since avoided much of the pain endured by other countries, such as Argentina, which went down the alternative route—dollarization—in their attempts at stabilization.

Of all the other Latin American governments only Brazil has had as high a degree of indexation of financial securities as Chile. Unlike the situation in Chile, however, there was no single reference unit, and adjustments often took place on an arbitrary and irregular basis. Moreover, indexation spread to labor markets, where it sustained ever-higher inflationary pressures. The introduction of a new currency, the real, pegged to the dollar succeeded in bringing down inflation. At the same time, the proportion of indexed debt in total debt decreased from about 70 percent at the beginning of 1994 to less than 30 percent by 2001.

The governments of Colombia, Mexico, and Peru have also recently begun to issue inflation-indexed securities. In the other Latin American countries, such as Argentina, Bolivia, El Salvador, and Uruguay, governments rely mainly on dollar-denominated securities. There has been much discussion about the benefits and drawbacks of both indexation and dollarization. Indexation can sustain and even augment inflationary expectations when it spreads to labor markets. Dollarization, on the other hand, exposes the government to significant currency risk because tax revenues from the nontradable sector are linked to the domestic currency.

Box 4.2 (continued)

This may explain why foreign investors generally have been unwilling to provide long-term financing denominated in U.S. dollars.
Source: Yermo (2002a).

Effects of Pension Funds on the Market for Government Bonds

There is little doubt that pension reform has contributed to the improved health of the Chilean public bond market. First, it may have encouraged fiscal restraint by the government. Second, it has provided "recognition" bonds with a long maturity. These bonds, issued by the government to compensate those who accumulated pension rights under the old system, became transferable in 1994 and have been traded in exchanges. The pension reform, therefore, contributed directly to the financial depth of the economy. Moreover, these bonds have relatively long duration (they are zero coupon bonds) and are therefore a stable source of funds for the Chilean government. Finally, the bonds have also helped the development of a benchmark yield curve that can be used for pricing private sector securities.

On the other hand, the role of pension funds in the development of the public sector bond market is less clear. Pension funds have certainly been a significant and reliable source of financing for the Chilean government and the central bank. In August 2002 more than 21 percent of the mixed fund portfolio consisted of central bank bonds with an average duration of three years and eight months. Nearly 6 percent of the same portfolio was invested in recognition bonds with an average duration of four years and seven months.

The Chilean experience contrasts with that of Peru, where the government has relied mainly on external financing. Only recently have pension funds been allowed to invest in these issues, so their contribution to the development of the market has been minimal. Unlike Chile, El Salvador and Peru have not yet permitted trading in secondary markets of recognition bonds. Given the lack of long-term government securities issued in domestic currency, such bonds would be a highly attractive investment for institutional investors such as pension funds. They would also assist in the construction of a yield curve that can be the basis for developing the corporate bond market.

As mentioned earlier, the role of pension funds in Mexico has been conditioned by investment regulations (pension funds are required to invest at least 51 percent of their assets in inflation-indexed securities). In

December 2002 the Specialized Retirement Fund Investment Societies (*Sociedades de Inversión Especializada de Fondos para el Retiro*) invested more than 70 percent of their assets in inflation-indexed government bonds. On the other hand, their contribution to the increase in maturities has been minimal because until December 2001, regulations impeded them from investing more than 65 percent in instruments with maturities longer than 183 days. The average maturity of the pension fund portfolios during the first two years of the system was in fact only 238 days (Rubalcava and Gutierrez 2000), well below the average maturity of Mexican government debt over that period.

The experience in other countries has been largely disappointing. Where pension funds have contributed to providing long-term funds, it has often been the result of government regulations or political pressures. In Argentina pension funds could invest up to 30 percent of their assets in an "investment account" where government bonds, mainly dollar-linked, were held up to maturity. After the 2001 crisis the government bonds held by pension funds were transformed into illiquid long-term loans to the government. In Bolivia the requirement to buy US$180 million worth of government securities per year has turned pension funds into the largest holders of these securities in the space of a few years. The pension funds must buy dollar-denominated government bonds that must be held to maturity (15 years) and that pay an 8 percent coupon. Sixty percent of the pension funds' assets were invested in these bonds in December 2001. In addition, in the secondary market pension funds buy government bonds that have maturities between one and three years. The government is also currently facing fiscal pressures and is considering replacing the dollar-denominated government bonds held by the pension funds by domestic currency–denominated debt.

Effects of Reforms on the Banking System

Except in Chile, bank loans are still the main form of external financing of the nonfinancial private sector. In Chile the stock market overtook bank credit as the main source of external funds in the late 1980s. Despite the slower growth of bank credit relative to the stock market, Chile stands out among Latin American countries for its high credit-to-GDP ratio—about 67 percent in December 2002, more than double the average for Latin American countries.

Pension funds can affect the evolution of the banking system through their investment strategies. In Latin America pension funds invest a large portion of their assets in financial instruments issued by banks. Only in Argentina, Costa Rica, and Mexico do pension funds allocate less than 14 percent of their assets to bank instruments. Pension funds therefore appear to play a complementary role to the banking sector.

Role of Pension Funds in the Development of the Market for Banking Sector Securities

Pension funds have played a central role in the growth of the mortgage bond market in Chile, by far the most developed in Latin America. Pension funds provide housing finance indirectly through two main types of investment: *letras hipotecarias* (mortgage bonds) and real estate investment funds. The *letras* are by far the most important type, making up more than 13 percent of the pension funds' portfolio. Pension funds own more than one-half of this market.

The *letras* are mortgage bonds backed by a portfolio of real estate and guaranteed by the commercial banks that issue these instruments. They are traded in exchanges and are thus eligible for investment by pension funds. They can have a maturity of 8, 12, or 20 years. The *letras* were introduced in 1977 and experienced rapid growth until the 1982–83 financial crisis. The loans financed through the *letras* have financed mainly the middle- and high-income residential sector.[9]

As with government bonds, the reason for the long maturity of *letras* has much less to do with pension fund investment per se than with the availability of price indexation for these securities and increased macroeconomic stability. Indexation to the UF itself has been possible thanks to the availability of a liquid market for UF-indexed government and Central Bank bonds of long maturity. These bonds provide the risk-free benchmark for pricing and, therefore, trading mortgage bonds.

Pension reform had a defining impact on this market. Pension funds, together with life insurance companies, have been the main investors in mortgage-backed securities since the early 1980s. Pension funds had 12 percent of their assets invested in *letras* in August 2002, with an average duration of four years and seven months. By providing medium- and long-term funding for house purchases, pension funds played a central role in the expansion of real estate investment that took place in the second half of the 1980s.

The only other country in Latin America that has seen significant growth in housing-related securities is Peru.[10] Leasing bonds account for more than 10 percent of the pension fund portfolios. The market is dominated by subordinated and leasing bonds that are issued by financial institutions. These bonds have replaced government debt as the reference benchmark because that market is small and illiquid. An increasing portion of private sector bonds is indexed to the *valor adquisitivo constante* (VAC, constant purchasing power), the currency unit that is linked to the consumer price level. As of September 2001 nearly one-fifth of all private bonds were denominated in VAC; the rest were mainly denominated in dollars. Peruvian bonds have also increased in maturity over the last decade. The share of bonds with a maturity longer than five years increased from 9 percent in December 1998 to 37 percent in September 2001.

Pension funds, however, cannot be held responsible for these changes because they invest largely in dollar-indexed bonds. In 1998, only 10 percent of total private bonds held by them were denominated in VAC. The limited interest in indexed bonds may be a sign of lack of credibility in the indexation unit in the context of a highly dollarized economy.

Unlike in Chile, the mortgage bond market in Peru (*Títulos de Crédito Hipotecario Negociable*) has not benefited from pension fund investment. These bonds have existed for many years but pension funds have hardly invested in them (less than 0.1 percent of the portfolio). This apathy derives from the low capitalization of the market. The main obstacle to its development is the inability of banks to issue such instruments directly without the authorization of the borrower.

Pension funds in other Latin American countries invest a smaller percentage of their assets in securities issued by banks. Most of the assets invested in the financial sector in other countries go to time deposits and liquid bank instruments. In Colombia, for example, pension funds invest more than one-quarter of their assets in the financial sector, but less than 1 percent is invested in mortgage or leasing bonds.

Impact on Bank Efficiency and Stability

Pension funds can help reduce the cost of issuing securities and hence reduce the market power of banks. As a result of this competitive pressure, net interest margins[11] may decrease. At the same time, pension funds can contribute to sustainable growth in bank credit. By helping promote capital markets, and in particular the stock market, pension funds stimulate information disclosure and monitoring and hence may reduce the credit risk borne by the banking sector. Pension funds may also be attracted by long-term deposits, helping reduce term transformation risk in the banking system.

In addition to their impact on bank efficiency and the growth of credit, pension funds can affect the maturity structure of bank loans. Depending on whether complementary or substitutive effects dominate, the average maturity of loans may increase or decrease. Levine (1997) argued that stock markets and banks tend to be complements rather than substitutes in emerging economies, and thus the maturity of loans would normally increase.

Impavido, Musalem, and Tressel (2001a) confirmed the complementary nature of the relationship between banks and institutional investors for a broad sample of countries, including four Latin American countries (Argentina, Brazil, Chile, and Mexico). Both bank profitability and the maturity of loans increase as pension fund and insurance company activity increases. They find that these increases result largely from a reduction in credit risk. Differences in bank efficiency across countries are also related to the level of development of the pension fund and insurance company

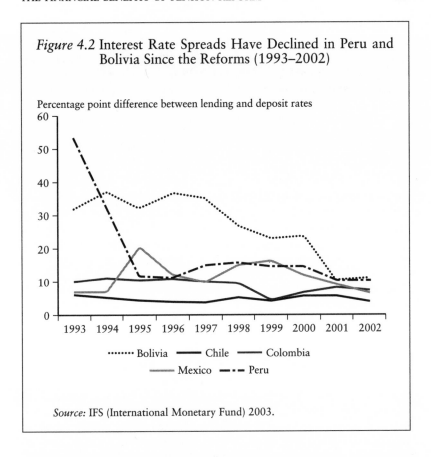

Figure 4.2 Interest Rate Spreads Have Declined in Peru and Bolivia Since the Reforms (1993–2002)

Percentage point difference between lending and deposit rates

········ Bolivia ⸺ Chile ⸺ Colombia
⸺ Mexico ⸻ Peru

Source: IFS (International Monetary Fund) 2003.

sectors. The positive correlation is larger at low initial levels of development, and it decreases as pension funds and insurance companies develop.

This trend is shown in figure 4.2, which plots the interest spread (lending rates minus deposit rates) in selected Latin American countries over the 1990s. The spread is lowest in Chile, the country with the most developed pension fund and insurance company sectors. But over the 1990s the spread did not decline much. This stability is related to the higher degree of competition faced by the banks in providing financing sources, which has led them to concentrate in alternative markets (such as personal banking or small- to medium-size firms), which are associated with higher costs. In other Latin American countries, such as Peru, the competition provided by pension funds and insurance companies is currently sufficient to stimulate a reduction in bank spreads but low enough to allow banks to maintain their financing of larger companies.

Another indicator of improved efficiency is the reduction in operating expenses. Chilean banks have operating costs that are less than 3 percent of total assets, less than one-half the level in other Latin American countries. Pension funds may have contributed to the increased competition in the banking system during the late 1980s and early 1990s by providing an alternative form of financing. However, there is no systematic evidence that the low interest rate spreads in Chile are related to the role of pension funds.

Effects of Reform on the Market for Private Sector Securities

In this section we look deeper into the operation of pension funds in Latin America to better assess their role in the development of the market for private sector securities.

Pension Fund Investment and Stock Market Liquidity

Only in Argentina, Chile, and Peru have pension funds been able to invest significantly in the stock market. Colombia is the only other Latin American country where such investments are permitted, but investment in stocks has been minimal (less than 3 percent in December 2002).

Most of the existing evidence on the impact of pension funds on stock market development is from Chile. The growth in the capitalization of the Chilean stock market after 1984 coincided with heavy investment by pension funds in shares. There is a high correlation between the amount of equities held by pension fund assets and the increase in the ratio of stock market capitalization to GDP, which has reached levels similar to those of the most developed OECD countries (greater than 100 percent). The evidence on market liquidity is also supportive of a causal link with pension fund investments. Iglesias (1998) provided evidence that transaction costs in securities markets fell in Chile after pension funds started investing in private sector securities. Fees charged by the Santiago Stock Exchange for market transactions dropped from 0.500 and 0.015 percent in 1985 to 0.120 and 0.000 percent in 1994. Holzmann (1997) identified a positive correlation between the growth of pension fund assets and monthly traded values in Chile, and Lefort and Walker (2000a) found corroborating evidence showing that the growth in pension investments has contributed to the growth in traded volumes in Chile since 1985.

Despite these positive findings the liquidity of the Chilean stock market is well below what would be expected from a country with one of the highest ratios of stock market capitalization to GDP and well-developed pension fund and insurance company sectors. The growth in pension fund investments and the rapidly growing allocation to domestic equities since 1985 have not been sufficient to raise turnover ratios (value traded as a percentage of market capitalization) to the levels observed in

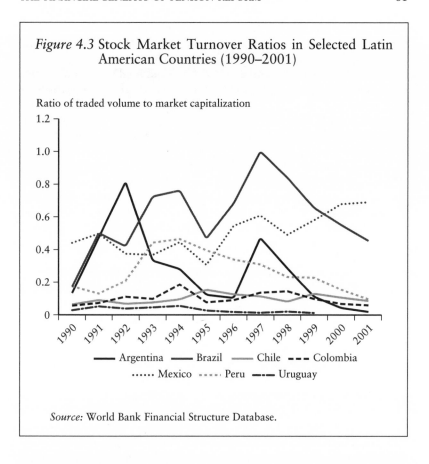

Figure 4.3 Stock Market Turnover Ratios in Selected Latin American Countries (1990–2001)

Ratio of traded volume to market capitalization

Legend: —— Argentina   —— Brazil   —— Chile   - - - Colombia   ······ Mexico   ····· Peru   —·— Uruguay

Source: World Bank Financial Structure Database.

countries like Brazil or Mexico, let alone in developed countries (see figure 4.3). In fact, this measure of liquidity is below the development threshold level of 15 percent proposed by Demirgüç-Kunt and Levine (1999) for the 1990s.

The low liquidity of the Chilean and most other Latin American stock markets can be partly explained by the high degree of ownership concentration and deficiencies in disclosure standards and in protection of the rights of minority shareholders that have been addressed only recently. Nonetheless, in other countries in the region, such as Brazil and Mexico, these deficiencies have been at least partly offset by foreign investors actively trading in local stocks (though mainly through ADRs). Foreign investors have helped make Brazil and Mexico the two most liquid markets in the region, accounting for more than 90 percent of all Latin American equity trading.

In Chile capital controls and an onerous tax treatment of foreign portfolio investment have prevented foreign investors from playing an active role in its markets. Despite their size, local pension funds have not been able to sustain levels of liquidity as high as foreign investors have in Brazil and Mexico. The high degree of synchronization in the choice and timing of stock purchases and the rapid accumulation in pension fund assets have contributed to creating a market where "buy and hold" is the only viable investment strategy. Chilean pension funds have no large counterpart that can buy their stocks when they are ready to sell. The positive liquidity effect of pension fund investment is largely a result of the monthly flow of mandatory contributions rather than the daily trading activities of the pension funds.

This situation may change with the liberalization of the capital account approved at the end of 2001. The Central Bank has since eliminated all administrative barriers that regulated capital flows and ADR issues. The Chilean Ministry of Finance eliminated the tax on short-term purchases and authorized short sales. Although the liberalization of the capital account may have a positive impact on stock market development, it may not be enough.

In fact, high exposure to foreign capital could actually make local markets less liquid and more volatile during a crisis than in more closed economies. The Asian and Argentine crises have dried up liquidity in most Latin American markets. The most prominent case is Argentina, where some of the companies with the largest capitalization have been delisted after being acquired by foreign players (for example, the oil company YPF was sold to Repsol). Even in Chile the presence of a large institutional investor industry did not prevent the fall of traded volumes of 55 percent observed between 1995 and 2000.

In Peru pension funds invest heavily in equity and the capital account is open, but just one Peruvian stock, gold producer Cia. de Minas Buenaventura, is liquid enough to attract foreign investment. The prevalence of workers' shares may deter foreign investors because of their attendant dividend and liquidation rights and the complexities and uncertainties associated with them.[12] At the same time the investment strategies of Peruvian pension funds do not seem to serve as a stimulant to market liquidity. Indeed, Lefort and Walker (2000a) did not find any causal relationship between pension fund investment in equities and market liquidity between 1993 and 1999.

Investment regulations (particularly those rules that limit investment to securities with the highest risk rating and those that limit the portion of capitalization that pension funds may own) are also not conducive to stock market liquidity. Additionally, they reinforce another negative aspect of Latin American stock markets: the high concentration of both capitalization and liquidity in a handful of stocks. The 10 most-traded companies in each country account for more than two-thirds of the local stock market's trading in all Latin American countries except Brazil (40 percent). In Chile and Argentina three companies account for almost 50 percent of current capitalization and turnover. In Mexico Telmex accounts for one-quarter of stock market capitalization and between 20 percent and 40 percent of daily trading.

Relaxing these investment rules within a prudential regulatory framework would go a long way toward improving the diversification of Latin American stock markets. Pension funds in Chile have steadily increased the number of issuers in their portfolios, thereby contributing to the broadening of the market. On the other hand, the continuing high concentration and herding of the industry can hardly be expected to bring about drastic improvements in liquidity. Only in Chile, where workers can now choose among five different funds, is liquidity likely to increase significantly. Diversity in options and preferences is an essential aspect of liquid markets.

Development of the Corporate Bond Market

Unlike the mortgage bond market, the corporate bond market has experienced very limited growth in Chile. Longer-term debt has become more dominant, but this seems to have much more to do with the availability of indexation than with the growth in pension fund assets. The development of the corporate bond market would also be unthinkable without the tight information disclosure standards introduced by the 1980 Securities Law. Nonetheless, pension funds have an important presence in this market and have been investing in longer-term maturities. In August 2002, 5 percent of their portfolios was invested in corporate bonds with an average duration of five years.

Chilean pension funds have also recently been permitted to invest in infrastructure bonds. These bonds are backed by insurance companies that guarantee repayment of the principal. The companies that issue these bonds are also guaranteed a minimum revenue by the state. Such investment is still very small, less than 1 percent of pension fund portfolios.

The availability of leasing and subordinated bonds in Peru has helped develop a local corporate bond market. However, these bonds cannot serve as a perfect substitute for treasury bills and bonds because they may have a significant credit risk. Without a reliable yield curve, trading corporate bonds in secondary markets exposes pension funds to liquidity risk. Pension funds have been avid buyers of corporate bonds, but they do not trade them regularly in secondary markets. The contribution of pension funds to the development of this market is also limited by risk-rating requirements. Pension funds are also relatively important investors in corporate bonds in Bolivia, Colombia, and Mexico. In Mexico, pension funds started to invest significantly in corporate bonds only during the past couple of years. So far their investment has been in short maturities, so their contribution to the breadth of the market has been very limited.

The corporate bond market has shown limited development in Argentina, where the bonds must be held until maturity (about two years) because they do not have a secondary market. Pension funds currently hold around 1 percent of their assets in corporate bonds. In Costa Rica, El Salvador, and Uruguay pension fund investment in corporate bonds has also been very subdued.

Venture Capital and Real Estate Funds

Pension funds are not permitted to invest directly in venture capital or real estate. In Argentina, Chile, and Peru pension funds can invest in these assets indirectly, by purchasing shares of investment and mutual funds that themselves own these assets (ceilings at 30 percent and 20 percent of the fund, respectively). Chilean pension funds invest less than 2 percent of their assets in venture capital funds (Enterprise Development Funds). These entities, which take the form of closed-ended mutual funds, were introduced in 1989 and pension funds quickly became their main investors. On the other hand, the real estate fund sector has hardly taken off.

An important obstacle to further investment in these funds is the body of investment regulations that limit the portion of the value of the securities issued by one such fund that can be owned by a pension fund. Given the small size of the private equity industry in relation to the pension funds, such limits are highly constraining. Pension funds are also discouraged from investing in such funds by performance rules because the valuation of venture capital funds is subject to much uncertainty.

In Argentina pension funds used to invest in this asset class before the crisis, but since then most of these investments have been sold. In Peru pension funds can invest in real estate funds but venture capital funds are not functioning yet. Investment in real estate funds is also very small, representing less than 1 percent of pension fund assets. In other countries investment in venture capital and real estate funds is not permitted. Indeed, in Mexico and Uruguay pension funds are barred from investing in any type of mutual funds.

It may be expected that pension funds' role as providers of finance for small- and medium-size enterprises and infrastructure projects will increase in the future. In a region where small businesses account for the bulk of sales and employment, and where there is need for massive infrastructural investment, such a development would be highly welcome. Governments can play an important role by ensuring that investment and performance regulations do not impede pension funds from investing sufficiently in private equity.

Conclusion

In this chapter, which is based on Yermo (2002a), we have shown that social security reform in Latin America has been accompanied by a set of corollary reforms that have had salubrious effects on capital markets.

Capital market development in some Latin American countries has been driven largely by the state-sponsored modernization of the financial sector infrastructure, tax and bankruptcy reform, and the regulatory structure developed by the authorities for the pension funds and other financial institutions.

Possibly the most important development in capital markets in the region during the 1990s has been the introduction of a new type of financial institution, the pension fund administrator, whose function is to invest pension contributions in financial assets. The reforms can therefore be credited with setting up a new financial industry that, at least in terms of institutional oversight, has been a role model for other financial institutions in the region. Although pension fund regulators in Latin America have erred on the side of caution, there is little doubt that the new systems have achieved some of the highest standards in the region in asset valuation, risk rating, and disclosure.

By subjecting the new financial intermediaries to high regulatory and supervisory standards, pension reform has also made a major contribution to the rapid modernization of the financial market infrastructure observed in the region over the last few years (especially custodial and risk-rating services). Furthermore, it has forced an adjustment of standards and practices in other financial institutions and in the capital markets. Transparency and integrity in financial markets have been dramatically improved as a result. In principle these improvements could have taken place independently of the pension reform. However, the mandatory nature of the funded pension systems provided the political justification for these much-needed developments.

There are some caveats to this generally positive assessment:

1. In terms of investment and performance objectives, pension funds are hardly different from mutual funds. Hence, it is possible that similar benefits could have been obtained had the pension fund regulatory framework also been applied to the mutual fund industry. An important question is whether the pension reforms necessitated establishing a new financial intermediary. It may be argued that if stricter regulatory and supervisory standards had been applied to existing financial institutions such as banks, insurance companies, and mutual funds, and these institutions had been allowed to manage the pension savings, the financial development indicators would have similarly improved. The liberalization of the market for voluntary pension savings in Chile (see chapter 7) may provide some ground for testing this hypothesis.

2. Although the private financial and nonfinancial sectors in Latin America have benefited from the growth of the pension industry, the main beneficiary has been the government debt market. Pension funds in some countries have participated actively in securing bank loans by investing in mortgage bonds (Chile) and leasing bonds (Peru). Pension fund investment

has also contributed to the growth of corporate debt and equities markets in these countries. Only in Chile, however, is there some evidence of a positive, causal relationship between pension fund investment and stock market liquidity. Similarly, Lefort and Walker (2000a) found evidence only in Chile that pension funds contributed to a lowering of the cost of capital to firms. In other Latin American countries investment in bank instruments has been limited largely to time deposits and other short-term securities. Investment in nonfinancial private sector securities has been muted (pension funds invest less than one-fifth of their assets in such instruments), partly as a result of investment and performance regulations. Regulations have also constrained the role of pension funds in the development of derivatives instruments.

3. Contrary to the situation in some OECD countries, where pension funds have been an independent driving force behind important financial innovations, the role of pension funds in the development of capital markets in Latin American countries is largely determined by government instructions that touch every aspect of their operations, from the amount of contributions that the industry receives to the investment of pension assets. The industry's structure and regulations reinforce the pension funds' preference for "buy and hold" investment strategies that are not conducive to market liquidity.

4. Although the illiquidity of pension investments coupled with the conservatism in investment strategies have brought stability to these markets, much of this stability is artificial. It is driven at least in part by portfolio rules that force pension funds to hold mainly domestic assets and in some countries oblige them to invest a minimum percentage of their assets in government bonds.

5. Macroeconomic stability is essential for capital markets to reap the benefits from pension fund investment, regardless of whether such investment is forced. The government debt market is most developed in Chile, where the government pursued fiscal consolidation prior to the reform and sustained this effort over later years. The pension reform also contributed directly to financial deepening because the transition debt was turned into tradable government securities. In Argentina, on the other hand, any positive short-term effect of pension fund investment on capital market development has been obliterated by the economic crisis.

Notes

1. The pension funds are pools of assets owned by the members (affiliated workers) of the pension fund and legally separated from the fund administrators. The only exception to this legal norm is Mexico, where the pension fund is itself an independent legal entity containing a board of directors.
2. Pension funds are also subject to ownership concentration limits as discussed later in this chapter.

3. An important exception is Argentina, where up to 30 percent of pension fund assets can be invested in government bonds held to maturity in an "investment account." The assets are therefore priced at book value. Bolivia also experienced a serious blow to the transparency of the system when the collective fund assets (which finance the BONOSOL program) were mixed with those of the individual accounts. The collective fund is invested in nonlisted companies and is subject to discretionary valuation.

4. Such a method was originally designed with a view to ensuring the comparability of pension fund portfolios and permitting adequate monitoring by the regulator, the National Retirement Savings Commission (Mexico). It is now expected that insurance companies and mutual funds will be required to use the same valuation method.

5. Concerns over the fiscal cost of pension guarantees can explain why Mexico does not allow investment in equities. The guarantee is equal to the salary-linked defined benefit under the previous social security regime for all workers who contributed to it. In other Latin American countries the state's liability in the funded system is limited to a minimum income guarantee (a flat benefit, at a level somewhat below the minimum wage), as discussed in chapter 9.

6. ADRs are certificates issued by banks in the United States that represent shares or bonds issued by a foreign company or a foreign subsidiary of a U.S. company. ADRs are backed by securities in custody in the country where the firm that issues the securities is based. ADRs can be converted at any time into the underlying securities. They serve as a signaling device and can therefore contribute indirectly to the liquidity of the local stock market.

7. Chile first liberalized the investment regimen for pension funds in 1985 by permitting investment in equities and corporate bonds.

8. Because pension funds in the region often concentrate their equity holdings in a small number of blue-chip firms, they can exert major influence on these companies' corporate governance. In Chile, for example, AFPs have become the most important minority shareholder in most of the country's listed corporations. As of December 2000 equity investments by pension funds accounted for more than 7 percent of total market capitalization.

9. Lower-income households are provided with very generous subsidies to buy their first home. Only a small loan is necessary to be able to access these governmental subsidies (Rojas 1999).

10. Pension funds are contributing to the financing of the housing market through other means in the other Latin American countries. In Mexico workers must make a separate contribution to the National Housing Fund for Workers Institute, a state-sponsored body that provides housing loans. In Uruguay the pension funds have a large part of their deposits in the *Banco Hipotecario*, the national mortgage bank.

11. The net interest margin is equal to total interest revenues minus total interest expenditures divided by the value of assets. This measure was proposed by Demirguç-Kunt and Levine (1999).

12. Workers' shares are nonvoting shares created during the military government in 1970 as a form of profit sharing and popular capitalism.

5

Social Gains from Pension Reforms in Latin America

SINGLE-PILLAR PUBLIC PENSION SYSTEMS in developing countries, particularly in Latin America, tend to generate regressive transfers from poorer workers to the relatively small number of higher-income workers covered by the systems. Simulations show that equity can be increased by moving from a purely PAYG system to a multipillar system with a large funded component by reducing this regressive character of transfers. However, the large proportion of the workforce employed in informal activities in developing countries hinders realization of an equitable pension system, even if a multipillar system is put in place. Informal workers will remain largely uncovered under the reformed system but nevertheless share the tax burden of financing minimum guarantees to the covered few. Therefore, increasing coverage is crucial not only to help households manage risks but also to generate equitable outcomes.

Economic theory would predict that, by reducing both the actual and the perceived tax on labor by establishing individual retirement savings accounts, pension reform will increase formalization of the labor force and its by-product, pension system coverage. Although there is no clear evidence of increased coverage in Latin American countries that have implemented pension reforms, Packard (2001) found that when controlling for other explanatory variables, there is a positive incentive effect of individual accounts on pension contributions. Nonetheless, pension coverage remains low and inequitably shared among income groups in Latin America, and this presents challenges even for countries that have implemented reform.

Inequitable Effects of Social Security and Progress with Reforms

Although presented as a model of solidarity when they were introduced decades ago, single-pillar social security systems in developing countries that define benefits on a PAYG basis can be regressive in a number of ways. First, pension benefits are based on earnings rather than on need and are often calculated to favor better-educated workers with steeper age/earnings profiles. Second, contributions from poorer workers with higher average mortality often subsidize benefits paid to longer-lived, higher-income workers. Third, and related to the previous point, poorer workers tend to begin working and contributing earlier than do those who are better off: workers in higher-paying jobs requiring more education tend to join the labor force later; because they start working sooner, the poor contribute longer during their active lives and receive a relatively shorter stream of benefits in retirement. Fourth, various exemptions, such as earlier retirement ages for select groups of workers including teachers and police, and lower contribution rates for civil servants often redistribute income from poorer to wealthier groups.

By replacing what were often regressive, single-pillar PAYG systems that frequently paid overly generous pensions to a privileged few with systems that diversify the risks to retirement income across multiple pillars, reforms were expected to introduce a more equitable system. Reformed systems would offer minimum income guarantees while they freed public resources for better-targeted forms of social assistance. The question is, have multipillar systems corrected the regressive impact of single-pillar public PAYG systems?

Very little evidence exists one way or another, largely because reforming governments are still paying transition costs and because the final impact of structural reforms on income inequality cannot be precisely measured until large segments of the population begin to retire with pensions financed primarily from individual retirement accounts. That said, there are important equity-related implications of the reforms that can be examined using simulation tools such as the World Bank's PROST.[1]

The introduction of multipillar systems is likely to have a substantial impact on distribution between beneficiaries of different income levels. Figure 5.1 shows the simulated effect of reform on the internal rates of return earned by poorer versus wealthier workers covered by formal retirement security systems. The figure shows the percentage-point difference between the internal rate of return earned by a representative wealthier-than-average worker and that earned by a poorer-than-average worker of either gender in each country. Both reform and no-reform scenarios are depicted, showing gains in equity under reforms in all cases.

Single-pillar PAYG systems in Latin America were notoriously regressive, conferring substantially higher returns on wealthier workers. In every country (for which data were available for PROST simulations) pension reforms that introduced multipillar systems lowered the regressive impact of single-pillar PAYG systems. In Chile and Argentina our simulations show that reforms even reversed regressive returns, increasing returns

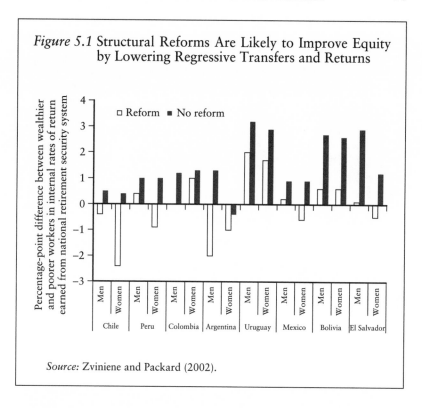

Figure 5.1 Structural Reforms Are Likely to Improve Equity by Lowering Regressive Transfers and Returns

Source: Zviniene and Packard (2002).

earned by poorer men and women covered by the systems relative to the return earned by wealthier workers of either gender.

Reforms have also had a notable impact on distribution of returns between genders. Figure 5.2 shows the percentage-point differential between the internal rates of return earned by men and women at average income levels (of covered workers) in each country. In Chile and Colombia reforms marginally increased the returns earned by women relative to those earned by men. Cox-Edwards (2000) claimed that the impact of reforms in Chile favoring women can be attributed to the minimum pension guarantee underpinning individual private savings in that country. In Peru reforms actually reversed distribution of returns from men to women. However, in every other country where the new retirement security model was adopted, women earn lower returns from the new systems relative to the returns earned by men.

That said, James, Cox-Edwards, and Wong (2003) used survey data and simulation techniques to show that poor women in Argentina, Chile, and Mexico have gained from reforms, receiving higher pension benefits than they would have received under the single-pillar PAYG systems. These gains are attributed to a better-targeted first pillar.

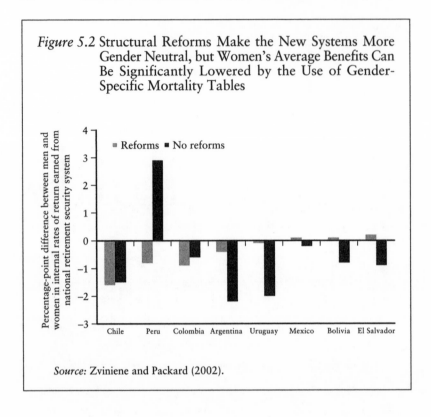

Figure 5.2 Structural Reforms Make the New Systems More Gender Neutral, but Women's Average Benefits Can Be Significantly Lowered by the Use of Gender-Specific Mortality Tables

Source: Zviniene and Packard (2002).

However, in Bolivia, Mexico, and El Salvador our simulations show that reforms replaced systems that subsidized benefits to women with systems that favor men. This shift may partially reflect the relatively greater importance of labor market participation and regular contribution in determining pension benefits under the new retirement security systems that are based on defined contributions (James, Cox-Edwards, and Wong 2003). The negative impact on the returns to women may reflect their relatively fewer years of employment and active contribution to the pension system. Men with fewer years of employment and those who work with fewer years of contributions would suffer a similar fall in returns with the introduction of individual accounts.

The internal rates of return calculated with PROST that are shown in Figure 5.2 assume that participating men and women have the same work and contribution histories. There is a more important factor increasing the gender-specific difference in returns between the two systems: the use of gender-specific mortality tables in calculating retirement annuities. Because women have relatively longer life expectancy at retirement, annuity providers using gender-specific mortality tables will calculate annuity payments that are significantly lower than payments made to men retiring with similar levels of accumulated savings.

Policies requiring a married male affiliate to retire with joint annuities that will cover his female spouse can improve the retirement security of surviving widows. Mandates requiring that private annuity providers use unisex mortality tables can correct disparities in returns from systems based primarily on individual retirement accounts, but they are highly controversial because they hinder the functioning of insurance markets. Attempts to meet equity objectives through further mandates in the operations of the private pillar—requiring insurers to use unisex mortality tables, in particular—can be detrimental to the development of private insurance markets and are better pursued through whatever first-pillar arrangements countries have put in place. There is evidence to suggest that the new first-pillar arrangements are succeeding in lowering the vulnerability of elderly women (James, Cox-Edwards, and Wong 2003).

Equity Implications of a Large Informal Sector

The equity issues examined in the sections above focus on the universe of workers actually covered by formal retirement security systems. However, the low rates of regular contribution among workers in Latin America, where many (if not most) workers are employed informally or self-employed, add another dimension to the inequitable impact that formal retirement security systems can have.

Because the majority of workers will not receive any benefits, the deficits of unbalanced, single-pillar public pension systems (where contribution revenue does not cover benefit expenditure) that are financed from current and future tax revenues can represent a transfer from uncovered workers to those covered by the systems—a relative minority of workers already benefiting from more stable, better-paying forms of employment. But even in the new multipillar pension systems with a large funded pillar, individual savings are almost always underpinned by some sort of public guarantee—often a minimum pension guarantee under which access to the minimum benefit is conditioned on a history of contributions to the system.

Figure 5.3 shows the marginal contribution to inequality of income (as measured by the Gini index) from public and publicly mandated pension systems (and primary employment, for comparison) in selected Latin American countries. Although any extrapolations have to be made with caution, the inequitable impact of pension benefits is notably greater in countries with unreformed purely PAYG systems (Brazil, Paraguay, Venezuela, and at the time Bolivia, although Uruguay is an exception) than in countries that introduced the multipillar model (Chile; Argentina's reform in 1994 was too recent for any impact to be apparent in the data shown). As explained above, however, even reformed pension systems

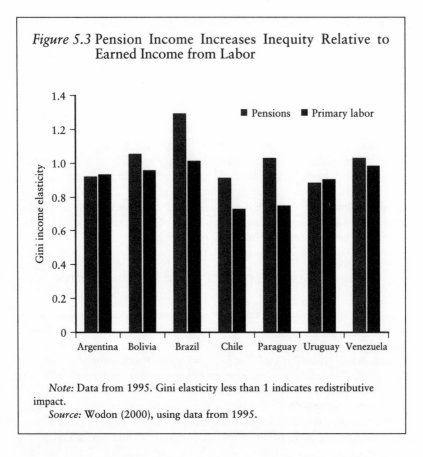

Figure 5.3 Pension Income Increases Inequity Relative to Earned Income from Labor

Note: Data from 1995. Gini elasticity less than 1 indicates redistributive impact.
Source: Wodon (2000), using data from 1995.

with large funded pillars will contribute to inequitable outcomes when a substantial portion of the labor force is not covered by the system.

Whether a pure PAYG system or a multipillar system with funded individual accounts and a minimum guarantee, pension systems that condition eligibility on a history of explicit contributions but pay benefits that are guaranteed by government transfers can redistribute income from all current and future taxpayers to those who have accumulated rights. This can lead to inequitable outcome in countries where most workers are not covered by the pension system. Even where the contribution and benefit parameters of a pension system are set to be "self-financing," government (society) still pays for shortfalls between benefits and contributions during economic downturns and for indexation to protect the real value of benefits during periods of inflation.

Thus all current and future taxpayers "contribute" in one way or another to maintain the number and value of pension benefits paid to a relatively smaller group of "covered" workers. This makes increasing

Box 5.1 Defining the Coverage Problem: What Is It and Why Do We Care?

At the turn of the 21st century fewer than 15 percent of the world's 6 billion people had access to a formal system of retirement income support (Holzmann, Packard, and Cuesta 2000). The majority of this population that goes without formal coverage lives and works in developing countries. To the extent that households in these countries can still rely on traditional arrangements to provide income security in old age, there may be little cause for worry. However, with the rapid aging of populations, urbanization, and economic development, many governments are increasingly concerned that their elderly people will have reduced access to traditional safety nets. Extending the coverage of social insurance therefore has become a policy priority.

Retirement pensions are typically the largest component of the set of public interventions that make up a social insurance system. Low coverage by the formal old-age pensions system, therefore, usually mirrors low coverage by other forms of social insurance, such as income support during unemployment, disability, access to family allowances, and in many cases access to public health care.

Low social insurance coverage presents several problems (Barr 1998, 2000). First and foremost is the problem for the individual and by extension the household. Workers who do not contribute to formal social insurance, either by choice or because of market or institutional barriers, are not accumulating rights toward the receipt of benefits should they become unemployed or disabled or when they lose their ability to work in old age. Nor are their dependents covered should the workers suffer untimely death. Household members may find it difficult to cope with losses resulting from these risks and can be forced into poverty when losses from an adverse shock are great.

Second is the problem for society. An individual's failure to save or insure imposes an externality. If he or she chooses to make no provisions for the risks to income, the costs of that decision fall on others. In countries where a significant number of workers fail to insure, governments face a "Samaritan's dilemma" in that politicians cannot credibly refuse to come to the aid of a large number of people who suffer a loss, and the burden of these losses can mount rapidly on current and future taxpayers.

Finally, low levels of coverage pose a problem for the social insurance institutions themselves. Low coverage can weaken a traditional PAYG pension system if not enough active workers and employers contribute to finance the benefits of the inactive retired, disabled, or unemployed population. If a substantial share of the population is not contributing, the system cannot pool risks efficiently and can quickly

(Box continues on the following page.)

Box 5.1 (continued)

lose financial viability. Similarly, where social insurance includes individual retirement accounts, the savings that can arise from scale in fund management are difficult to obtain when a large number of workers do not participate; persistently high administration costs eat into the savings of those who do participate.

The growing "informal," unregulated sector in many developing countries is important in the analysis of coverage to the extent that informal employment opportunities lift the constraint on choices by allowing individuals to avoid government mandates to pool risks or save in the formal retirement security system.

We define "coverage" both as a "stock" and a "flow" concept. The stock of the population that is covered includes all those people of retirement age and older who are receiving a formal retirement pension. The flow are those individuals of working age who are members of the workforce and currently are accumulating rights toward a retirement pension, either by contributing within the parameters of a PAYG benefit formula or by regularly depositing savings into a private individual retirement account. Thus, the "coverage gap" also has stock and flow dimensions. The stock consists of the current mass of elderly people (of most concern, elderly poor people and those living close to the poverty line) with no formal income protection. The flow consists of the likely stream of current active workers who would fall into the former category year after year. Evidence shows, for example, that Peru's coverage gap is particularly wide.

Source: Packard (2002).

coverage of formal retirement security arrangements (and indeed the wider social insurance system) critically important for individuals and households that need instruments to manage the risks to their income that arise in old age (see box 5.1) and to eliminate institutional determinants of inequality.

Has Reform Increased Coverage?

Low rates of coverage of the working population under pure PAYG systems were a strong motivating factor for pension reform (box 5.2). By tightening links between contributions and benefits (second pillar) and cutting the pure-tax component of payroll deductions, the reformed systems were expected to eliminate a substantial labor market distortion arising from pure defined-benefit PAYG regimes, lower incentives to evade mandated contributions, and encourage greater formalization of the workforce.

In most developing countries only a small share of workers sell their labor in a regulated "formal" sector that is subject to a mandated minimum

---

Box 5.2 Was Increasing Coverage an Objective of Pension Reform?

Pension reform literature and policy discourse have been consistently critical of the low coverage levels of purely public PAYG pension systems and the distortions they introduce to labor markets, particularly in developing countries. Because pension benefits in defined-benefit PAYG systems often have little relationship to mandatory contributions, both workers and firms can view contributions to these systems as a tax rather than as savings. In developing countries with dual labor markets, this perceived tax creates incentives for evasion, thereby reducing participation in the pension system and lowering coverage levels. Furthermore, the high payroll tax rates required in the formal sector to keep the system solvent restrain labor demand while the incentives for early retirement in many PAYG systems reduce labor supply.

Increasing coverage by reducing flight to the informal sector was considered more than just a fortunate consequence of introducing "multipillar" pension systems with a large privately funded component. Increasing coverage has been presented as a core objective of the multipillar model. In 1994 the World Bank's *Averting the Old Age Crisis* presented clear evidence of the impending insolvency, inequitable benefits, and unacceptably low coverage rates of purely PAYG systems in the developing world. Among the "main aims of any structural reform of a pensions system" is "to increase the incentives to participate" (Devesa-Carpio and Vidal-Meliá 2002, p. 9) and stem the flow of workers to the informal sector. The result is greater coverage and a more efficient labor market. Indeed, reductions in "effective tax rates, evasion and labor market distortions" are presented among the objectives and principal benefits of the multipillar reform model (World Bank 1994, p. 22).

It has been extensively argued that reforming from a single-pillar, PAYG, defined benefit system to a multipillar system with a fully funded, defined contribution pillar achieves this increase in coverage by reestablishing the broken link between contributions and benefits. The link is particularly crucial in reducing evasion in developing countries: "When escape to the large informal sector and other means of evasion are easy, it is more important than ever to . . . link benefits closely to [payroll-based pension] taxes" (World Bank 1994, p. 320). If workers' pension benefits depend on the contributions they make during their working lives, then there will be "positive effects on workers' incentives to participate in the formal sector" (Mitchell 1998, p. 15).

In addition to its salutary effect on coverage, the multipillar approach also "is designed to reduce labor market distortions" caused by public PAYG systems (James 1997, p. 10). On the demand side, broadening the tax base, shifting the tax burden to the worker, or both reduces payroll

(Box continues on the following page.)

Box 5.2 (continued)

taxes paid by firms, thus increasing "employers' ability to hire and keep their employees" (Mitchell 1998, p. 15). On the supply side, linking benefits to contributions not only induces workers to leave the informal sector, but also "encourage[s] people to remain in work longer" by removing the incentives to early retirement present in many PAYG systems (Disney and Whitehouse 1999, p. 30). In short, literature on pension reform clearly states that increasing coverage is both an objective and a predicted result of implementing a multipillar system with a large privately funded component.

Source: Contributed by Todd Pugatch.

---

wage and is covered by a social security system. The remainder work in an unregulated, uncovered "informal" sector where wages are solely determined by the market and where both workers and employers escape the mandate to contribute to social security.[2] A country's social security institutions can determine the allocation of labor between the sectors because social security contributions are one of the main components of nonwage labor costs. Thus "informalizing" production allows firms to reduce their costs. In Latin America the costs imposed by social security are estimated to be as high as 20 percent of the operating expenses of small firms (Tokman and Martinez 1999).

Theory suggests that at the margin a higher contribution rate for social security distorts labor allocation if workers do not consider their contributions "appropriable" in the future at the market rate of interest (Corsetti 1994; Schmidt-Hebbel 1998a). When the link between mandated contributions and perceived benefits is ambiguous, social security acts simply as a tax on labor (Atkinson and Stiglitz 1980; Summers 1989). In the case of public pensions where the payoff to workers' "investment" in the system lies far in the future, this perceived tax can be even more onerous if discount rates are high and access to credit is constrained (Samwick 1997; James 1999). In addition, in many developing countries public institutions like social security lack credibility (i.e., workers may strongly believe that they will receive no pension at all), thereby further increasing the perceived tax burden of current contributions (James 1996).

Several authors have shown that the extent of distortion to the labor market is independent of whether a country opts for a purely public PAYG system or for private individual retirement accounts (Diamond 1998; Barr 1998; Thompson 1998; Barr 2000). Corsetti (1994) found that to the extent that workers link current contributions to future pension benefits at the margin, individual retirement accounts do not necessarily produce fewer labor market distortions that determine the size of the informal sector than does a public PAYG system. In fact, when contributions and benefits are actuarially linked there may be more income incentives to work in the formal sector under a PAYG regimen than in a fully funded system. Orszag and Stiglitz (2001) and Barr (2000) presented similar arguments. Corsetti (1994) acknowledged that although the link between contributions and future benefits is unambiguous in a system of individual retirement accounts, such an actuarial balance must be carefully built into the design of the benefit formula for a PAYG system. James (1997) stressed this point, showing that rarely do PAYG formulas clearly link benefits to contributions, and even when they do, the balance is frequently upset by demographic and political pressures, especially in developing countries. Rather than enter into this debate, in this section we focus on studies that attempt to measure the impact of Latin American pension reforms that were expected to lower labor market distortions and improve workers' incentives to contribute. Have the incentives to participate in formal retirement security systems been improved by reforms? And has the share of the working population covered against the loss of earnings ability in old age increased?

Attempts to arrive at a common, cross-country indicator for coverage of social security systems have been confounded by differences in legislation and institutional structures. Coverage may be determined by citizenship, residence, or income status, or it may be restricted to workers who make contributions for a minimum number of years (Palacios 1996; Palacios and Pallares-Miralles 2000). In Latin America and the Caribbean region 25 countries legally require that all salaried workers contribute to be covered.[3] Despite legislation, however, numerous opportunities for unregulated employment and limited enforcement capacity allow large segments of the working population to escape these mandates. Figure 5.4 tracks the evolution in the most commonly used indicator of coverage—the share of the economically active population accruing rights by contributing to the national social security system.[4]

In several cases the time series shown in Figure 5.4 match the 1995 cross-section data on contributors in the labor force reported in Palacios and Pallares-Miralles (2000) for selected Latin American countries and years during the 1990s. Coverage is higher (between 30 percent and 60 percent of the economically active population (EAP)) in relatively affluent countries like Argentina, Chile, Colombia, Mexico, and Uruguay[5] and lower (between 10 percent and 20 percent) in poorer countries like Bolivia, El Salvador, and Nicaragua. It is interesting to note the relative stability in the share of the economically active population that contributed to social security throughout the long recessions of the 1980s. Another trend that is evident is the rise in contributors with economic growth in the early 1990s in all but three of the countries shown.

The most dramatic change in labor force participation in the retirement security system has been in Chile, where after the introduction of mandatory individual retirement accounts in 1981, and until only recently, the

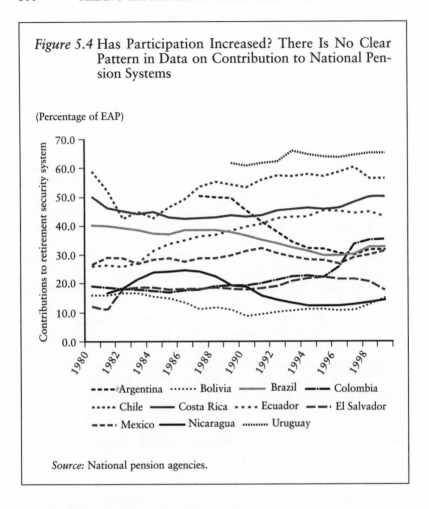

Figure 5.4 Has Participation Increased? There Is No Clear Pattern in Data on Contribution to National Pension Systems

(Percentage of EAP)

- - - Argentina   ······ Bolivia   ―― Brazil   ―·― Colombia

····· Chile   ―― Costa Rica   ···· Ecuador   ―·― El Salvador

- - · Mexico   ―― Nicaragua   ········ Uruguay

Source: National pension agencies.

share of contributors to the retirement security system (the statistic presented shows all branches, including the closed PAYG plan in the separate regimens for police and the military) climbs steadily, but only to reach a level similar to that in 1980. Also noteworthy, however, is the dive in the share of contributors in Argentina since 1989, five years prior to the introduction of individual accounts in that country.

Almost a decade after reforms—two decades in the case of Chile—the evidence of a change in the levels of coverage (proxied by contributors in the workforce) that is attributable to the introduction of individual retirement accounts has been mixed. It is difficult to discern a pattern from the data on contributors in figure 5.5. Several studies found that the share of the Chilean workforce covered by the reformed system has increased

(Corsetti and Schmidt-Hebbel 1994; Schmidt-Hebbel 1998b; Edwards and Cox-Edwards 2000a; Corbo and Schmidt-Hebbel 2003). Others claimed that there has not been an improvement in incentives and that there has even been a fall in the share of workers who contribute (Cortazar 1997; Arenas de Mesa 2000; Arenas de Mesa and Sanchez 2001; Mesa-Lago 2001). Palacios and Pallares-Miralles (2000) showed that in a large and varied sample of countries the share of contributors to a formal pension system in the labor force is almost entirely explained by income per capita and varies little by the type of pension system in place.[6]

Until very recently, however, most studies relied on simulations, casual observation of data on labor force participation, or single-variable analysis. Furthermore, most analysis of participation in the pension systems fails to control for macroeconomic conditions or for policy variables unrelated to social security that affect the labor market. Despite the time that has passed since reforms were implemented in several countries, the expected improvement in incentives attributable to the introduction of individual retirement accounts has not been rigorously tested.

In a background paper for this book, Packard (2001) employed the model presented by Edwards and Cox-Edwards (2000a) to estimate the impact of a transition from a purely public PAYG system to one with privately managed individual accounts on the share of the workforce that contributes to retirement security systems. The aim was to identify the incentive effect on participation expected by the proponents of reform by controlling for development, cyclical, and country-specific features. The results of panel analysis on 18 countries observed from 1980 to 1999 indicate that, after controlling for level of development and for the impact of the economic cycle, introducing individual retirement accounts has a positive but small incentive effect. These results are reported in table 5.1.

The results also suggest that the *extent* of private provision influences the level of participation: the greater the share of mandated payroll contributions that accumulates as private savings, the larger the portion of the workforce that contributes after reforms.[7] However, this increase in contributors may only occur gradually after individual accounts are introduced, as employers and workers overcome uncertainty and become familiar with the set of new institutions that reforms put in place.[8] It should be pointed out that the results do not rule out improved incentives from simply aligning contributions and benefits within a PAYG system (as with reforms in Brazil and the establishment of "notional" accounts in several Eastern European countries), without having to incur the costs of introducing individual accounts.

In accompanying background papers, Packard (2002), using household data from Chile, and Barr and Packard (2002), using data from Peru, showed that the contribution density (the share of their working lives individuals have contributed to a formal pension system) of workers who joined the labor market after the introduction of individual accounts is

Table 5.1 Evidence That Pension Reforms Positively Affect Incentives

Independent variables	Pooled OLS	Random effects	Fixed effects
Income per capita	0.035	0.124	0.094
	(0.016)**	(0.025)***	(0.033)***
Life expectancy	0.011	0.009	0.007
	(0.002)***	(0.003)***	(0.003)**
Change in unemployment	−0.428	−0.246	−0.263
	(0.203)**	(0.072)***	(0.070)***
Female labor supply	0.473	−0.059	0.085
	(0.144)***	(0.265)	(0.315)
Total payroll tax	0.36	−0.388	−1.189
	(0.107)***	(0.217)*	(0.355)***
Portion of payroll tax going to individual account	0.272	0.057	0.153
	(0.110)**	(0.064)	(0.076)**
Years since reform	−0.012	−0.025	−0.025
	(0.024)	(0.009)***	(0.008)***
Years since reform^2	0.002	0.004	0.004
	(0.004)	(0.001)***	(0.001)***
Years since reform^3	−0.00009	−0.0001	−0.0002
	(0.0001)	(0.000)***	(0.000)***
Year dummies included?	yes	yes	yes
Observations[a]	287	287	287
Number of countries[a]	18	18	18
R-squared	0.53	0.29 (within)	0.31 (within)

F test of joint significance of fixed effects, H_0: OLS accepted
$F_{(17, 241)} = 131.50$ P > F = 0.0000
Hausman specification test, H_0: difference in random and fixed effects not systematic

$$\chi^2 (28) = 27.68 \text{ P} > \chi^2 = 0.4816$$

Notes: Contributors to national pension system as share of EAP, various estimations. OLS ordinary least squares. Standard errors in parentheses. Specification tests indicate that the fixed effects estimator in the last column is preferred.

[a] Colombia removed from the sample; 20 observations dropped.
* Significant at 10 percent level.
** Significant at 5 percent level.
*** Significant at 1 percent level.
Source: Packard (2001).

significantly greater than that of workers who contributed to the pension system prior to reforms.

Although the reported analysis found evidence of an improvement in incentives attributable to the shift to individual retirement accounts, other factors directly and indirectly linked to the reformed pension systems are found to determine rates of participation among workers. In another background paper for this inquiry, Valdés-Prieto (2002c) showed that a broader set of policies have a significant and substantial impact on coverage. Changes in labor and social legislation that impose costs on participation in the formal labor market or confer benefits to covered workers affect the overall coverage of the pension system. Using time-series analysis of the labor force in Chile that contributed to the pension system from 1990 to 2001, Valdés-Prieto presented evidence that the share of contributing workers in the labor force falls with increases in the minimum wage. This effect did not result from workers being excluded from formal employment—as has been argued in the past—but because increases in the minimum wage also increase the minimum that workers are mandated to save in the AFP system. This increases the amount that those who contribute only the minimum are forced to save. Furthermore, increases in the flat commissions charged by the AFPs also lower the number of workers who contribute. Finally, participation in the pension system increases with increases in the subsidy the government pays to cover the health expenses of workers who contribute to Chile's public health system.

Conclusion

Despite the positive impact of pension reforms on workers' incentive to seek coverage, the share of workers who contribute to the formal retirement security systems is still low relative to OECD countries, even in the wealthier countries in Latin America that offer individual accounts. Totals reach barely above 65 percent in a few cases. That finding warns strongly against complacency. The relatively small share of contributors in the labor force indicates that the wedge created by the payroll tax to public PAYG systems prior to reform was just one of many possible factors that still lead certain groups of workers to turn away from government-mandated retirement income protection.

In analyzing coverage outcomes—that is, the share of the new elderly population who receive pension benefits each year—Rofman (2002) found that coverage is falling in Argentina. Fewer elderly people among every new cohort in Argentina receive pension benefits. Furthermore, whether one considers participation rates or the incidence of pension benefits, coverage indicators show a regressive pattern (see table 5.2), and indicate that more needs to be done to increase access to at least minimum levels of protection against the risks to income that accompany old age.

Table 5.2 Participation Rates and Incidence of Benefits Show a Regressive Pattern of Coverage by Formal Pension Systems

a. Contributors as a percentage of population aged 15 to 65 years

Income Group	Argentina	Bolivia	Chile	Colombia	Costa Rica	El Salvador	Nicaragua	Peru	Venezuela
Total	36.0	10.3	62.7	22.3	22.9	25.5	11.0	13.0	33.1
Quintile 1	18.7	0.6	43.4	9.8	8.9	3.6	—	1.6	14.4
Quintile 2	14.8	2.5	57.4	10.3	25.2	7.3	—	6.1	28.8
Quintile 3	34.7	9.2	64.3	16.1	25.5	18.2	—	10.6	32.9
Quintile 4	47.4	14.6	67.9	26.0	27.0	34.6	—	17.0	37.7
Quintile 5	58.4	25.8	72.0	42.1	23.2	49.5	—	25.1	44.3

b. Pension recipients as a percentage of population older than 65 years of age

Income Group	Argentina	Bolivia	Chile	Colombia	Costa Rica	Dominican Republic	El Salvador	Peru	Venezuela
National	66.2	11.9	41.4	15.2	33.2	14.6	8.8	23.5	9.4
Quintile 1	54.1	0.3	15.0	0.2	25.5	10.7	1.6	8.2	2.2
Quintile 2	66.5	6.3	41.6	12.4	31.5	10.8	9.3	17.5	6.1
Quintile 3	70.4	13.3	50.2	15.8	41.0	17.1	11.1	26.2	9.7
Quintile 4	70.0	28.9	57.4	22.8	48.3	19.8	11.4	34.4	15.8
Quintile 5	71.2	29.0	55.0	32.5	35.0	19.2	20.6	41.8	16.1

— Not available.

Source: National household surveys (Argentina, EPH 2002; Bolivia, ECH 2000; Chile, CASEN 2000; Colombia, ENH 1999; Costa Rica, EHPM 2000; Dominican Republic, ENFT 2000; El Salvador, EHPM 1998; Mexico, ENEU 2001; Nicaragua, ENMV 1999; Peru, ENAHO 2000; Venezuela, EHM 2000).

Notes

1. For the assumptions employed in the simulations presented here, see the technical annex at the end of this volume.

2. Recent evidence (Maloney 2003) shows that factors favoring the nontradable sector, such as recessions and currency appreciations, increased the size of the informal sector in the 1990s.

3. Only 13 countries require self-employed workers to pool risks or save along with the rest of the working population, whereas 10 countries invite self-employed workers to participate on a voluntary basis. Self-employed people are required to contribute in Argentina, Brazil, Cuba, Honduras, Uruguay, and Venezuela. Almost all the countries in the Caribbean region require that self-employed workers participate in the national social security system, with the exception of Antigua and Barbuda. Participation is voluntary in Bolivia, Chile, Colombia, Costa Rica, Ecuador, El Salvador, Mexico, Nicaragua, Panama, and Peru (Mesa-Lago 2000).

4. This indicator is second best because it does not capture coverage of public (or publicly mandated) disability and survivor insurance, which often extends for a determined period after a worker stops contributing toward a retirement pension. The share of contributors in the workforce at any given point in time also excludes workers who may have contributed in the past and acquired *some* rights, and it fails to take account of rights of dependent spouses and children in the workforce. Although working spouses and children may not contribute themselves, they are likely to be covered for survivor and health risks through the contributions of the head of household.

5. With the option to switch between the defined contribution AFP and the defined-benefit PAYG system every three years, the data from Colombia may count contributors twice and overstate the rate of coverage, thus data should be interpreted with caution.

6. Although the correlation presented by Palacios and Pallares-Miralles (2000) is indeed high, one would expect analysis of a large sample of diverse countries to show that per capita income explains most of the variation in almost any indicator of interest, whether it is contributors to a pension system, education, longevity, or household ownership of consumer durable goods.

7. An important caveat to this result should be made with respect to Argentina. After the 1994 reform workers could choose between a reformed PAYG system and private accounts for the earnings-related portion of their pensions. To increase the participation in individual accounts, the government assigned workers who did not make an explicit choice to the private branch of the system by default. In a background paper for this book Rofman (2002) found that as many as 2.8 million affiliates to the private branch of the system never explicitly chose the private option. Although this could affect the results cited above, the dependent variable in the panel analysis is the share of pension-system contributors among workers, not the share of affiliates. Furthermore, each reforming country was dropped from the panel one at a time to see if the positive incentive results were particular to any single reform. The results withstood this experiment.

8. Packard (2001) found evidence of a J-curve effect in the share of workers who contribute after the introduction of individual accounts, but the effect was very weak and not robust to small changes in the sample.

II

Analytical:
How Governments Can
Help Individuals Deal with
Retirement

6

How Individuals View
Social Security

CHAPTERS 3, 4, AND 5 PRESENTED EVIDENCE showing that countries in Latin America that adopted the multipillar model—distinguished best by the presence of mandatory savings accounts—experienced improvements in the economic sustainability and socioeconomic orientation of social security systems and have increased financial sector depth. These outcomes were often the stated goals of the reform, and the evidence shows that countries have been successful to varying degrees.

But it is fair to ask if these objectives should be ends in themselves or simply means to improving the welfare of citizens. Having a fiscally healthy government, a well-functioning labor market, and a growing financial sector are important because they can make individuals and their families better off. But the main question is, Are people in the reforming countries better off because of the adoption of multipillar systems of social security? This is the question addressed by part 2 of this volume. This chapter presents a simple analytical framework centered on the behavior of an individual—a rational "representative agent"—to help in answering this question. The theory yields important clues for the role of government in a setting where individuals make decisions under risk; the implications are similar to those drawn by Barr (2000; see box 6.1). Chapter 7 provides evidence that Latin American workers may not judge the new system quite as kindly as do fiscal and financial specialists. Chapter 8 provides both an argument that Latin American workers deserve to be trusted more in deciding how best to save for their old age and some empirical clues to how governments can best help workers address the risks associated with aging.

It is important to stress here that the framework used is not novel; it is borrowed from the economics of insurance literature, building on the seminal work of Ehrlich and Becker (1972, 2000).[1] The novelty lies only in extracting the implications for public policy.

Box 6.1 The Welfare State as a Piggy Bank to Reduce Old-Age Income Insecurity

Barr (2000) proposed a simple and elegant rationale for the role of government in a real-world scenario of risk and imperfect information. Using this simple Fisher framework of individual choice, Barr derived the principles for realistic expectations from and effective design of pension systems.

Contrasting these principles with thinking inspired by the Chilean reforms, Barr listed 10 myths concerning the macroeconomics of pensions, the design of pension systems, and the role of government:

1. Funding resolves adverse demographics.
2. The only way to pre-fund is through pension accumulations.
3. There is a direct link between funding and growth.
4. Funding reduces public pension spending.
5. Paying off debt is always good policy.
6. Funded schemes have better labor market incentive effects.
7. Funded pensions diversify risk.
8. Increased choice is welfare improving.
9. Funding does better if real returns exceed real wage growth.
10. Private pensions get government out of the pensions business.

It would be fair to say that chapters 3, 4, and 5 provide considerable evidence from Latin America during the last two decades that supports the argument that the elements of Barr's list are genuine myths, not self-evident truths.

This volume also takes seriously Barr's advice that analysis of pensions "needs to draw on several perspectives, including microeconomics, macroeconomics, financial economics, and an understanding of the theory of social insurance" (2001). Chapters 3, 4, and 5 address the first three aspects; this chapter applies simple principles of insurance to the economics of pensions.

In applying the basic principles of insurance to the problem of social security, this volume characterizes the challenges associated with pension design as the matching of instruments to the two fundamental losses associated with aging in a world of increasing prosperity: the loss of the ability to earn in old age and the loss associated with poverty during old age. Changing demographics imply that the former is an increasingly frequent loss, and the greater availability of saving instruments for old age imply that the latter is an increasingly rare loss. The economics of insurance suggest that frequent losses cannot easily be insured against (or only at prohibitively high premiums) but that rare, idiosyncratic losses can be pooled. The preferred risk management strategy for frequent losses is a combination of saving and measures to reduce risk.

Box 6.1 (continued)

Our approach differs from that of Barr in one respect. Whereas Barr treated the poverty relief role (the "Robin Hood" function) of government as distinct from its role in redistribution over the life cycle (the "piggy bank" function), we subsume the responsibility of old-age poverty relief within the set of decisions associated with the life cycle. As a result of this we arrive at a "size of government" that is somewhat different: government–defined benefit pensions serve only a poverty-relief function. But expanding the insurance function of government to cover poverty relief actually strengthens Barr's argument that the "welfare state is here to stay" (2001, p. 1) because the insurance function of governments will not diminish as economies grow, and may indeed increase.

Source: Barr (2000, 2001).

The Advantage of Taking the Individual's Viewpoint

The attractiveness of an approach that is centered on the individual is not just that it refocuses attention on what really matters in designing public policy—that is, the welfare of individuals and their families. Another attractive feature is that it uses a well-developed literature on the economics of insurance to draw implications more carefully rather than attempting to build a conceptual framework from scratch. There are two main payoffs from the improved analytical rigor that comes from this overtly incremental approach to conceptualization of old-age income security. First, it brings the appropriate role of government into sharper relief and, second, it reliably points at directions in which policymakers should take their countries to provide better income security in old age. "Better" here is understood to mean sustainable, secure, and sufficient support for more people.

The next section in this chapter provides the reasons why saving and not pooling should be the main instrument for dealing with the loss of earning capacity during old age, that is, smoothing consumption over the life cycle. Using the same approach we discuss the rationale for having a pure pooled plan as well—to deal (largely) with the risk of poverty in old age. Readers will see the potential payoff in policy formulation: it provides some guidance on the relative sizes or "weights" of the pooling and savings components in the multipillar system of any country, depending on measurable parameters such as life expectancy at retirement and the incidence of old-age poverty.

Unlike much of the pension literature that assumes at the outset that individuals do not behave rationally (e.g., are reluctant to prepare for old age), we begin with assumed rational individuals who maximize lifetime utility for themselves and their families. We then extend the analysis to deal with a commonly assumed market failure—that individuals may not save "enough" for old age. Using a paper commissioned for this book (Valdés-Prieto 2002b), we discuss the basis for benevolent policy—a justification for a government-imposed mandate on individuals to save for old age. The analysis yields useful guidance on the relative sizes of the mandatory and voluntary pillars of the savings component. Finally, we examine another widely assumed rationale for a government-imposed mandate to save for retirement—that savings are somehow "underproduced" at an aggregate level when the benefits of saving for financial sector development and growth are considered.

Saving as the Mainstay of Old-Age Income Security

The principles of insurance are clear on the matter of income security in old age. In the face of a possible loss, a "comprehensive insurance" approach would suggest that individuals can insure against the loss, take steps to lower the likelihood that the loss will occur, or do nothing and simply "take their lumps" (see, e.g., Ehrlich and Becker 1972, 2000; and box 6.2). The purchase of insurance transfers income from "good" to "bad" times to lower the size of losses in the latter. Individuals can insure themselves in two ways: through mechanisms that pool the risk of the loss occurring among those who are exposed to this risk, or through individual savings or "self-insurance." The cost of pooling risk (equal to the insurance premium, assuming an actuarially fair price) is set according to the probability that the loss will occur. Thus, as the probability of a given loss rises, the cost of pooling to insure against that loss will also increase. In contrast, the implicit or shadow price of saving—the other way to transfer income from good times to bad—does not vary with the probability of the loss. As the likelihood of the loss increases, the price of pooling risk relative to the price of saving will rise. Rational individuals confronted by actuarially fair prices will then prefer saving to pooling to insure against the loss.

The loss in question here arises from the inability to earn an income because of the body's natural deterioration in old age. As life expectancies rise as a result of improvements in basic hygiene, medicine, and education, the probability that most people will face a period of life in which they will need to consume but be unable to work can also rise. As such a state of the world becomes more likely, rational individuals should increasingly turn to saving to smooth consumption over their lifetimes and step up "self-protection" efforts to lower the impact of this loss of earning capability.

If individual preferences are not argument enough, the same logic can be applied at the aggregate level to support a transition to individual savings accounts. Improvements in longevity increase the share of the population that faces a relatively predictable loss. Pooling risk by defining

---

Box 6.2 A Theory of "Comprehensive Insurance"

In the Ehrlich and Becker (1972, 2000) characterization there are two states of the world: bad and good. Faced with risk a person may purchase insurance that involves paying a premium. The individual also spends resources on self-insurance (transferring income from good to bad states by themselves) and self-protection (lowering the probability of the bad state). The individual chooses the levels of market insurance and self-insurance where the price of market insurance (the premium) equals the shadow price of self-insurance. Resources spent on self-protection are optimized where the marginal gain from reducing the probability of loss equals the marginal loss from having to pay for self-protection.

The framework has several implications for pension policy. First, market insurance and self-insurance are substitutes. As the price of market insurance rises relative to self-insurance, the person will prefer the latter as a way to transfer resources from the "good" state of the world (working age) to the "bad" one (old age). Second, the individual will prefer market insurance to self-insurance for insuring relatively rare losses because the shadow price of self-insurance does not fall as the probability of the loss decreases, but the price of market insurance does. Third, although imperfect information or weak institutions may result in a thin or missing market for insuring against some losses, and governments would feel justified in stepping in to address these "market failures," the basic principles of insurance still apply: where the losses are relatively rare the preferred mode of intervention should involve pooling of risks; where losses are frequent the emphasis should be on providing or facilitating instruments for self-insurance or saving. Finally, although the possibility of adverse selection necessitates a mandate to participate in a public plan that involves pooling (namely, that mimics a market insurance plan), the rationale for mandatory participation in a private savings system is much weaker; that is, government-provided instruments for pooling imply a strong *insurance-related* rationale for mandating participation, but the rationale for coerced participation in a self-insurance scheme is based on weaker reasoning (e.g., moral hazard in the presence of a public pooled plan and political economy reasons in the presence of an existing—and inappropriately designed—social security system).

Source: Ehrlich and Becker (1972, 2000); de Ferranti et al. (2000); Packard (2002).

---

retirement benefits financed on a PAYG basis will become more expensive relative to individual savings as the number of old people rises relative to the number of young people. Although advances in health can postpone the loss of earnings ability, in most countries the legal retirement age has not risen commensurately. Little wonder then that social security systems that relied on pooling to deal with this increasingly frequent loss ran into trouble unless they altered the very definition of the risk in question to keep it relatively rare, for example, by raising the age at which retirement benefits commence as retirees' life expectancy increased.

The main point is that if the loss of earnings ability while living is widespread—as it is in much of Latin America—simple economics of insurance dictate that saving, not pooling, is the appropriate insurance mechanism to smooth consumption across these "states of the world." All this is not to say that there is no room for a pooled scheme. Pooling is the appropriate instrument for the rarer losses associated with disability and untimely death—in the terminology of Ehrlich and Becker (1972, 2000), "market insurance." So the reliance on saving for old-age income security to smooth consumption does not imply that there is no room for pooling instruments such as disability and survivors' insurance and annuities. For simplicity, however, we refer to the consumption-smoothing part of a pension system as the savings component.

In a useful survey of the gains from pension reform around the world, Lindbeck and Persson (2003) identified the "individualization" of social security as a prominent feature of reform efforts, reflected in a shift to individual accounts, either notional or real. But that survey ended by emphasizing that these "reforms do not diminish the need for basic, or guaranteed, pensions. Quite the contrary; growing reliance on quasi-actuarial and actuarially fair systems, which in themselves do not encompass any systematic intra-generational redistributive elements, makes it even more imperative to maintain a safety net to prevent poverty in old age" (p. 109). We discuss this issue next.

Pooling to Insure Against the Risk of Old-Age Poverty

In contrast to the incidence of old age, and assuming rising incomes, the prospect of poverty during one's retirement years will become relatively rare in Latin America over time. For this reason the cost of insuring against the risk of poverty will become relatively low, providing justification for defined benefit programs financed either through payroll or general taxes that pool the risk of old-age poverty among taxpayers.

In the absence of sufficiently flexible statutory benefit entitlement ages, the extent of pooling in defined benefit plans increases over time as populations age. As the cost of pooling increases, governments are forced to raise taxes to finance these systems. Such costs may be bearable for a pure pooling arrangement designed to prevent or alleviate indigence in old age. On the other hand, the growing cost of pooling arrangements, which are geared to addressing the consumption-smoothing motive of individuals, can overwhelm government finances. Defined contribution regimens (whether PAYG or funded) introduce an automatic rebalancing mechanism because benefits depend on the life expectancy of a given generation. The growing preference for defined contribution plans among employer-provided pension systems in OECD countries and the shift to notional defined contribution systems in countries such as Italy, Latvia, Poland, and Sweden are evidence of the increasing relative costs of pooling for old-age income security.

The comprehensive insurance approach has immediate and obvious implications for the size of the first pillar (the pooling component, which has a poverty-prevention objective) as compared with the second and third pillars (the savings component, which has a consumption-smoothing, income-replacement objective) in dealing with risks related to old age, namely that it should be much smaller. Under reasonable assumptions the role of government in providing an instrument to pool against the risk of old-age poverty also emerges as important (asymmetric information), as does the need for mandating participation (adverse selection). But the analysis does not shed nearly as much light on the relative importance of the mandatory versus voluntary savings components, namely, the weights of the second and third pillars. It is to this issue that we turn next.

Justifying Mandatory Saving—Individual Welfare

Most fields within economics that seek to justify a role for government begin with the premise of individual rationality. The case for government intervention usually hinges on some failure of market mechanisms to induce individuals and firms to choose optimal levels of consumption and production.

In the case of underconsumption or underproduction of something good—for example, vaccines against tuberculosis or automobiles that run on solar energy—the usual solution proposed is to subsidize its production or consumption. This "rule" arises from the principle that quantity restrictions are more distortionary in terms of unintended effects than interventions to manipulate prices. When an activity is mandated by societies (e.g., compulsory enrollment of children in basic education), the government is generally expected to provide this service at a lower price than could be asked by the market.

Somewhat in contrast, pension policy discourses usually presume irrationality on the part of individuals. Where this is not assumed, external benefits to saving for old age are often asserted. And more often than not the prescription is to rely on mandated minimum savings levels instead of, say, providing fiscal incentives to induce individuals to save more than they would without such inducements. The result has to be that many people are coerced into saving more than they should (the distortion discussed above), given their tastes for current consumption or the needs of people at their stage in life. Young people and poor people are often the main targets of such paternalistic policies, and they are most likely to end up worse off than had there been no interventions.

We started this chapter with the assumption of rationality and arrived at the conclusion that under most circumstances, the mainstay of old-age income support should be saving. Now we examine the possible rationale for *mandating* this saving, relying on a paper commissioned for this book.[2] Valdés-Prieto (2002c) examined the five most frequently used arguments for justifying a policy that mandates savings for retirement: myopia, moral hazard caused by the first pillar, incentives for intergenerational abuse, adverse selection in annuity markets, and "improvidence" or a systematic mistake in assessing the length and cost of old age until it is too late for the individual to correct. After reviewing the evidence and internal consistency of these theories, only improvidence survives critical evaluation as a plausible basis for benevolent policy (see table 6.1). However, as the gains from eliminating improvidence are bounded—after all, the case is that voluntary savings are low, not zero—this implies a limit on the social costs of the mandate that should be tolerated.

Even pro-mandate or interventionist interpretations based on individual behavior imply a second pillar that is relatively small, with savings only enough to allow purchases of annuities that yield the same level of benefits as first-pillar pensions. The main rationale for the large second pillars that we observe in the countries that have adopted multipillar reforms must then be the existence of *oversized first pillars*. Presumably this is because people were accustomed to high replacement ratios in the old PAYG systems, and it was difficult for governments to lower this ratio suddenly. If this is the case, then a gradual decline in the size of the second pillar is all the more sensible because it will enhance the equity of *both* mandatory components—the defined benefit first pillar and the defined contribution second pillar.

The implications for the third pillar are ambiguous. Given rational individual behavior, large first and second pillars imply little room for voluntary saving. The distortion in old pooling-dominated systems was a lack of emphasis on saving; the distortion in reformed systems may be a large second pillar at the expense of the third pillar.

Justifying Mandatory Saving— Economy-Wide Externalities

The case for mandating saving for old age—that is, for setting up a second pillar—has also been made in a more circular manner than individual myopia or improvidence. Mandatory savings programs are believed to increase the economy-wide savings rate, thus increasing access to credit for firms that would otherwise be starved of capital. It is argued that a second pillar fosters capital market development and thereby provides better financial

Table 6.1 Justifying a Government-Imposed Mandate to Save for Old Age—Microeconomic Reasons

Rationale	Definition	Evidence	Consistency checks	Implication
Myopia with respect to saving for the future or lack of self-control	Broadly defined as high preference for consumption *now* relative to *later*; also includes self-control failure	No evidence of psychic externalities (that society would be made better off if people are protected from their own weaknesses) important enough to justify large second pillar	Paternalism against myopia inconsistent with democracy; people have voluntary instruments (e.g., mortgages) to overcome the problem of self-control	Myopia, poor self-control, and presence of psychic externalities useful for studying individual behavior, but fall far short of justifying a government second- or third-pillar intervention
Moral hazard arising from the first pillar	The presence of a pooling plan or safety net (e.g., first-pillar pension) implies perverse incentive not to save enough	Second pillar is usually far larger than this moral hazard would justify—accumulation should not be greater than what is needed to afford a pension of 1 or 2 times the minimum salary	Given presence of first pillar, introduction of second pillar makes poor workers worse off	Introducing a second pillar to reduce moral hazard is not Pareto-desirable because it makes poor people worse off, and may even be Pareto-worsening; third-pillar interventions likely to help the wealthy
Intergenerational abuse in pooled plans	PAYG systems allow massive transfers from future generations of workers, but mandatory savings do not	Timing of introduction of such systems—removal of wealth requirements for voting—such that median voter was manual worker	Assumes median voter is "egotistic" or selfish, but same voter makes unselfish decisions about environment and public support for basic research	Not convincing enough to be taken as the explanation for second-pillar pensions

(Table continues on the following page.)

Table 6.1 (continued)

Rationale	Definition	Evidence	Consistency checks	Implication
Adverse selection in annuity markets	If insurance provider has less information than worker, only the most long-lived people purchase insurance in voluntary markets because good and bad risks are all charged the same premium	No evidence that workers have more information on their own longevity than do specialized insurance providers	Even if true, the intervention should be limited to the annuity market, rather than mandating saving; implies no government intervention at accumulation stage, only at dispersion stage	Probably not adequate justification for mandating saving; if true, choice between annuity and programmed withdrawal should not be permitted
Improvidence or systematic miscalculation	Systematic mistake in assessing the length and cost of old age until worker is too old to rectify this mistake at modest cost	Evidence raises doubts about individuals' ability to distribute lifetime wealth over time because of psychological constraints	The best solution is to provide information on correct length of retirement	Educating workers about old-age needs is best policy; third-pillar institutions better suited for this because their success depends on attracting voluntary saving

Source: Authors' interpretation of Valdés-Prieto (2002b).

instruments for saving. The argument here is that having a second pillar stimulates the growth of the third pillar by hastening the growth of "institutional capital." Table 6.2 summarizes the different macroeconomic reasons for setting up a second pillar.

These arguments again imply that an individual left to himself or herself would underproduce savings for old age, not relative to what would be optimal for the specific individual—the rationale discussed in the previous section—but compared with what would be optimal for the economy as a whole. This is again a market failure and it makes a case for government intervention. Paradoxically, this argument is generally made by people who distrust governments and ostensibly trust markets. And the case made is for quantity controls, not for price subsidization.

This issue cannot be resolved except by appeal to data. Schmidt-Hebbel (1997) found some evidence that part of the increase in national savings observed in Chile can be traced to the pension reform, both directly through limited crowding out of voluntary savings and indirectly through capital market development and higher productivity growth. Most of the increase in savings, however, results from an increase in public savings (that were not fully offset by private dissaving) and by other structural changes, such as a comprehensive tax reform, that triggered a sharp increase in corporate savings rates.

For three of the Latin American countries that have adopted multipillar reforms (Argentina, Chile, and Peru), Walker and Lefort (2002) examined whether there is evidence of links between mandated saving and capital market development. They found that some of the key improvements in the capital market infrastructure, such as the development of depositary and risk-rating services, have been linked intrinsically to pension reform. In addition, the regulatory oversight of the financial system, and in particular of the new pension fund industry, has been modernized to increase the security of retirement savings.

Pension funds can also contribute to capital market development by improving the liquidity of securities markets and lowering the cost of capital for firms. As shown in chapter 4, this evidence is clearest in Chile, where pension funds have become the largest minority shareholder of many companies traded in the stock market. Chilean pension funds also appear to be playing an increasingly important role in corporate governance by voting for independent directors and demanding greater transparency in company accounts. In other countries that permit pension fund investment in corporate securities, such as Argentina and Peru, too little time has passed since the inception of the system to extract conclusive evidence.

The main recipients of the new retirement savings, however, have been governments and financial institutions. Pension fund administrators and especially life insurance companies have been avid buyers of medium- and long-term government bonds in the region and have contributed to reducing the dependency on foreign capital. The greater degree of market

Table 6.2 Justifying a Government-Imposed Mandate to Save for Old Age—Macroeconomic Reasons

Rationale	Definition	Evidence	Consistency checks	Implication
Savings	The mandate increases national savings because of limited crowding-out by voluntary dissaving in countries with credit-constrained households.	Some evidence of increase in savings as a result of pension reform in Chile, but main cause is government savings, not mandate.	Sound fiscal management and inflation protection mechanisms are central to promoting savings; Chile is the exception in Latin America.	Transition debt needs to be financed explicitly, and mandate needed to finance this debt, leaving little ground to increase savings.
Capital market development	The mandate creates a pool of long-term savings that is channeled into the capital markets and contributes to their development.	Some evidence of greater liquidity of stock market in Chile as a result of pension fund investment; the modernization of capital markets is driven mainly by regulatory reform, not pension funds.	The mandated savings are managed by a handful of pension fund managers who invest in more or less the same way; such concentration of decisionmaking is not conducive to dynamic markets and is prone to political capture.	Capital market development can be achieved without mandating savings, the United Kingdom and the United States being the two prime examples.
Economic growth	Funds are channeled into productive investments; there is a more efficient allocation of resources in the economy.	Most funds are channeled into government debt and deposits, so there is little left for direct financing for the corporate sector.	Investment regulations determine asset allocation; regulations limit investment in projects without history and securities of lower credit rating.	Mandated savings call for strict prudential regulations that constrain innovative investment.
Labor market efficiency	Social security contributions are no longer perceived as a tax.	The new funded system is perceived as more risky than alternative investments, so the tax element is not eliminated.	Lower contribution rates increase participation and improve compliance in mandatory pension systems.	Labor market efficiency is best served by voluntary savings.

Source: Authors' compilation.

discipline over government debt has not always been forthcoming (Argentina is the prime example), but pension reform has been at least a catalyst for concomitant reforms aimed at improving the management of the government debt.

The health of the banks' balance sheets has also improved with the influx of new capital. Both pension funds and life insurance companies have allocated a significant portion of their assets to deposits, thereby contributing to raising lending rates and lengthening the maturity of loans. In Chile pension funds and life insurance companies have also played a key role in the development of the mortgage debt market, thus contributing to development of the real estate market.

In general the evidence supporting capital market development is clearest in the case of Chile. This is certainly a result of the longer history of the system, which permits more accurate empirical estimations. At the same time some developments in Chile, such as growth of the mortgage debt market or the increasing maturity of bank loans, would have been impossible had inflation protection mechanisms not existed (fixed income markets are indexed to a measure of the cost of living) and had there been no serious and credible policy of fiscal discipline, as argued in chapter 4.

Conclusion

The relevant point is that rare and idiosyncratic losses can be pooled or insured against, and frequent or systemic losses should be saved for, or self-insured against. With life more frequently extending beyond the point where earning ability declines and with more systemic loss resulting from the welcome development of increased longevity, the mainstay of old-age income security becomes self-insurance or savings. The role of government is to ensure that inter-temporal contracts are honored—hence the importance of regulation of private long-term savings plans.

By the same token, however, there are two risks that are rare and idiosyncratic and that justify pooling, whether facilitated by markets or by governments. The first risk is old-age poverty. This loss is difficult for markets to insure against because of moral hazard, potential adverse selection, and the social nature of the definition of poverty. Hence there is a clear argument for a mandated scheme—"first-pillar" pensions in World Bank (1994) terminology, "first-tier" pensions in Barr's (2000) words, and so on. The second risk is outliving one's savings because of unexpected longevity, which is rare by definition. So the retiree buys an annuity, which allows the transformation of the stocks of saving into retirement income flows. But while there may be a problem of adverse selection (where only those expecting to live longer buy annuities, and the others opt for withdrawing their pension savings in lump sums), there is no problem of moral hazard here, and the definition is technical rather than social. This consumption-smoothing instrument is something the private sector can provide. There is, of course, the problem of adverse selection that may require help from the government in the form of a mandate to participate in annuity plans or may be addressed privately through employer-sponsored retirement plans. Here again the role of government is to ensure that inter-temporal contracts are honored and to offer inflation-indexed savings instruments to the annuity providers because some of the losses may result from inflation.

Savings plans that are not mandatory but are tax advantaged are called "third-pillar" (World Bank 1994) or "third-tier" (Barr 2000) pensions. If the savings plans are mandatory, they are called "second-pillar" or "second-tier" plans, and the role of government in ensuring reasonable management and investment fees is (arguably) greater. But although these two components can be broadly characterized as savings, both have critical components that involve the pooling of risk in the form of annuity schemes. This is why in chapter 1 (see table 1.1) we argued that the main distinction among the three components of the multipillar system is not whether they are purely saving or self-insurance schemes, or purely pooling or market-type insurance. Rather, the distinction lies in the principal objective for the program and the role of government in ensuring that the objective is achieved:

• In the first pillar the government *defines the benefits* to facilitate the sharing of losses associated with old-age poverty.
• In the second pillar the government *defines the contributions* to ensure adequate consumption smoothing over the life cycle.
• In the third pillar the government *defines the incentives* to encourage the maintenance of a reasonable standard of living during old age.

To conclude, in a world of uncertainty and imperfect information one may summarize the interactions among workers, markets, and the government as follows: Individuals save for old age and often are encouraged to do so by preferential tax treatment for long-term saving. This personal saving is the mainstay of old-age income security. Workers also buy insurance from governments in case they do not save enough to stay out of poverty, or if they have bad luck with their savings. Upon reaching old age—defined broadly as losing the option of labor earnings—people have a lump sum of savings, but they face another uncertainty: they do not know how to spread this money over their remaining lives. So they insure against this lack of knowledge by converting the lump sum into a flow that ensures they will have retirement income even if they live longer than expected. Had they relied on individual rather than group solutions to address the problem of unexpected longevity, many would outlive their savings and others would leave behind larger bequests or estates than desired.

Notes

1. Gill and Ilahi (2000) employed the Ehrlich-Becker concept of "comprehensive insurance" to address the potential role of government in augmenting individual efforts to lower the probability of losses (self-protection), to pool risks (market insurance), and to undertake precautionary savings (self-insurance). De Ferranti et al. (2000) used this extended framework to structure a discussion of economic risk management in Latin America and the Caribbean region. Packard (2002) used the comprehensive insurance framework to analyze the losses associated with old age.

2. See Valdés-Prieto (2002b). This reliance notwithstanding, the views expressed in this chapter are not necessarily those of the author of this background paper.

7

How Well Has the "Savings" Component Performed from the Individual's Perspective?

EARLIER CHAPTERS HAVE TAKEN STOCK OF structural reforms of retirement security systems in Latin America largely from the perspective of the policymaker, assessing the new multipillar pension systems in terms of their impact on laudable socioeconomic objectives. There is evidence that pension reforms in the region have increased the fiscal sustainability of remaining public pension promises; contributed to the development of the financial sector and to the deepening of capital markets; corrected what were regressive institutions; and even removed distortions in the labor market to improve workers' incentives to participate in formal pension systems.

However, stalled progress with one of these objectives, increasing coverage, is cause for concern among the region's governments. The share of the workforce that contributes to a formal pension system remains low. Rates of worker participation by level of household income even show a regressive pattern. In several Latin American countries the share of the elderly population receiving pension benefits is falling. For at least some individuals the new funded, privately managed individual savings pillars are not as attractive as they are made out to be.

Furthermore, few workers have found it worthwhile to make voluntary contributions to their individual retirement accounts even in those countries where these are relatively liquid, impose no additional commissions, and offer attractive tax benefits (at least relative to savings in other financial instruments).[1] This chapter, which is based on Yermo (2002b), explores why this is the case, evaluating how well individuals have fared under the savings component with respect to their consumption-smoothing objectives.

We find that the earnings ceilings used to calculate mandatory contributions are relatively high, which leaves little space for voluntary contributions. Mandatory contributions may also place a heavy burden on young and poor workers who have pressing consumption needs. We also evaluate some aspects of the performance of the new funded pillar that may make them less attractive than those of other formal and informal instruments available to secure adequate retirement income. These factors may also help explain why many workers in Latin America still choose to ignore formal pension systems despite reforms.

Risks to Old-Age Income Security

Structural reforms of Latin America's purely public pension systems were intended to have three main benefits for individuals. First, the introduction of a fully funded system based on a defined contribution formula would grant individuals full legal ownership over a financial asset—the accumulated fund in their individual account—that could not be appropriated by third parties, even in the case of personal bankruptcy.[2] Second, the partial replacement of state administration of a PAYG system with private management of pension funds would insulate workers' pension savings from political manipulation and ensure higher efficiency and professionalism. Third, the shift from a defined benefit formula to a defined contribution plan would encourage each age cohort to procure enough resources for their own retirement. Overall these improvements should have permitted more efficient consumption-smoothing.[3]

One can evaluate whether reforms delivered these benefits by referring to the four main risks that individuals are exposed to in retirement income security systems (see box 7.1), as well as the administration costs involved in establishing and operating different pension arrangements. The first two improvements should have translated into lower policy and agency risks for individuals. The last improvement should have led to better management of investment and longevity risk.

Investment risk tends to vary significantly across countries, depending on the extent of development of the domestic financial markets (cost, volatility), the legal protection of property rights and contracts, and access to foreign assets. The management of investment risk in a funded system depends primarily on the importance (relative weight) of the system in the provision of total retirement income. All individuals have a minimum level of income that they wish to attain in old age. Reaching this target with a high degree of certainty requires significant investment in risk-free, long-term assets. From the government's perspective providing such assets is indispensable to permit efficient consumption smoothing by households. In countries where macroeconomic management and fiscal prudence are the norms, such an asset would normally be an inflation-indexed long-term government bond. PAYG defined benefit systems can also offer implicit rates of return that are inflation protected, but they are relatively inflexible with respect to changes in life expectancy. On the other hand, recent reforms of public pension

---

Box 7.1 The Four Fundamental Risks in Retirement Income Security Systems

Investment Risk

Investment risk arises from the variation in account balances and portfolio values as a result of inflation and changes in the prices of assets held by a pension plan. In defined contribution plans this risk is borne by the individual. In defined benefit plans the risk is borne by the plan sponsor (the government or employer). Normally one can trade off investment risk against the expected reward from the investment. The more risk averse is an individual the less risky will be his or her optimal investment portfolio.

Longevity Risk

Longevity risk refers to the uncertainty surrounding the length of retirement—or the time between retirement and death of the retiree or survivor. This risk is in principle borne by the plan sponsor in defined benefit plans, and shared between the retiree and the annuity provider in defined contribution plans.

Policy Risk

Policy risk arises from interference by policymakers in the operation of a pension system. Intervention can range from arbitrary changes in plan rules (e.g., benefits, tax treatment) to more direct intrusion in the operation of the pension fund (e.g., strict investment rules that do not permit adequate diversification of investment risk.

Agency Risk

Agency risk refers to risks arising from private management of pension plans. The most serious forms of agency risk include the misappropriation of assets and outright fraud. More commonly, agency risk surfaces in circumstances where there is a conflict of interest, such as when a pension fund manager engages in an investment transaction with a related party. A weaker but no less harmful form of agency risk is negligence or ignorance on the part of the pension provider.

Sources: Yermo (2002b); Barr (2000).

---

systems introduced in Italy, Latvia, Poland, and Sweden, which are based on notional defined contribution (NDC) formulas, do not suffer from this problem. NDCs are comparable to a funded system in which the assets resemble a portfolio of inflation-indexed government bonds, but there are some important differences (described in box 7.2). In particular, it may be

Box 7.2 Comparing Notional Defined Contribution Systems
and Pension Funds Invested in Inflation- and
Wage-Indexed Government Bonds

Notional defined contribution (NDC) systems are publicly managed individual account-based retirement systems that are run on a PAYG basis, like publicly managed, defined-benefit plans. Their investment and longevity risk management properties, however, are closer to those of the funded, defined contribution systems introduced in Latin America than to those of defined-benefit plans. Individual accounts are credited annually with a return that is normally linked to some macroeconomic income measure such as the wage base or output, and accumulated funds are converted into income streams only near retirement. There is an automatic adjustment to increasing life expectancy. Later generations pay higher premiums than earlier generations for the same degree of protection against longevity risk.

NDCs can be thought of as an investment in short-term, wage-indexed government bonds. In the absence of PAYG pension systems, such bonds, if they existed, would have valuable risk management properties, especially later in life when a greater proportion of a household's wealth is invested in financial assets. NDCs also offer some protection against inflation. The actual extent of inflation protection will depend on the income measure used to calculate the return and the correlation between this measure and inflation. In the European countries that have introduced NDCs a measure of the wage base is used, which in normal circumstances would offer a high degree of inflation protection. An inflation-indexed bond, on the other hand, offers full protection against inflation.

One disadvantage of NDCs with respect to long-term government bonds is that the return on both current and past contributions is determined annually, whereas a long-term government bond offers a fixed coupon payment until the maturity date. There is therefore less interest rate uncertainty with a long-term government bond. NDCs, however, can have return-smoothing mechanisms to mitigate the inherent volatility of the indexing factor.

NDCs may also be subject to more policy risk than the explicit debt issued by the government to meet pension liabilities. Explicit pension debt is subject to the scrutiny of foreigners as well as the local population. It may therefore be more costly for governments to default on explicit debt than on implicit, NDC debt.

The main advantage of notional defined contribution systems is that they are cheaper to run. The difference in administrative cost is of a high order of magnitude because under an NDC system there is no need to assign fund management to financial institutions. The cost of an NDC is not much higher than that of a PAYG defined-benefit plan. The extra cost arises from the need to maintain a detailed record of individual accounts and additional disclosure to participants.

argued that the political risk of the implicit government debt of an NDC is greater than that of the explicit debt of a funded system. Where inflation-indexed bonds or similar assets are not available domestically, pension funds may find them by investing abroad.

In practice the optimal investment portfolio in the savings component of a social security system will vary significantly among individuals, depending on the rate at which they discount the future, their degree of risk aversion (both of which may be age dependent), the extent to which they face unexpected shocks to their wealth and income (and hence their need for liquidity), the correlation of these shocks with their investment portfolio, their desire to pass on some of their assets to their descendants, and their access to defined benefit pension plans and other statutory pooling instruments (Campbell et al. 1999). In general, however, inflation-indexed bonds, NDCs, and similar assets offering inflation protection are attractive investment instruments for long-term income smoothing, especially as individuals approach retirement. Housing also tends to offer good protection against inflation over the life cycle of an individual (at least in urban areas), but house prices can experience much volatility over short periods. Education and children are also traditional forms of saving for retirement used around the world.

The management of longevity risk in funded systems depends primarily on the type of plan chosen. Defined benefit plans, whether funded or PAYG, privately or publicly managed, do not provide automatic adjustment for increasing life expectancy and hence are less suitable for managing intergenerational longevity risk. Given the inflexibility of statutory retirement ages, defined contribution plans are better endowed for this purpose. In a defined contribution system the cost of increases in life expectancy of earlier generations cannot be easily shifted to later generations as it can in a defined benefit formula.[4] Instead, every generation must either save more or retire later to maintain its standard of living in old age.

The introduction of a defined contribution system, however, does not guarantee the efficient management of intragenerational longevity risk.[5] Financial instruments such as annuities that offer protection against such risk lose their attractiveness as a result of adverse selection and high commissions. Workers also need flexibility in the purchase of annuities to ensure adequate smoothing of investment risk.

In principle, policy risk will affect private plans less than publicly managed ones. Unwelcome forms of government intervention, however, can affect private plans as well. For example, governments can impose quantitative investment regulations and performance rules whose consequences may not always be desirable for individuals.

Agency risk is specific to privately managed systems. Governments play a central role by regulating such plans to ensure that they are managed in the best interest of plan members and other beneficiaries.

In addition to their risk management properties, funded systems differ in administrative costs. These costs can be made considerably higher if a new infrastructure is created to manage individual accounts. More generally, however, commissions can remain high as a result of marketing expenses incurred as private providers fight for market share in captive markets, such as those of mandatory funded programs.

Performance of the New Funded Pillars in the Accumulation Stage

In a multipillar pension system with a prominent funded savings component structured on a defined contribution basis, affiliates participate in an "accumulation stage" (when contributions accumulate as savings) and a drawdown or "distribution stage" (at retirement age when workers receive their pension benefit either as a lump sum, programmed withdrawal or as an annuity, depending on pension laws). The following sections focus on the performance of the newly funded pillars in the accumulation stage, and the distribution stage.

Returns from Investment High But Volatile

Table 7.1 shows the annual real returns obtained by the pension fund industry from the time when private pension systems were established until December 2002. The rate of return is calculated net of any asset

Table 7.1 Gross, Real Returns to Pension Funds Have Been High

(December 1994–December 2002)

Country	Real return (percent per annum)
Argentina	10.4
Bolivia	17.1
Chile	10.3
Colombia	9.9
Costa Rica	7.0
El Salvador	10.9
Mexico	10.4
Peru	6.6
Uruguay	15.0

Note: Real returns are annualized cumulative values. Returns for Chile are for *Fondo 1* (in 2001) and *Fondo C* (in 2002). Colombian average pension fund return is measured from inception until December 2000. For Mexico returns are net of asset management fees.

Source: AIOS 2002, Colombian Banking Superintendency.

management fees (only permitted in Mexico), but is not adjusted for salary- or contribution-based charges (the only form of charge permitted in countries other than Bolivia, the Dominican Republic, and Mexico). These commissions do not have an impact on the accumulated fund because they are paid on top of the mandatory contribution that goes into the individual account. To calculate net investment returns one would need to calculate the equivalent fee as a percentage of assets and subtract it from the gross return. Using a 40-year contribution horizon to translate contribution-based fees into asset-based fees, the net real return in Chile between 1994 and 2002 would be 9.1 percent, compared with the gross return of 10.3 percent.

The highest real return by December 2002 was obtained by the pension fund industry in Bolivia, a 17.1 percent annual average return in real terms. The lowest was Peru's 6.6 percent return rate. Overall, real gross returns of Latin American systems appear attractive.

The pattern of pension fund returns has been largely determined by investment regulations that either prohibit or substantially limit investment in foreign securities, as well as by floors on investment in domestic government bonds.[6] As a result of these regulations, pension fund portfolios in all Latin American countries (with the exception of Peru) are concentrated in domestic government bonds, deposits, and other instruments issued by financial institutions (e.g., mortgage-backed securities). As shown in figure 7.1 these instruments account for more than 70 percent of all pension fund assets in all countries except Peru.

Because investment regulations are the main determinants of investment performance, there is a strong element of policy risk in the new savings systems. In some countries, such as Chile, where fiscal rectitude and macroeconomic stability are well established, individuals may be content if their pension fund portfolios are heavily invested in domestic government debt. Indeed, as argued above, such investment makes much sense for a large part of an individual's income, especially when PAYG pensions are no longer available.

Generally, investment restrictions on domestic assets have not hindered pension fund performance relative to other instruments available in the domestic market. Interest-bearing assets have been attractive investments in an environment of high interest rates designed to rein in inflation and stabilize the currency. This was the case in Chile in the early 1980s. The historical performance of Chilean pension funds has been largely driven by the extraordinary rates of return during the early years. These rates were the result of high bond returns as interest rates fell in the early 1980s.

In at least one case, however, the strict investment regulations have exposed workers to the vagaries of a local bond market whose recent high yields basically reflected a high default risk (and hence a high premium over the yields of government bonds of the United States and countries in the Euro zone). This risk ended up materializing in Argentina in late 2001

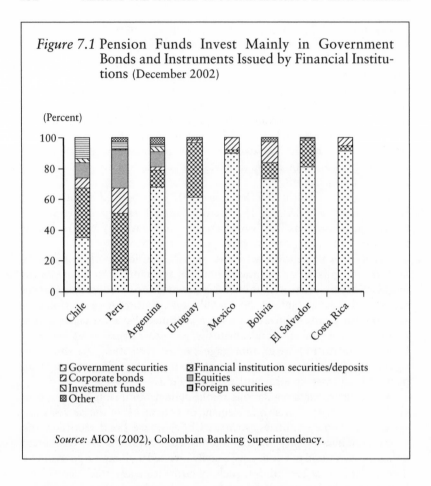

Figure 7.1 Pension Funds Invest Mainly in Government Bonds and Instruments Issued by Financial Institutions (December 2002)

Source: AIOS (2002), Colombian Banking Superintendency.

(see box 7.3). The Argentine experience raises serious concerns about the ability of governments to ensure the performance and indeed the sustainability of mandatory funded plans that replace PAYG systems—even only partly—when the right macroeconomic conditions are not in place.

To the extent that the transition costs imposed by pension reform overwhelm government finances, mandating saving that ends up invested largely in government bonds exposes workers to policy risk similar to that of the old system. Nonetheless, it may be argued that even under imprudent governments, workers are better protected against political intrusion by investing in explicit government bonds rather than implicit pension debt. Defaulting on explicit government debt has repercussions on the country's access to foreign capital. Capital inflows may dry up, leading to further deterioration in economic conditions. As discussed in chapter 3, defaulting on implicit government debt, such as PAYG debt, often has less

---

Box 7.3 Argentina's System in Crisis: Do Private Accounts
Protect Workers from Policy Risk?

It is often claimed that mandating individual retirement accounts administered by private dedicated providers gives workers' retirement pensions
a greater degree of protection against political interference than they
would have under a purely public PAYG regimen. However, the degree
of protection against policy risk offered by privatizing a large portion of
mandated pensions can be exaggerated. The recent economic and political
crisis in Argentina illustrates how any government-organized retirement
security system—whether directly administered or simply mandated—
can fall prey to politicians.

Argentina's private pension system was vulnerable even before the crisis. Since the start of the system in 1994, nearly 50 percent of the privately
managed assets were invested in government bonds. This concentration
of portfolios, usually explained and excused by the lack of alternative instruments and the high-risk premiums paid on government bonds, left the
pension funds dangerously exposed to the government's fiscal problems.

In the midst of a long economic recession a fiscal crisis flared in early
2001. The authorities pursued a number of "urgent" policies to cope with
the pressures of an overvalued currency, mounting debt, and disintegrat-
ing investor confidence. The government's attempts to cope have had a
direct impact on the pension system by altering the value of current
benefits, contribution rates, and investment rules for the private fund
managers. Although some of the system's parameters did in fact need
adjusting (see Rofman 2000), the actions taken by the authorities were
shortsighted, hasty, lacked adequate analysis, and circumvented critical
political institutions. Most of the policies implemented would have
normally required changes in legislation but were approved by decree
because of "exceptional circumstances," or were enacted by regulatory
authorities using procedural technicalities to bypass the legislative
process. The government's expediency is an important factor in analyzing
recent events because the lack of political support in Argentina's congress
for many of the measures taken has deeply wounded the system's credibility in the public eye and greatly increased the likelihood of a backlash
against the structural reforms of 1994.

In a desperate effort to cut government spending, the authorities first
went after pensions paid by the public branch of the system. In July 2001
monthly benefits greater than 500 pesos paid by the PAYG branch were
reduced by 13 percent. This cut affected about 15 percent of beneficiaries. By the end of the year the government had lowered the maximum
pension paid by the PAYG system from $3,100 to $2,400 a month. During
the first quarter of 2002, as the government decided to abandon a failed
currency board, there was no attempt to index pensions to mounting

(Box continues on the following page.)

Box 7.3 (continued)

inflation. Accumulated inflation of about 40 percent in 2002 has not been compensated, thereby reducing the real value of benefits for many retirees with no other source of income.

The private system, however, was not spared. In the closing months of 2001 the government executed a swap of bonds held by domestic investors, mostly banks, insurance companies, and pension funds in the private second pillar. In exchange for the old bonds (which had a market value and were regularly traded on the local stock market and exchanges abroad), new instruments backed by a "guaranteed loan" were issued. These new instruments had a lower interest rate and no secondary market, which made their valuation subjective. Although the swap was "voluntary," strictly speaking, the government exerted strong political pressure to accept the swap on the private fund managers both directly and indirectly through the industry regulator. Furthermore, in the following weeks the government enacted a deposits swap by issuing a decree ordering that all pension assets invested in certificates of deposit be applied to buy treasury bills directly from the government.

In the wake of Argentina's chaotic peso devaluation, in March 2002 the government decided to convert the instruments backed with guaranteed loans—still denominated in U.S. dollars—to pesos, at an exchange rate of 1.4 pesos per dollar. These new loans were indexed to inflation and receive an annual interest rate of between 3.0 percent and 5.5 percent. The first scheduled payment of interest, in April 2002, was made by the industry regulator applying the 1.4 exchange rate. This conversion resulted in a significant increase in the real value of assets, if compared with inflation (by 40 percent) or average wages (82 percent). Although the government has not defaulted since it began repayments on the swap, in several cases the pension funds have legally challenged the conversion and refused to receive interest payments on the new instruments. The government continues to deposit these payments in custodian accounts.

The government's heavy hand in setting private pension portfolios (in addition to cuts in the rate of contribution to the private system restored in 2002, and a temporary ban on new annuities that restricted new retirees from the private system to scheduled withdrawals) will have a long-lasting effect on the system's credibility. The increasing concentration of investments in government debt has raised the share of bonds in combined pension portfolios to 78 percent. This concentration would be dangerous in normal times but, considering that the Argentine government has defaulted on part of its debt, it becomes a major concern. The authorities have declared their intention to honor the guaranteed bonds and other papers, and although the government has met its obligations to the funded system to date, the instability of the general economic situation raises the risk of further default.

Box 7.3 (continued)

The most likely outcome of the events of 2001 and 2002 is reduced confidence in any form of mandated retirement security provision. Argentina's mixed pension system suffers from weak public confidence in institutions in general and, after the crisis, financial institutions in particular. The pension system did not attract workers' interest even prior to the crisis. In the years leading up to the crisis, among the minority of the labor force that participated in the system more than 75 percent of new participants failed to make an explicit choice to join either the funded or the PAYG branch, and had to be assigned through a default process. However, recent events and public debate about the funds losing most of their assets in the devaluation are likely to lower confidence further. This is likely to keep the number of participants in the system low, and the general lack of support could increase political support for new reforms that would deeply damage the efficiency of the system.

Source: Rofman (2002).

---

dramatic repercussions on investors' perceptions of the fiscal stance of a government.

Diversification into domestic equities, however, has not significantly helped improve the returns of pension funds, and when it has done so, as in Chile, it has made the pension funds a relatively risky investment.

Adjusting for volatility—proxied by the standard deviation of returns—and comparing with alternative instruments provides an idea of the real value of pension funds to individuals. When adjusted for risk the performance of the Peruvian pension funds—those most exposed to domestic equities—lags far behind that of other countries. As shown in figure 7.2 the pension fund industry return was the lowest of the group (0.5 percent per month on average), but the standard deviation was one of the highest in Latin America, at 1.2. Hence the ratio of return to standard deviation (i.e., the return per unit of risk) was by far the lowest in the region. Given the earlier discussion of sovereign risk, this measure of investment risk must be considered along with some important caveats (see box 7.4).

Although high pension fund returns help generate higher pensions (as long as contribution periods are also long), their volatility will lead to significant differences in pension benefits across cohorts. An example, based on Chile's historical returns, will help show the impact of return volatility on the accumulated fund.

Figure 7.3 shows the pension fund average cumulative annual return for 20 different cohorts. Each cohort represented in the figure, except 1981, starts contributing at the beginning of the year. The 1981 cohort starts contributing in July, the month the system was launched. As of

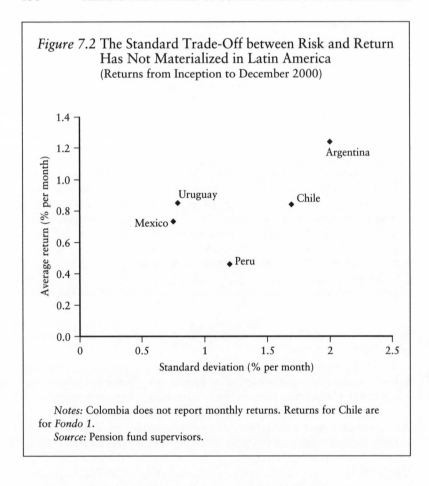

Figure 7.2 The Standard Trade-Off between Risk and Return
Has Not Materialized in Latin America
(Returns from Inception to December 2000)

Notes: Colombia does not report monthly returns. Returns for Chile are
for *Fondo 1.*
Source: Pension fund supervisors.

December 2000, cohorts that started contributing in the 1980s earned
cumulative returns that range from a minimum of 8.7 percent (1987
cohort) to a maximum of 10.9 percent (1981 cohort), with an average of
9.4 percent. Cohorts of the 1990s, on the other hand, have earned cumulative returns that range from a minimum of 4.1 percent (1995 cohort) to
a maximum of 10.2 percent (1999 cohort), with an average of 7.0 percent. Such differences in returns will generate a gap between the average
accumulated balance of 1980s and 1990s cohorts on the order of 35.0
percent.

Some participants will find the volatility of pension fund returns excessive, especially at a time when alternative—in principle more liquid and
safer—domestic investments such as bank deposits were also yielding
high returns. As shown in figure 7.4, Chilean pension fund real returns
before fees have certainly been higher on average than real yields on bank

Box 7.4 Points to Keep in Mind When Comparing Risks in Pension Fund Portfolios in Latin America

In a pension plan based on defined contributions in individual retirement accounts, the accumulated savings of affiliated workers earn variable returns from investment in domestic and international capital markets. The skill of AFPs at maximizing returns and minimizing investment risk will have a direct impact on the retirement benefit affiliates can expect to earn from their savings.

A first-glance comparison of the risk of AFP portfolios shows that Peru's AFP investments are relatively more risky than those of other mandatory private pension systems in the region (when the measure of risk used is the average statistical volatility or standard deviation of the combined investment instruments held by the AFP industry). However, some important caveats have to be made with respect to this measure of risk. For Peru the high standard deviation in the price of AFP investment securities can be explained in large part by the relatively greater allocation of pension funds in private equities compared with that of other countries, whereas funds invested in government securities constitute a relatively small share of Peru's AFP portfolios. This is true because until only very recently the Peruvian government had a policy of not issuing domestic debt securities to maintain fiscal discipline—most funding was obtained in the external dollar market. Hence the level of treasury securities in Peru's domestic capital market is extremely small compared with most other countries in the region, although holdings of private equities (which are typically more volatile) are higher.

Government (treasury) securities in most countries in the region, with Chile being one of the few exceptions, generally have short to medium maturities (typically between 30 days and three years). These relatively short maturities mean that, as fixed income instruments, their duration and price volatility are low. In other countries where AFPs hold extremely large shares of government securities in their investment portfolios, such portfolios will reflect less volatility and presumably less risk than portfolios such as those held by Peruvian AFPs, which rely primarily on private sector securities, including significant shares of corporate stocks.

Finance textbooks assume that government securities are risk free. However, the experience of Argentina as well as the precarious economic condition of many countries in the region demonstrate that this is hardly the case. Government securities, particularly in countries with chronic fiscal deficits, are far from risk free. Their price may not be very volatile, but if governments default on their debts, as happened in Argentina, the price volatility essentially becomes 100 percent because at the default event the market price for the defaulting government's bonds falls to zero.

(Box continues on the following page.)

Box 7.4 (continued)

Statistical series on portfolio volatility seldom show these drastic events because governments default in crisis situations.

Thus, the holding of large shares of government securities in AFP portfolios in Bolivia, Colombia, El Salvador, Mexico, or Uruguay may not reflect a low-risk strategy at all. The absence of default-induced price volatility data for these securities in historical statistical series of AFP portfolio performance does not mean that the potential for default is not present, as recent events in Argentina poignantly demonstrate. In fact, recent expert views on this matter propose that government securities should be assigned risk ratings according to the fiscal and macroeconomic situation of each country. If this were done portfolio risk would be measured not only by historically observed volatility trends but also by the risk categorizations or default probabilities of each security in the AFP's (and other institutions') portfolios. When the proper methodology for realistically rating government securities is fully developed, it may very well be that the investment portfolios of Peruvian AFPs are much less risky because they have low holdings of government debt.

Source: Lasaga and Pollner (2003).

---

deposits. But during the 1990s when domestic equities investment accounted for about one-quarter of the total portfolio, the difference decreased significantly (6.6 percent real yield on deposits, 9.8 percent real return on pension funds), and may not have compensated for their much greater volatility (1.1 against 8.5 percent).

The rather dismal performance of Peruvian pension funds compared with bank deposits should caution other countries against a rushed liberalization of pension fund investment in domestic equities. The Latin American equity markets went through an unstable period during the 1990s and underperformed bonds in practically every country in the region. As shown in figure 7.5, in Peru, the country with the highest exposure to domestic equities, U.S. dollar–denominated Peruvian government bonds (Brady bonds) offered higher and more stable yields between 1993 and 2000. Pension funds, however, were only allowed to invest in these instruments after 1999.

For Latin American countries the only effective way to improve diversification, lower aggregate portfolio risk, and possibly even enhance returns is by investing in foreign securities. Currently, however, only Argentina, Bolivia, Chile, Mexico,[7] and Peru permit investment in foreign assets. Chile had the highest limit of 13 percent at the end of 2000. Early in 2002 the legislated limit was raised to 30 percent, but the actual limit was set at 20 percent. In Argentina there was a low investment in foreign securities relative to the limit until 2001, which is largely explained by the

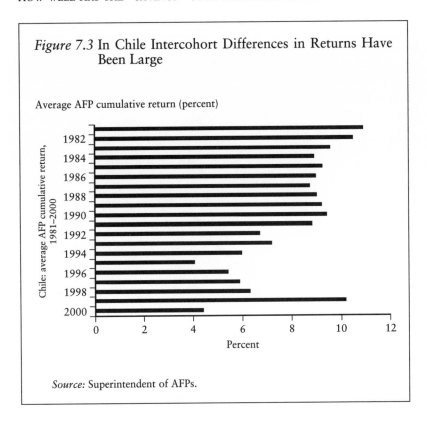

Figure 7.3 In Chile Intercohort Differences in Returns Have Been Large

Average AFP cumulative return (percent)

Chile: average AFP cumulative return, 1981–2000

Source: Superintendent of AFPs.

government's efforts at forcing pension funds to buy government bonds. Since the devaluation foreign investment in the pension funds' portfolio has more than doubled and is now close to the ceiling. In Peru foreign investment was not permitted until 2000 and the Central Bank sets an actual ceiling on the share of permitted foreign investment to prevent volatility in the foreign exchange market. This explains why investment abroad remains somewhat below the limit. In Bolivia the limit on investment in foreign securities was set by the legislation at the time of the reform at 50 percent of the pension fund's portfolio, the highest in Latin America. The Bolivian supervisor, however, only established the regulatory framework for foreign investment at the beginning of 2002. The pension funds, therefore, are only starting to increase the diversification of their portfolios overseas.

With the exception of Bolivia, the demand for greater investment in foreign securities is demonstrated by the fact that AFP investments allocations are close to their permissible ceiling (see table 7.2). At the same time the limited gains from diversification into domestic equities are

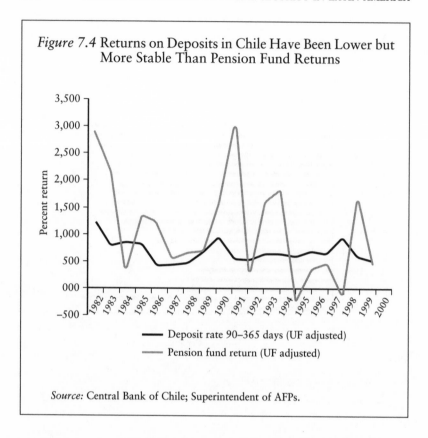

Figure 7.4 Returns on Deposits in Chile Have Been Lower but More Stable Than Pension Fund Returns

— Deposit rate 90–365 days (UF adjusted)
— Pension fund return (UF adjusted)

Source: Central Bank of Chile; Superintendent of AFPs.

demonstrated by the large gap between the actual and permitted investment in this class of securities.

The gains from diversification into foreign equities are understandable given the limited liquidity and high volatility of stock markets in the region. Using time-series data extending back to 1976, Srinivas and Yermo (2000) found that equity investors in Argentina, Chile, Mexico, and Peru would have achieved much higher risk-adjusted returns by investing a large portion of their assets in foreign benchmarks such as the Standard & Poor's index (for the United States) and the Morgan Stanley Capital International Europe, Australia, Far East index (for non-U.S. equity investments). In some cases (e.g., Peru since 1990, Argentina 1976–90) domestic investors would have done best by investing their whole equity portfolios in foreign equity. In all other cases investors would have benefited by investing at least half their equity portfolios in foreign equity.

International diversification of bond portfolios is also valuable for investors in countries where government debt has a high default risk.

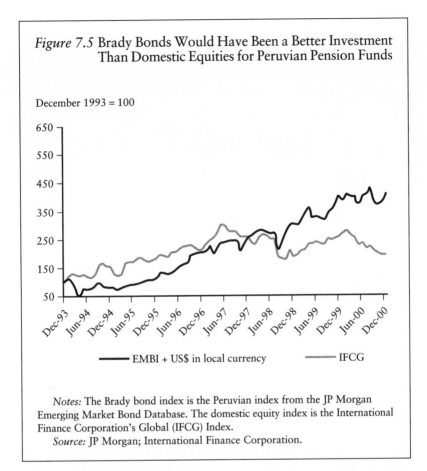

Figure 7.5 Brady Bonds Would Have Been a Better Investment Than Domestic Equities for Peruvian Pension Funds

December 1993 = 100

——— EMBI + US$ in local currency   ——— IFCG

Notes: The Brady bond index is the Peruvian index from the JP Morgan Emerging Market Bond Database. The domestic equity index is the International Finance Corporation's Global (IFCG) Index.
Source: JP Morgan; International Finance Corporation.

Dollar-linked bonds issued by local governments may offer protection from devaluation and high returns to pension funds in the short term, but these returns are often the consequence of premiums demanded by investors to hold bonds of a high default risk. On the other hand, investment in foreign government bonds is less valuable for pension funds in countries (e.g., Chile) that have a liquid market of indexed fixed income instruments and where government debt is rated highly.[8]

The experience of Argentina shows how even relatively well-diversified domestic portfolios cannot guarantee a decent performance when macroeconomic conditions—economic growth and government finances in the case of Argentina—are in a dire state. In such countries the return on domestic equities is closely linked to that of fixed income securities. Only by investing abroad can pension funds reduce risk by diversifying away from domestic currencies, investing in more stable equities markets, and offloading domestic government debt with a poor credit rating. The

Table 7.2 Asset Allocation and Portfolio Limits

(December 2002)

	Domestic equities			Foreign securities		
	Actual investment	*Limit*	*Difference*	*Actual investment*	*Limit*	*Difference*
Argentina	6.5	35.0	28.5	8.9	10.0	1.1
Bolivia	0.0	0.0	0.0	1.3	50.0	48.7
Chile	9.9	37.0	27.1	16.2	20.0	3.8
Colombia	2.3	30.0	27.7	0.0	0.0	0.0
Costa Rica	0.0	0.0	0.0	0.0	0.0	0.0
El Salvador	0.5	5.0	4.5	0.0	0.0	0.0
Mexico	0.0	0.0	0.0	0.0	0.0	0.0
Peru	31.2	35.0	3.8	7.2	10.0	2.8
Uruguay	0.0	0.0	0.0	0.0	0.0	0.0

Note: Data for Colombia are for December 2000.
Source: AIOS 2002, Colombian Banking Superintendency.

Argentine experience, however, clearly shows also that mandatory savings systems can easily fall prey to desperate governments irrespective of the investment regimen in place. In Argentina the AFJPs were allowed to invest abroad (up to 10 percent of their portfolio), but the government still found ways to elevate their exposure to increasingly risky government bonds.

The Cost to Affiliates of the New Savings Component

In addition to the relatively high volatility of investment returns and the exposure of the new funded pillars to substantial policy risk, affiliates of Latin America's new funded pillars with individual accounts face steep commissions that reduce their accumulated balances drastically relative to what they could have been had these commissions been invested in the retirement accounts.[9] As discussed by Valdés-Prieto (1998) the relatively high commissions can be traced partly to strategic competition between the pension fund administrators that resulted in high costs. Pension fund administrators have relied heavily on sales forces to attract new affiliates, which has pushed up the cost of their services. In Chile, for example, marketing and sales costs accounted for more than one-half of operational expenses in the late 1990s (SAFP 1998). The resulting high cost–high price equilibrium also depends critically on a low price elasticity of demand. Mastrángelo (1999) showed that the marketing elasticity of demand is 18.5 times greater than the price elasticity. Similar results have been found in Argentina.

Furthermore, workers do not appear to react to differences in returns, although this could be the result of the limited variability in returns across AFPs. Pension fund administrators, therefore, face a strong incentive to spend on marketing and sales forces to attract new affiliates. In addition to marketing costs, the fees can be explained by the set-up costs of the new industry that in some cases have fallen largely on earlier cohorts.

There are two main measures of charges that may be used: the reduction in yield and the charge ratio. The reduction in yield shows the effect of charges on the rate of return, given a set of assumptions about the rate of return, the time profile of contributions, and the term of the plan. The charge ratio, on the other hand, is calculated by dividing the accumulated balance that the charges by themselves would have generated had they been invested by the sum of the accumulated balance resulting from the actual contributions and the charges (had they been invested). One can also calculate the cumulative charge ratio at retirement, which results from including in the calculation all contributions and fees paid over the career of a worker. As discussed by Whitehouse (2001), the use of the charge ratio can provide a misleading picture of the cost of a private pension system when commissions are set as a percentage of the accumulated fund. On the other hand, the charge ratio is a more useful and appropriate measure of the cost efficiency of the system in Latin American countries where commissions are charged mainly only on contributions or salaries.

The commission structure is regulated in all Latin American countries. Commissions to cover administrative costs (account and asset management expenses) can be set as a percentage of salary or contribution in all Latin American countries. Additional, fixed commissions are permitted in Chile, in Mexico, and (for one pension fund) in Uruguay.[10] In Bolivia and Mexico pension fund managers can also set commissions as a percentage of returns, and in Costa Rica the fund managers can set fees on the performance. The commissions must be the same for all affiliates of a given pension fund administrator. The only exception to this rule is loyalty discounts (reductions in fees for remaining with the same administrator), which are permitted in Argentina, El Salvador, Mexico, Peru, and Uruguay. Most countries also do not permit fees to be charged on voluntary contributions. Some countries directly limit commission levels through explicit caps. In Bolivia the caps on both the contribution- and the asset-based charges were set during the tender process through which the fund managers were selected. Colombia and El Salvador set a ceiling on the sum of commissions and insurance premiums. In Costa Rica, there is a cap of 8 percent on fees set on the performance of the pension fund. A ceiling has also been set on contribution-based charges, which were first allowed in 2003.

Variable commissions (those calculated as a percentage of contribution/salary) are nonetheless the most important component of the total cost in most Latin American countries (Bolivia, Costa Rica, and Mexico are the exceptions). These commissions vary significantly across countries, as shown in table 7.3. For a worker of average income the lowest variable commission was Bolivia's, at 0.5 percent of the affiliate's salary in December 2002. The highest charge was Peru's, at 2.27 percent. This comparison, however, ignores the additional asset-based fee in Bolivia of approximately 0.2 percent, which is equivalent to approximately 0.5 percent of the average salary (over a 40-year contribution period). The total fee-to-salary ratio in Bolivia is therefore closer to 1.0 percent, which brings it closer to other Latin American countries but still far below the Peruvian level.

The ratio of variable commissions to total contributions (excluding insurance premiums) in December 2002 is shown in the last column of table 7.3. For countries in which commissions are set only as a percentage of the worker's contributions or salary, this measure is equivalent to the charge ratio over a one-year period.[11] In Argentina the charge ratio in 2002 was 36.19 percent, by far the highest of any Latin American country. The large gap in charge ratios between Argentina and the other countries is the result of the decision made in December 2001 to halve the mandatory contribution to the funded pillar. Given the significant fixed costs in account and asset management, lower contribution rates are translated into higher charge ratios. For the same reason, the number of contributors in the country will affect the charge ratio.

Table 7.3 Workers Still Pay High Commissions in Some Countries

(December 2002)
(Percent)

	Administration fee/salary (item a)	Contribution to fund/salary (item b)	Fee/total contribution (item c = a/(a+b))
Argentina	1.56	2.75	36.19
Bolivia	0.50	10.00	4.76
Chile	1.76	10.00	14.97
Colombia	1.63	10.00	14.02
El Salvador	1.58	11.02	12.54
Peru	2.27	8.00	22.10
Uruguay	1.92	12.27	13.53
Average	*1.60*	*9.15*	*16.87*

Notes: Administration fee includes only account and asset management charges set as a percentage of contribution/salary. Insurance premiums are excluded. Information for Colombia refers only to the mandatory pension fund system for December 2000. Information for Bolivia includes only the contribution charge (the asset management charge varies from zero to 0.23 percent, depending on the amount of assets in the portfolio). Information for Uruguay excludes an additional commission for custody, which averaged 0.00293 of total assets under management in December 2002.
Source: AIOS 2002, Colombian Banking Superintendency.

However, contribution rates and the number of contributors cannot explain all the differences in charge ratios between countries. Chile, for example, has the same contribution rate as Bolivia and a much higher number of contributors (3.4 million vs. 0.4 million in December 2002). But its charge ratio of approximately 18 percent (including fixed commissions) in 2002 is much higher than Bolivia's, which is approximately 9.1 percent (including both the contribution- and the asset-based fee). The difference in the annual commission charge per person between the two countries is even greater: US$90 in Chile in December 2002 vs. US$31 in Bolivia. The greater gap in this measure of commissions between the two countries is explained by the different charge structures. The Bolivian asset-based fee collects increasing commissions over time as the funds accumulate.

Chile's charge ratio (the second highest among the countries listed in table 7.3 when fixed commissions are included in the measure of the charge ratio) also seems inconsistent with the maturity of the system, which should have helped make the industry more efficient and competitive. The longer period since the inception of the new system also should have given the Chilean pension fund administrators more time to amortize the set-up (fixed) costs from their own establishment and that of the pension funds that they manage.

For the same reasons, commission rates should be expected to fall over time. Figure 7.6 shows the evolution of the ratio of variable commissions to total contribution at the end of various years in three countries. Argentina and Peru have both experienced a sudden jump in variable commission rates, in 2001 and 1995, respectively. These increases in commissions resulted from reductions in the mandatory contribution rate (from 11 percent to 5 percent in Argentina and from 10 percent to 8 percent in Peru). Allowing for this policy shift, the variable commission rate has fallen somewhat between 1997 and 2002 in both Argentina and Chile. In Peru, on the other hand, the variable commission rate has remained at more than 20 percent since 1997.

The different evolution of charges in these countries can be largely explained by regulatory policies aimed at containing operational costs (such as restrictions on switching between funds and greater control of sales forces) and direct pressure from the supervisor aimed at lowering commissions in Argentina and Chile. The imposition of restrictions on the frequency with which affiliates can switch among fund managers also applies in Peru, but this policy by itself can also foment collusion in the industry—and the evidence from Peru presents some worrisome trends. Since 1997 there has been a dramatic decline in the operational costs of the pension fund industry, accompanied by increasing return on equity to the fund managers, but little change in the fees charged to affiliates (Lasaga and Pollner 2003).

Nevertheless, even the Peruvian commission rates do not appear high when compared with mutual fund and professional asset managers in both Latin American and abroad. A 22 percent charge ratio as in Peru is equivalent over a 40-year horizon to an asset-based fee of approximately 1 percent. While fixed income and indexed mutual funds are able to achieve somewhat lower fees in large, mature markets such as that of the United States, this is not the case for such funds in Latin America (see chapter 10 for further evidence on the cost of retail fund management).

The higher commission rates that older workers faced when they entered the pension fund system also translate into much higher charge ratios for these earlier cohorts. Figure 7.7 shows the cumulative charge ratio at retirement (including all fixed and variable commissions charged over the whole contribution period) for Chilean male workers earning the average wage in successive cohorts, where each cohort is identified by the year in which it would normally retire, starting with the cohort that retired in 1982.[12,13]

The cumulative charge ratio at retirement was highest for the cohorts who retired soon after the inception of the new system and fell gradually for later cohorts. During the early years of the system more than three-quarters of the total contributions were consumed by management fees.

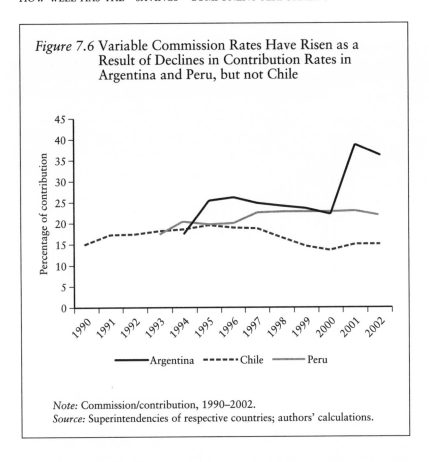

Figure 7.6 Variable Commission Rates Have Risen as a Result of Declines in Contribution Rates in Argentina and Peru, but not Chile

Note: Commission/contribution, 1990–2002.
Source: Superintendencies of respective countries; authors' calculations.

Because the first workers to retire from the new system started to do so only in the second half of the 1980s, few workers suffered from such exorbitant fees. Nonetheless, for the first workers to retire from the new system individual retirement accounts were expensive, although at least until 1987 there were few retirees.[14] For a worker earning the average wage who retired in December 2000 and who had contributed each year to the system (choosing the average pension fund), management fees would have consumed approximately one-half of his or her total contributions.[15]

For younger workers who started contributing only after 1982 and who will start retiring after 2022, the cumulative charge ratio drops to significantly lower levels (25 percent to 35 percent). After a secular decline, however, the cumulative charge ratio has begun to creep up again for the youngest cohorts (those who will retire after 2034). This increase is attributable to the increase in the fixed commission because the variable

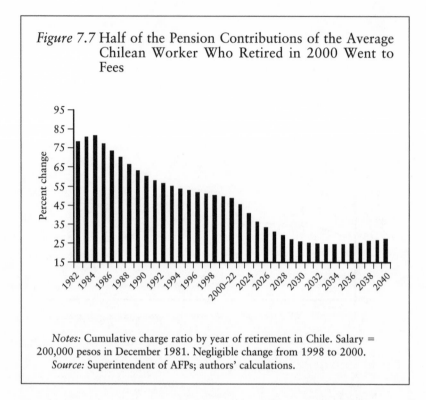

Figure 7.7 Half of the Pension Contributions of the Average Chilean Worker Who Retired in 2000 Went to Fees

Notes: Cumulative charge ratio by year of retirement in Chile. Salary = 200,000 pesos in December 1981. Negligible change from 1998 to 2000.
Source: Superintendent of AFPs; authors' calculations.

commission in Chile has actually fallen somewhat over the last few years (see figure 7.6).

The earlier cohorts who chose the funded system, therefore, have borne a disproportionate share of the set-up costs of the new pension fund industry; the evolution of the fee structure has led to a redistribution of income from early (older) to later (younger) participants. Unwittingly, pension reform of the Chilean kind has at least on this aspect reversed the bias inherent in generous PAYG systems in which future generations paid for current retirees. In the new funded system current workers subsidize the administrative cost of the system for future generations.[16] Such redistributions are more generalized when older workers are obliged to switch to the new system as in Bolivia and Mexico.

Although expected, such large intergenerational transfers are avoidable.[17] It is also possible to lay the cost of these redistributions on the richer households of a given cohort. Uruguay's reform, which required contributions to the new savings pillar only for higher-income individuals, has ensured that the new industry is subsidized in its early stages by those most able to create "thickness" in the market and endure high charges.

The flat commissions charged by pension funds in Chile and Mexico can also act like a regressive tax, creating income inequalities within the same cohorts. In Mexico any regressive effect is more than offset by the *cuota social*, the flat contribution subsidy of one peso per day paid by the state into each individual account (Azuara 2003). In Chile, even in the best of cases where workers choose the combination of flat and contribution-linked commissions most appropriate to their salary levels (i.e., the one that minimizes the total commission as a percentage of salary), poor people end up paying a higher percentage of their salaries in commissions than do the rich. The regressive nature of the commission structure is clear from figure 7.8, which shows how much higher is the cumulative charge ratio of the cheapest AFP for a middle-income worker who started contributing in 1990 (salary of 300,000 Chilean pesos in 1990, 2 percent real growth annually) than the cumulative charge ratio of the cheapest AFP for a high-income worker who started contributing that same year (salary of 900,000 pesos in 1990, 2 percent real growth annually).[18] The gap was greatest at the beginning of the period, at more than 3 percentage points. By the end of the decade it had fallen to about 0.7 of a point, largely

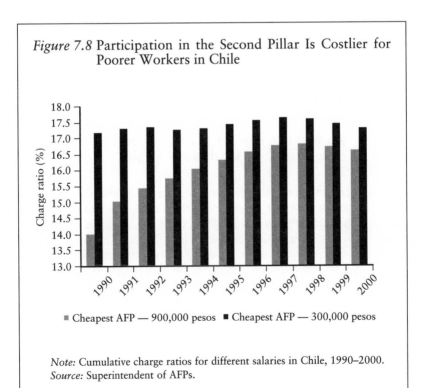

Figure 7.8 Participation in the Second Pillar Is Costlier for Poorer Workers in Chile

■ Cheapest AFP — 900,000 pesos   ■ Cheapest AFP — 300,000 pesos

Note: Cumulative charge ratios for different salaries in Chile, 1990–2000.
Source: Superintendent of AFPs.

as a result of the sustained increase in the cumulative charge ratio for higher-income workers.

Of course a regressive charge structure would be less worrisome if those AFPs chosen by poorer households offered a better service or performed better in terms of gross rates of return. There is no evidence that this is the case. Indeed, there is no correlation between the level of commissions and the performance of a pension fund. As for the service offered, more frequent or detailed communications on a worker's accumulated balance are unlikely to compensate him or her for a lower replacement rate or net salary. Moreover, it would appear that many low-income workers may not be choosing the lowest-priced option, given their earnings level, as demonstrated by the low price elasticity of demand calculated by Mastrángelo (1999) for Chilean AFPs. For Argentina, where AFJPs could also set fixed charges before November 2001, Rofman (2000) has calculated that the average commission (including the insurance premium) would be less than 3.0 percent instead of 3.4 percent if each contributor chose the cheapest AFJP for his or her income level.

These distributional consequences of the pension reform deserve more attention by policymakers. The costs of the system, and in particular fixed commissions, can also be a strong disincentive to participation for low-income households who may mainly desire a minimum pension guarantee that insures them against poverty in old age. In Mexico, where pension fund administrators have complete freedom to set charges, the *cuota social* account subsidy more than offsets these adverse distributional effects and may also increase the incentive to participate in the formal pension system.

Performance of the New Funded Pillar in the Distribution Stage

Workers affiliated with the new funded pillars are generally allowed a greater degree of choice at retirement in the distribution phase than during the accumulation phase. As shown in table 7.4, in all Latin American countries, with the exception of Bolivia and Uruguay, participants may choose between (at least) a private annuity and scheduled withdrawals. Some countries also permit a sequential, but not simultaneous combination of the two (deferred annuities). Lump-sum distributions, meanwhile, are highly restricted, which is consistent with the mandate to save.[19]

Depending on which option is chosen, the effect on risk-bearing is radically different. The scheduled withdrawal option lays all investment and longevity risk on the individual. An annuity, on the other hand, insures the policyholder against the risk of outliving his or her resources and therefore lays longevity risk on the insurance company that sells the policy. Insurers, however, price annuities according to the life expectancy of

Table 7.4 The Form of Benefits Is Usually Inconsistent with an Assumption of Retiree Irrationality with Respect to Saving

Country	Form of benefit
Argentina	Annuity, scheduled withdrawal (up to five years after retirement)
Bolivia	Only annuity
Chile	Annuity, scheduled withdrawal, deferred annuity
Colombia	Annuity, scheduled withdrawal, deferred annuity
Costa Rica	Annuity, scheduled withdrawal, deferred annuity. Not implemented because products are not available. During the first 10 years workers can withdraw full accumulated balance as a lump sum at retirement.
Dominican Republic	Annuity, scheduled withdrawal
El Salvador	Annuity, scheduled withdrawal, deferred annuity
Mexico	Annuity, scheduled withdrawal
Peru	Annuity, scheduled withdrawal, deferred annuity
Uruguay	Only annuity

Notes: Lump-sum distributions are permitted in all countries except Bolivia and Uruguay, but there are substantial constraints. Relevant data can be consulted in Devesa, Martínez, and Vidal (2000).

Sources: Devesa, Martinez, and Vidal (2000); and relevant national legislation.

the age cohort to which an individual belongs. Hence, annuities normally offer protection only against the risk of outliving the average individual of the cohort, while passing on the cost of anticipated increases in the average life expectancy of the cohort.[20] The extent of protection offered against investment risk, meanwhile, varies depending on the type of annuity sold.

In general, the scheduled withdrawal option is preferable when interest rates are very low and unlikely to increase within the time frame permitted for purchasing a deferred annuity. Pensioners, however, are not free to choose the amount they wish to withdraw as a benefit. Scheduled withdrawals are recalculated every year by the pension fund administrator as a function of the pension fund's return and the life expectancy of the worker and his or her family members. The scheduled withdrawal option is mandatory for workers in Chile and El Salvador who have accumulated funds that are insufficient to generate annuities above the minimum pension. At retirement they must draw down a pension equal to the minimum pension. When the funds run out, the government pays the remaining amount necessary to finance the minimum pension.

Annuities are attractive instruments for workers with above-average life expectancy because the price they pay reflects the average life expectancy of the population. Mandatory annuitization of the balance of accumulated savings in individual retirement accounts may, therefore, be beneficial for these individuals—and it may correct failures in annuities markets as a result of adverse selection.[21] However, it can be costly for some disadvantaged groups in society with a low life expectancy because the premiums charged by annuity providers (based on the average life expectancy of the whole population) are above what would be actuarially fair for these groups. Annuities are mandatory in Bolivia and Uruguay for all workers at the time of retirement, and in Argentina, Chile, El Salvador, and Peru for workers who wish to obtain their pensions before the official retirement age.[22]

Given the attraction of early retirement for many workers, the early retirement rule acts as an indirect form of compulsion of annuities. In Chile, for example, more than one-half of annuities are of the early retirement type. Other than adverse selection, the only main justifications of mandatory annuitization are the moral hazard of minimum pension guarantees and workers' improvidence. The moral hazard problem justifies annuitization of the portion of the accumulated balance sufficient to meet the minimum pension guarantee. Such argument is certainly not applicable to countries such as Argentina or Uruguay that have contributory, PAYG-financed first pillars that fulfill the poverty-prevention function. In the other countries it would justify lower levels of compulsory annuitization for early retirement. The improvidence argument, although valid, needs to be weighed against the costs of forcing low-income individuals to buy annuities. Low-income workers often have lower life expectancies and greater consumption needs in retirement than richer individuals and may therefore suffer most from mandatory annuities.

There are also certain restrictions on annuity sales that can be costly for individuals. Workers cannot combine them simultaneously with the scheduled withdrawals option. Since, in addition, all annuities are of the single-premium, fixed type, workers face considerable risk in the timing of the annuity purchase. Permitting partial and gradual annuitization would go a long way toward smoothing out this investment risk. Variable annuities—whereby investment risk is borne by the pensioner and longevity risk is borne by the insurance companies—may be particularly attractive for higher-income workers or for those who work where the public pension system still offers generous pensions. Variable annuities may also be provided more cheaply by insurance companies than fixed annuities because, with the exception of Chile, the financial instruments needed to underwrite fixed annuities and hedge investment risk over long periods (inflation-indexed bonds of long maturities) are in short supply.

In Chile, Colombia, and Peru annuity benefits must be indexed to a measure of prices, also transferring inflation risk to the insurance company. In Uruguay annuities must be indexed to wages. In Argentina, benefits may be denominated in U.S. dollars, which offers protection against devaluation (and hence at least partial protection against inflation). An inflation-indexation requirement, however, is feasible only to the extent that there is a liquid market of inflation-indexed securities that insurance companies can rely on to build portfolios that match their inflation-indexed liabilities. Only Chile has such a market. In countries like Colombia and Peru insurance companies are likely to charge a hefty premium for underwriting inflation-indexed annuities. In Uruguay premiums are likely to be even higher because growth in wages often outstrips prices.

In Chile, Colombia, El Salvador, and Peru workers can also buy deferred annuities and in the meantime draw down part of the accumulated balance as part of a scheduled withdrawal. Deferred annuities may be attractive when interest rates are expected to increase. Nonetheless, annuity purchases may still be badly timed because workers are not able to buy deferred annuities before retirement and only one- to three-year deferrals are permitted at retirement. In Argentina, Bolivia, and Mexico, where deferred annuity purchases are not permitted, the investment risk that workers face is even greater.

However, as long as workers are able to move into conservative, fixed income portfolios as they approach the time of annuity purchase they can minimize this risk. If interest rates fall the value of the annuity that can be purchased with the accumulated balance declines, but the market value of the fixed income investments in the individual account rises. Restrictions on worker choice of investment portfolios are therefore a source of unnecessary volatility in retirement benefits.

An indicator of the impact of interest rate volatility on annuity values in Chile is shown in figure 7.9.[23] This graph shows the value of the annuity that a premium, fixed in real terms, would buy at the end of each year since 1988. The value of the annuity is expressed in terms of the replacement rate, with the replacement rate of 1988 set arbitrarily at 50 percent. The interest rate used to calculate the benefit paid by the annuity is the annuity yield for workers retiring at the official retirement age, as reported by the *Superintendencia de Valores y Seguros*. As shown in figure 7.9 there is some variation in the annuity value over time. The difference between the highest and lowest replacement rates is 22 percentage points, the average replacement rate over the period is 60 percent, and the standard deviation is 6 percent. These differences in replacement rates across cohorts are caused by the volatility of interest rates over the period. In particular, the decline in interest rates in the late 1980s lowered the value of annuities for cohorts retiring in these years. Workers retiring in 1998 and 1999 especially would have been better off deferring the purchase of the annuity for two and one years, respectively.

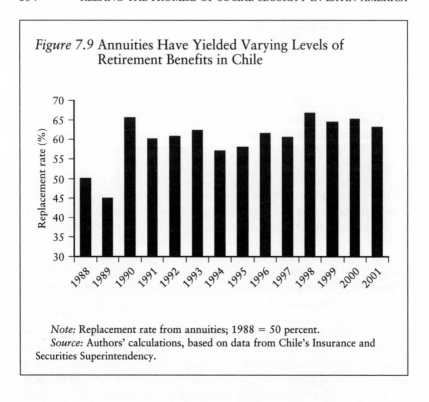

Figure 7.9 Annuities Have Yielded Varying Levels of
Retirement Benefits in Chile

Note: Replacement rate from annuities; 1988 = 50 percent.
Source: Authors' calculations, based on data from Chile's Insurance and
Securities Superintendency.

Investment and Longevity Risk Management
Properties of the Funded System

The new funded pension systems are a potentially attractive new instrument for managing intergenerational longevity risk during the accumulation stage. By moving to a defined contribution formula the new pension
pillars ensure a more fair and efficient allocation of the cost of increasing
life expectancy between generations. However, annuities, the instruments
that insure individuals against intragenerational longevity risk are only
available at retirement. It may be desirable, therefore, to permit the purchase of annuities before retirement, although this may expose insurance
companies to greater risk of misjudging increases in life expectancy.

It is considerably less clear whether the design of the new funded pillars
is consistent with the efficient management of investment risk. Restricting
individual choice and limiting portfolios to mainly interest-bearing assets
make sense for mandatory contributions intended to meet minimum
income requirements in old age (most if not all of the mandatory contributions of poorer households and part of the contributions of richer
households in countries where the PAYG plan is being phased out).

Indeed, it could be argued that mandatory contributions should be invested exclusively in inflation-indexed government bonds of appropriate maturity and of the highest possible creditworthiness. These bonds are essential to building portfolios that will ensure the attainment of basic retirement income needs. Such a limited investment regimen, however, would call into question the rationale for decentralized, competitive private management of the new funded pillars. To the extent that society agrees on the need to set a minimum pension guarantee (defined in reference to the minimum or average wage), a flat-rate benefit offered as a part of a PAYG system would achieve the objective of providing a basic retirement income much more effectively and at much lower cost. This proposal is taken up in more detail in chapter 9.

Individual investment choice is desirable for the portion of contributions whose main objective is to ensure income smoothing above the basic income level. Richer households in countries where the funded pillar is the only source of mandatory pensions may therefore wish to invest their portfolios in a riskier manner than that permitted by current regulations. Similarly, both low- and high-income households in countries such as Argentina, Costa Rica, or Uruguay may also wish to invest their additional mandatory contributions to the funded pillar in a riskier manner. Workers in these countries are still covered by a contributory PAYG system that provides for basic retirement income objectives. In other words, individual portfolio choice becomes most desirable for retirement savings that are complementary to those intended to keep households out of poverty in old age.

For contributions above the level needed to meet basic income needs in old age, the current restrictive design on the new funded pillars can impose costly restrictions on risk management in two ways:

1. The current mandate to save forces individuals to manage investment risk through a single instrument until their retirement. Individuals are not allowed to invest their mandatory, tax-advantaged pension contributions in assets that may offer a more suitable risk–return trade-off or may be cheaper to manage, such as bank deposits, property, children's education, or foreign assets. Moreover, prior to retirement participants cannot pool smooth investment risk through, for example, deferred annuities, guaranteed investment contracts, or term deposits.

2. During the accumulation stage the mandated savings instrument offers a risk–return trade-off that is determined by investment regulations and the fund managers' choices. Hence, it is not possible to adjust portfolios over the life cycle in accordance with affiliates' risk, time, liquidity, and bequest preferences.

The only country that has been moving away from this design is Chile, where a second fund was introduced in 2000. Since May 2000 and until late 2002 Chilean workers close to retirement were offered the opportunity to trade out of the so-called *Fondo 1* (the original pension fund) into a fund invested exclusively in fixed income securities (*Fondo 2*). At the end of 2001 only men older than 55 and women older than 50 were permitted to switch their accumulated balance to this second fund.

The *Fondo 2* had limited popularity among those workers eligible to switch, however. The option to switch was only taken up by a handful of (lucky) workers who have benefited since then from bonds' superior performance relative to equities. Figure 7.10 shows the performance of *Fondo 2* over *Fondo 1* in terms of a higher annual real rate of return (gross of contribution fees) during every month between June and December 2001. This bumpy start of the *Fondo 2* appears to be caused by the limited

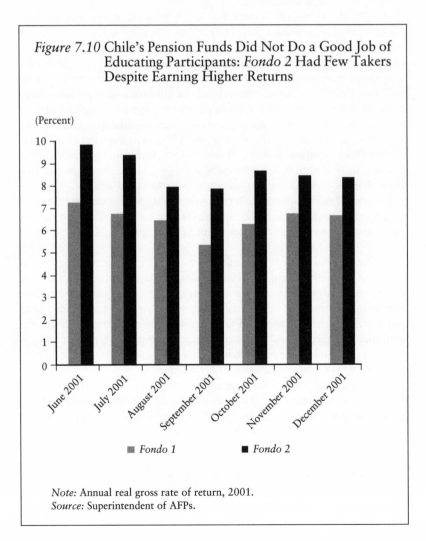

Figure 7.10 Chile's Pension Funds Did Not Do a Good Job of Educating Participants: *Fondo 2* Had Few Takers Despite Earning Higher Returns

(Percent)

■ *Fondo 1*   ■ *Fondo 2*

Note: Annual real gross rate of return, 2001.
Source: Superintendent of AFPs.

Table 7.5 The Five New Funds in Chile Vary by Proportion
of Equity Investment

(Percent of total assets in each type of fund)

	Minimum	*Maximum*
Fund A	40	80
Fund B	25	60
Fund C	15	40
Fund D	5	20
Fund E	0	0

Source: Ministry of Economy and Finance, Chile.

publicity extended to the switching option. The pension fund administrators had little incentive to engage in advertising and information campaigns because the switch to *Fondo 2* would not translate into any additional income from commissions. In addition, the fund managers were under heavy pressure from the government to cut commissions and had reduced the number of sales agents they employed. Nor did the government sufficiently promote the second fund.

The government drew important lessons from the experience with *Fondo 2*. Despite the low acceptance of the second fund, a law passed early in 2002 extended individual choice over the investment of mandatory savings even further. A multifund system has been approved that permits workers to choose among five funds, all with varying exposure to equities. The five funds are characterized by the level of investment in equities. The equity limits for each fund are shown in table 7.5. Men 55 and under and women 50 and under are able to choose among all five funds. Men older than 55 and women over 50 are able to choose among funds B to E. Pensioners who have maintained their accumulated assets with the AFPs (instead of opting for an annuity) are able to choose among funds C to E.

Those workers who do not select a specific fund when they enter the workforce will be assigned one according to their age: workers up to 35 years of age are assigned to fund B. Men between 36 and 55 and women 36 to 50 are assigned to fund C. Men 56 and older, women 51 and older, and pensioners are assigned to fund D.[24] The same default options were applied 90 days after the introduction of the multifund system for those workers who had not selected a fund within that period. Men and women who have their accounts invested in fund A but do not move to one of the other funds within 90 days after they turn 56 or 51, respectively, are shifted to fund B in a gradual manner over a four-year period.

Although workers' reaction to *Fondo 2* does not augur well for the new multifund system, the government has made a greater effort to publicize the new funds. Since September 2002, when funds A, B, and D were

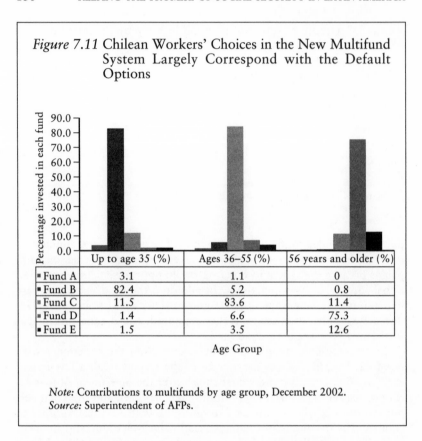

Figure 7.11 Chilean Workers' Choices in the New Multifund System Largely Correspond with the Default Options

	Up to age 35 (%)	Ages 36–55 (%)	56 years and older (%)
▪ Fund A	3.1	1.1	0
▪ Fund B	82.4	5.2	0.8
▪ Fund C	11.5	83.6	11.4
▪ Fund D	1.4	6.6	75.3
▪ Fund E	1.5	3.5	12.6

Age Group

Note: Contributions to multifunds by age group, December 2002.
Source: Superintendent of AFPs.

introduced, investment in the funds has been more promising.[25] By June 2003 nearly 1.4 million workers had chosen a fund, representing 40.5 percent of contributors. It is interesting to note that the choices made largely correspond with the default options. As shown in figure 7.11, between 75 percent and 85 percent of the workers in the three age groups chose the portfolio assigned as the default option.

The government has a fiduciary responsibility to ensure that workers are properly advised on the choices they face and their potential impact on retirement income. This responsibility may be laid on the pension fund administrators, but because private fund managers enjoy a trapped market of mandated demand, they have little incentive to incur the costs of educating individuals on optimizing their returns from the system by shifting their portfolio allocations. Indeed, the mandate may be partly responsible for some of the internal inconsistencies of the system. Because the number of competitively priced voluntary savings and insurance instruments in Chile is increasing, the possibility that distortions in the financial sector and capital markets could arise from the government mandating a particular form of private retirement saving should be investigated with increased scrutiny (Shah 1997; Lasaga and Pollner 2003).

The new Chilean design also intermingles the poverty prevention and income smoothing objectives of a formal pension system. In its drive for individual responsibility it has put poor households in a situation where investing in equities seems to be a one-way bet. Workers who do not expect to accumulate much more than the minimum pension guarantee have an incentive to invest in riskier portfolios (with a higher allocation to equities). If returns are high, they receive higher income, but if they are low, the government picks up the bill through the minimum pension guarantee. The data available in fact show that poorer workers choose portfolios similar to those of richer households (see figure 7.12). Hence, the government, as guarantor of the minimum pension, will face an additional source of risk in the form of the volatility of the equity portfolios of poorer workers. The increasing international diversification of equity portfolios will

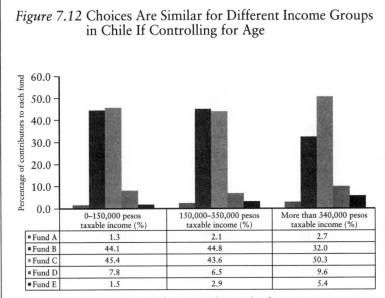

Figure 7.12 Choices Are Similar for Different Income Groups in Chile If Controlling for Age

	0–150,000 pesos taxable income (%)	150,000–350,000 pesos taxable income (%)	More than 340,000 pesos taxable income (%)
▪ Fund A	1.3	2.1	2.7
▪ Fund B	44.1	44.8	32.0
▪ Fund C	45.4	43.6	50.3
▪ Fund D	7.8	6.5	9.6
▪ Fund E	1.5	2.9	5.4

Taxable income (thousands of pesos)

Note: Percentage of contributors to each fund by income group, December 2002.
Source: Superintendent of AFPs.

reduce this risk, but the fact remains that the government is offering poor workers an incentive for risk taking, when such liabilities may best be matched through investment in inflation-indexed government bonds. If the purpose of the guarantee was a form of redistribution through the back door, this could have been done in a way that did not create perverse incentives for risk taking and distortions to capital markets.

A similar risk of moral hazard may arise in Peru, which passed legislation along Chilean lines to allow fund managers to offer affiliates multiple funds. On the other hand, this problem does not arise in those savings components that are not covered by state guarantees, such as the voluntary savings pillar of all Latin American countries and the mandatory pillar in Argentina, Costa Rica, and Uruguay (the countries that have retained a basic PAYG pillar). A move away from the one-size-fits-all model and toward more worker choice of investment may therefore be considered in these cases. Nonetheless, it is critical that the authorities ensure the comparability and transparency of fee structures and fund performance and that they engage in a serious effort to raise the financial literacy of the population.

Conclusion

Although the savings systems have delivered relatively high gross returns and the administrative costs do not appear high when compared with retail fund managers in the region, there are still some worrying issues. Young and poor workers may be discouraged from participating by the relatively high mandatory contribution rates. Poorer workers also suffer from fixed commissions in Chile, which may further reduce their incentive to participate and which have a regressive income effect. The earnings ceiling used to calculate mandatory contributions is also very high in all Latin American countries (they are actually among the highest in the world for mandatory retirement security systems), which leaves little space for the voluntary system to develop.

There are other explanations for why rational workers may not find the new savings component satisfactory in Latin American countries: the cost of pension fund administration, the lack of investment choice, the absence of international diversification, the regulatory bias toward government securities, and the obligation to buy annuities. In every Latin American country that has introduced savings components, at least one of these features is present. Chile is probably the country with the least of these negative features (high fees and obligation to buy annuities for early retirement).

There are signs that the savings systems are becoming more efficient over time, at least in some countries. Variable commission ratios have fallen in recent years in Chile, but nowhere near as much as the administrators' operating expenses. Investment regulations are gradually being relaxed (including on foreign investment) in Bolivia and Mexico. Chile introduced portfolio choice in 2002 and Peru will do so in 2005. Other countries, such as Mexico, may soon follow. Policymakers are also reconsidering the high contribution rates of these systems, although, at least in Argentina, they do not seem to have taken into account the impact that lower mandatory contributions have on variable commission rates in an industry with high fixed costs. Argentina halved the contribution rate to the mandatory system in 2001, which led to a sharp increase in the ratio of fees to contributions.

As policymakers reconsider these and other features of the savings components, it is essential that they take into account the interaction of the savings component with the rest of the retirement income system. High contribution rates and maximum taxable earnings are particularly detrimental for the growth of mandatory and voluntary pension savings when a large public pillar is still in place (as in Costa Rica and Uruguay). Similarly, diversification into foreign securities and riskier domestic instruments may be more valuable for workers if they know that they will be able to rely on defined benefit promises to cover their basic retirement needs. Finally, mandating savings into a particular instrument may be costly for workers if they can find better investment alternatives elsewhere.

Notes

1. In Mexico there were US$0.16 billion in the voluntary accounts in December 2001. In Chile at the end of 2001 there were 1 million voluntary savings accounts that held US$0.2 billion. Only one of six affiliates had a CAV, despite their relatively high liquidity (withdrawals are permitted four times a year) and absence of commissions.

2. "Funding" does not necessarily imply private management, but the reverse is nearly always the case, especially for mandatory plans. Some publicly managed plans, like the provident funds found in several Asian countries, are funded. In some OECD countries public plans that were traditionally run on a PAYG basis are starting to build up reserve funds to meet future liabilities. For ease in terminology we use the term "funded" or "savings" component to refer to the privately managed individual accounts that are such a prominent feature of pension reforms in Latin America.

3. We abstract here from the poverty prevention objective because this is the subject of chapter 9. Readers should note, however, that the systems in some Latin American countries (e.g., Bolivia, Chile, El Salvador, and Mexico) play a poverty prevention role with the support of minimum income guarantees.

4. This will only happen to the extent that the annuity providers do not accurately estimate increases in life expectancy. The later in life that people are allowed to purchase annuities, the less likely this will be the case. It should be noted that annuities are similar to defined benefit plans in their investment and intragenerational (generation-specific) longevity risk management properties.

5. The rest of this chapter focuses on the first type of risk.

6. Investment floors are only in place in Bolivia, Mexico, and Uruguay. The Argentine government also used nonlegislated forms of persuasion before the 2001

crisis to increase the allocation of pension funds to government bonds above the legislated limit.

7. Mexico lifted the ban on investment in foreign securities in June 2002.

8. Chile was an exception in Latin America in the 1990s, being the only country whose government debt was rated investment grade by the main rating companies. Since then Mexico has obtained investment grade as well.

9. As explained previously, in addition to these commissions workers must pay monthly premiums for disability and life insurance.

10. In Peru fixed commissions were permitted until 1996. Argentina banned fixed commissions at the end of 2001.

11. In Mexico the two measures are not equivalent because some providers charge commissions on assets and returns. In Bolivia the commission is set on assets under management. In Chile the AFPs also charge fixed commissions.

12. The cumulative charge ratio at retirement measures the total impact of charges on retirement income over a person's career. To calculate this ratio for Chile, both fixed and variable charges need to be taken into account. It is assumed that the representative worker is charged the industry average commission, where the weights are the contributions collected by each AFP. It is assumed also that the participant contributes to the system on a regular basis. In the Chilean case, the cumulative charge ratio at retirement is an accurate measure of administrative costs for older participants who made contributions from the start of the system and retired before the year 2000. We also project the cumulative charge ratio at retirement for workers who will retire after that date. The projected cumulative charge ratio at retirement is calculated assuming that the fee levels remain constant until retirement.

13. The salary for the cohort that retired in December 2000 was set at 285,000 Chilean pesos, the average wage of the contributors to the pension. Wages are assumed to grow at 2 percent a year in real terms and the contribution for disability and life insurance is assumed to be a constant 0.7 percent of the worker's salary, its average level during the past 10 years. Precise information on insurance premiums prior to 1990 is not available.

14. Only 393 people retired in 1983 from the funded system. Even by 1987 the number was less than 8,000.

15. The contrast of these results with previous evidence (e.g., James, Smalhout, and Vittas 2001) stems from focusing on commissions at a point in time instead of focusing on their cumulative effect over a worker's career (as shown by the cumulative charge ratio).

16. Despite this fact, the net intergenerational impact is probably still positive for earlier generations because of the recognition of their accrued rights under the previous, generous system and the high gross returns during the first years of the funded system.

17. If an asset-based structure had been chosen instead of the salary- and contribution-based one, any up-front costs could have been more evenly spread over time. On the other hand, workers with low contribution densities—often the poorer ones—may have been worse off than those workers with higher densities because under an asset-based structure commissions are normally deducted every month even when there are no contributions. Moving to an asset-based charge now, moreover, would be a very complex process.

18. The cumulative charge ratio in 2000 for someone who started contributing in 1990 is much lower than the one shown in figure 7.7 for someone who retired in 2000 because the worker in the later cohort did not contribute in the 1980s, the period of highest commissions. Moreover, this simulation is based on the lowest-cost fund, whereas that in figure 7.7 is based on the average fund.

19. In chapter 6 we identified "improvidence," or regretting not having saved enough when old age is reached, as the main justification for mandating savings for

retirement. It would be inconsistent to mandate savings during the accumulation stage but permit lump-sum payments at retirement, unless improvidence disappears gradually as the individual gets older and realizes the need for providing an adequate level of retirement income.

20. Of course, insurance companies may miscalculate increases in the average life expectancy of a specific age cohort and inadvertently provide protection against this longevity risk to those cohorts.

21. Valdés-Prieto (2002b) argued that there is limited empirical evidence of adverse selection in annuities markets in Chile.

22. In Chile workers who want to draw their pension—and retire from the mandatory pension system, although not necessarily from the workforce—before the official retirement age (60 years for women, 65 years for men) are required to have a benefit that exceeds 110 percent of the state-guaranteed minimum pension and must be greater than 50 percent of the worker's average real wage over the last 10 years prior to the retirement request. If the benefit exceeds 70 percent of the worker's average real wage over the last 10 years prior to the retirement request and 120 percent of the statutory minimum pension, the rest of the accumulated balance can be taken as a lump sum. Similar rules are in place in Argentina, El Salvador, and Peru.

23. We abstract here from the impact of interest rates on the value of the accumulated balance.

24. The assets are transferred between funds on a gradual basis over a four-year period.

25. The previous *Fondo 1* and *Fondo 2* have been renamed C and E, respectively.

8

The Preferences That Individuals Reveal

AS POPULATIONS GROW OLDER THE economics of insurance prescribe individual saving as the most efficient and sustainable means of ensuring adequate income in old age. At the aggregate level it becomes increasingly costly for a shrinking labor force to finance the pensions of a growing number of retired elderly purely through public PAYG pooling arrangements. At the household level workers will be increasingly reluctant to pay the higher payroll taxes necessary to sustain pure pooling PAYG systems. However, pooling remains an important insurance instrument to lower losses from the relatively rare risks of poverty in old age, unexpected longevity, disability, and untimely death.[1] Because the market for insurance often fails, and even where it flourishes cannot provide private pooling instruments to insure against certain loses relevant to retirement income—such as inflation—there is a role for government in augmenting the set of instruments at households' disposal through social insurance.[2]

Governments in Latin America have taken up this role with enthusiasm, as shown by the proliferation of publicly administered and/or mandated health, disability, retirement, and unemployment insurance systems in the region since the 1920s. However, these social insurance institutions can be detrimental if designed with little regard for the changing nature of the risks they seek to cover, if they ignore privately available alternatives and if they pay no attention to what individuals and households reveal as their preferences for what governments should provide. When social security is designed with little regard for individual incentives and household preferences workers are likely to turn away from the systems, thereby jeopardizing the plans' financial sustainability and effectiveness at pooling risks.

This chapter focuses on the low rates of participation in Latin America's national retirement security systems. We particularly emphasize the impact of pension reforms on the *incentive* for workers to seek formal coverage when the mandate to participate in a national pension system can generally be evaded and where alternative saving and investment options exist—from financial instruments like bank deposits and private annuities taken up voluntarily to nonfinancial assets such as housing, other property, small enterprise, and even the accumulation of human capital (education and training that make workers more productive). As in other chapters of this book, rather than discuss the government's objective of *covering* the population, we focus on the household's objective of adequately insuring itself against the loss of earning ability that comes with aging: whether households have *access* to adequate coverage and whether they choose to *participate* or opt out of government-administered or -mandated pension systems.

There are three main findings. First, after analyzing individual and household behavior with respect to national pension systems (using data from regularly deployed surveys as well as two surveys focused on risk, savings, and insurance in Chile and Peru), we provide evidence that people generally are more likely to make rational decisions with respect to securing adequate retirement income than is typically assumed. This manifest rational behavior regarding savings and investment choices makes it all the more important for governments to provide the instruments that people want to secure adequate income in old age. After all, if on the whole people behaved irrationally with respect to retirement income it would matter little what they wanted, and governments would be justified in stepping in to tell them.

Second, this chapter presents evidence that people expect from governments what governments can credibly deliver. In Chile, where there is considerable trust in government, the contribution behavior of workers suggests that what they want from government is some insurance against poverty in old age. Workers tend to contribute to the public system just enough to qualify for government topping-up—namely, the assurance of a minimum pension to insure against old-age poverty. This behavior may reveal a preference for government-provided instruments for pooling over saving.

Third, in Peru, where there is considerably less trust in government, survey data suggest that workers may value regulatory oversight of privately managed pension plans more than instruments to insure against the losses associated with old-age poverty. The latter result is "contaminated" by the fact that the Peruvian government has not implemented a poverty prevention component for the majority of affiliates to the reformed pension system, but the results in Peru indicate that even with weakly enforced property rights investment in real estate acts as a substitute for the formal retirement savings system.

Is Low Participation Evidence of Social Exclusion or Individual Choice?

Much of the literature on coverage of pension systems argues that workers' access to protection is determined by the degree of unionization in a particular sector and industry of employment (Mesa-Lago 1991; Tokman 1992; World Bank 1994; Uthoff 1997; Marquez and Pages 1998; Mesa-Lago 2000). Several studies have pointed out that with the changes in occupational structure in Latin America over the past two decades—that is, an increasing proportion of the workforce that is self-employed or working in small firms (ILO 1999; de Ferranti et al. 2000)—a growing number of workers are excluded from pension programs because coverage in these sectors is far lower than is typically found in public and private large-scale manufacturing and in the civil service (IADB 2000). This strand of the literature characterizes low rates of coverage as evidence of broader social exclusion linked to segmented, discriminatory labor markets and the failure of governments to provide greater access through better education and opportunities for social advancement.

Access to social security is determined by occupational category and the size of the firm where workers are employed (Mesa-Lago 1991; Uthoff 1997). Levels of participation differ according to the amount of political pressure for inclusion in the national system that certain groups of workers can bring to bear (Mesa-Lago 1991, 2000). Countries with greater rates of urbanization, industrialization, and unionization and with a greater share of salaried employment (relative to self-employment) will have higher rates of coverage. Countries that still have predominantly rural, agricultural economies, where labor is less unionized and where there is a large share of self-employed people in the workforce, have lower levels of coverage. Workers in part-time jobs and people temporarily employed without a contract are also less likely to be covered. Thus, the workers that national pension systems are especially intended to protect are those least likely to enjoy the benefits of protection (Marquez and Pages 1998).

The social-exclusion literature does provide plausible arguments and convincing empirical evidence to explain why workers go without coverage; however, it does not tell the whole story. Barrientos (1998a), James (1999), and Holzmann, Packard, and Cuesta (2000) looked beyond the social-exclusion arguments and presented a number of hypotheses to explain why *rational, nonmyopic* individuals and households may *choose* to avoid formal retirement income security systems, even if these are actuarially fair and/or include privately owned and administered savings accounts.

Where formal retirement security is bundled with unrelated government programs and regulations, the costs of compliance to the individual (or small firm) may be prohibitive. Coverage under a formal social security system is often nested deeply within the broader regulatory and taxation framework of the economy. Even where single-pillar pure PAYG systems have been replaced with less centralized systems based on individual retirement accounts, participation may require payment of taxes, compliance with regulations, and adherence to labor standards totally unrelated to income security in old age (Holzmann, Packard, and Cuesta 2000).

The constraints imposed by formal pension systems on many work-ers—especially poorer entrepreneurs—may be more binding on their in-vestments in productive enterprise than they are beneficial to smoothing consumption. Avoiding the pension system may be optimal given capital and credit constraints on investment choices. The opportunity costs of vesting scarce capital in a formal retirement security plan, no matter how actuarially fair, may be too high. The inability to draw on saved funds in times of hardship can place unacceptable liquidity constraints on workers. This is especially true of entrepreneurs, farmers, and rural nonfarm self-employed populations whose wealth is held in illiquid forms or whose in-come is largely seasonal (Holzmann, Packard, and Cuesta 2000).

Furthermore, mandatory contributions to social insurance can lead to welfare losses for poorer people with high rates of discount. Where household income may be just sufficient to meet immediate, basic needs for survival, saving for old age may not be rational (James 1999; Will-more 2001b). Poorer households will place greater value on consumption today than on consumption tomorrow or far into the future. If the time preference rate is higher than the market rate of interest and credit is ex-pensive or rationed, the shadow discount rate is even greater. Thus, for lower-income households mandatory contributions can lead to major welfare losses, and participation in a formal social security system may place an intolerable constraint on household efforts to smooth consump-tion (James 1999).

Additionally, income security in old age may not be the primary risk concern in poorer households. The profile of risks faced by the poor may feature the less predictable shocks to income, such as disability and sud-den illness, more prominently. This line of argument is strengthened by the link between income (nutrition/health) and mortality; that is, poorer peo-ple would rather consume income today than save and consume in the fu-ture when, because of their relatively higher mortality rate, they may not be around to collect a pension. These factors augment the implicit tax component of mandated retirement contributions for poorer households, whether they live and work under a single-pillar pure PAYG regimen or one that includes mandatory retirement savings accounts.

For many households in developing countries, traditional, family-based systems of old-age security may provide superior income smoothing and cover against the risk of poverty in old age. There is ample evidence that agents (as individuals, as households, and within households) engage in consumption smoothing and risk management to mitigate the impact of fluctuating incomes. Where formal insurance markets have failed to coa-lesce or have broken down because of moral hazard and adverse selection, the extended family and community still fill the gap. The majority of the world's elderly people rely solely on informal and traditional arrange-ments for retirement income security (World Bank 1994; James 1999).[3] Traditional structures involving resident elderly parents or expected reliance on children (Becker and Tomes 1976; Appelbaum and Katz 1991; Hoddinott 1992) are still prevalent in Latin America (IADB 2000) and may act as a superior, more flexible substitute for the formal social insurance system.

Furthermore, poor and nonpoor households may put little stock in the promises of government. Even reformed pension systems may be suffering from an inherited lack of credibility in formal social security institutions. Even if workers were fully aware of the benefits defined by social security legislation they might perceive a high political risk to their promised pension stemming directly from a government's lack of credibility. If governments have a track record of frequently changing the rules of the game (vesting requirements, the benefit formula, indexation, or minimum pension guarantees), if inflation taxes are high, and if funds earmarked to pay retirement benefits are mismanaged or depleted, workers may consider the risk of not receiving a pension to be too high and may heavily discount the returns of investing in being covered.

Where private individual accounts have been introduced, households may find the burden of financial risk in reformed systems to be too high. A criticism of the new multipillar model is that it requires workers to assume a greater share of risk to their income security in retirement than do pure PAYG systems (Diamond 1993, 1998; Orzag and Stiglitz 2001; Barr 2000). Under purely public PAYG regimens government assumes a hefty share of risk (demographic, macroeconomic, and financial), and workers' only risk is largely political (i.e., that their benefits will be cut or their accumulated rights ignored in the political process of setting government budgets). Under the reformed systems based on privately invested savings in individual accounts, workers are burdened with the weight of a wider range of risks to adequate retirement income. In a system of individual accounts, although there may be relatively greater certainty of receiving some pension there is substantially greater uncertainty as to the amount of the pension—that is, of accumulating a balance sufficient to guarantee an adequate stream of income in old age.[4] A significant number of workers may consider mandated arrangements where the bulk of the pension is determined by variable returns from private investment to be too risky. The perception of risk in the reformed systems my be even greater in countries with poorly regulated capital markets, in economies vulnerable to frequent external shocks, or where the full faith and credit of government are called into question and even publicly issued. Fixed-income securities, which typically dominate the portfolios of the new pension funds in Latin America, pay substantial risk premiums. Recent events in Argentina are a poignant illustration of this argument.

The mix of retirement investments adopted by households will necessarily depend on the relative costs and benefits of each investment and its efficiency in balancing returns with risk. A portfolio of formal and informal assets (financial assets, own home, other property, own business) and household-based strategies (education of a child, reciprocal arrangements among members of the extended family) may have higher returns and lower risks (beholden children and relatives) than do the portfolios offered by the national pension system. Ultimately, pension systems based on compulsory contributions to either a purely public PAYG system or one including individual savings accounts may simply crowd out voluntary household arrangements and what are often considered supplementary third-pillar retirement investments offered privately by the formal financial sector.

Who Contributes to Social Security? Survey Evidence from 13 Latin American Countries

In a background paper for this book Packard, Shinkai, and Fuentes (2002) analyzed the contribution behavior of workers using household-level data from 13 Latin American countries. As in Barrientos (1996, 1998a) for Chile and Holzmann, Packard, and Cuesta (2000) for Chile and Argentina, the authors performed separate probit maximum likelihood estimations of the probability that working individuals are contributing to the national retirement security system in their country. Table 8.1 summarizes the results by presenting the positive or negative impact of selected individual, employment, industry, and household characteristics on the likelihood that workers are contributing to the national pension system in each country.[5] Although the authors are restricted in the set of specific hypotheses that can be tested by using survey data from a large number of very diverse countries, interesting regional trends emerge from their analysis.

It is not surprising that better-educated workers earning higher incomes are more likely to be contributing to the national pension system. It is interesting to note that working women, often considered an "excluded" group, are more likely to contribute in 8 of the 13 countries examined. This finding may reveal greater prudence with respect to old age among working women relative to men, but it may also be explained by their relatively greater numbers in professions traditionally well covered by public social insurance systems such as public administration, nursing, and teaching.

As shown in table 8.1, however, structural barriers clearly remain between formal coverage and workers in certain sectors and industries. Certain segments of the working population face a lower likelihood of access to formal income protection in old age. These people include married women (although many of these may be covered through the contributions made by their husbands), workers in rural households and people employed in agriculture, transportation, retail and services, and the construction industries (relative to workers in manufacturing). The probability

Table 8.1 Probability That Workers Contribute to Social Security Is Determined by Individual, Household, and Labor Market Factors

	Bolivia	Brazil	Chile	Colombia	Costa Rica	Dominican Republic	Ecuador	El Salvador	Mexico	Nicaragua	Paraguay	Peru	Venezuela
	1993	1997	1996	1998	1997	1998	1995	1998	1996	1998	1995	1997	1997
Individual characteristics													
Age	+	+	+	+	+	+	+	+	−	+	+	+	+
Elderly		+	−	−	+		−	−		−	+	−	−
Income	+	+	+	+	+	+	+	+		+	+	+	+
Education		+	+	+	+		+	+	+	+	+	+	+
Woman		−	+	+	+		+		+	+	+		+
Married			+	−	+	+	+	+	−	+	+	+	+
Wife			−	−			−		−		−		−
Rural			−		+	−	+	−	−		−	−	
Employment characteristics													
Single job		+	+		+	+		+	+			+	−
Subordinate	−	+	+	−	−	−				−	−	−	+
Professional		−	−	+	+	+	+		+	+	+	+	+
Self-employed		−	−	−		−		+					
Only self-employed		+	+		−	−	−			−			
Self-employed professional						+					+		
Work hours				+					+			+	+

(Table continues on the following page.)

171

Table 8.1 (continued)

	Bolivia	Brazil	Chile	Colombia	Costa Rica	Dominican Republic	Ecuador	El Salvador	Mexico	Nicaragua	Paraguay	Peru	Venezuela
	1993	1997	1996	1998	1997	1998	1995	1998	1996	1998	1995	1997	1997
Part-time	+	+	+					–			–	–	–
5+ years with firm		+	+					+		+	+	+	–
Contract	+	+	+					+	+	+	+	+	–
Industry of employment (standard International Standard Industrial Classification categories, where manufacturing is omitted)													
Manufacturing													
Agriculture		–	–	–	–	–		–	–	–		–	–
Mining	+	–	–			+	+		–				
Utilities			–	+	+					+			
Construction		–	–	–	–	–	–		–	–	–	–	–
Retail		+	–	–	–	–		–	–	–	–	–	
Transportation		+	–	–	–	–	–	–	–	–		–	–
Finance		+	–	+	–	–			–		–		
Community	+	+	–	–	–			–	–		–		–
Household characteristics													
Size	–	–	–	–	–	–					–		–

	4,374	136,420	45,718	36,528	11,828	6,881	11,180	18,021	23,455	6,554	5,486	8,112	12,426
Number of old people		+				+	−	+	−				
Number of male children		+	+		+	+		+	+	+	+	+	
Number of female children		+	+		+				+		+		
Extended family		+	+	−	+			+	+		+		
Observations	4,374	136,420	45,718	36,528	11,828	6,881	11,180	18,021	23,455	6,554	5,486	8,112	12,426
Pseudo R^2	0.23	0.58	0.48	0.31	0.18	0.31	0.28	0.52	0.48	0.46	0.38	0.59	0.37

Notes: The table presents probit regressions; dependent variable "contributes to social security."
"+" and "−" indicate variable has at least a 10 percent statistically significant positive or negative effect, respectively, on the probability of contribution to the national retirement security system. Blank cells indicate the variable is not statistically significant to the probability of contribution.

Source: Packard, Shinkai, and Fuentes (2002).

of access to the social security systems is also lower for workers in small firms and those without a legal employment contract. Although this hypothesis was not tested, this may reflect small firms' costs of affiliating workers and making regular contributions, including the costs of compliance in heavily regulated and taxed product and factor markets.

The results summarized in table 8.1 also show that workers who hold what have been traditionally considered "better" jobs in Latin America—in larger firms, in manufacturing, and in the civil service—are more likely to be contributing. Indeed, many workers and their households may be excluded from retirement security systems and other forms of social insurance in countries with deeply segmented labor markets. The evidence in table 8.1 suggests that the growing concern among policymakers for workers in these sectors may be justified, especially in countries where workers queue for covered, formal employment. However, such conclusions can only be drawn from a thorough country-specific analysis of labor market dynamics: how individuals insert themselves in different sectors and industries, whether workers choose the sector in which they work, and whether "covered" formal employment is indeed rationed.[6]

Finally, in table 8.1 there is little evidence of traditional forms of retirement income security substituting for formal institutions. In fact, a larger share of elderly people and dependent children in the household seems to complement participation in the formal system in most countries. The positive influence of children and elderly people on the likelihood of contribution to formal pension systems may not be as surprising as it seems. Workers who have many dependent children and who are more likely to face the risk of disability and sudden death may have a higher demand for coverage under the social security system and thus may be more likely to contribute (Barrientos 1998a). Furthermore, older children and resident elderly men and women may take charge of household chores such as cooking and caring for younger children, thereby freeing parents—especially women—to take up remunerated employment and increasing the probability that they will accrue rights in the social security system. Only in Mexico is the anecdotal preference for (male) children as insurance against destitution in old age—the most frequently cited traditional old-age security arrangement— borne out by the data. In Mexico a larger share of male children in the household significantly lowers the likelihood that workers contribute to the pension system.

The failure to find evidence of traditional arrangements substituting for formal institutions, however, may be more a consequence of the poor proxy variables available in the existing data to capture these arrangements and other factors effecting demand for formal coverage and the choice to participate. Without quantitative data on the role played by children and elderly people in the household economy, and qualitative data on the expected/desired number of children of each gender, or the motivation for having larger families, it is difficult to detect and test the significance of traditional retirement security arrangements. Analysis conducted in background papers for this book using recently collected data from surveys focused on risk, savings, and social insurance in Chile and in Peru shows that these and other factors significantly determine individual and household demand for formal coverage, and that when taken into account they render most of the access variables discussed above statistically insignificant.

Do Low Participation Rates Reflect Lack of Demand?

The analysis presented in the last section, taken from Packard, Shinkai, and Fuentes (2002), placed greater emphasis on factors affecting access to formal coverage in Latin America. This is primarily the result of the limitations of regularly deployed household surveys in most of the countries in the region. For example, among the variables available it is difficult to find data on asset holdings that may be preferred as alternative forms of retirement savings. Few surveys ask about access to credit, thereby hindering examination of the effects of capital constraints on consumption-smoothing behavior. Furthermore, there are few qualitative data on the role played by resident elderly people in the household or the motivation for having children. Surveys deployed recently in Chile (where individual retirement accounts have been in place for the longest period of time) and Peru (the second country in Latin America to introduce individual retirement accounts) correct these limitations and allow a fuller analysis of factors affecting individuals' decisions whether to participate in government-mandated retirement security systems (see box 8.1).

Before presenting the results of the PRIESO surveys (social risk management surveys), it is important to review the set of instruments for retirement income security that the governments in Chile and Peru either provide directly, mandate, or regulate. Table 8.2 presents the features of the reformed pension systems in both countries discussed in chapter 2, and provides additional relevant information that will help readers put into context the econometric results reported in this section.

The reformed pension systems in the two countries are similar. In both countries dedicated private pension fund managers invest workers' accumulated savings in individually owned retirement savings accounts. Employee participation is mandatory, but the self-employed freely choose whether to participate in the formal system. Part of workers' contributions pay for the services of the fund managers as well as the premiums for privately provided life and disability insurance.

Although the reformed systems are similar, crucial differences are also apparent. It is most important to an analysis of individual and household savings and insurance behavior that workers who choose to participate in

Box 8.1 PRIESO: Social Risk Management Surveys in Chile and Peru

Until recently, analysis of participation in the reformed retirement security systems in Latin America has been constrained by the limitations of regularly deployed household surveys. Several previously unavailable variables used in background analysis for this book were constructed from data collected in specially designed surveys on risk, savings, and social insurance (in Spanish, *Encuestas de Previsión de Riesgos Sociales*— PRIESO) conducted first in Santiago, Chile, in January 2000 and repeated in Lima, Peru, in May 2002. The PRIESO surveys are specifically designed to identify the strategies taken by households to mitigate risks to income. In addition to traditional questions dealing with household composition, income, and labor market activity, the surveys elicit respondents' opinions of the reformed pension systems, their preferences for alternative retirement security strategies, their access to credit, perceptions of their own mortality, income shocks, and strategies for coping with risk.

Although both surveys were limited to a sample of workers from the largest metropolitan region of each country, the results in several instances reflect national statistics. For example, among the sample of workers in Santiago who are affiliated with the pension system, only 62 percent were making contributions at the time of the survey, approximately the same contribution level found by Edwards and Cox-Edwards (2000a) using nationally representative data. Among working men, 64 percent were contributing. Only 58 percent of working women made contributions; and 42 percent of the women of working age who were neither working nor searching for a job received some coverage from the system through the contributions of a spouse, leaving 58 percent of this cohort without formal coverage.

The PRIESO protocol includes questions never previously asked combined with more traditional questions on household composition and labor market activity. For instance, the surveys include a wide range of questions about informal instruments to mitigate poverty in old age, and about how these instruments might substitute or complement the formal pension system. The data collected in the PRIESO surveys thus provide an important empirical resource to buttress an area of research that has largely relied on qualitative and anecdotal evidence.

To illustrate that point, two questions were posed to capture whether and how parents expected their children to care for them in their old age. Even a casual analysis of responses from Chile shows the rural/urban disparities frequently referred to in the literature on informal intrahousehold risk management (Alderman and Paxson 1992; Hoddinott 1992; Deaton 1991, 1997; Cox, Eser, and Jimenez 1998). Although 47 percent of

---

Box 8.1 (continued)

respondents from rural areas expected to live with a son or a daughter in their old age, only 19 percent of urban respondents held the same expectation. Similarly, rural respondents seemed more confident that they would receive some sort of care from their children, with 67 percent giving an affirmative response and only 14 percent unsure. Only 17 percent of rural respondents did not expect to be cared for by their children. Urban respondents, on the other hand, were more evenly distributed between those who anticipated care from their children (34 percent), those who did not (30 percent), and those who did not know (19 percent). When asked why they did not expect either a son or daughter to care for them (28 percent of all respondents), the answer most frequently given was that they did not want to become a burden. In formal econometric analysis workers who expected to either reside with or otherwise receive care from their children were significantly less likely to contribute to the formal pension system than were those who did not expect to be cared for (Packard 2002).

Readers can find more details on the PRIESO surveys (sample questionnaires, survey field reports, and sampling techniques) in Chile and Peru in Packard (2002) and Barr and Packard (2002a, 2003), online at Web page of the Office of the Chief Economist, Latin America and the Caribbean Region: www.worldbank.org/keepingthepromise, or bancomundial.org/cumpliendolapromesa.

---

the formal retirement security system in Peru are allowed to choose between a downsized public PAYG plan and private individual accounts for their earnings-related pensions. Furthermore, although workers' retirement security in Chile is underpinned by poverty prevention benefits—both a pension guarantee for workers who have made a minimum number of contributions and a targeted (but rationed) social assistance benefit to elderly, indigent people—neither type of public pooling instrument to prevent poverty is available to the majority of workers affiliated with the reformed pension system in Peru (see box 8.2).

In analyzing the coverage of an old-age income security system—especially the demand for coverage—a revealing *choice* variable is an individual's period of contributions to the pension system as a share of his or her life as part of the labor force—or the *density* of his or her contributions. This measure has long been unavailable to researchers in developing countries, even those countries in Latin America that have introduced individual accounts.[7,8] Respondents to the PRIESO surveys were asked the month and year that they first contributed to the social security system.

Table 8.2 Reformed Pension Systems in Chile and Peru Are
Similar, but There Are Important Differences

	Chile	*Peru*
Year of reform	1981	1992–1993
Earnings-related public PAYG system?	Closed	Remains for workers who choose publicly managed second pillar
Total payroll tax rate, pre-reform (%)	33	18
Total payroll tax rate, post-reform (%)	20.0	20.5–22.0
Participation of new workers?	Mandatory	Voluntary (but workers must choose a second-pillar system: either AFPs or the downsized PAYG)
Participation of self-employed workers?	Voluntary	Voluntary
Remaining separate system for civil servants?	No	No (with exceptions for some subnational systems)
Dedicated fund managers	AFP	AFP
Contribution to AFP/IRA (% of wage)	10	8
Fees and insurance premiums (% of wage)	2.31	3.73
Switching between fund managers?	Two times annually	Once annually
Payout options	Annuity or scheduled withdrawal	Annuity or scheduled withdrawal
Minimum return on investment?	Relative to average	Relative to average
Minimum contributory pension?	Yes	Only for affiliates of PAYG and of the AFP system who were born before 1945
Social assistance pension ?	Yes	No

Note: IRA individual retirement account.
Source: Authors' compilation.

They were then asked to estimate the total period (in years and months) during which they had failed to contribute for whatever reason—inactivity, unemployment, employment without a contract, or self-employment—since they started. A "contribution density" variable was constructed from these responses.[9]

Box 8.2 Peru's Reformed Pension System: Multipillar in Name Only

Proponents of mandated individual retirement accounts are often unfairly accused of paying little attention to the remaining pillars of the multipillar model. However, the history of Peru's pension reform provides evidence to support this accusation. Since the December 1992 passage of the law that introduced privately managed retirement savings accounts, Peru's retirement security system has been multipillar in name only.

Peru is exceptional among recent reformers in the region for not providing a poverty prevention pension to the majority of workers who affiliated with the new system of private accounts. A first-pillar minimum pension guarantee still exists for workers affiliated with the reformed PAYG plan, and a guarantee similar to the minimum pension guarantee in Chile was put in place in July 2002 for older affiliates of the private plan. But the majority of workers covered by a formal retirement security system are not covered against poverty in old age. The failure to set up a contributory pillar is particularly worrisome because Peru does not have a social assistance benefit targeted at its elderly indigent population.

For most of Peru's workers the set of institutions put in place by structural reforms in 1992 does not yet represent a diversification of the risks to income in old age as envisioned by the reformers. Rather, it is more a transfer of the bulk of these risks from the state to households. The government is currently exploring how this imbalance can be redressed in an equitable and fiscally sustainable way.

Source: Barr and Packard (2003), available online at: www.worldbank.org/keepingthepromise.

In figure 8.1 the sample of affiliated men and women who responded to the PRIESO survey in Santiago, Chile, is divided into deciles by their contribution density. Taking eligibility for the minimum pension guaranteed by the government as the minimum level of coverage offered under the retirement security system, the required months of contribution for the guaranteed benefit (240 months, or 20 years) are divided by the average number of working months for men and women. The resulting ratio is the "contribution density threshold" that affiliates must cross to qualify for the minimum pension guarantee (the bold, horizontal axis of each graph).[10] Assuming that workers will maintain their reported rate of contribution to the system, affiliates whose contribution density places them above the threshold will qualify for (at least) the minimum level of coverage, but those below will not.[11]

Econometric analysis shows that the contribution density of workers who entered the labor market and began participating in the system after the introduction of individual accounts in 1981 is significantly greater than that of workers who began contributing prior to reforms (Packard 2002). This microeconomic evidence of an improvement in workers' incentives to participate in formal retirement security systems lends support to the country-level evidence of an improvement in incentives discussed in chapter 5. However, it is immediately apparent in figure 8.1 that a large gap in coverage remains. A greater share of affiliated women—about half—lies below the threshold of contributions necessary to qualify for the minimum pension guarantee. Although this raises concern, many of these women may be entitled to some benefit through the current and past contributions of a husband. What is particularly worrying is that if we assume no change in workers' current contribution behavior, 30 percent of *affiliated* men are unlikely to qualify for the minimum benefit. Readers should also note that the PRIESO in Chile is only representative of greater metropolitan Santiago, and thus is likely to understate the shortfall in regular contributions reported in national surveys that include less-industrial rural

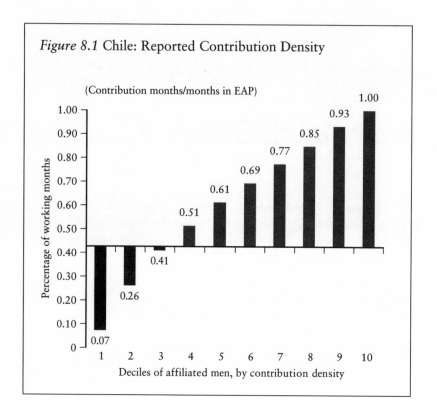

Figure 8.1 Chile: Reported Contribution Density

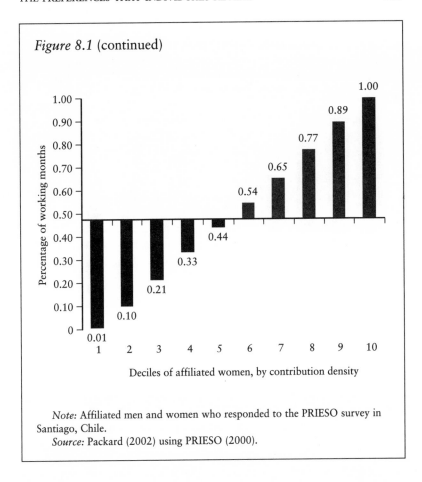

Figure 8.1 (continued)

Note: Affiliated men and women who responded to the PRIESO survey in Santiago, Chile.
Source: Packard (2002) using PRIESO (2000).

areas where access to the pension system is relatively limited. Indeed, a national survey of affiliates based on the PRIESO and conducted by the Chilean government reveals that average contribution density among affiliates of the pension system is significantly lower.

Additionally, because preferences for time and risk are fundamental to the decision to insure and to save, particular attention was paid to collecting and analyzing empirical measures of risk aversion and time preference. In a background paper for this book, Barr and Packard (2002a) analyzed how time and risk preferences determine contribution behaviors among a subsample of respondents to the PRIESO in Chile. The results of experimental techniques used to measure individuals' aversion to risk are presented in figures 8.2 and 8.3.

The first point to note is that although people who start their own business are often thought to have a greater tolerance for risk, there are no

Figure 8.2 There Is No Difference in Risk Preferences between Employees and Self-Employed Workers
Who Responded to the PRIESO Survey in Chile

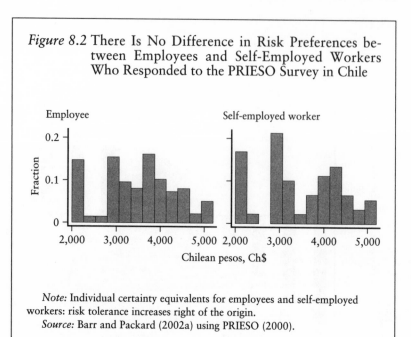

Note: Individual certainty equivalents for employees and self-employed
workers: risk tolerance increases right of the origin.
Source: Barr and Packard (2002a) using PRIESO (2000).

significant differences in risk preferences between self-employed workers
and wage employees in the PRIESO sample in Chile. This finding indicates
that self-employed people are of particular interest when studying contribution behavior, given that in Chile as in other countries in the region self-
employed workers are allowed to freely choose whether to contribute. Because they are free to reveal their preferences with respect to the pension
system although wage employees are explicitly constrained by the mandate to contribute, and because no significant difference in the relevant
preference indicator (in this case, risk aversion) can be found, inferences
can be drawn about the behaviors of all workers from the contribution decisions of those who are self-employed.[12] Furthermore, as shown in figure
8.3, despite the assumption that the formal pension system is the only
source of insurance against poverty in old age, the authors found that self-
employed contributors to the pension system—those workers in Chile
who are completely free to manifest their preference with respect to
retirement saving—are significantly more tolerant of risk than the self-
employed workers who choose not to contribute to the AFP system. This
suggests that the Chilean pension system may be viewed with some trepi-
dation by workers considering whether to contribute. This may be because
those who are more risk averse prefer to rely on alternative forms of
retirement income security, or may be deterred by the financial risks associated with the capital markets in which retirement savings are invested

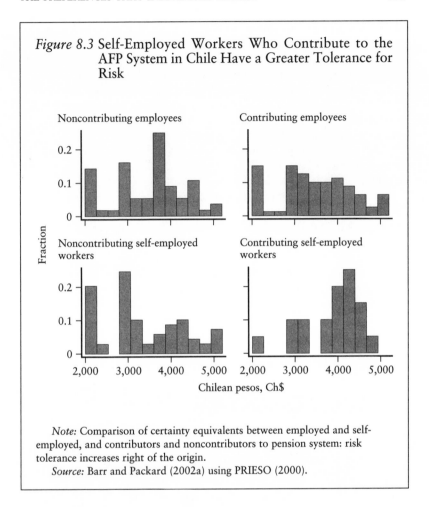

Figure 8.3 Self-Employed Workers Who Contribute to the AFP System in Chile Have a Greater Tolerance for Risk

Note: Comparison of certainty equivalents between employed and self-employed, and contributors and noncontributors to pension system: risk tolerance increases right of the origin.

Source: Barr and Packard (2002a) using PRIESO (2000).

under the reformed system. Alternatively, these potential clients may be poorly informed about the system and the performance of the private fund managers.

Packard (2002) took the analysis of savings and insurance preferences in Chile a step farther, using a wider range of variables from the PRIESO survey, including the risk and time preference measures, in contribution regressions similar to those presented in the last section to capture the impact of household preferences and alternative investments. The expectation of care from children and the amount spent on their education significantly lower the likelihood of contribution to the system. Investments in tools and machinery also lower the likelihood of contribution to the system.

By including the contribution history variable shown in figure 8.1 in the analysis of the contribution behaviors of all workers (not just those who are self-employed), we are able to separate the public risk pooling element of the Chilean pension system (the minimum pension guarantee) from the dominant private savings element and find evidence of portfolio behavior among the sample of affiliates. Workers who have met the contributory requirements to qualify for the minimum government-guaranteed retirement pension by contributing for at least 20 years are significantly less likely to continue contributing to the AFP system. The likelihood that these workers make additional contributions beyond the eligibility threshold decreases as the rental value of their homes increases.

Finally, after taking account of alternative strategies and investments for retirement security as well as workers' contribution histories, the earlier finding that individuals with a greater tolerance for risk contribute to the pension system is confirmed. This suggests that there are retirement investments in Chile that are perceived as relatively less risky than saving in the reformed pension system. The results provide evidence that housing, household enterprise, and even the education of children are among the alternative investments being pursued by individuals.

It is important to note that including this wider range of variables in the analysis of contribution behavior in Chile renders most of the "access" variables—found to be significant in table 8.1 in the last section—

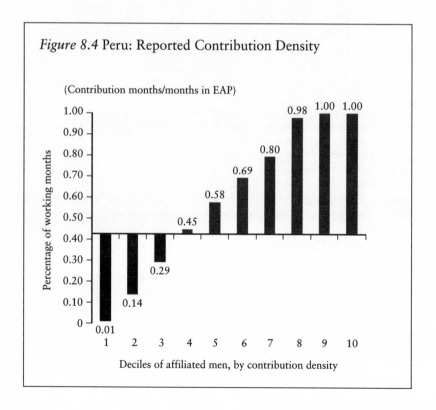

Figure 8.4 Peru: Reported Contribution Density

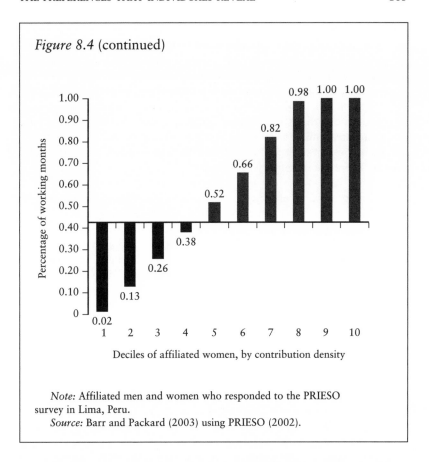

Figure 8.4 (continued)

Deciles of affiliated women, by contribution density

Note: Affiliated men and women who responded to the PRIESO survey in Lima, Peru.

Source: Barr and Packard (2003) using PRIESO (2002).

statistically insignificant to the likelihood that men participate in the pension system. Thus levels of participation in the retirement security system in Chile are likely to reflect relatively low household demand for the system as a savings and investment vehicle. That said, there are still significant barriers to women's participation in the pension system, related primarily to the size and place of employment and their (lack of) contractual relationship with employers.

The second PRIESO survey was conducted in May 2002 with a representative sample of working individuals in Lima, Peru, where since the introduction of the multipillar model workers choose between alternative forms of government-mandated coverage for the earnings-related (second pillar) portion of their pensions. As described earlier, since the reform was implemented every new cohort of workers in Peru chooses between individual accounts and the reformed public PAYG plan. (The same system exists in Argentina and Colombia, although in Colombia workers can choose every three years.) Figure 8.4 plots contribution densities calculated from the history of contributions of men and women in the PRIESO sample who are affiliated with either branch of Peru's retirement security system. Although very similar to the contribution densities of affiliated workers in Chile (shown in figure 8.1), noteworthy differences are apparent.

In figure 8.4 the bold, horizontal axis represents the threshold density of contributions that would be necessary to qualify for a minimum pension guarantee similar to Chile's guarantee. However, as discussed in box 8.2, Peru does not offer a first-pillar benefit to younger affiliates of its AFP system. There are three main differences:

1. Twenty percent of men and women affiliated with Peru's pension system have a perfect (1.00) contribution density. Although there is only a small sample of countries in Latin America that have introduced individual accounts, a drop in the share of regular contributors among affiliates of the new systems is found to be common over time. Thus the large share of affiliates with perfect contribution density relative to Chile may simply reflect a younger system.

2. A greater share of affiliated women in Peru (60 percent) than in Chile would be likely to fulfill the contributory requirements to receive a minimum pension guarantee. Furthermore, those women whose contributions fall short of the threshold would be closer to qualifying for the minimum benefit than would affiliated women in the same contribution decile in Chile.

3. The coverage gap—measured by contribution density below the minimum eligibility threshold—for affiliated men in Peru is worse. As in Chile, 30 percent of affiliated men from the PRIESO sample would not be likely to meet the contribution requirements to qualify for the minimum level of coverage. However, the 30 percent of affiliated men whose contributions fall short in Peru have greater shortfall to make up.

As is true in Chile the data on contribution history affirm the policy shift away from pure public PAYG pooling and toward some private saving, and they indicate that the introduction of individual accounts led to an improvement in the incentives to participate in Peru's pension system. Among workers who were affiliated with the national retirement security system before the introduction of individual retirement accounts, those who switched to the AFP system have a significantly (at 1 percent confidence level) greater contribution density than those who remained affiliated with the reformed PAYG system. Furthermore, even among workers who affiliated after 1993 when the pension reform came into full effect, those who chose the AFP system over the reformed PAYG have a greater density of contributions.

Turning to the measures of risk preference gathered in Peru (presented in figures 8.5 and 8.6), as was found in Chile there is no significant differ-

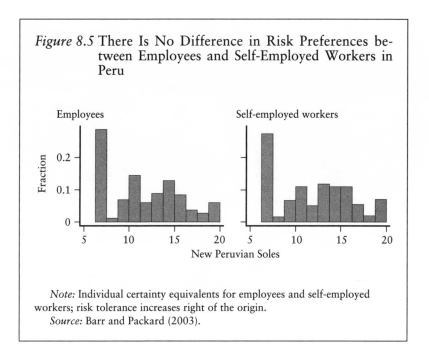

Figure 8.5 There Is No Difference in Risk Preferences between Employees and Self-Employed Workers in
Peru

Note: Individual certainty equivalents for employees and self-employed
workers; risk tolerance increases right of the origin.
Source: Barr and Packard (2003).

ence in the risk preferences between employees and self-employed workers.
Unlike the situation in Chile, however, self-employed workers with a
greater aversion to risk contribute to Peru's retirement security system.
Among contributing self-employed people, those most averse to risk choose
the private branch of the pension system and make contributions into an
individual retirement account.

Two sets of choices can be analyzed: the choice to switch from the public to the private system made by workers affiliated prior to 1993, and the
choice of one branch of the system over another made by individuals joining the labor market for the first time since 1993, namely, those workers
for whom competing public and private options existed the first time they
made a choice with respect to the formal retirement security system.

Among workers affiliated with the pension system prior to reforms,
those who switched to the private system after 1993 have a significantly
greater aversion to risk than those who stayed (although the statistical significance of this result is very weak). Furthermore, among individuals who
affiliated after the introduction of individual accounts in 1993, those with
a greater aversion to risk also chose the private AFP system over the reformed PAYG still administered by the government. The inverse also
holds. Among affiliates who joined the system after reforms, those who
contribute to the public PAYG branch have a significantly greater tolerance for risk.

Figure 8.6 Self-Employed People in the AFP System in Peru Are More Risk Averse

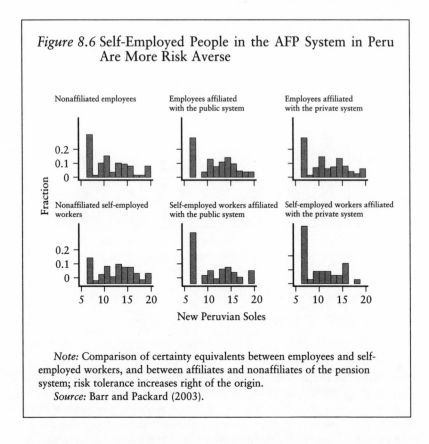

Note: Comparison of certainty equivalents between employees and self-employed workers, and between affiliates and nonaffiliates of the pension system; risk tolerance increases right of the origin.
Source: Barr and Packard (2003).

What of those workers who do not contribute to either branch of the formal pension system in Peru? As in Chile investment in housing and other residential property acts as a substitute for the formal retirement savings system, despite weakly enforced property rights in Lima. Workers for whom the mandate to save is not binding hold the greater share of their accumulated assets in the form of housing. Additionally, the greater the share of children in their households, the less likely workers are to contribute to the formal pension system. If investment in housing and children can be considered substitute strategies for securing well-being in old age, workers' participation decisions are rational and consistent.[13]

Although there is no minimum pension guarantee in Peru's AFP system, the cutoff in workers' contributions to the pension system is similar to that observed among workers who cross the eligibility threshold for the guarantee in Chile. The missing first pillar in Peru limits the conclusions that can be drawn and the comparisons that can be made with results from Chile, but this behavior could reveal perceived falling marginal returns to workers' investment in the formal pension system and a preference for greater diversification among saving options.

Implications of Household-Level Analysis: The Preferences Individuals Reveal

Public interventions to help households mitigate loss of earnings ability and poverty in old age—and other adverse shocks to income over the life cycle—are a relatively new phenomenon even in industrial countries. In most developing countries the majority of households still rely on mechanisms that lie in the private domain—provided formally through the market or informally though family and social networks. However, evidence that investments for income security that require cohesive social networks are increasingly less reliable (Deaton 1991; Hayashi, Altonji, and Kotlikoff 1996) indicates that a role for government clearly exists. That said, it is important in assuming this role that careful attention is paid to complement and not distort private choices or to displace private options.

Latin America's experience with overly generous guarantees from poorly managed social security institutions that privileged a relatively small, select group at an unsustainable cost to the majority of households provides an example of what policymakers should seek to avoid. It is often argued that failing formal public institutions have caused the majority of workers to turn away from social security. Pension reforms that introduced the multipillar system, based primarily on individual retirement accounts, were intended to bring workers back to the formal economy by increasing incentives to contribute. Evidence presented in this book suggests these reforms have had a positive impact on worker participation.[14]

Despite the positive impact of reforms, policymakers still have cause for concern. Although reforms have increased the incentives to contribute, the low share of regular contributors in the labor force provides the best argument against complacency. The empirical evidence summarized in this chapter suggests that although reforms to social security were intended to sever the link between coverage and a worker's sector or place of employment, barriers to access remain. Across the region certain segments of the working population may still be excluded. Binding minimum-wage legislation, tenure-based employment security provisions, overly regulated product markets, or even the transaction costs of affiliation and contribution to the pension system could increase the costs of participation for small businesses above what they can afford to remain in operation. If structural reforms to the social security system and to related institutions succeed in eliminating explicit barriers to participation (e.g., conditioning access on employment in a certain industry or sector), remaining implicit barriers (primarily to do with transaction costs) may be lowered as reformed systems become more efficient.

However, the data on contributors to government-administered and/or
-mandated pension systems ignore other forms of insurance and savings
that individuals and households may engage in on their own, and thus can
overstate the degree of vulnerability to the loss of earnings ability and the
risk of poverty in old age. Because the actions households take to secure
income in retirement mostly lie outside government-mandated systems (reliance on family, private savings, house purchases, and take-up of private
insurance policies) and are not reflected in participation rates, the truly
"vulnerable" population—households that really are facing the likelihood
of poverty in old age—is probably smaller than that reflected in official
statistics.

More households may be covering themselves and securing an adequate
retirement income. For this reason it is important to take account of alternative assets, savings, and insurance in the widely applied simulation
analysis of retirement savings in developing countries where data are available, and to collect these data where not available. Although some barriers to access remain even after structural reforms, the analysis presented in
this chapter, using new data on private savings and insurance and the retirement investments preferred by households, indicates that researchers
and policymakers concerned with low rates of participation should focus
relatively less on issues of social exclusion and relatively more on the factors affecting household demand for formal coverage.

The results of our analysis of PRIESO data from Chile indicate that
with respect to individual preferences the Chilean pension system may be
overly engineered. Workers seem to be using a system intended to act primarily as a vehicle for savings—with a small pooling component—primarily as a risk pooling device. Each cohort of workers that completes the
minimum required months of contributions to the system may be content
to receive the government's pension guarantee. Given the modest amount
of the guarantee (which has averaged between 80 percent and 90 percent
of the minimum wage in the last 10 years), one would hope that these
workers would continue to save or invest for retirement outside the
system. Contrary to the default assumption of worker irrationality, the
evidence drawn from the PRIESO survey in Chile suggests that many do,
because the likelihood of further contribution to the pension system is
lower as the market value of affiliates' property increases.

Several researchers have attributed the fall in regular contribution after 20 years to rational moral hazard because simulations will show that
for lower-income workers every additional contribution above the
threshold necessary to qualify for the minimum pension benefit is a pure
tax (Vittas 1996; Cox-Edwards 2000; Edwards and Cox-Edwards 2000a;
James, Cox-Edwards, and Wong 2003).[15] It is important to point out that
the portfolio behavior apparent among affiliates of the pension system in
Chile is seen not among the working poor (for whom the rational moral
hazard explanation applies) but among respondents in the fifth income

decile and higher. When they have contributed for 20 years, affiliates have the right to the minimum benefit—the pension system's remaining public pooling instrument—but only if they suffer a dramatic fall in their accumulated assets and actually need it, because eligibility is also means-tested. Given their likely lifetime earnings, many workers will not qualify. Each contribution to the AFP system above the eligibility threshold for the minimum pension guarantee is purely a form of savings for this group. If affiliates perceive the AFP system to be a relatively risky, costly, and illiquid savings instrument, it comes as little surprise that they manifest a preference for alternative, voluntary forms of savings (such as housing and life insurance programs) when they have secured the guaranteed minimum annuity.

Furthermore, the analysis from Chile indicates not only that households save outside the mandated system—but also that with regard to the portion of their retirement portfolios the government has mandated, they may place a relatively greater value on security than on real rates of return. In Chile those workers who freely choose to contribute to the system show a significantly higher tolerance for risk. Households are content to gain eligibility for the low, government-guaranteed annuity and continue to save outside the system, despite the variable but high real returns they could earn in the system.[16]

In Peru, on the other hand, workers averse to risk choose the private AFP system over the government's reformed PAYG option. Rather than contradicting the findings from Chile, however, the result may reveal a similar preference for security when set against data indicating that private financial institutions are trusted more than all three branches of the Peruvian government (Barr and Packard 2003). Given recent revelations of systemic corruption in Peru's public institutions and the events leading to the ouster of the Fujimori regime, these findings may not be surprising. Furthermore, the relative youth of the new pension system, the failure of Peru's government to effectively implement the promised minimum pension guarantee for workers who choose private individual accounts, and the lack of secure third-pillar instruments are likely to lead to very different patterns of saving and investment behavior than that seen in Chile. Despite precarious property rights in Peru relative to Chile, however, there is evidence of workers replacing investment in the pension system with investment in housing and other residential property.

Conclusion

Contrary to the assumption often made by policymakers with respect to retirement security, the results presented from Chile and Peru indicate that workers make rational choices. The results from Chile—where individual retirement accounts have been in place for more than 20 years—suggest that what households may be seeking from a government-mandated instrument is a greater degree of security relative to the retirement investments that they undertake freely. This may also indicate that when a social safety net to prevent households from falling into poverty in old age (either because of an exogenous shock or their own improvidence) is in place and reflects the particular degree of redistribution valued in that society, mandating private savings should be considered a largely transitory policy device.

Publicly mandated but privately owned and managed individual retirement savings may be most effective as a transition institution to substitute for missing or inadequate instruments until private capital markets can provide efficiently priced savings and insurance vehicles. In the longer term the role of the state in mitigating loss of earnings ability and poverty in old age may be reduced to protecting households against systemic shocks to which private insurance cannot respond (such as inflation, through privately traded indexed instruments), and ensuring that a retirement income safety net, financed with pooled tax payments, is securely in place. Further investigation of the level at which such a safety net should be placed so as to effectively protect households from improvidence and governments from moral hazard and a Samaritan's dilemma is sorely needed.

In the medium term the optimal role of governments concerned with mitigating the loss of earnings ability and the risk of poverty in old age may be to spend less on trying to increase compliance with the mandate to save and more on ensuring that the economic and regulatory conditions enable markets to offer a greater array of secure, voluntary private savings and insurance instruments. In the relatively developed, middle-income countries of Latin America where households are already engaging in strategic portfolio behavior and where sophisticated savings and insurance products are increasingly available at competitive prices, mandating a particular form of private savings instrument can present a new set of distortions. A government-mandated savings instrument offered by a small number of dedicated private providers may produce adverse effects on the supply of private and potentially more competitive alternatives.

Notes

1. The distinction among the appropriate instruments to mitigate investment versus longevity risk is discussed in chapter 10.

2. The importance of indirect government intervention (such as the regulation of private providers of contractual savings and the provision of inflation-indexed securities) is also addressed in chapter 10.

3. These traditional strategies can take the form of larger families or preferences for male offspring, especially in agricultural economies and in labor markets whose wage structure discriminates against women (Hoddinott 1992). Furthermore, there is ample evidence that households still rely heavily on reciprocal relationships within

the extended family; remittances arising from rural-to-urban and international migration of household members (Hoddinott 1992); strategic marriage arrangements; intrahousehold arrangements; establishment of a portfolio of assets with uncorrelated risks; purchase of livestock or jewelry; forward sale of agricultural crops (Alderman and Paxson 1992); and community-based credit systems.

4. Of course this argument rests on the strong assumption that governments are less likely to default on public pension promises. A fair counterargument is that most purely public PAYG systems in Latin America were bankrupt prior to reforms, and the likelihood of government default on its public pension promises made workers' investment in the pre-reform systems just as risky if not more so.

5. As described in Packard, Shinkai, and Fuentes (2002), specification tests strongly (at the 1 percent level) rejected pooling the data from the different countries into a single regression.

6. Several recent publications have focused on whether individuals are queuing for formal employment in Latin America (see Maloney 1998a, 1998b, 1999, 2000, 2003). Contrary to a large body of literature on labor markets in developing countries, these studies found little evidence that self-employment is the residual sector. Data on transitions in and out of the labor market and across sectors in Argentina, Brazil, Chile, and Mexico show that movement into self-employment is more consistent with an entrepreneurial "pull" than the popular notion that workers are "pushed" out of formal jobs into small enterprise. However, informal wage employment often does exhibit many of the characteristics of a residual employment safety net. Individuals in this branch of the informal sector are often indistinguishable in their age and education from the unemployed population. In Chile informal employees are more likely to have a greater number of dependents as parents and heads of household than those still searching for a job, and thus are more likely to take up informal employment out of greater income necessity. This raises the concern that informal employers may be unwilling to incur the costs of "formalizing" their workers by providing access to the national retirement security system.

7. Ironically, although a worker's density of contributions is relatively more important in assessing whether he or she is covered in a defined contribution system than under a purely PAYG regimen, the private and decentralized structure of the reformed system in Chile has made data on contribution history unavailable to government researchers interested in exploring contribution patterns. The private fund management industry resisted earlier efforts for the government to gain access to these data, even successfully arguing their case in Chile's courts. The government has found a second-best avenue around this obstacle by surveying a random sample of AFP affiliates. The nationally representative data on affiliates will soon be available to researchers.

8. Cox-Edwards (2000) and James, Cox-Edwards, and Wong (2003) used cross-section survey data to estimate longitudinal patterns of contributory behavior and wages. Because information on years of contributions was previously unavailable, the researchers were forced to create synthetic cohorts to estimate years of contributions. They found that men typically accumulate 40 years' worth of contributions from the age of 16 to 65. Women tend to have more interruptions, especially women with lower levels of education.

9. Contribution density is constructed by first calculating respondents' history of contributions in months and dividing that number by their number of months in the labor force, using the Mincer (1974) formula for labor market experience: (age minus years of education minus 5). For further details see Packard (2002).

10. Eligibility for the minimum pension guarantee in Chile is not only determined by a minimum contribution requirement, but also by an income test. However, poor elderly people who have not contributed for at least 20 years can only

receive the noncontributory social assistance pension, roughly equal to 50 percent of the contributory minimum pension guarantee.

11. The contribution densities shown are a cross-section. Affiliates of different ages are grouped together by contribution density. However, it is likely that workers may increase their contribution density as they age, and even as they approach retirement age. However, plotting contribution densities by age does not reveal a clearly increasing pattern. Regression analysis shows that affiliates may even perceive diminishing marginal returns from contributions, leading many to slow their contributions well before retirement age.

12. There is also no difference in time preferences between employees and self-employed workers. Furthermore, self-employed contributors to the pension system show lower rates of time preference, as traditional life-cycle consumption and savings theory would suggest, thereby validating the techniques used to gather the data.

13. However, the security of investments in housing depends greatly on securing property rights; and the ease with which wealth held in physical assets can be used to finance consumption will depend on the functioning of the market for land and real estate. Neither can be taken for granted in a developing country like Peru. Furthermore, the prevalent mode of investing in children may become an unreliable source of income security in old age because of greater migration, urbanization, and the resulting dispersion of family groups. As an additional note of caution, although respondents are behaving in a manner consistent with their current preferences, this is no guarantee that these preferences will remain stable with age or over time.

14. However, the results presented cannot be used as evidence that a transition to private individual retirement accounts is the *only* way to improve incentives and achieve greater rates of participation. A similar improvement in incentives may arise from aligning contributions and benefits within a PAYG system—as with the establishment of notional defined contribution (NDC) retirement accounts in several Eastern European countries. In Latin America, although not an NDC reform strictly speaking, only Brazil has chosen to align benefits and contributions while maintaining the PAYG financing structure of its retirement security system. Not enough time has passed since the Brazilian reform in 1999 for a conclusive analysis of its impact on incentives to be made. The analyses in background papers written for this book indicate that workers respond to improvements in incentives to contribute to formal retirement security systems. To the extent that public social security institutions in developing countries lack credibility, and that privately managed, individually owned retirement savings are perceived as wholly owned, the impact on participation brought about by a transition to private individual retirement accounts may be greater than adjustments in the parameters of PAYG systems. Time will tell as more evidence becomes available.

15. Simulation analysis conducted in the past (Edwards and Cox-Edwards 2000a; Cox-Edwards 2000) indicates that the minimum pension guarantee in Chile may be set too high relative to average income and may foster moral hazard among workers with lower lifetime earnings. The analysis in Packard (2002), however, shows that meeting the minimum contribution requirement for the guaranteed benefit has no significant effect on the contributory behavior of workers in the fourth income decile and below. On the other hand, workers in the fifth income decile and above who become eligible for the minimum guaranteed annuity are less likely to continue contributing. The likelihood of additional contributions is lowered even more as the market value of their homes rises.

16. There is an interesting alternative interpretation of workers' observed behavior. A saver's risk does not stem solely from the risk in the investment opportunities. The risk of unforeseen cash needs is also important. Thus a risk-tolerant

worker accepts a larger amount of liquidity risk. Middle-income workers may cease contributing to the second pillar after completing 20 years because the size of the second-pillar replacement rate they have accumulated by then (say, 30 percent) is adequate for their needs (and is optimal given the illiquidity of second-pillar savings). Middle-income workers may value the minimum pension because it is a subsidy they can access by choosing programmed withdrawal and living longer (the programmed withdrawal pension falls with survival, but the state subsidizes a floor). High-income workers have a tax motive to stop contributing for 20 years: second-pillar pensions are subject to the income tax, whereas profits from the holding and sale of houses are exempt—and profits in other investments can be hidden by creative accounting. We are grateful to Salvador Valdés-Prieto for pointing this out. As in the first interpretation, however, the weight of this alternative interpretation rests on a greater assumed rationality and informed choice on the part of affiliates rather than on the default assumption of irrationality so prevalent in the pension policy literature, and would justify only a minimal mandate to save.

III

Prospective:
The Future of Social
Security in Latin America

9

Preventing Poverty in Old Age: Improving the Pooling Component

HISTORICALLY, GOVERNMENT-ORGANIZED (mandated and/or administered) retirement security systems have been designed with two complementary functions in mind: maintaining levels of consumption in retirement by replacing a portion of individuals' incomes when they are no longer able to work, and preventing widespread poverty among elderly people by fixing an income floor below which covered workers will not fall. In the past two decades social security reforms in Latin America and elsewhere have focused mainly on restructuring the *income replacement function* of pension systems, whereas the *poverty prevention function* (once explicitly identified and separated into a first or even a zero pillar) has not received the attention it deserves. In fact, this component should be the main attraction of a social security system, not a sideshow. Building on the evidence and reasoning in earlier chapters, this chapter shows why the lack of attention to this core component of government policy is a serious mistake.

Government's Essential Role: Preventing Poverty Among Elderly People

In earlier chapters we saw how changing economic fundamentals imply the growing importance of saving over pooling for income replacement in retirement where longevity is increasing (although some degree of pooling through the purchase of annuities is appropriate to cover longevity risk among members of roughly the same age cohort).[1]

Figure 9.1 shows how longevity is likely to evolve in selected Latin American countries, providing an empirical basis for this shift in policy

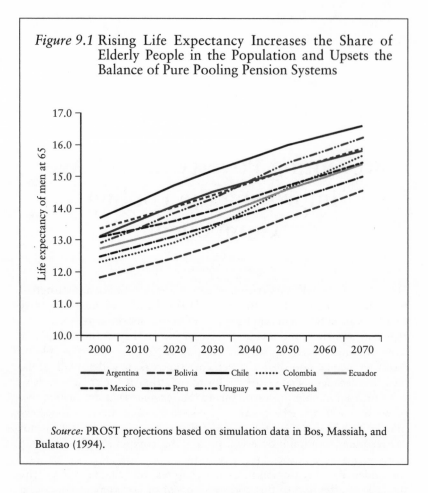

Figure 9.1 Rising Life Expectancy Increases the Share of Elderly People in the Population and Upsets the Balance of Pure Pooling Pension Systems

Source: PROST projections based on simulation data in Bos, Massiah, and Bulatao (1994).

with the passage of time: the average 65-year-old man is likely to live almost 20 percent longer in 2050 than he did in 2000. With the loss of earnings ability while living becoming more frequent, countries that still rely on traditional "defined benefit" systems will experience strong fiscal pressures to reform.

In contrast, as countries develop, poverty among the elderly portion of the population should become increasingly rare relative to poverty among other age groups. Table 9.1 shows head-count poverty rates for selected Latin American countries calculated using income reported in household surveys. The incidence of poverty among elderly people by this measure can actually be significantly greater than among the population as a whole. Indeed, in 11 out of the 19 countries shown in table 9.1 this is the case, seemingly contradicting our assertion that poverty among old men and women should be relatively rare.

The numbers, however, often fail to capture wealth.[2] When the value of accumulated assets is taken into account (see figure 9.2 using data from the PRIESO survey in Lima, Peru), elderly people are somewhat better off. In the context of economic development, all else being equal, average life-time incomes should rise, the opportunities to save and accumulate assets should increase, and poverty among the elderly population (measured in wealth—accumulated assets) should become even more rare. In a review of poverty among elderly men and women in 44 countries—largely wealthier, industrial countries—Whitehouse (2000) found that although the incomes of elderly people are 80 percent of the incomes of the population as a whole, these people are not typically poor. Old people are either represented proportionately or underrepresented among the poor population.

For this reason minimum PAYG benefits need not be justified on the basis of solidarity. As a relatively rare loss, risk pooling is the most appropriate and efficient insurance mechanism to mitigate poverty in old age. To the extent that poverty among old people is increasingly rare, and effective targeting instruments are in place to accurately measure household wealth, a social insurance mechanism to keep elderly men and women out of poverty should become more affordable. Obviously, in making this argument the legal and financial institutions that protect property rights and allow households to convert illiquid assets into income for consumption in old age are critically important. The existence and efficiency of such institutions cannot be taken for granted in Latin America or elsewhere.

Over time, therefore, the rationale to pool the risk of old-age poverty has grown stronger, not weaker. Comprehensive insurance strategies imply a growing importance of the pooling pillar because it is increasingly well matched in terms of design to the risk of old-age poverty. In most cases, however, its *size* should shrink relative to the savings pillar.

It is curious that the poverty prevention function of pension systems should have been relatively ignored until quite recently and that the income replacement function should have received so much attention from policymakers and the pension specialists who advise them. After all, the public policy objectives of mandating participation in retirement security systems are to counteract individuals' improvidence and myopia during their working years and to prevent elderly poor people from becoming an economic burden on society. Although it is determined by specific social values that can vary widely from country to country, the minimum level of income required in retirement to fulfill these two policy objectives is relatively modest—certainly less than the benefits promised by pre-reform, single-pillar PAYG systems in Latin America, and often less than the level of income replacement targeted by the architects of structural reforms in the region.[3]

Indeed, the poverty prevention features of a retirement income security system should be at the center of policy discussions rather than at the

Table 9.1 Poverty among Elderly People Is as Frequent as among Other Age Groups When Measured by Current Income (Percent)

	Per capita income under $2[a]			Per capita income 50% of median[b]			Equivalent income 50% of median[c]		
	All	60+	65+	All	60+	65+	All	60+	65+
Argentina	16.64	5.29	4.49	20.71	6.40	5.22	18.60	9.48	8.48
Bolivia	46.98	47.96	50.17	28.36	30.16	31.35	27.86	36.59	38.38
Brazil	22.21	6.32	5.38	25.58	7.45	6.28	23.46	10.33	9.44
Chile	8.88	4.41	3.78	13.11	6.58	5.74	11.81	7.89	7.34
Colombia	30.37	29.91	31.19	26.57	26.43	27.61	25.75	29.20	30.79
Costa Rica	11.75	16.83	19.06	18.12	22.22	24.19	17.30	30.38	33.63
Dominican Republic	13.84	19.81	21.75	25.18	34.07	36.39	23.76	38.09	40.89
Ecuador	40.92	47.27	49.38	26.52	33.53	34.69	26.02	38.39	40.03
El Salvador	36.86	33.71	33.63	30.46	28.48	28.37	30.06	30.35	37.74
Guatemala	36.60	—	44.70	36.60	—	44.70	34.10	—	45.90
Honduras	36.58	28.89	30.28	27.45	19.91	20.87	26.81	24.27	25.67
Jamaica	17.50	17.50	18.19	26.21	24.57	26.44	25.02	29.71	32.29
Mexico	27.22	30.23	30.95	22.86	27.44	28.04	21.89	30.50	31.27
Nicaragua	38.26	31.83	32.55	20.34	15.81	16.20	19.70	18.25	18.95
Panama	21.35	18.14	17.97	22.16	18.80	18.66	20.64	21.71	21.69
Paraguay	30.21	23.32	23.22	25.91	19.40	18.60	24.46	24.35	23.92
Peru	31.80	21.90	21.56	24.70	15.78	15.24	24.17	18.32	18.69
Uruguay	1.41	0.14	0.15	21.95	6.52	5.43	17.84	8.67	7.45
Venezuela	29.52	24.98	25.28	19.95	17.36	17.49	19.69	20.85	21.18

Notes: Poverty rates for older age groups (over age 60 and 65) in selected Latin American countries; — not available.

a Per capita income equal to or less than US$2 per day.

b Per capita income equal to or less than 50 percent of median income.

c Income equal to or less than 50 percent of median income using OECD equivalence scale. OECD scale is equal to 0.5 + 0.5 × number of adults + 0.3 × number of children (age 16 or less).

Source: Bourguignon, Cicowiez, Dethier, Gasparini, and Pestieau (2004).

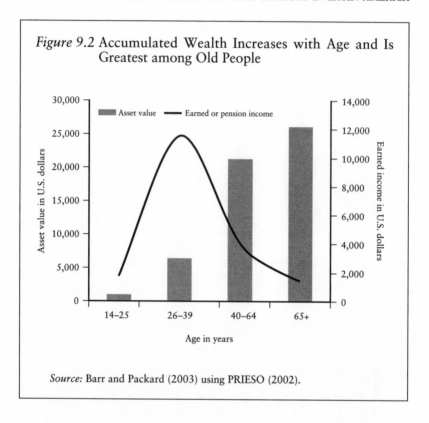

Figure 9.2 Accumulated Wealth Increases with Age and Is Greatest among Old People

Source: Barr and Packard (2003) using PRIESO (2002).

margin. When a pension system that will prevent poverty among elderly men and women at a fiscally sustainable cost is in place, government has largely fulfilled its role with respect to retirement income security and should then concentrate on ensuring the efficient and secure supply of private savings and insurance options.

In this chapter we briefly set the earnings replacement function of pension systems aside and place the poverty prevention function at center stage. We examine the emerging distinction between contributory "pillar one" and noncontributory "pillar zero" public pension benefits, using the theoretical framework employed in chapter 6. Next we describe three different options for structuring the poverty prevention pillar, drawing on international and regional experience. Finally, we present the results of simulations to show the cost of each public pooling alternative in the Latin American countries that have undertaken structural reforms to motivate a discussion of how best to structure public poverty prevention systems for elderly people.

Readers should note that we do not advocate any particular option over the rest because the optimal poverty prevention institution or set of institutions will vary widely by country, level of development, and administrative capacity. We do, however, place poverty prevention (i.e., covering the risk of poverty in old age) at the top of the list of objectives of pension policy, and we present the set of issues that policymakers should keep in mind when determining what sort of poverty prevention pillar to put in place.

Pillar Zero vs. Pillar One: Does the Distinction Matter?

Since the publication of *Averting the Old Age Crisis* (World Bank 1994), in which the basic architecture of the multipillar system of public and private pension provision was described, a curious distinction has emerged between two types of pensions still directly administered by government: *first-pillar* pensions paid to individuals with a history of contributions to an earnings-related retirement security regimen, and *zero-pillar* pensions offered universally or targeted at the elderly poor population regardless of whether they have contributed to an earnings-related pension regimen. This distinction is probably more helpful to pension specialists (who are confronted with public pension systems that, even after structural reforms, can exist alongside other transfers to elderly people) than it is to policymakers or to the individuals and households they represent. Conceptually we find the distinction unnecessary.

According to the analytical framework borrowed from the economics of insurance (presented in chapter 6), when the policy objective is to prevent poverty among elderly men and women, the distinction between a first pillar that conditions benefits on contributions and a zero pillar that pays pensions regardless of contribution history is largely political. Both pillars pool the risk of poverty in old age; both pillars are directly administered by government; both pillars are typically financed on a PAYG basis; and both pillars receive "contributions" either from payroll taxes or from other levies with a broader base such as taxes on income or on consumption.

By definition, a pooling or insurance instrument will always have fewer "losers"—those who receive a payoff from the pool if they suffer the bad state that the instrument seeks to cover—than the number who contribute to the pool. After all, there has to be a sufficient number of "winners" to compensate the "losers" or the instrument will not be able to pool risks effectively (Barr 2001). The payment to contributors who suffer the bad state may be actuarially fair, but not all contributors are guaranteed payment.

When the logic of prescribing public, defined benefit, PAYG pooling to cover the relatively rare risk of poverty in old age is accepted, and the level of pooled benefits is set with care not to upset individual and household incentives to save privately, to insist on separating a zero pillar from the first appears politically expedient at best. At worst, perpetuating a distinction between the two pillars can lead to perverse outcomes and even increase the vulnerability of the poorest segment of society.

On the one hand, public pooling PAYG systems that deny minimum pensions to individuals who lack a history of explicit contributions but that pay benefits guaranteed by government transfers, can redistribute income from all current and future taxpayers to those who have accumulated minimum pension rights. Even where the contribution and benefit parameters of pillar one are set to be "self-financing," who pays for shortfalls between benefits and contributions during economic downturns, or for indexation to protect benefits during bouts of inflation? All current and future taxpayers "contribute" to maintain the number and the value of benefits paid to a relatively smaller group of covered workers.

On the other hand, separate, seemingly noncontributory transfer arrangements to the elderly poor population are perceived as charity rather than just another instrument with which households can manage risks to income, and are often only reluctantly considered in budget allocations. Small budget allocations to "social assistance" pensions separated from the first pillar typically count on the support of small, relatively weak political constituencies, and historically have been vulnerable to budget cuts.

Options for Preventing Poverty among Elderly People

There are at least three basic alternatives for structuring the public pooled component of a government-organized retirement security system with a poverty prevention objective (Willmore 2001a). These are (1) a minimum pension guarantee or benefit top-up to workers who have contributed for a specified number of years to a retirement security regimen; (2) a benefit targeted at the elderly poor population; and (3) a universal flat pension, sometimes called a "demogrant," paid to all men and women over some threshold age, regardless of their means. In several countries these alternative poverty prevention pension structures overlap.

Each option has its particular merit, but all impose a cost. A minimum pension top-up will cover workers with low lifetime earnings who contribute to the retirement security system, and may provide some incentives for participation in the earnings-related pillar, but it leaves workers without a history of payroll contributions uncovered. A targeted pension will provide benefits to only those elderly people whose income or accumulated wealth lies below some specified level, but accurate targeting may lie beyond the capacity of many governments and can introduce poverty traps and opportunities for corruption. A universal pension covers all individuals of a certain age regardless of their income, accumulated wealth, or contribution history, but can entail considerable and even prohibitive fiscal costs.

Many countries have at least one of the three arrangements, and most countries in Latin America offer both the contributory minimum pension guarantee and an often poorly targeted benefit for the elderly poor populace. Chile's minimum pension guarantee ensures that affiliates with at least 20 years of contribution history to the pension system retire with a minimum annuity amount, which is initially financed out of the accumulated balance in the affiliate's individual account and then by the government directly when these savings are exhausted. This model has been adopted in Colombia, Mexico, and El Salvador. Mexico offers to all affiliates an additional account subsidy that has an important poverty prevention role for poorer affiliates (see box 9.1). Few countries offer a universal flat pension. We are not aware of any Latin American country other than Bolivia that offers such a plan (see box 9.2).

Judging from the conceptual discussion in the previous section, in a country where all individuals contribute to the earnings-related pension system, a contributory minimum guarantee structured as a top-up is a satisfactory public pooling arrangement: it encourages workers to save privately and guarantees a minimum level of retirement income at a minimum cost to taxpayers. As we already pointed out, however, in countries where most workers will not have a sufficiently long history of contributions to the earnings-related pension system, a top-up conditioned on a long history of participation can not only exclude large segments of the population, but also can lead to perverse transfers. Readers are reminded of the large share of affiliates in the reformed pension systems in Chile and in Peru that may not have a sufficient contribution density to qualify for the minimum pension guarantee (i.e., if this guarantee is eventually implemented for all affiliates of the private second pillar in Peru). Incentives can also be distorted if low-income workers are offered their choice of investment (as in Chile) because the pension guarantee eliminates downside risk, thereby turning high-risk investments into a one-sided bet.

Targeting public pensions at the elderly poor population is the public pooling arrangement closest to the risk pooling ideal for middle-income countries in which many workers fail to contribute regularly to an earnings-related pension pillar. This is especially true if the targeted benefit is financed with a broad-based tax, such as the value-added tax.

Means testing to target the benefit efficiently, however, comes with complications and costs. Means tests increase administrative costs and provide opportunities for corrupt behavior on the part of public officials (World Bank 1994; Willmore 2001a). Furthermore, just as overly generous social assistance benefits can lead to moral hazard, so means tests can discourage private saving and wealth accumulation for retirement (Hubbard, Skinner, and Zeldes 1993, 1994) as well as continued work in old age. Finally, as mentioned in the previous section, means-tested benefits are often regarded as charity, which reduces their political appeal, makes the benefits vulnerable to budget cuts—especially in economic downturns

Box 9.1 The *Cuota Social*: Preventing Poverty among Elderly Men and Women in Mexico

To strengthen the efficacy of Mexico's new multipillar pension system in preventing poverty among elderly men and women, the government of Mexico introduced a flat contribution subsidy along with private individual accounts in 1997. The government makes a daily payment to the individual retirement accounts of all workers affiliated with the new private defined contribution pillar whose contributions are up to date.

This contribution, called the *Cuota Social*, is commission-free and does not vary with workers' income. When the new AFORE pillar came into effect in July 1997, the *Cuota Social* was set at 5.5 percent of the minimum wage and now equals 6.05 percent, reflecting adjustments for inflation. Because all contributing affiliates of the reformed pension system in Mexico receive the same amount of *Cuota Social* contributions in their individual retirement accounts, the share of total pension contributions represented by the *Cuota Social* is inversely proportional to workers' incomes. That is, the *Cuota Social* bolsters the value of low-income workers' pension accounts more than the value of high-income workers' accounts. In fact, *Cuota Social* contributions represent more than one-quarter of the value of retirement contributions for the 68.5 percent of the Mexican workforce earning three times the minimum wage or less; it accounts for almost 55 percent of the retirement contribution for a worker earning the minimum wage.

The *Cuota Social* introduces a poverty prevention mechanism directly into the defined contribution pillar created by the Mexican pension reform of 1997. For workers earning up to three times the minimum wage the *Cuota Social* is greater than commissions charged to their individual contributions taken from wages, thereby allowing their future pension benefits to be larger than their individual contributions. This could serve as an incentive for low-income workers to join or remain in the formal sector by contributing to the defined contribution system. It is still too early to adequately estimate the effects of the *Cuota Social* on workers' incentives to join the AFORE system and to keep their contributions up to date.

The contribution subsidy, however, is not the only poverty prevention instrument in Mexico's multipillar system. AFORE affiliates with at least 25 years of contributions who have not accumulated savings sufficient to finance a determined minimum annuity qualify for a minimum pension guarantee top-up similar to that in Chile's AFP system. This poverty prevention instrument is more targeted at the likely elderly poor population than is the *Cuota Social*.

The *Cuota Social*'s fiscal burden on the Mexican government will be substantial in the first decade of reform. At 0.33 percent of GDP at the outset of reform, it is the largest cost item among government

---

Box 9.1 (continued)

contributions to the reformed pension system. However, as GDP and real wages grow the relative burden of the *Cuota Social* will decline, even allowing for increases in pension coverage. Grandolini and Cerda (1998) projected that *Cuota Social* liabilities will decrease to 0.2 percent of GDP by 2025 and increase again, to 0.5 percent by 2067. Furthermore, Azuara (2003) projected potential fiscal savings by increasing the *Cuota Social* as a percentage of the minimum wage and investing the amounts over time, thereby reducing the government's liability at the time of retirement to finance the minimum pension guaranteed by the reform.

Source: Contributed by Todd Pugatch, based on Grandolini and Cerda (1998) and Azuara (2003).

(Snyder and Yackovlev 2000)—and may discourage eligible applicants dissuaded by social stigma (Barr 1992; Willmore 2001b). Despite this, some countries have improved their targeting efficiency at modest cost, notably Mexico and Chile.

A universal flat pension does not strictly comply with the conceptual ideal of a public risk pooling mechanism to ensure against poverty in old age because all individuals above a specified age would receive some benefit, not only those suffering poverty. However, Willmore (2001a, 2001b) claimed that of the three public options for pooling against the risk of poverty in old age, universal pension benefits have numerous advantages over both systems that condition coverage on a minimum period of contributions and those that target benefits to poor people. He argued that because universal pension benefits provide coverage to all individuals of pensionable age they are the simplest public poverty prevention mechanism to administer, with the lowest transaction costs. Willmore believed that universal flat pensions prevent governments from creating the disincentives to work and save that are often inherent in means testing.

In a review of public poverty prevention pensions around the world, however, Willmore noted that most governments regard this type of program as a luxury that will be difficult to sustain. He demonstrated algebraically that where per capita income is growing, the cost of providing a universal benefit to a growing share of elderly people need not imply an onerous levy on taxpayers and that this can even be true when income growth is kept constant. Figure 9.3 compares the generosity and cost to taxpayers of public poverty prevention pensions in a first set of countries that provide universal benefits, with a second set of countries that means-test to target benefits at the poorest individuals and households.

Willmore claimed that government can easily regain a large portion of the transfers to elderly men and women by taxing universal pensions as

Box 9.2 BONOSOL: Bolivia's Universal Pension Program

A unique feature of Bolivia's pension reform was the creation of the BONOSOL program, which uses income from privatization of state enterprises to fund an old-age social assistance pension. The Sanchez de Lozada government (1993–97) partially privatized Bolivia's six largest public enterprises, selling 50 percent of the firms to foreign companies. Noting the poor results of recent public sector projects (a possible alternative use of the funds generated), the absence of a safety net to prevent old-age poverty, and the Bolivian people's status as the ostensible owners of the state enterprises that had been capitalized, the government decided to distribute the proceeds of privatization to all Bolivians 65 years old and older. Political considerations were also important in establishing the program: distribution of dividends from capitalization would galvanize support for privatization and for pension reform.

BONOSOL pays an annuity to all Bolivians 65 or older. The initial annuity was scheduled at US$248 per year for the first five years of the program, with adjustments to follow every three years thereafter to reflect changes in portfolio income and life expectancy. Citizens who were 21 or older in 1995 are eligible to receive the BONOSOL annuity when they reach 65 on the grounds that this group paid for the state enterprises that were sold to finance the program. No similar benefit has been planned for subsequent generations. The portfolio through which the program is financed was US$1.65 billion at its inception, representing 22 percent of Bolivia's GDP. Bolivia's two AFPs manage this portfolio.

Although the BONOSOL annuity is not means-tested, the program serves as the poverty prevention pillar in Bolivia's multipillar pension reform. Because all Bolivians 65 or older are eligible for the benefit, its coverage is much greater than for those receiving pension income under the old PAYG system or the new defined contribution system. At just 27 percent of average per capita income and 11 percent of average earnings in 1997, BONOSOL payments are intended to provide a broadly shared subsistence income in old age, not a replacement income to a small segment of the workforce. BONOSOL replaces 85 percent of the income of extremely poor people and 50 percent of the income of the other poor people (1997 figures). Early results indicated that the program would be a major success: of the more than 300,000 Bolivians eligible to receive the benefit at its inception, 63 percent received the annuity within the first two months of the program, with only 14 cases of attempted fraud reported.

The BONOSOL program is also less onerous to the government than most other poverty prevention pillars. The program enabled the Bolivian government to establish a poverty prevention pillar without minimum pensions or minimum return guarantees, thereby reducing its contingent liabilities. And because the program is financed by capitalization income rather than payroll taxes, it does not distort labor markets.

Box 9.2 (continued)

The political risk inherent in the program was apparent when, after the new government came to power in 1997, the BONOSOL program was renamed BOLIVIDA and payments were reduced to US$60 per year. The reduction was made based on a Ministry of Finance study that concluded that the higher BONOSOL benefits would be exhausted in 30 years, rather than the 70 years for which the program was envisioned. Nevertheless, the new Sanchez de Lozada government that came to power in 2002 restored the BONOSOL program at its original benefit levels, fulfilling a campaign promise but disregarding financial simulations that indicated the program's lack of sustainability. Current and future beneficiaries of BONOSOL remain subject to portfolio and political risk, but the latter can be minimized by establishing a sense of ownership over BONOSOL among its beneficiaries to increase the political cost of diverting its assets elsewhere.

Source: Contributed by Todd Pugatch, based on Von Gersdorff (1997) and Escobar (2003).

any other form of income, and he cited New Zealand's universal flat pension as an ideal poverty prevention system. Assuming a large part of universal benefits paid to the elderly population could be clawed back through taxation channels, the administrative ease of a universal flat pension might provide a public pooling model that effectively and efficiently covers the risk of poverty in old age.

Contributory Minimum Pension Guarantees

Minimum pension guarantees are used in most Latin American countries to set a minimum level of benefits in mandatory pension systems. The minimum benefit is usually set at a level close to the minimum wage, but there are significant differences between countries. For example, in Colombia the minimum pension is fixed at the same level as the minimum wage. In Chile, on the other hand, the minimum pension is fixed discretionally by the government and is currently equivalent to approximately two-thirds of the minimum wage. All countries apply minimum contribution requirements that range from 20 years in Chile to 30 years in Argentina, the Dominican Republic, and El Salvador.

These guarantees can distort incentives and lead low-income workers to contribute only for the period needed to qualify for the guarantee. In chapter 8, however, we showed that the contribution behavior of poorer workers in Chile and Peru did not change significantly after they qualified

Figure 9.3 Relative Generosity and Cost of Alternative Public Poverty Pension Arrangements in Selected Countries

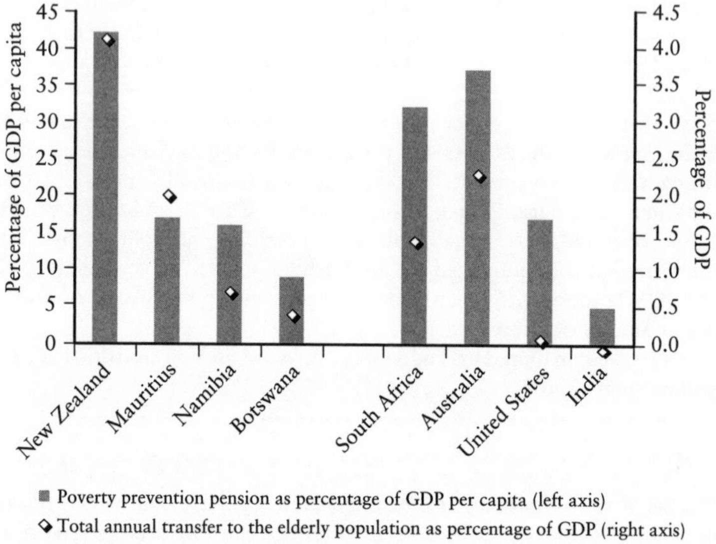

■ Poverty prevention pension as percentage of GDP per capita (left axis)
◇ Total annual transfer to the elderly population as percentage of GDP (right axis)

Notes: Countries in the first group (Botswana, Mauritius, Namibia, and New Zealand) provide a minimum universal benefit. Those in the second group (Australia, India, South Africa, and the United States) target minimum benefits at elderly poor people.
Source: Willmore (2001a).

for the minimum pension guarantee (whereas the contribution behavior of workers in the fifth income decile and higher did change).

A more worrisome issue is that minimum pension guarantees can distort incentives for risk taking in savings-based pension systems. A minimum pension guarantee is a pooling instrument to prevent poverty, but access to this instrument in most Latin American countries[4] is conditioned on a minimum contribution to the savings system with a consumption-smoothing objective. There is an inherent tension between the need for risk pooling to counter poverty and the need for individual choice to achieve efficient consumption smoothing that can only be resolved if different instruments (pillars) are assigned these separate functions. Minimum pension guarantees work well in defined benefit and notional defined contribution systems, where there is no individual choice, but are not adequate for the savings-based systems of Latin America, where it is only a matter of time before individual choice of investment portfolio is more widely introduced.

To date, only Chile permits investment choice in its mandatory pillar (the one that guarantees protection to workers). In June 2002 a new multifund structure was introduced that allows all young workers to choose among funds that allocate different percentages of their assets to equities. Poorer workers, knowing that they are covered by the minimum pension guarantee, have a strong incentive to choose the portfolio with the high-risk, high-return profile. Other countries are likely to follow the Chilean example. These countries face a significant challenge if they continue to exercise their poverty prevention goals through minimum pension guarantees conditioned on participation in the mandatory funded system while trying to improve the design of the funded component's consumption-smoothing properties by permitting workers to invest a higher proportion of their mandatory savings in equities and foreign securities than is currently permitted.

Calls for more flexibility in investment and greater individual choice are already being heard in other Latin American countries. In Mexico the liberalization of individual choice and investment portfolios is particularly worrisome for the government, because workers who contributed to the old system are covered by a guarantee equal to the benefit under the old PAYG plan. If they were offered the choice these workers would quite rationally opt for the riskiest portfolios, knowing that they will be bailed out by the government if the funds perform badly. Only those countries in which there is no minimum pension guarantee in the funded component, such as Argentina, Costa Rica, and Uruguay, can safely relax restrictions on individual choice and investment because workers there still benefit from a defined benefit pension that provides a basic income.

No country in the rest of the world has completely done away with a basic defined benefit pillar. This feature of several of the Latin American pension systems is practically unique by international standards. The only country that comes somewhat close to facing a similar moral hazard problem is the outsourced pension scheme in the United Kingdom. In the United Kingdom there is a minimum pension guarantee, but this is set at 20 percent of national average earnings, a level only slightly higher than that of the mandatory basic pillar that offers a flat-rate benefit equivalent to 16 percent of average earnings. But given current requirements for minimum contributions into outsourced plans, the risk of moral hazard is minimal.

The moral hazard problem of individual choice has not emerged in any Latin American country other than Chile. This problem has been addressed by restricting individual choice and limiting investment to interest-bearing assets. By the same token, however, these restrictions damage the consumption-smoothing properties of the funded component, as argued in chapter 7. To the extent that the savings system is to become the mainstay of retirement income in countries such as Chile, Colombia, El Salvador, Mexico, and Peru, it should be complemented with a poverty prevention, risk pooling pillar that has separate financing. Policymakers in these countries should consider transferring the part of contributions sufficient to combat old-age indigence into a separate pooling mechanism offering flat-rate,[5] basic benefits, as is done in Argentina. The savings component could then be freed of any state guarantees and evolve into a flexible consumption-smoothing system offering workers meaningful investment choices.

Noncontributory Poverty Prevention Pensions in Latin America

Prior to structural reforms retirement security systems in Latin America often combined the poverty prevention and earnings replacement functions into a single, defined benefit PAYG system. When a single policy instrument is designed to meet both objectives, it is difficult to take stock of its success in preventing poverty—the subject of this chapter. Some stocktaking of Latin America's experience with PAYG systems was briefly presented in chapter 3 where the substantial fiscal impact of these systems and their negative effects on equity were also discussed.

In this section we briefly review experience in the region with pension systems explicitly designed (in most cases) to prevent poverty—the so-called noncontributory pension programs.[6] A telling statistic is that three of the countries reviewed in this book (El Salvador, Mexico, and Peru) do not have noncontributory pension systems. In the countries where they exist, these programs developed alongside the contributory, payroll tax–financed, single-pillar PAYG systems to become a dominant instrument among the battery of targeted social assistance benefits. We draw the comparative statistics on noncontributory pensions from an extensive (and highly recommended) review by the International Labour Organization (Bertranou, Solorio, and Van Ginnekin 2002).

Noncontributory systems have developed in countries in the region with a longer history of formal social security. Whereas the noncontributory component of the larger social insurance infrastructure in these countries usually developed parallel with the contributory programs, in many cases (Brazil being a prime example) noncontributory programs may still be bound within the contributory programs. Tables 9.2 and 9.3 compare noncontributory pension programs in Argentina, Brazil, Chile, Costa Rica, and Uruguay according to the criteria commonly used to assess social protection programs: fiscal cost, coverage, generosity, and effectiveness at reducing poverty.

Table 9.2 presents expenditure on noncontributory pensions in the five countries studied by the ILO, as a percentage of GDP; as a share of total public spending on social security; and as a share of spending on the wider

Table 9.2 Expenditure on Noncontributory Pension Programs

Country	Expenditure as percentage of GDP	Expenditure as percentage of total expenditure on social security	Expenditure as percentage of total social sector spending	Percent financed from general revenues
Argentina	0.2	3.6	1.1	100.0
Brazil (Assistance)	0.3	5.3	2.0	100.0
Brazil (Rural)	1.0	17.2	6.7	91.6
Chile	0.4	5.5	2.3	91.6
Costa Rica	0.3	7.0	1.8	48.3
Uruguay	0.6	5.5	2.6	100.0

Note: Brazil's assistance pensions include the purely noncontributory BPC (*beneficio de prestação continuada,* continuous pension benefits), which replaced the RMV (*renda mensal vitalícia,* lifetime monthly income) in 1996. Brazil's rural pensions program is a regimen of preferential contribution parameters for rural sector workers that acts implicitly as a noncontributory pension program because it is poorly enforced.

Source: Bertranou, Solorio, and Van Ginnekin (2002).

social sectors (including education and health). Public spending on noncontributory pensions is highest in Brazil (by all three measures). Although contributing to Brazil's precarious fiscal situation (along with the egregiously generous pension regimen for civil servants in that country), this spending has had positive impact on reducing poverty among elderly men and women. As shown in table 9.1, poverty among old people in Brazil is among the lowest in the region. Uruguay is the second-highest spender on noncontributory benefits (as share of GDP), followed in third place by Chile. The final column shows the source of financing for the noncontributory programs. In each of the countries (with the notable exception of Costa Rica) noncontributory pensions are financed almost entirely from general revenues.

The first important point about coverage to note in table 9.3 is that benefits paid to the elderly poor populace are just a portion (although frequently the dominant portion) of noncontributory pension programs. These programs typically mirror the benefits paid by payroll tax–financed systems, namely old-age, survivor, and disability benefits. The share of noncontributory pensions paid for old age is shown in the third column of table 9.3. Brazil's rural pensions program—a special regimen of preferential contribution and eligibility criteria nested within the country's social security regimen for workers in the private sector—pays the greatest share of benefits for old age, followed closely by Costa Rica. Argentina's noncontributory pension system pays the smallest share of

Table 9.3 Noncontributory, Poverty Prevention Pensions Cover a Significant Portion of Pension Recipients

Country	Number of beneficiaries	Number of beneficiaries for old age	Percentage of benefits for old age	Beneficiaries as percentage of all pension recipients	Old-age beneficiaries as percentage of elderly poor population
Argentina	350,660	40,152	11.5	10.1	47.0[a]
Brazil (assistance)	2,022,708	706,345	34.9	11.1	86.3[b]
Brazil (rural)	6,024,328	4,012,127	66.6	33.0	—
Chile	358,813	165,373	46.1	22.6	36.5 and 78.7[c]
Costa Rica	76,009	46,597	61.3	31.2	44.5[d]
Uruguay	64,053	18,515	28.9	9.0	17.3 and 11.9[e]

— Not available.

[a] Share of indigent population aged 65 and older who receive a public pension based on *Encuesta de Desarrollo Social* (Social Development Survey 1998), in Arriagada and Hall (2000).

[b] Share of recipients among population 67 and older with per capita household income less than the minimum wage, receiving a public pension (Assistance and Rural), September 1999.

[c] Share of population 65 and over in deciles 1 and 2, urban and rural areas, respectively, in 2000.

[d] Share of poor people aged 65 and older in 2000.

[e] Share of poor people aged 50 and older in Montevideo and the interior of Uruguay, respectively, in 1997.

Source: Bertranou, Solorio, and Van Ginnekin (2002) and others where noted.

benefits for old age. The next point to note in table 9.3 is the importance of noncontributory programs in the overall retirement security infrastructure of the countries examined. Beneficiaries of noncontributory pensions make up more than a third of pension recipients in Brazil and Costa Rica. In Chile, 22.6 percent of pension recipients receive the noncontributory *pensiones asistenciales* (PASIS, social assistance pension). The share of noncontributory benefit recipients among pensioners in Argentina and Uruguay is much smaller (11.5 percent and 9 percent, respectively).

Figure 9.4 shows the relative generosity of the old-age noncontributory pensions in the countries studied by the ILO. Uruguay's noncontributory pension is the most generous as a percentage of the average contributory pension, followed by those of Chile and Argentina. However, the generosity of noncontributory benefits in Chile and Costa Rica is slightly overstated because the minimum rather than the average contributory pension is used for comparison.

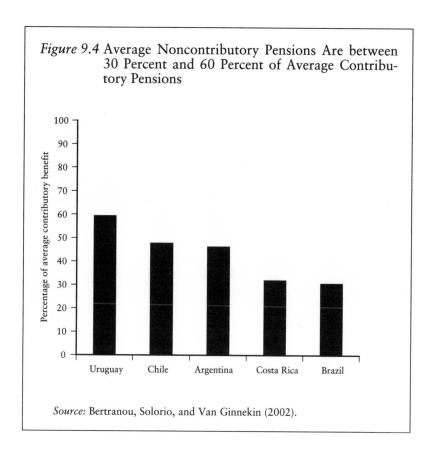

Figure 9.4 Average Noncontributory Pensions Are between 30 Percent and 60 Percent of Average Contributory Pensions

Source: Bertranou, Solorio, and Van Ginnekin (2002).

As discussed in greater detail elsewhere (Bertranou, Solorio, and Van Ginnekin 2002), noncontributory pension programs have had an important effect on poverty. Case studies show that in 2000 and 2001 noncontributory pensions lowered the rate of poverty among elderly men and women by 67 percent in Argentina, 95 percent in Brazil, 69 percent in Chile, and 21 percent in Costa Rica. But many elderly poor people still go without an old-age pension of any kind, as shown in the last column of table 9.2.[7]

Forecasting the Cost of Public Pooling Alternatives

How much would each of the alternative public, poverty prevention pooling arrangements described in earlier sections cost? We present at least a preliminary answer to this question in this section, along with the results of simulations using the same income and demographic data and the same macroeconomic assumptions employed in the simulation results presented earlier in this book.[8]

Rather than try to find a minimum level of public pension benefit that would be both a salient and a socially acceptable lower boundary on income across a set of very diverse countries, we decided to use each country's legal minimum wage to reflect the lowest level of income that even populist politicians would find politically acceptable.

Setting minimum pension benefits at the minimum wage is a very generous decision with dangerous consequences for incentives to save and fiscal sustainability. In most of the countries in our sample the minimum wage as a share of average wages is high (table 9.4). The minimum wage

Table 9.4 As a Share of Average Wages, Minimum Wages Are Relatively High in Chile, Colombia, and Some Other Latin American Countries

Country	Year	MW/mean	MW/median	MW/10th percentile wage
Argentina (urban)	1998	0.26	0.33	0.67
Bolivia	1997	0.22	0.34	0.80
Brazil (all)	1998	0.24	0.43	1.00
Brazil (urban)	1998	0.22	0.37	1.00
Chile	1996	0.34	0.55	1.09
Colombia (urban)	1998	0.40	0.68	1.00
Honduras	1999	0.62	0.90	2.26
Mexico (urban)	1999	0.34	0.48	0.87
Uruguay (urban)	1998	0.19	0.27	0.64

Note: Ratio of the minimum wage (MW) to comparison wages.
Source: Maloney and Nuñez (2001).

is often set above the market-clearing wage by governments acting on political pressure from trade unions. Furthermore, although the minimum
wage is presented as the lowest level of income that society is prepared to
let workers earn legally, this judgment often assumes that during their
working lives individuals have dependents to support and other expenses
that retired households no longer have to meet. If we assume that, other
than health expenses, elderly people consume less than households headed
by individuals of working age, poverty prevention benefits should typically
be set as some fraction of the minimum wage. In Chile the minimum pension guarantee oscillated between 80 percent and 90 percent of the minimum wage during the 1990s (Cox-Edwards 2000). In Colombia the contributory minimum pension is set equal to the minimum wage. In Peru the
minimum pension guaranteed in the reformed PAYG system is actually a
bit higher than the minimum wage.

By selecting the minimum wage as the level of the poverty prevention
benefit in these simulations we are not advocating this as the optimal size
of the public pooling pillar. To the contrary, given the typical distribution
of wages in Latin America, setting the public poverty pension equal to the
minimum wage would provide a strong disincentive for workers to save
privately. Indeed, in Colombia, where the minimum wage is binding, there
is strong emerging evidence that the consequently high minimum pension
lowers the share of workers who contribute to the formal pension system
and threatens fiscal sustainability.

Nor are we advocating one type of pooling structure over another. We
are simply addressing a fiscal concern often faced by policymakers when trying to determine the appropriate size of their poverty prevention pillar. We
provide cost projections of what we believe to be a likely upper-boundary
benefit—that which even the most ardent populist politicians might be
willing to support as the acceptable level of the minimum pension in their
country—to arrive at conservative estimates of the cost of restructuring the
pooling pillar in different ways. In this spirit we have also generously indexed
the minimum benefit to current wages. Significant cost savings can be had
by indexing benefits to inflation or to a combination of prices and wages.

To calculate the cost of the targeted benefit we have simply assumed
that the current rate of poverty among the elderly population (as shown
earlier in this chapter in table 9.1) will remain constant throughout the
simulation. In light of the earlier discussion of the likely level of poverty
among elderly people, when poverty is measured by income or by accumulated wealth, our assumed poverty rate is likely to be very conservative
(i.e., to overstate poverty or need among the elderly population) in some of
the countries included in this exercise and less so in others. The cost of paying the targeted benefit is simply derived by multiplying this poverty rate by
the cost of the universal benefit. This cost will in some cases vary significantly from the costs of the noncontributory programs reviewed in the
previous section largely because we assume that the targeted benefit reaches
all the elderly poor people. The simulation results are presented in table 9.5.

Table 9.5 Cost of Providing and Guaranteeing a Public Pension Equal to the Minimum Wage
(Alternative public pooling arrangements as a percentage of GDP)

	Uruguay					Argentina					Mexico			
	Current transfer (%)	Top-up (%)	Targeted[a] (%)	Universal (%)		Current transfer (%)	Top-up (%)	Targeted (%)	Universal (%)		Current transfer (%)	Top-up (%)	Targeted (%)	Universal (%)
2001	4.00	0.00	0.14	1.90	2001	2.50	0.80	0.34	4.00	2001	0.50	0.50	0.41	1.30
2010	2.60	1.00	0.14	1.90	2010	2.20	0.80	0.36	4.30	2010	0.60	0.40	0.44	1.40
2020	2.10	0.70	0.14	1.90	2020	2.30	0.80	0.39	4.60	2020	0.70	0.40	0.59	1.90
2030	2.20	0.40	0.16	2.20	2030	2.80	0.90	0.44	5.20	2030	0.70	0.30	0.75	2.40
2040	2.50	0.30	0.19	2.60	2040	3.60	1.30	0.55	6.50	2040	0.70	0.30	1.06	3.40
2050	2.80	0.30	0.22	2.90	2050	4.40	1.60	0.64	7.60	2050	0.60	0.40	1.34	4.30

	Bolivia					Colombia					Chile			
	Current transfer (%)	Top-up (%)	Targeted (%)	Universal (%)		Current transfer (%)	Top-up (%)	Targeted (%)	Universal (%)		Current transfer (%)	Top-up (%)	Targeted (%)	Universal (%)
2001	3.50	0.00	1.57	4.10	2001	—	0.20	1.08	3.50	2001	7.20	0.00	0.25	3.40
2010	2.20	0.20	1.42	3.70	2010	—	0.40	1.14	3.70	2010	4.60	0.40	0.27	3.70
2020	2.10	0.30	1.54	4.00	2020	—	0.80	1.57	5.10	2020	3.40	0.90	0.33	4.50
2030	2.10	0.20	1.80	4.70	2030	0.70	1.60	2.31	7.50	2030	1.50	1.50	0.48	6.60
2040	1.70	0.30	2.23	5.80	2040	3.40	3.30	2.96	9.60	2040	0.50	1.30	0.60	8.20
2050	0.90	0.60	2.99	7.80	2050	5.40	4.70	3.45	11.20	2050	0.80	1.30	0.64	8.70

	El Salvador					Peru			
	Current transfer (%)	Top-up (%)	Targeted[a] (%)	Universal (%)		Current transfer (%)	Top-up (%)	Targeted (%)	Universal (%)
2001	1.40	0.10	1.74	4.60	2001	0.70	0.00	0.36	1.90
2010	2.20	0.10	2.00	5.30	2010	0.90	0.20	0.37	2.00
2020	3.20	0.10	2.34	6.20	2020	0.90	0.30	0.45	2.40
2030	2.90	0.00	2.98	7.90	2030	0.90	0.40	0.56	3.00
2040	2.60	0.20	4.23	11.20	2040	0.80	0.50	0.75	4.00
2050	0.50	0.50	5.36	14.20	2050	1.00	0.70	0.93	5.00

a. Poverty rates used to calculate the cost of the targeted benefit are those presented in the last column of table 9.1, as 50 percent of equivalent mean income in each country (Bourguignon et al., 2004).

Source: PROST simulations using same assumptions as Zviniene and Packard (2002), documented in the technical annex at the end of this volume.

There are few surprises in the projected costs of structuring the pooled benefit according to the three alternatives discussed earlier. Limiting public pooled benefits to a top-up paid to those who contribute to the earnings-related pillar is often the cheapest option but also the one that leaves large segments of the population uncovered against the risk of poverty in old age. Targeting benefits at the elderly poor population will be cheaper than the exclusive top-up in countries like Argentina, Chile, and Uruguay, where poverty among the elderly population is low—but more expensive than a top-up in countries like Bolivia, Colombia, and El Salvador, where old-age poverty is more widespread.

The surprise arises from the cost of the universal flat benefit. Assuming countries could start from scratch (admittedly, a very strong assumption, but helpful nonetheless), the cost of paying benefits to all individuals over age 65 is in many cases not too different from what governments are currently paying to cover the deficits of their reformed pension systems (much of which is made up of transition costs, and the payment of benefits covering risks other than those of old age). The difference in costs of the universal benefit become apparent, however, later in the simulation horizon when countries have finished paying the transition costs of reforms and longer life expectancy makes the universal benefit paid at 65 exhorbitant.

The projected costs of the universal benefit in Uruguay would be less than the current pension deficits the government has to pay until 2030, and then is roughly equal to annual transfers to elderly people if there is no change in the current system. In Argentina, even when the benefit is generously set equal to the minimum wage and indexed to wage growth, the cost of the universal pension, although higher than the deficits of the current public pillar, mirror costs of a similar benefit in New Zealand. However, even in wealthier New Zealand, the transfer to the elderly populace is forecast to grow to 9 percent of GDP by 2050 (Willmore 2001a). The cost of the universal pension is highest in El Salvador, Colombia, and Chile—countries considered to be outliers in the region with respect to the level at which they set the minimum wage.

Readers should keep in mind that these are simple simulations intended only to inform an important debate on the size and structure of the poverty prevention pillar. Clearly, the cost of setting benefits to the minimum wage and indexing to wage growth would make universal pensions inviable in most Latin American countries. The simulated costs of the different poverty prevention benefits are shown alongside current spending on public pensions to give readers an idea of their relative size. Much of the current cost of public pensions represents acquired rights that governments would find difficult to ignore in favor of purely poverty prevention programs. Furthermore, these simulations are only preliminary and are intended to motivate a closer investigation of options for a poverty prevention pillar in each country. There is much that could be done to improve these cost estimates in a country-specific study of viable options. The projected costs do not take account of (a) the portion of the current transfers to the elderly population that is still financing the transition cost of introducing individual retirement accounts; (b) the cost of excluding workers without a contribution history from receiving benefits; (c) the revenue that the government could claw back by setting a surcharge on pension payments for workers above certain income levels or by simply making the universal flat benefit taxable; (d) the administrative costs of means tests to efficiently target a benefit to elderly poor people; and (e) the costs of corruption and leakage to people who are not poor that must be kept in mind, given the track record of public pension administration in the region. Adjusting the minimum retirement age to match changes in life expectancy would go far toward containing the costs of this benefit. Each of these considerations can change the projected costs of poverty prevention benefits considerably and should be examined carefully in country-specific analyses using PROST or other actuarial simulation tools.

Conclusion

We have argued that there is little distinction between contributory and noncontributory public pension systems when the public policy objective is to prevent poverty in old age. The origin of this distinction between contributory and noncontributory benefits is political. Indeed, there may still be sound political economy grounds for requiring workers to pay some premiums to social insurance to maintain a strong constituency to protect budget allocations to these poverty prevention programs.

That said, in countries where labor is very mobile among sectors and the informal economy is large, structuring the premiums for social insurance programs as payroll taxes is an increasingly ineffective and unreliable way to finance social insurance. A more reliable source of financing for public pooling mechanisms may be a value-added tax. In fact, financing public poverty prevention pensions through taxes other than payroll taxes would erase the distinction between the covered and uncovered sectors of the labor force. This requires that public poverty prevention pensions be viewed not as the social assistance charity of the state and society but as an additional instrument available to individuals and households to manage shocks to their income should they need it.

As pointed out in *Averting the Old Age Crisis* (World Bank 1994), greater reliance on a broad tax base, such as an income or consumption tax instead of a payroll tax, is the most efficient course for policymakers to pursue in the long run because it reduces the tax rate needed to finance benefits. It is also most consistent with the poverty prevention and redistributive functions of the remaining public pooling pillar after introduction of the multipillar model (Willmore 2001b).

We have also argued in this chapter that if Latin American countries decide to continue to meet poverty prevention objectives through contributory systems (coupled with means testing for the uncovered population), the contributory part should ideally be assigned to a separate pooling pillar offering a minimum benefit to all qualifying contributors. Making the minimum pension guarantee conditional on participation in the savings component creates an unnecessary tension between the need for risk pooling to optimize poverty prevention and the need for individual choice to tailor consumption smoothing to individual preferences. Policymakers in El Salvador, Mexico, and Peru should also consider the introduction of means-tested social assistance for the elderly population. Another promising avenue is outreach to elderly households in programs that target poverty broadly like Chile's *Puente* and Mexico's *Oportunidades*. Without these additional instruments the basic promise of old-age social security, poverty prevention among elderly men and women, will not be kept.

Ultimately the experience with single-pillar, defined-benefit, PAYG arrangements in Latin America teaches us that the proverbial devil in public pooled pension plans is in the details. The details can only be deciphered with more focused, country-specific analytical work conducted with an eye to competing demands on limited fiscal resources, such as social assistance transfers to other, perhaps needier groups in the population. This analysis should address at least the following questions: (a) Should a separate, poverty prevention first pillar be universal or targeted? (b) Will political considerations allow a new minimalist, universal public pooled pillar to replace partly or wholly other contributory and noncontributory benefits mandated and guaranteed by governments? (c) In a country where the informal sector is large and tax evasion is rampant, how could the benefit best be financed? (d) Would the benefit be a flat amount or related to the number of years of contributions? (e) What would be the maximum old-age poverty prevention benefit the government could credibly guarantee and sustain? (f) How would the benefit be indexed to protect its real value? (g) Would the benefit be taxable? and (h) At what age should individuals be eligible?

Notes

1. This is not to say that the market for private annuities can be taken for granted. Even in middle-income countries like those in Latin America that introduced private individual accounts, much still has to be done to ensure that there is a well-regulated, transparent, and competitive annuities market to cater to the demands of affiliates retiring under the new pension systems.

2. Poverty statistics typically are calculated using current income from employment, pensions, or public and private transfers reported in representative household and labor market surveys. Older respondents, many of whom are likely to be retired, will report lower levels of income, which will naturally place them in the lower tail of the income distribution.

3. Purely public Bismarkian PAYG systems typically defined benefits of between 80 percent and 100 percent of average wages earned in the last few years (and in many cases the last month) prior to retirement. Although based primarily on defining contributions in individual accounts, the replacement rates envisioned by policymakers setting the contribution parameters of the new multipillar systems ranged from 60 percent to 70 percent of some average of earnings prior to retirement (Pinera 1995; Valdés-Prieto 2002b; Rofman 2002).

4. Only Argentina, Costa Rica, and Uruguay have assigned the poverty prevention role to a separate pillar based exclusively on risk pooling.

5. The targeted or minimum benefit of this component could be set as is currently the case in most Latin American countries, as a percentage of the minimum wage. Alternatively, it could be set, as in the richer OECD countries, in relation to average earnings. In Latin America, as in OECD countries, the minimum pension benefit tends to be somewhere between one-quarter and one-half of average economywide earnings.

6. Notable exceptions are the *pensiones graciables* found among the noncontributory pension programs in Argentina and Uruguay. These pensions were created to recognize notable contributions made by citizens to what were deemed national interests (e.g., in recognition of military service or international distinction in the arts, sports, and science). In both cases these pension programs have deteriorated into fiscally regressive and costly tools of political patronage.

7. The case study for Chile in Bertranou et al. (2002) reported that many more PASIS benefits were being paid than there were elderly poor people in the country in 2000. Taking the share of PASIS beneficiaries as a percentage of the elderly poor population gives a coverage rate of 154 percent. Because PASIS benefits are paid to poor disabled people and to widows, the rate reported in Bertranou et al. (2002) is likely to overstate coverage of the elderly poor populace. The figures reported for Chile in the last column of table 9.2 are taken directly from the CASEN (2000) household survey.

8. PROST simulations reported in this section were performed by Asta Zviniene (HDNSP; World Bank Human Development Network, Social Protection Unit), using the same macroeconomic assumptions employed in the simulations reported earlier and presented in Zviniene and Packard (2002).

10

Facilitating Consumption
Smoothing: Improving the
Savings Component

IN THIS CHAPTER WE EVALUATE various policies aimed at improving the functioning of the savings pillar so that it best serves its consumption-smoothing role. In some countries, however, the funded system has a dual role, serving also a poverty prevention function. In chapter 9 we examined alternate ways to deal with the poverty prevention goal and argued that it would be best served by a separate defined benefit pillar, which should be financed by general tax revenues. The discussion in this chapter focuses only on the goal of consumption smoothing for most of the population, above what is required to prevent poverty in old age.

The evidence provided in chapters 7 and 8 raises some concern over the ability of Latin American governments to mandate a retirement savings instrument that is attractive for a reasonably high proportion of individuals. The low density of contributions to the mandatory pillar and the reported strategic behavior by workers to qualify for the minimum pension guarantee may be primarily a consequence of widespread informality, low disposable incomes, and pressing consumption demands that leave little space for long-term savings. However, we also saw in chapter 8 that Latin American workers are saving and investing through other means, such as buying a house. It is therefore possible that the size of the mandate may be too large, that some of the mandated products' characteristics (cost, risk, and liquidity) are not sufficiently attractive, and that the products' weaknesses are not compensated for by preferential tax treatment of retirement savings.

High contribution rates may discourage poor and young workers from participating in the mandatory pension system because these groups are most likely to have competing demands on their income. One policy option that may be considered is to reduce the size of mandatory contributions for these groups. Poorer workers may even be exempt from the mandate to save. After all, their basic needs should already be taken care of by the poverty prevention pillar. We also suggest reducing the earnings ceilings for mandatory contributions so that the voluntary pension system can develop.

The limited acceptance of opportunities to make additional, voluntary contributions to individual accounts in countries such as Chile, Colombia, Mexico, and Peru could be taken as further evidence of problems in the funded system. In these countries voluntary retirement savings in the new private second pillar are relatively liquid and therefore compete directly with alternative investment instruments. Although voluntary saving in the products offered by the AFPs is relatively stagnant, saving in alternative financial instruments has grown at fast rates in Chile, even if those instruments often have a less advantageous tax treatment and involve additional costs of intermediation.

Aside from the size of the mandate on many formal workers, the lack of interest in voluntary savings could be explained by a desire among individuals to diversify their savings into other products. It seems strange, however, that workers would prefer to save through instruments that are nearly always more expensive than the pension funds (bank deposits being the main exception) and that offer significantly lower tax benefits.

We suggest several changes to the new private second pillar to lower administrative costs and improve the management of investment and longevity risks, drawing on work commissioned specifically for this book as well as a large and growing body of literature. These recommended changes in the structure of the private second pillar (changes such as greater competition, enlarging fund choice, centralizing account management and record keeping, and diversifying investment in foreign securities more widely) can indeed lower administrative costs of the new systems and further improve investment performance, but it is critical that governments ensure that these benefits are passed on to affiliates of the pension system, and not simply kept by the fund managers to increase their profit margins.

As in most areas, the critical ingredient to ensuring that affiliated workers benefit from the improved performance of the new private second pillar is *competition*. Competition might be introduced with small but important changes to the structure of the dedicated financial industry. But it is even more likely to arise from creating an enabling environment for private providers of voluntary savings and insurance instruments that can substitute for mandated savings and insurance in the private second pillar, and from ensuring a level playing field with respect to the forms of long-term saving and investment the government rewards with efficient regulatory oversight and moderately favorable tax incentives. Fortunately, this is the direction that governments already seem to be headed in countries where structural reforms have begun to mature.

Improving the Mandatory Savings Pillar: Lowering Costs to Affiliates

In this section we focus on ways to improve the income-smoothing role of the mandatory funded pillar. We propose various reforms aimed at eliminating some of the failings of the existing systems identified in chapter 7, such as the high cost and lack of efficient management of investment and intragenerational longevity risk. The objective of the proposed reforms is to offer workers a better (risk- and cost-adjusted) return than alternative investment products offer. The last subsection discusses the mandate itself and how it affects populations such as the vast majority of Latin Americans who live with monthly incomes of less than US$500.

Helping People Meet Their Differing Life Cycle Needs

The main difficulty in designing mandatory savings programs that complement poverty prevention pillars as described in chapter 9 is that individuals have different consumption needs and objectives and face innumerable investment choices throughout their life cycle. While their ultimate goal is recognized to be consumption smoothing, individual time and risk preferences will determine specific consumption paths and investment choices, which may include not only financial assets but also housing, education, and for some people even their own business. Provident workers who recognize their needs and the value of saving for retirement may even have negative savings rates when young because of expectations of higher labor earnings in subsequent years. Indeed, efficient consumption smoothing may dictate that such individuals borrow when young.

Mandating savings can be costly for such workers in two ways. First, the mandate may force workers to borrow even more than they would do in the absence of the mandate, at rates that are typically higher than the returns earned on their savings. This spread is highest in developing countries and alone may be sufficient reason to evade the mandatory system. For those people who are unable to borrow, the mandate may force them to bypass other investment opportunities (e.g., housing and education) and may leave them unprotected against income shocks. Second, the opportunity cost of mandatory savings is compounded in Latin America by the fact that the new system duplicates the fixed costs of financial intermediation.

Poorer and improvident workers are likely to suffer the most from the mandate. Low-income workers normally face greater credit constraints and may therefore be less able to adjust their consumption to any mandate to save. Although they may suffer the least in terms of spread costs between borrowing and savings rates, they suffer the most in terms of lowered disposable income, missed investment opportunities, and exposure to un-expected income shocks. The duplication of fixed costs of financial inter-mediation also impinges most on the income of poorer workers. High mandatory contributions can also bring these workers closer to the poverty line during their youth.

Mandating contributions of poorer workers above the level required to prevent poverty in old age is therefore contentious. By limiting mandatory contributions of poorer households to a level sufficient to ensure a mini-mum income at retirement, the negative effects of the mandate can be minimized. Such contributions should be directed toward a separate plan with purely poverty prevention objectives, as discussed in chapter 9. Some Latin American countries, however, do not have separate contributions for poverty prevention and for consumption-smoothing purposes. While it is possible in principle to organize the first pillar as a minimum pension guarantee on fully funded individual accounts (as in Chile or El Salvador), the operational cost of such an arrangement can be exacting. The advan-tages of fully funding poverty-level benefits are also debatable when one considers that pension contributions that have a poverty prevention ob-jective should be invested in long-term, inflation- or, even better, wage-indexed bonds with minimal credit risk. Such conservative investment strategies are needed in order to ensure that the minimum pension is reached with a high degree of certainty.

To the extent that lower-income workers are covered by a separate poverty prevention pillar, there seems to be little need to require them to make additional contributions to the pillar that serves a consumption-smoothing role.[1] The level of retirement income that brings poor people out of poverty is similar to that needed for consumption-smoothing purposes.[2]

For higher-income workers one can also question to what extent the consumption-smoothing objective should be achieved through a mandatory savings plan. Improvident workers, regardless of their income, suffer from the mandate. Improvident workers are likely to borrow more than provi-dent workers and as a consequence pay a higher price in terms of the spread charged by credit institutions. How much both provident and improvident workers pay in terms of higher intermediation costs will depend on their access to credit. Improvidence, however, is a function of age. In general, older workers tend to be more provident because they realize the conse-quences of having insufficient resources in old age. Hence they are more likely to accept mandatory contributions to a retirement savings plan.

There is evidence that workers in Latin America may be evading the mandatory system to invest their limited spare savings in housing (Packard 2002a; Barr and Packard 2003). This fact is hardly surprising given the acuteness of housing deficiencies and the importance individuals attach to home ownership as a shock absorber. Permitting investment of mandatory pension contributions in housing could be a necessary first step to help individuals meet their consumption and savings objectives throughout their life cycle. Doing so would require reform of the pension system to permit affiliates to use accumulated funds as down payments to obtain mortgages from banks. Controlling the final use of such withdrawals, however, can be a daunting task for governments. For example, it may be difficult to prevent those people who already own a house from selling it to qualify for a fund withdrawal.

Withdrawals could also be permitted for investment in human capital, such as education and health care. Such a possibility is particularly important for low- and middle-income households who have limited sources of savings and who face the greatest borrowing constraints. The fungibility of funds withdrawn, however, may make it very difficult for policymakers to control the use of withdrawals destined for these specific purposes. It would also add tremendously to costs. Similarly, permitting withdrawals in cases of emergency, such as unexpected income or wealth shocks, may make sense from the perspective of individual welfare, but the monitoring costs would be very high. Introducing such flexibility into the system, moreover, can create incentives for moral hazard. Poorer workers wishing to access their accumulated savings may hide their assets or join the informal sector.

In general the more governments aim to satisfy individual preferences over investment, the more complicated the monitoring of the system becomes and the greater the risk that governments will be called to bail out unfortunate workers who made bad choices. Hence, if it is deemed that mandatory contributions may be unnecessarily high for many workers, a better policy response is to lower the mandate rather than permit withdrawals. High contributions coupled with a liberal policy on withdrawals may lead to mistaken perceptions about the adequacy of accumulated retirement funds among both individuals and the government.

The ease with which individuals avoid the mandate in Latin American countries casts doubt on its usefulness, at least at current contribution levels. It is likely that the extent of evasion is partly linked to the level of mandated contributions. That is, if mandatory contribution rates are decreased and the maximum taxable wage reduced, the contribution frequency is likely to increase.

Participation is especially likely to increase among poorer and younger workers who have many competing consumption demands (purchasing a home, professional education, raising children). Saving for retirement may therefore come at a high cost for them. For richer and older workers closer to retirement, mandatory contributions may be less costly because there are fewer urgent demands on their income. At the same time, however, these workers are the least improvident and therefore the least likely to change their behavior as a result of a mandate to save.

Overall, the goals of maximizing social welfare translate into establishing contribution rates and maximum taxable wages that overcome the problem of improvidence in youth but that minimize the costs of financial intermediation and leave workers sufficient disposable income for other purposes (maintaining a family, buying a home, or meeting unexpected income shocks). Contribution rates should also be set to minimize moral hazard from the first pillar (reduction in voluntary savings).

To achieve these goals, mandatory contribution rates above the level required to finance the poverty prevention pillar could be linked to the age and income of the individual.[3] A useful reference is the Swiss system in which mandatory contribution rates in the mandatory occupational pension system (Switzerland's second pillar) increase gradually with a worker's age (from 5 percent in the 30s to 15 percent in the 50s). Earnings-linked contribution rates are also applied in Colombia and in some OECD countries.

The maximum contribution rate and taxable wage consistent with social welfare objectives are likely to be much lower in Latin America than in countries where disposable household incomes are much higher. Although mandatory contribution rates (to the PAYG or funded component) are generally lower in Latin America than in OECD countries (Argentina, Brazil, and Uruguay are the main exceptions), the maximum taxable wage is much higher. Except in Chile, the maximum taxable wage in Latin American countries is more than five times average earnings, whereas in OECD countries it is often less than twice the average wage.

From a social welfare perspective, therefore, it seems appropriate for mandatory contributions above those that finance the poverty prevention pillar[4] to be related to both the income and age of the individual.[5] The ceiling on taxable earnings could also be gradually lowered from its current level in countries with a high ceiling, such as Bolivia or Mexico, and a ceiling could be introduced in countries that do not currently have one, such as Costa Rica and Peru. This would free up resources that could be invested in a wider array of financial instruments and other attractive long-term assets such as housing or education.

Such a solution may not be perfect because it does not take into account all possible variations in the degree of improvidence or access to credit among workers of a similar age cohort or income group. It would be unreasonable to expect governments to manage a mandated system in the best interest of all individuals because such an ideal system would require governments to cater to each individual's specific needs and constraints. By reducing the size of the mandatory funded pillar for the young and the poor, however, policymakers can reduce distortions to individual choice while still helping to mitigate the dangers of improvidence.

Enacting Reforms to Decrease Administrative Costs and Commissions

One of the central policy concerns in any mandatory pension system that is privately managed is the cost of administration. The Latin American systems have been generally successful at reducing costs, but it appears that this has come largely by restricting individual choice and competition among the pension fund administrators. In particular, marketing and distribution expenses have been reduced by restricting the number of times per year that an affiliated worker can switch between pension fund administrators (once in Mexico, Peru, and Bolivia; twice in other countries). These restrictions essentially have created a captive clientele for each pension fund administrator and institutionalized what was already an oligopoly. Even under such restrictive conditions, however, commissions may still be unacceptably high for a large percentage of the population. More can still be done to lower costs. Indeed, the high returns on capital for the pension fund administrators in some countries prove that only a small portion of the decline in operating expenses is being passed on to affiliates as lower commissions.

In Peru, for instance, profit margins for the fund managers are growing with efficiency, yet the price of the private pillar paid by affiliates has remained stubbornly high. Fees charged by AFPs in Peru were the highest—30 percent of affiliates' net contributions (that is, contributions net of fees and premiums for insurance)—considerably above the regional average of 15 percent. Carranza and Morón (2003) argued that Peruvian fees are much closer to the regional average when one allows for the lower contribution rate in Peru. Despite this, the average cost to affiliates has persisted for almost five years—even though the number of contributors has increased and the industry has had more time to become more efficient and amortize the initial set-up costs (see figure 10.1). The minimal variation in that percentage across all four AFPs during the past five years is another indication of the weakness of competitive market forces in the industry.

Lasaga and Pollner (2003) attributed persistently high AFP fees in Peru to a number of structural factors that hamper competition among the fund managers and may have contributed to forming an oligopoly. These factors include (a) the high start-up costs of entering the dedicated private pension fund administration industry; (b) the difficulty of comparing AFP fees (assessed on a prepaid, percentage-of-income basis) with the charges of similar service providers in the private financial sector (often assessed as a percentage of assets under management); (c) opaque and outdated provision of insurance services tied to mandatory retirement savings; (d) the high transaction costs to affiliates opting to switch from one AFP to another; and (e) the model of "dedicated provision" itself and its implied exclusion of other regulated financial sector actors (some, like commercial banks, with established and farther-reaching supply networks) from the managing of mandated retirement savings.

As the Latin American funded systems become more flexible and permit participants to exert some degree of portfolio choice, policymakers will have to search for more creative solutions to the problem of administrative costs. Possible solutions fall into two main categories: those that aim to reduce operational costs through supply-side measures or caps on

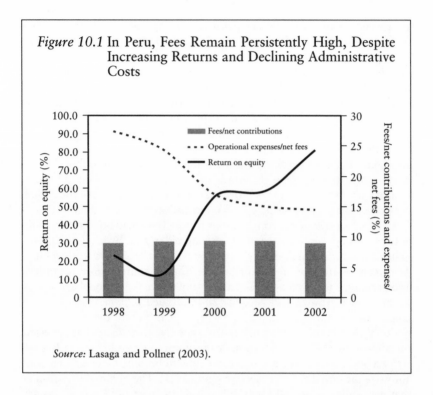

Figure 10.1 In Peru, Fees Remain Persistently High, Despite Increasing Returns and Declining Administrative Costs

Source: Lasaga and Pollner (2003).

commissions (see table 10.1), and those that employ demand-side measures aimed primarily at increasing the price elasticity of demand (see table 10.2). Supply-side measures are certainly the most effective. One promising measure is to permit group contracts. This would involve raising the profile of employers in pension plan administration. Firms use retirement plans as part of their human resources policies to attract and retain talented employees. A greater involvement of employers in pension provision could therefore result in higher voluntary pension contributions and a better diversification of retirement income sources.

The possible role of the employer could range from record keeping and assistance in the selection of investment products and providers to direct provision of pension plans. Nonetheless, it is unlikely and possibly undesirable for any but the largest Latin American employers to offer defined benefit plans. Such plans require expensive administrative structures and regular supervision. Moreover, the trend toward greater transparency in company accounts (as international accounting standards are adopted) is increasing the visibility of the pension liabilities of employers, who in turn are shrinking or altogether closing down these plans and substituting plans with more limited guarantees or purely defined contribution plans.[6]

Table 10.1 Reform Options to Reduce the Operational Expenses of the New Private Second Pillar

Reform proposal	Rationale	Country case	Potential problems
Limit the frequency with which workers can switch between pension fund managers.	Marketing costs are lowered because the ability to attract new members is curtailed.	All Latin American countries limit switching to one or two times per year. In Bolivia switching was prohibited after the two pension fund administrators merged.	Competition among pension fund administrators is further limited. The government's fiduciary responsibility is even greater because the only element of choice (and therefore of market discipline) is removed.
Allow group contracts, permitting the establishment of occupational pension plans where the employer negotiates the commission with the pension fund administrator.	Employer is a countervailing force to the pension fund administrator, with much more bargaining power than individuals have in the retail market.	No Latin American country has yet permitted group contracts.	Self-employed workers are not able to benefit from commissions as low as those available to wage and salaried workers.
Separate pension services and centralize some services, such as record keeping related to the management of individual accounts. These services may be auctioned off by the government in an international open bid. Alternatively, employers may be responsible for record keeping.	Record keeping and individual account management are services with significant economies of scale. In addition, if pension fund administrators cannot know the identity of the account holders, marketing costs are significantly curtailed.	Mexico and the Dominican Republic have centralized record-keeping systems. The new funded system in Sweden also has centralized contribution collection and record keeping.	The auctioning process is subject to political risk.

(Table continues on the following page.)

Table 10.1 (continued)

Reform proposal	Rationale	Country case	Potential problems
Allow other financial sector institutions to manage pension fund assets.	Economies of scale in asset management and additional investment expertise will lead to lower costs and better investment performance.	No country permits other than dedicated providers to manage pension funds.	Big financial institutions will dominate the pensions market even more. Monitoring conflicts of interest could become more difficult.

Source: Authors' compilation.

That said, there is much to be gained from the employer acting as an intermediary between pension service providers and employees in defined contribution plans. Latin American governments have a lot to learn from the long, international experience in occupational pension provision. There are many generally successful examples of mandatory occupational plans based on defined contribution formulas, such as those in Australia, Denmark, Hong Kong (China), and Switzerland.[7]

Of all Latin American countries that have introduced mandatory individual retirement accounts, only Costa Rica permits employers to contract the funds management directly with pension fund administrators. This authorization, however, only extends to voluntary pension contributions. Costa Rica has also permitted the continuation of occupational defined benefit plans for some public sector workers, some of which are complementary to the individual account system.

Arrau and Valdés-Prieto (2001) proposed reforms to the mandatory pension system in Chile along the lines of the United States' 401(k) system, but with limits on investment in company stock. The Chilean parliament has considered a similar proposal. Further discussion of this policy option is needed in other Latin American countries. Occupational pension plans that involve the employers in the negotiation of fees with pension service providers (asset managers) can help keep costs down and simplify investment choices for workers. If other countries follow Chile and liberalize product and provider choice in their funded pension systems, the employers' role will become all the more valuable for securing retirement income for affiliates.

One important caveat that should be considered here is that employer plans are notoriously subject to agency risk. However, regulations can be designed to ameliorate this problem, as has been done in the current system to minimize conflicts of interest between plan members and fund managers. A potential conflict of interest could arise in an employer-intermediated plan if workers pay commissions that are negotiated between employers and fund managers. It may, therefore, be better for employers to pay commissions, as proposed by Arrau and Valdés-Prieto (2001). Nonetheless, it should be noted that supervision of conflicts in occupational schemes may be much more expensive than in the current personal plans, given the large number of employers present. That said, one could argue that employees already have means of monitoring their employers' actions via labor market institutions in many countries.

Another problem of the proposal is that self-employed workers and those working for small employers (the majority of workers in Latin America) may be left at a disadvantage. In fact, salaried workers already benefit from voluntary employer contributions in the existing system. Small employers could also sponsor plans jointly (multi-employer pension plans are common in Brazil, for example). If the government is concerned about the interests of the self-employed population, the adequate response should be to subsidize contributions by these workers rather than impede access for salaried workers to more efficient retirement arrangements.[8] This solution was recently put into practice in the Dominican Republic and should be monitored closely and evaluated carefully, particularly with regard to its fiscal costs.

It may also be argued that employer intermediation, although superior to personal arrangements in terms of cost efficiency, may still be more expensive than a more centralized solution. Bolivia is the Latin American country that comes closest to a centralized model, especially because the two Spanish banks that owned the two pension fund administrators merged in 2000. The Bolivian reform also included caps on commissions and the auctioning of licenses for pension fund administration. Another example of a bidding contest for assigning fund management was the Chilean auction for managing the individual accounts of the new unemployment insurance program. This contest led to commission levels close to US$4 per worker per year. Chilean pension fund administrators charge 20 times this amount for managing individual retirement accounts.

One could argue that full centralization of pension administration would obliterate the benefits of competition in private pension fund management. Evidence from Latin America, however, clearly shows that the current pension fund industries are anything but good examples of competition. The Bolivian case also demonstrates that governments can organize transparent bidding contests for pension fund management that are less vulnerable to political risk.

An alternative to full centralization (as in the case of the de facto Bolivian monopoly) is to centralize only certain services, such as contribution collection and record-keeping functions that have significant economies of scale and lower policy risk. Centralized contribution collection is already in place in some Latin American countries, such as Argentina and Mexico, but it does not seem to have led to lower costs than in countries with decentralized mechanisms (Demarco and Rofman 1998). An assessment of the causes is now overdue.

Outside Latin America, Sweden and Estonia have embraced centralization in pension administration services other than asset management. Sweden has centralized account management, record keeping, and benefit payment (in the form of annuities). Only asset management is in the hands of the private sector. Workers choose among the full range of mutual funds licensed in the country.[9] The advantage of this system is that mutual fund managers ignore the identity of the owners of the assets that they manage. As a result, sales agents that have proved so costly, because there is no way to check whether a person targeted by an agent, has actually become a new client of the fund manager.

Such proposals are certainly worthy of consideration in Latin America, although the experience with public pension systems raises doubts about the ability of governments in the region to manage centralized systems as is done in Sweden.[10] One way to avoid this problem is to transfer the record-keeping function to employers. Employers are already required to ensure that contributions are paid on time and must maintain a record of the contributions made to the pension system on behalf of their employees.

Parallel efforts should be made also to promote competition and choice of provider in asset management and insurance services. Competition could be enhanced by opening up the pension fund management industry to other financial institutions that would act as professional asset managers. Greater competition is also needed in the market for insurance products (e.g., annuities) in countries such as Argentina, where the affiliates are offered only the products of the company that is tied to the pension fund administrator.

Caps on commissions would also seem to be highly relevant for Latin America, where financial literacy is lower than in OECD countries and financial products are still relatively standardized given the limited investment opportunities (table 10.2). Caps are also becoming popular in some OECD countries such as Ireland, Sweden, and the United Kingdom. Under the United Kingdom's stakeholder proposal private providers may only charge fees on assets under management, subject to a 1 percent limit. In Sweden fees are also capped as a percentage of assets, but they vary depending on the size of the fund.

Governments can also do much to increase the affiliates' responsiveness to commissions so that they choose those providers who offer the lowest fees. The transparency of fees can be enhanced by requiring the disclosure of fees for the whole industry (clearly separating administration fees from insurance premiums), deducting the fees from the accumulated balance (though still calculated on the basis of contributions or salaries), and simulating their impact on the expected pension benefit. Such information could be provided in the regular account statements that affiliates receive. A similar degree of disclosure could be used for annuity rates. Another, more interventionist mechanism is to allocate indecisive workers to the fund manager offering the lowest commissions. Finally, pension fund administrators could be permitted to offer lower commissions for "loyal" affiliates who stay for a certain period with the same administrator. This is currently only permitted in some Latin American countries. There is much ongoing experimentation in this area, and no one-size-fits-all solution is likely to emerge.

Improving Risk Management of Mandated Retirement Savings

The second key feature of the consumption-smoothing component that should be reformed is the design of investment regulations and of individual choice in the system to ensure (a) a better fit with the affiliates' appetite for risk and liquidity and (b) better management of investment and longevity risk. Reforms are needed in both the accumulation (saving) and the distribution (retirement) phases, although probably more radical

Table 10.2 Reform Options to Ensure That Savings Are Passed on to Affiliates as Lower Commissions

Reform proposal	Rationale	Country case	Potential problems
Place caps on commissions.	This is an effective way to limit fees. When accompanied by regulations on fee structures it ensures a high degree of transparency for investors.	All Latin American countries except Mexico already regulate commission structures, but only Bolivia has actually imposed limits on fees.	The cap may be set too low and will need to be adjusted as technology and market conditions change.
Improve the visibility and comparability of commissions by requiring that all commissions be deducted from the accumulated balance rather then deducted directly from payroll. Visibility can also be enhanced by disclosing comparative fees across pension fund administrators.	Commissions paid out from the accumulated balance are more visible to workers than are commissions deducted from payroll.	Since November 1998 Chile requires that all information regarding commissions be included in the quarterly statements sent to participants, including a comparison of commissions. Since May 2000 the types of commissions charged (fixed, variable, and transfer fees) must also be clearly disclosed.	The participant may pay higher fees for the stricter disclosure requirements.
Establish an information process for transmitting information about benefit options to plan members, so that they can compare annuity rates and other relevant variables.	Lack of transparency in annuity sales has driven costs up. Workers take cash rebates instead of focusing on annuity rates.	In Chile pension fund administrators must disclose various annuity options available to the plan members prior to annuity sales.	There is a danger of cartels being formed between pension fund administrators and insurance companies if they are allowed to exchange information about plan members.

Allocate workers who enter formal sector jobs for the first time and do not choose a pension fund administrator, to the cheapest administrator (according to the expected income level).	By choosing the lowest possible commission the average cost of the system is reduced.	This mechanism for allocating indecisive workers was introduced in Argentina at the end of 2001.	The only element of individual choice in the system is eliminated. All key decisions are made by the pension fund administrators under the surveillance of the state.
Permit pension fund administrators to offer lower commissions for "loyal" affiliates who stay with the same administrator for a certain period.	"Loyalty" discounts create an incentive for workers to choose their fund administrator more carefully because when they change they forgo the reduction in commissions.	Argentina and Mexico allow "loyalty" discounts.	Discounts may not discourage other administrators from offering rewards to workers who change affiliation.

Source: Authors' compilation.

changes are needed in the former given the practical lack of individual choice.

Some basic reforms are needed to improve the management of investment risk (table 10.3). First, investment in securities issued by foreign entities should be permitted. Chile is currently the country that has gone farthest in liberalizing overseas investment by pension funds, raising the ceiling to 20 percent of the pension funds' portfolios. Diversification abroad is especially important in small countries with limited opportunities for domestic investment, and in countries with unstable macroeconomic conditions. But it is precisely these countries that typically impose the strictest limits on foreign investment. By steering investments toward domestic markets governments hope to develop their capital markets and reduce dependency on volatile foreign capital. They instead increase workers' investment risk.

Second, the single-fund model should be relaxed and at least two other funds should be introduced. One of the funds should be a low-risk fund invested mainly in debt of the highest credit rating (both domestic and international), inflation-indexed as far as possible, and covering long maturities. The second fund should be a diversified portfolio of riskier assets, including corporate debt and equities. The third fund would consist of a domestic money market portfolio. Workers would be allowed to choose among these three funds, but limits might be imposed on the last two funds for prudential reasons.

The logic of this arrangement is as follows. The first fund would be, to the extent possible, the long-term risk-free asset that an investor needs to build an optimal portfolio for retirement. In countries such as Chile, where there is a liquid market for inflation-indexed, long-term government debt of high credit standing, such a portfolio could consist mainly of debt instruments. In other countries where domestic debt has a higher default risk there would be a need to permit greater investment in debt issued by foreign governments and corporations. The second fund would permit workers with greater appetites for risk to invest in a well-diversified portfolio of bonds and equities. Such a fund would contain both domestic and foreign securities, depending on the quality of the former. The third fund would permit workers near retirement to increase the liquidity in their portfolio to cash out some of their savings.

This basic three-fund system is similar to the five-fund system introduced in Chile in 2002 and legislated in Peru in 2003 (to be introduced in 2005), as well as the three-fund system of the thrift savings plans (TSPs) for federal government employees in the United States.[11] The main difference is that the three-fund model would allow for greater flexibility in the choice between domestic and foreign assets, and would clearly identify a portfolio that is as far as possible a long-term risk-free asset. In the TSP, the G fund approximates this because Treasuries are arguably the safest securities in the world. However, because most of the instruments in this portfolio are

Table 10.3 Reform Options to Improve Investment and Longevity Risk Management

Reform proposal	Rationale	Country case	Potential problems
Liberalize investment abroad by pension funds.	Given high volatility of domestic securities, foreign investment (especially equities) can significantly improve risk–return trade-offs.	Chile is the country that has gone farthest in liberalizing foreign investment. Mexico is the last country to permit such investment.	Foreign investment may bring undesirable macroeconomic consequences, institutionalizing capital flight. It is also difficult for governments to allow such investment when the domestic economy has insufficient access to financing.
Introduce a multifund structure with different portfolio allocations.	Individuals would be able to adjust their portfolios to suit their risk preferences.	Chile introduced a five-fund structure in 2002. Peru legislated a similar multifund structure in 2003.	Some individuals may find it difficult to make choices. In the Chilean case undecided people are allocated to a fund according to their age.
Authorize variable annuities.	Some individuals may prefer to bear investment risk during the retirement age and thus aim at higher benefits.	Bolivia is the only country that has authorized variable annuities.	Variable annuities expose individuals to the volatility of financial markets. If the funds are largely invested in equities there can be massive changes in the pension benefit during retirement.
Authorize purchase of annuities with multiple premiums.	By spreading the purchase of an annuity over many years, one reduces timing risk (the risk that interest rates are low at the time of purchase).	No Latin American country allows individuals to spread out the annuitization of the accumulated balance.	The administrative cost of multiple-premium annuities tends to be greater than that of single-premium annuities because money has to be collected and annuitized on many occasions.

(Table continues on the following page.)

Table 10.3 (continued)

Reform proposal	Rationale	Country case	Potential problems
Authorize deferral of annuity purchase after retirement, opting for scheduled withdrawals in the meantime.	The value of annuitization increases as a worker becomes older: there is a higher risk of outliving one's resources, the bequest motive is less important, and the cost of annuities is lower because of the higher probability of death.	Chile and Peru allow workers to switch from scheduled withdrawals to annuities after retirement.	Workers may be forced to enter annuity contracts under adverse conditions (at times of low interest rates) if they leave the annuitization option until late in their working lives.
Modernize mortality tables.	Mortality tables should be based on recent historical experience of annuitants in the country.	Chile created mortality tables based on annuitants in the 1970s; the tables are used in Peru, too.	Local annuity tables require sufficiently large samples and history to reduce statistical errors.
Permit saving through other financial instruments such as mutual funds and savings products offered by banks and the life insurance industry.	Mutual funds are very similar to pension funds but offer a much broader array of investment choices. Banks and life insurance companies can offer interest rate guarantees that may be attractive for workers.	No country has opened up the mandatory funded component to competition. Chile opened up the voluntary component to other financial instruments and providers in 2002.	The lack of transparency in performance and fees may impede appropriate individual choices. Allowing a wider set of financial sector actors to manage mandated savings makes supervision more difficult and could increase the risk of losses from mismanagement.

Source: Authors' compilation.

not inflation-indexed (the U.S. government only started issuing such bonds in the 1990s), there is no protection against inflation over a long investment horizon.

The introduction of individual choice in investment allocation would not only permit the construction of optimal retirement savings portfolios, but would also help further insulate the pension system from political risk. In its current form, where a handful of investment directors control all pension assets, it is too tempting for governments to change the investment regimen on an ad hoc basis to meet their needs or objectives, such as easing a fiscal deficit or veering investment toward unprofitable or risky industries that support the elected government. It is crucial also that the introduction of portfolio choice is accompanied by intensive financial education campaigns.

Reforms are also needed during the retirement stage to permit better management of investment and longevity risk. Some aspects of the design of the distribution stage appear problematic. First, while a case can be made for mandating annuities for the portion of the accumulated balance needed to keep the worker out of poverty in old age, this is better accomplished by a separate poverty prevention pillar. For contributions above this level, mandating annuities is less compelling. Poorer workers tend to have shorter lives and greater consumption needs, so obliging them to buy annuities can have regressive effects on the income distribution. Yet in Bolivia and Uruguay annuities are mandatory at the retirement age.

Second, variable annuities, in which investment risk is borne by the pensioner and longevity risk is borne by the insurance companies, do not yet exist in any country and are only permitted in Bolivia. These annuities may be particularly attractive for higher-income workers or for workers in areas where the public pension system still offers generous retirement income.

Third, the requirement to buy annuities with a single premium impinges on the ability of individuals to smooth the risk of mistiming the annuity purchase. Some people will find that at the time of retirement long-term interest rates, and thus the payout that insurance companies offer them, are lower than they had expected. Ideally, an individual would buy an annuity in installments or would purchase successive annuities to smooth this volatility.

Fourth, more flexibility is also needed to enable workers to switch from scheduled withdrawals to annuities at some point during their retirement, as is the case in Chile and Peru. The value of annuitizing the remaining balance increases as a worker grows older: bequest motives become less important as the fund is drawn down, the risk of outliving one's savings becomes higher, and the cost of annuitizing decreases.

Fifth, the requirement that private annuities be indexed to inflation in countries that lack liquid inflation-indexed government bonds (such as Colombia and Peru) seems irresponsible. Although the intention behind this requirement is good (protecting elderly people against price increases), the results are likely to be detrimental to workers. Private insurance companies will charge hefty fees for protecting benefits against a risk that ultimately only the government can affect.

Reforms are also needed to improve information on life expectancy of annuitants. Some Latin American countries (e.g., Argentina) rely on mortality tables from OECD countries that may be out of line with developments in the "younger" Latin American populations. Countries with young funded pension systems may be better off using data from countries with older systems, such as Chile, although there is a need to modernize the mortality tables even in Chile because they date from the 1970s.

Latin American governments should also consider more generally whether there are other financial instruments available that would be suitable for retirement savings purposes. In principle, well-regulated financial systems can offer suitable alternative retirement products, such as mutual funds and insurance policies. Mutual funds are in fact likely to come into close competition with pension funds in Chile because the nature of the investment products they offer is similar. Indeed, in many ways Latin America's new mandatory pension funds are simply a special type of mutual fund.[12]

Life insurance companies are also in a position to offer products over the accumulation stage that are attractive for more risk-averse individuals. In Chile insurance companies already market a life insurance policy in the new voluntary pension system (the so-called *seguro de vida con ahorro*, or life insurance with savings) with a savings component that can be covered by a real return guarantee. Such a guarantee can be offered because there is a liquid, long-term, inflation-indexed bond market that insurance companies can tap to hedge their liabilities. Chilean insurance companies already rely on these bonds to hedge liabilities arising from the underwriting of annuities contracts. The life insurance industry in Argentina and Peru offer similar (if admittedly less sophisticated) products that combine insurance and savings features.

The long-term guaranteed rate of return offered by insurance companies in Chile may be superior to the bond portfolio offered in an individual pension fund account for many workers because the companies can tie down a real rate of return on contributions over a long investment horizon. A portfolio of bonds of different maturities is subject to reinvestment risk and may therefore be less attractive for risk-averse investors. Nonetheless, insurance companies are not able to offer interest rate guarantees over a period longer than a few years in other Latin American countries because of their higher interest rate volatility and lack of long-dated instruments.

The only countries that resemble Chile in the extent of capital markets development are Brazil and Mexico. Both of these countries have a more developed equity market that accounts for more than 90 percent of all stocks traded in the region, although their debt markets are still concentrated in shorter maturities and have not developed as liquid, inflation-indexed securities markets. Hence products offering investment guarantees are still some time away for even these relatively developed Latin American countries.

The problem with permitting choice over savings products in the mandatory system arises from the difficulty of comparing different fee structures. If Chile and eventually other Latin American countries were to open up their mandatory pension system to other financial products, they should first ensure that commissions structures are comparable, perhaps by permitting only commissions based on accumulated assets. In addition, many Latin American countries have not reinforced the regulatory and supervisory framework for mutual funds and insurance companies. It would be unwise to open up the mandatory system to these financial institutions in their current state. Of course, if all the resources that have been dedicated to establish and supervise the new private second pillar effectively had instead simply been used instead to improve the regulation and supervision of other financial institutions, these conclusions may have been different.

Improving the Voluntary Savings Pillar: Increasing Options and Incentives

Ideally, in an enlarged voluntary retirement savings pillar the decisions of how much to invest and in what instrument to invest should be left to the individual. To avoid distortions to inter-temporal consumption choices, all suitable retirement savings products should be subject to the same expenditure tax.[13] To maximize the extent of flexibility of the system workers should be allowed to carry forward unused tax deductions to later years.

There are two main drawbacks with this liberal model of voluntary retirement savings. The first is that individuals may not have a sufficient level of financial literacy to make adequate investment choices. Even if they do the extent of differentiation among financial products may make it too complicated or time consuming for the average worker to compare fees and performance across savings vehicles. The liberal model of voluntary savings, therefore, calls at the very least for a regulatory framework that ensures the transparency of the cost and benefit of different financial products.

Another real-world drawback with this ideal model is that richer workers often take most advantage of the tax incentives offered by governments to encourage retirement saving to reduce their tax liability. This problem can be significantly ameliorated by offering instead a public subsidy to workers who contribute to a savings plan, as is done in the Mexican mandatory funded pillar and in the mandatory pillar for self-employed workers in the Dominican Republic.[14] Such a subsidy would probably be necessary in Latin American countries where a large section of the population (sometimes more than half) are not subject to income taxes. The progressive impact of the subsidy can be ensured by fixing it in absolute amounts (as in Mexico) and by setting an upper ceiling on taxable earnings for subsidy eligibility.

In all Latin American countries (except Chile since 2002 and Brazil) the regulation and taxation of voluntary pension savings are far from this liberal model. Chile has recently extended the preferential treatment of voluntary retirement savings to financial products offered outside the AFP industry (see box 10.1). In addition to bank deposits (which provide a less volatile return than pension funds), mutual funds and insurance policies are competing as voluntary pension savings products in Chile since the beginning of 2002.

Box 10.1 The Big-Bang Approach to Voluntary Pension Savings Reform in Chile

Since March 2002 Chilean workers have been able to save up to 50 UFs[1] of their monthly pre-tax income in any voluntary pension plan authorized by the securities and insurance regulator, as well as in voluntary savings accounts managed by the private second-pillar AFPs. There are no restrictions on the number of plans or AFPs in which workers may deposit their voluntary savings. Workers also may cash out these plans at any time before retirement, subject to a 10 percent special excise tax (in addition to the relevant income tax). Employer contributions, however, may only be liquidated at retirement.

The development and performance of the voluntary market in the coming years will be followed closely by Chilean policymakers, who may use the voluntary pensions market as a testing ground for a possible reform of the mandatory system. Two of the most complicated issues in the operation of the voluntary pensions market will be the transfers between plans and providers and the commissions charged.

Although the law does not envisage any limits in switching among plans, it does regulate the commission structure firmly. AFPs may only charge a fixed commission for collecting voluntary contributions and transferring them to the plan chosen by the worker. This fixed commission must be the same regardless of the plan chosen. AFPs and voluntary pension plan providers may not charge a commission, however, for partial or full transfers of the accumulated balance in the individual's voluntary account to another AFP or to a different voluntary plan. The voluntary pension plan providers and the AFPs may charge commissions for fund management based on the stock of accumulated assets.

Note: *Unidades de fomento* are inflation-indexed monetary units used for all financial transactions in Chile.

Prior to the 2002 reform in Chile the only option available to individuals wishing to benefit from tax incentives was to park their voluntary savings up to retirement in the mandatory, illiquid AFP accounts. Other savings vehicles, including the more liquid *Cuenta 2* offered by the pension fund administrators, were not as tax advantaged. The *Cuenta 2* itself, however, was less popular than other financial products even though there were no additional commissions and it had a somewhat more attractive tax treatment than mutual funds and savings products offered by life insurance companies before March 2002. Probably the only negative feature of the *Cuenta 2* is that withdrawals are only permitted twice a year. Despite its benefits there has been a net withdrawal of voluntary savings from the AFP *Cuenta 2* over the last two years, while there has been sustained growth in premiums for savings products offered by life insurance companies (see figure 10.2).

Prior to Chile's reform in March 2002, Brazil was the Latin American exception in permitting a high degree of choice for tax-advantaged,

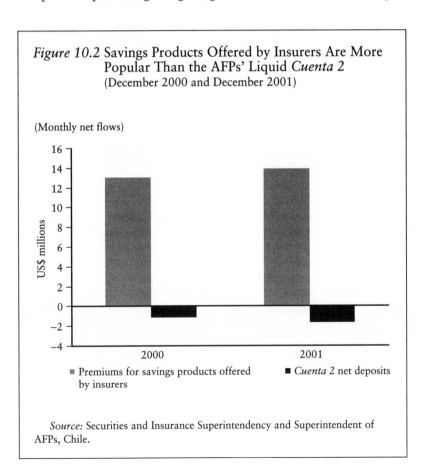

Figure 10.2 Savings Products Offered by Insurers Are More Popular Than the AFPs' Liquid *Cuenta 2*
(December 2000 and December 2001)

(Monthly net flows)

■ Premiums for savings products offered   ■ *Cuenta 2* net deposits
by insurers

Source: Securities and Insurance Superintendency and Superintendent of AFPs, Chile.

long-term savings. Its mutual fund industry is highly developed and offers both occupational and personal pension plans (see box 10.2). The mutual funds are in fact at the center of the new voluntary personal pension plans that have been instituted since the mid-1990s. Life insurance companies also participate actively as providers of personal pension plans and can sell retirement savings products to companies.

High contributions to the mandatory pension system (both the PAYG and the funded second pillar), the illiquidity of voluntary contributions to

---

Box 10.2 The Role of the Financial System in Brazil's Voluntary Pension Savings Plans

The voluntary pensions system in Brazil consist of two distinct sectors— the occupational and the personal sectors. Although occupational plans still dominate the pensions landscape, accounting for the vast majority of members and assets, their growth has been disappointing over the last two decades. Personal pension plans, however, are expanding at a rapid pace (contributions to personal plans grew at an average annual rate of 38 percent between 1994 and 2001).

Occupational plans are established by employers and have been traditionally of the defined benefit variety, financed through the establishment of pension funds. The importance of mutual funds and professional asset managers in this system cannot be overstated. Mutual funds account for one-half of all assets held by occupational pension funds. Professional asset managers handle more than one-quarter of all occupational pension assets.

Three main types of personal plans exist—the traditional pension plans, the personal pension plans without benefit guarantees (*plano gerador de benefício livres*, PGBLs), and the individual programmed pension funds (*fundo de aposentadoria programada individual*, FAPIs). All receive a favorable tax treatment (deductibility up to 12 percent of salary) but have different liquidity requirements. Although traditional personal plans and PGBLs must be kept until retirement, investments in FAPIs must be kept for at least 10 years to receive tax benefits. If savings are withdrawn before that time a penalty is imposed.

Both the traditional plans and the PGBLs are administered by insurance companies or specialized providers. The traditional plans are essentially deferred annuity contracts. They offer guaranteed real rates of return that may become unaffordable for insurance companies as soon as macroeconomic conditions improve and interest rates fall. On the other hand, the more recent PGBLs are unit-linked products in which contributions are invested in mutual funds. At retirement the accumulated balance must be transformed into an annuity. FAPIs are managed by banks but must also offer a set of investment options consisting largely of mutual funds.

Box 10.2 (continued)

In addition to the PGBL and the FAPI, a new generation of products combining life insurance and savings has recently gained approval by the insurance supervisor. Like its Chilean equivalent (*seguro de vida con ahorro*, or life insurance with savings), the life insurance plan without benefit guarantees (*vida gerador de beneficio livre*, VGPL) offers a lump-sum payment in case of death during the accumulation stage and benefits in the form of annuities when the policyholder retires. The benefits depend on the funds accumulated at the time of the claim.

Given the rich variety of products and financial service providers, to the extent that the government of Brazil considers a partial shift from PAYG financing to funding for income replacement in old age, it would rely on its existing financial institutions and products rather than establish new ones (as other countries in the region have done).

Source: Gill, Packard, Schwarz, and Yermo (2001).

---

the pension funds, and limited tax advantages for saving in other retirement products may explain in part why saving in Latin America is low. Economists still dispute whether the net effect of structural pension reforms has been positive to household savings, and in particular whether mandatory savings "crowd out" or "crowd in" voluntary savings (Schmidtt-Hebbel 1998a). Even in Chile, the only country in Latin America where total contribution rates to the pension system fell after the reform, household savings in 2000 were at only a slightly higher level than in 1987.

There is little doubt that by excluding other financial products from the benefits of both the mandatory and the tax-advantaged voluntary retirement savings pillars, their development has been handicapped. Saving in financial instruments such as mutual funds and life insurance (other than the mandatory insurance for death and disability) is much lower than pension fund saving. Except in Brazil, employer-sponsored retirement programs are also rare, covering only some public sector plans and a few multinational corporations. Nonetheless, opening up the sector to competition from alternative products and providers would require a tremendous regulatory effort to ensure the transparency of the cost and benefits of different products and adequate supervision of their providers.

Do Mutual Funds Have a Role in the Voluntary Savings Pillar?

Savings in mutual funds was less than 10 percent of GDP in all Latin American countries that had introduced a mandatory private pension pillar as of 2001. In contrast, Brazil's mutual funds have experienced

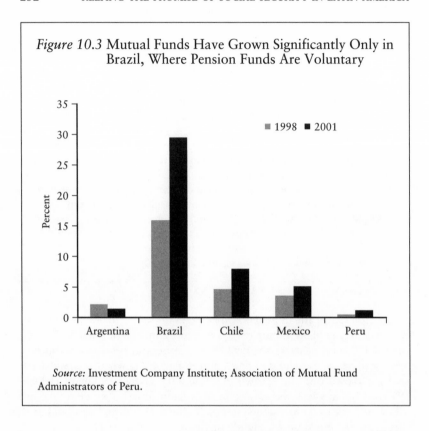

Figure 10.3 Mutual Funds Have Grown Significantly Only in Brazil, Where Pension Funds Are Voluntary

Source: Investment Company Institute; Association of Mutual Fund Administrators of Peru.

tremendous growth in the past decade. As shown in figure 10.3, mutual fund assets grew from 15 percent to nearly 30 percent of GDP between 1998 and 2001. This growth can be largely accounted for by pension funds and other corporate investors who invest in mutual funds because they are not subject to the tax on financial transactions. Up to one-half of pension fund assets were invested in mutual funds in December 2001, whereas pension funds and other corporate investors accounted for more than one-half of mutual fund balances.

The limited development of mutual funds in Latin American countries other than Brazil offers some interesting insights on the implications of introducing a mandatory private pension system for the development of a voluntary savings pillar. The new second-pillar pension funds and mutual funds have a lot in common. They both operate on the principle of individual ownership of a quota of a fund that is invested in financial instruments by a company that is dedicated exclusively to that purpose. The few differences between the two industries are in fact driven by regulatory requirements, which tend to be more onerous for the new second-pillar pension funds. Although individual investors face no restrictions in the type and number of mutual funds in which they can invest, mandatory saving in second-pillar pension funds is highly regulated. Workers may save in only one fund (except in Chile and soon in Peru where five funds are available), which is subject to strict investment and performance regulations. Of course, the prohibition against accessing savings until retirement also affects the functioning of the pension fund industry. Pension fund administrators have benefited enormously from this captive market, which has helped boost their profitability.

The obligation to save through pension funds has set a lower boundary on the potential saving in mutual funds because it has reduced the disposable income of workers.[15] Had workers been free to place their mandatory savings in different financial products, there is little doubt that mutual fund growth would have been more pronounced. Even in the voluntary savings market, however, the mutual fund industry has been placed at a disadvantage relative to pension funds.

First, mutual fund savings have been subject to a less attractive tax treatment than voluntary contributions to the pension fund system. This asymmetry in tax treatment exists because voluntary contributions to the pension funds cannot be cashed out before retirement in most Latin American countries. Even in those countries where they can be cashed out (Chile, Costa Rica, Mexico, and Peru) there is a maximum frequency for distributions.[16]

A second bias against mutual funds is that governments have made less of an effort at regulating and supervising them than they have at overseeing new pension funds. The disclosure of mutual fund performance and commissions in particular is far less transparent than that of pension funds. In most Latin American countries mutual funds can charge commissions on entry and exit, as well as an annual management charge (set normally as a percentage of assets under management). Competition in the mutual fund market of countries such as Argentina, Chile, or Mexico does not take place via commissions and performance. Instead, the main determinant of the mutual fund administrators' profitability is access to a distribution channel. In Chile, for example, mutual funds sold through bank branches by administrators tend to have a higher profitability than those sold by independent administrators. The Chilean mutual fund industry has also been hampered in the past by regulations requiring separate administrators for open-ended, closed-ended, and real estate mutual funds. This artificial separation was lifted during the capital markets reform in 2002.

Investment regulations for mutual funds at times have verged on the side of imprudence, failing to address conflicts of interest effectively. In Mexico, for example, mutual funds can invest freely in assets of the administrator's parent company. In the past mutual funds have been used by the main Mexican financial groups to obtain financing for their operations. Even today such investments are permitted. Latin American pension funds, on the other hand, are subject to an investment limit of 5 percent (less in some countries) on assets of companies related to the pension fund administrator.

These policy decisions (tax treatment and regulatory framework) have further weakened the attractiveness of mutual funds relative to pension funds and probably explain the slow development of mutual funds in Spanish-speaking Latin America relative to Brazil. The mutual fund industry has not been able to reap the benefit from economies of scale present in financial markets as have the second-pillar pension funds, and it has been subject to less scrutiny of its market practices. As a result competitive forces have been weak in driving commissions lower.

The fees charged by open-ended mutual funds are certainly much higher than those charged by pension funds. Maturana and Walker (1999) showed that average commissions (including entry, exit, and annual management fees) for the Chilean mutual fund industry represented 3.1 percent of total assets managed in 1996 (down from 3.8 percent in 1990). Pension fund commissions are significantly lower, verging currently toward a level equivalent to approximately 0.7 percent of assets under management.[17] The commissions charged by equity mutual funds in Chile also seem high when compared with other countries. By the end of 2001 annual management fees for equity mutual funds in Chile were 5 percent of assets under management, whereas in Brazil they were only 3 percent.

The evolution of annual fund management commissions charged for the three main types of mutual funds during the 1990s is shown in figure 10.4. It is noteworthy that commissions charged by equity funds have remained stubbornly high despite the sustained growth in total assets under management. This suggests that the problem of high commissions is not just the result of economies of scale but that there are barriers to entry in the industry that allow players to keep commissions high.

A priori, however, it would seem that operational costs and hence economies of scale may account partly for the higher fees charged by Chilean mutual funds relative to second-pillar pension funds. The operating expenses of Chilean pension fund administrators equaled 0.5 percent of assets in 2001, whereas the figure for mutual fund administrators was much higher (0.9 percent).

As shown in figure 10.5, however, economies of scale operate largely at low levels of assets under management (less than 100 billion pesos) and thereafter they stabilize rapidly. Indeed, the two mutual fund administrators that had cost-to-asset ratios similar to those of the pension fund administrators (0.7 percent) managed less than 150 billion pesos. Another important factor that may explain the higher fees for mutual funds is the lower transparency of fee structures and greater extent of product differentiation. That there are 20 mutual fund administrators but only 5 pension fund administrators in Chile despite the much larger size of the pension fund industry, demonstrates that it may be easier to create a competitive advantage in the mutual fund industry.

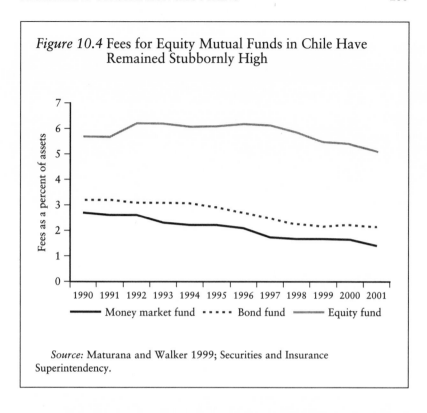

Figure 10.4 Fees for Equity Mutual Funds in Chile Have Remained Stubbornly High

Source: Maturana and Walker 1999; Securities and Insurance Superintendency.

Looking ahead, what role should the mutual fund industry play in Latin America's reformed pension systems? The similarities in the operation of second-pillar pension funds and mutual funds raise doubts about the efficiency of maintaining separate administrators for each type of fund and supervising the two systems under different regulatory authorities. Indeed, to the extent that a mandatory savings system requires additional prudential regulations (such as performance rules, and quantitative investment regulations), there is no reason why regulators could not apply them also to mutual fund administrators. Maintaining separate administration and supervision for pension funds and mutual funds is particularly costly in poorer countries where skilled labor is in short supply in both public and private sectors.

In many Latin American countries, however, the mutual fund industry is not ready to play a central role in retirement savings. Transparency and conflicts of interest with related financial groups are rife, and commissions seem to be even higher than those charged by second-pillar pension fund administrators. Before policymakers consider opening up the voluntary pension pillar to mutual funds they should ensure that the industry is ready to compete with second-pillar pension funds as the agent

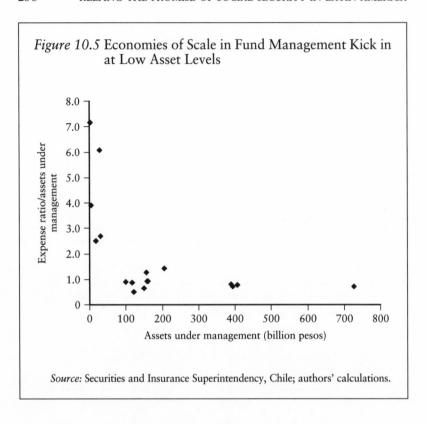

Figure 10.5 Economies of Scale in Fund Management Kick in at Low Asset Levels

Source: Securities and Insurance Superintendency, Chile; authors' calculations.

of workers in channeling their pension contributions into productive investments.

Is There a Role for Life Insurance Providers in the Voluntary Savings Pillar?

Unlike mutual funds, the life insurance industry has not been excluded from the new mandatory private pension pillars in Latin America. On the contrary, death and disability insurance is also mandatory and managed by life insurance companies in all countries that have reformed their pension systems (except Mexico and Costa Rica, where the social security institute administers these benefits). Life insurance companies also play a central role in the retirement stage of the new systems selling annuities. They are not allowed, however, to manage funds from forced savings during the capital accumulation phase before retirement.

Some savings products sold by insurance companies could have been used, like mutual funds, as vehicles for long-term saving. Life insurance companies in Latin America often provide policies with savings accounts. In some cases, as in Chile, the rate of return on these accounts is protected by absolute return guarantees, which are attractive for risk-averse, long-term investors. In the context of a volatile interest rate environment, however, such guarantees may only be affordable over relatively short periods. Insurance companies in some OECD countries have experienced severe difficulties in recent years as a result of guarantees offered during the 1970s when interest rates were at much higher levels. The availability of inflation-indexed government bonds would ease asset liability management by insurance companies because the interest rate volatility of real bonds tends to be much lower than that of nominal bonds.

Exclusion from the accumulation side of the mandatory pension pillars and a less advantageous tax treatment than voluntary contributions to the second-pillar pension funds have handicapped the development of the market for savings policies sold by life insurance firms. Questions remain even now about the readiness of the industry to become a viable competitor with the second-pillar pension fund administrators. Historically the supervision of insurance companies has been less effective than that of second-pillar pension funds. One continuing problem is the lack of separation of life insurance and non–life insurance operations, which creates risks for potential savers in life insurance products. This is probably more of a problem for investors in small countries close to the Andean Mountains and in the Caribbean region where risk of natural catastrophe can be high. The licensing process is also deficient in several Latin American countries. Specifically, some countries do not require the submission of a business plan or they require a feasibility study that covers only certain aspects of the insurance operation. The work of the supervisor is made more difficult by the fact that the appointment of actuaries is not obligatory.

The consequences of the weakness of the regulatory and supervisory framework are evident in the number of insurance company bankruptcies over the past few years. The OECD (2001) reported a total of 57 bankruptcies in seven Latin American countries between 1996 and 1998, distributed as shown in figure 10.6. Only in Mexico and Venezuela were policyholders spared financial losses. In Argentina and Colombia losses were limited by the existence of policyholders' protection funds (only for retirement insurance and workers' compensation).

Despite its turbulent past the insurance industry has recently begun a slow process of modernization in many Latin American countries. Part of the impetus is provided by structural pension reforms, because insurers play a central role in providing coverage against the risks of death and disability before retirement—and can sell annuities during the retirement stage. Chile, the country with the longest-lived private second-pillar pension system, was understandably also the first to tackle some of the problems in the insurance sector.

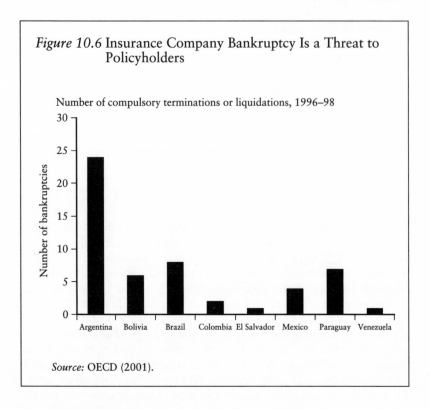

Figure 10.6 Insurance Company Bankruptcy Is a Threat to
Policyholders

Number of compulsory terminations or liquidations, 1996–98

Source: OECD (2001).

Are There Options to Improve the Voluntary Funded System?

The evidence discussed in the previous section raises two main policy questions for Latin American governments that have undertaken reforms of their pension systems:

1. Does the limited liquidity for accumulated funds in the tax-advantaged voluntary retirement savings system of Latin America help or hinder the growth of retirement savings?
2. Are other financial products (such as mutual funds and other savings products managed by financial institutions) attractive as vehicles for long-term saving in the tax-advantaged voluntary pillar?

Although part of the reason for the lack of interest in voluntary saving in pension funds may be lack of public trust in institutions linked to the social security system, the illiquidity of such savings would seem to be a more dissuasive factor. The reform of voluntary pension savings in Chile demonstrates the difficult challenge faced by policymakers when designing a voluntary pillar.

Until March 2002 workers wishing to make additional savings for retirement while benefiting from the same tax treatment as the mandatory contributions could deposit their contributions only in the mandatory pension fund accounts (*Cuenta 1*). Furthermore, workers were able to make voluntary contributions to separate accounts managed by the pension fund administrators, the so-called *Cuenta 2* (or voluntary savings account). As many as four withdrawals from these accounts were permitted in a year. The tax treatment of *Cuenta 2* contributions, however, was not as attractive as that of voluntary contributions to the mandatory accounts. Despite the less advantageous tax treatment of the *Cuenta 2*, its liquidity made it the preferred choice for most Chilean workers. As of December 2001 there were more than 1 million *Cuenta 2* accounts, but only 155,000 mandatory *Cuenta 1* accounts had received voluntary contributions. Only the richer tax-paying individuals have found it attractive to place more of their voluntary savings in the mandatory account rather than the *Cuenta 2*. This explains why the total funds accumulated in the *Cuenta 2* were approximately half of those in the mandatory accounts (US$213 million versus US$453 million in September 2002).

Since March 2002 Chilean workers have been able to place the voluntary savings that were originally destined for the mandatory account in a variety of financial products. In addition, the requirement to maintain the balance up to retirement has been eliminated and workers can withdraw as much of their funds as they wish at any time, subject to tax penalties. As a result, voluntary contributions have increased dramatically. According to Chile's superintendent of AFPs, voluntary contributions to the mandatory pension fund accounts over the period March to September 2002 were 14.7 percent above those of the same period in the previous year.

Reform of the voluntary savings market in Chile is also expected to give a huge boost to the mutual fund and life insurance industries. Premiums paid for voluntary retirement savings products sold by life insurance companies between March and September 2002 equaled US$5.7 million, a sizable amount but significantly less than the voluntary deposits made into the mandatory pension fund accounts over the same period (US$59 million).

The boost to voluntary savings since the 2002 reform calls into question the logic of the prohibition against withdrawal of funds before retirement to the extent that it dissuades workers from participating in the pension system. It would seem that, at least for voluntary retirement savings, expecting workers to accept parting with their assets until retirement is not very reasonable. The Chilean evidence clearly shows that voluntary retirement savings can be increased by allowing greater access to the accumulated funds before retirement. Tax benefits can be clawed back if funds are cashed out before retirement, thereby creating an incentive for long-term saving. Such mechanisms have been successfully implemented in many OECD countries and could be explored in Latin America.

As to the role of mutual funds and other savings products sold by financial institutions in the pension system, the Chilean evidence clearly shows that these products can also be attractive for workers. The fact that life insurance companies have captured 10 percent of the second-pillar pension funds' market is a clear indication of the competitive pressure to which the second-pillar funds are now subject.

At the same time, however, it is not clear whether the appeal of mutual funds and other savings products is the result of an inherent superiority in performance terms or whether their popularity is simply a result of marketing efforts. In particular, mutual funds in Chile benefit from an extensive bank-branch network through which these products are sold. Insurance companies, meanwhile, can use the same sales agents and brokers to sell both insurance policies and voluntary savings products. Indeed, the savings products authorized for life insurance companies carry a life insurance policy.

The lack of transparency in the commission structure of both mutual funds and life insurance companies is certainly a cause of concern and would caution against a rushed opening of the voluntary retirement savings system to product choice. The past experience of high commissions in the mandatory private second pillar is likely to be repeated in the context of a voluntary savings market where commissions on pension funds are not directly comparable with those on mutual funds and on life insurance companies. Pension fund commissions are applied exclusively to contributions, but mutual fund commissions are primarily applied to the accumulated assets. The complexity of some insurance products and their opaque commission structure do not bode well for a population with low levels of financial literacy.

Extending choice over different financial instruments under these conditions can be a recipe for confusion and ill-informed decisions. Governments bear less fiduciary responsibility in voluntary retirement systems—but to the extent that individual choice among different products is permitted, governments may be blamed for inadequate choices and may be called on to provide compensation for unfortunate workers. The first task, therefore, is to improve the regulation of these financial products and their providers.

A useful reference in this respect will be the Mexican experience with fee calculators that were introduced by the supervisory authority in 2002 to make it possible to compare fees among second-pillar pension fund administrators.[18] New regulations require pension fund members to sign a form that states what effect switching administrators will have on their account balance as a result of different commissions. The pension fund administrators are now also required to inform plan members about any increase in fees. Although it is yet to be seen how effective these policies are at increasing investors' awareness of the relative impact of different fee structures, a simpler and more effective solution would seem to be the one implemented in Chile's new voluntary pension pillar, where only asset-based charges are permitted.

Conclusion

The reform proposals that have been put forward in this chapter have considered how to improve the management of investment and longevity risk and reduce administrative costs of consumption smoothing in the savings pillar, assuming that the primary goal of poverty prevention is met through a separate pillar.

As readers will recall from chapter 7, the other main risks that individuals bear in funded systems are policy and agency risk. We did not dwell extensively on the latter because governments generally have been successful at ensuring the proper functioning of the new second-pillar pension funds. Fortunately fraud and conflicts of interest are issues that have not yet surfaced on a large scale in countries where the new private pillars were introduced with high standards of disclosure and transparency.

Regulation and supervision in other parts of the financial system, however, have yet to achieve the same level of rigor as that of the second-pillar pension fund industry. The mutual fund industry is a case in point. To the extent that greater space is created for voluntary savings and free choice of product and provider is introduced, there will be an even greater urgency to improve the regulation of the financial system. Countries with limited resources should also consider the benefits of consolidated supervisory structures through which the scarce professional staff can be more effectively used in a variety of financial service markets. To the extent that individual choice of savings products and providers is permitted, regulations will also be needed to ensure the comparability of fees and performance. The more choices that people face, the greater the need for access to clear, independent, and timely information about retirement products. Financial literacy programs should be given the highest priority at both government and employer levels.

The Chilean experience with the five funds in the mandatory private pillar and with the liberalization of the voluntary savings pillar will be a good testing ground for these proposals. Peru's experiment with offering greater investment choice to affiliates of the mandatory private pillar also can provide valuable lessons. The approaches taken should be evaluative rather than dogmatic.

It is clear that neither the poverty prevention nor the income-smoothing pillars can be completely insulated from the dangers posed by policy risk. Poverty prevention instruments require a government-mediated transfer of resources among workers. Hence, policy risk will always be present in such plans, especially when governments are unable to maintain fiscal discipline and macroeconomic stability. Funded, privately managed programs, as the Argentine example clearly shows, can also easily fall prey to cash-strapped governments. Just as the repayment promises of a fiscally profligate household are not taken seriously, the promise of old-age income security by a fiscally imprudent government will not be credible. Fiscal prudence is therefore essential to ensure the population's confidence in both the PAYG and funded pillars of the pension system.

Countries that require retirement savings to be mainly invested in government bonds with a high default risk are not in a good position to mandate savings. For such countries policy risk is likely to be overwhelming for the new funded system, as was illustrated by Argentina in 2001. Yet eliminating the mandate is hardly the best solution, even when a basic PAYG pillar still exists. In Argentina the sale of even a small part of the pension funds' government bond portfolio could send waves of panic through the market and interest rates may rise, further damaging the country's fragile economy. This option is not even currently open to the pension funds, as the government debt they hold is in the form of nontradable loans. On the other hand, gradually reducing both the ceiling on earnings subject to the mandate and contribution rates can serve as a disciplining device for the government, which will not be able to make promises it cannot keep.

In general, governments should focus their attention on poverty prevention and prudent macroeconomic management. Mandating investment in government bonds during the initial years of the new system can be a useful vehicle to ease the fiscal cost of structural reforms and to ensure a stable performance of the new second-pillar pension funds, but only as long as governments have previously built a track record of prudent macroeconomic policy. The Chilean government significantly strengthened its primary fiscal surplus prior to the pension reform in 1981 and was therefore in a position to limit pension fund investment to investment-grade bonds. As the transition costs decreased over time, investment restrictions were gradually lifted. Argentina presents the exact opposite scenario. The fiscal deficit of the Argentine government deteriorated significantly in the years following structural pension reform, and that forced the government to rely increasingly on the second-pillar pension funds as a source of captive financing for the ballooning debt. There is a similar risk in other countries, such as Bolivia.

The main lesson from these diverse experiences is that a significant fiscal tightening is a basic *precondition* for the success of structural pension reforms, especially for governments that start from a fragile fiscal stance. Having already reformed its system, Argentina is not in a position to start afresh. To guarantee the sustainability of its retirement system, however, the government's first step should still be to put its internal finances in order. It could then turn the current inflation-indexed loans that it extended to the pension funds into tradable government bonds of increasing maturity.

As long as the fiscal situation is under control, such bonds could help strengthen interest in long-term saving.

In Latin America only Chile has managed to develop a liquid market of investment-grade, long-term, inflation-indexed government bonds. Chile is the only country in the region where long-standing fiscal discipline has successfully raised government bonds to investment grade. Thanks to the development of the government debt market, Chilean insurance companies are able to offer performance guarantees and annuities at competitive prices. Second-pillar pension funds also find Chilean government bonds an attractive and safe source of investment income. At the very least, countries insisting on a retirement security model inspired by the Chilean experience should remain cognizant of these developments. The persisting differences between Chile and these countries over the past decade may even provide cause for reflecting on whether such an approach is suited for all the countries in the region.

The importance of providing these types of sound financial instruments cannot be overestimated. The shift from a defined benefit to a defined contribution system in Latin America involved not just a fair and welcome transfer of cohort-specific longevity risk to individuals, but also laid all investment risk on workers. Prudent governments, however, are in a position to offer long-term investment guarantees that protect individuals from improvidence and governments from their own myopia.

Moving forward, policymakers will need to reconsider the design of their savings pillar. Some of the reforms proposed in this chapter hang on the ability of governments to regulate markets and promote consumer protection. Some basic questions need to be answered: (a) Can the efficiency of centralized record keeping and account management be spared from political manipulation? (b) Can governments ensure as effective supervision for mutual fund administrators and other financial providers as they do for pension fund administrators? (c) Can they ensure transparency in performance and fee structures across products and providers? (d) Can conflicts of interest in employer pension plans be adequately addressed? (e) Is the level of financial literacy of the population sufficient to permit introducing individual choice of investment portfolio or even financial product? (f) Can limits on pension fund investment abroad be relaxed without endangering macroeconomic stability? and (g) Is it politically acceptable to introduce age- and earnings-specific contribution rates and to reduce maximum earnings subject to the savings mandate?

Notes

1. There is no reason why low-income workers should be prohibited from making contributions to the funded pillar, especially if the savings product offers better performance than other financial instruments available in the financial system.

2. Uruguay is the only country that somewhat conforms with this arrangement because poorer workers are not obliged to contribute to the funded system but are covered by a public defined benefit pillar. However this pillar offers earnings-related pensions (the replacement rate is about 50 percent) rather than just a level of income sufficient to avoid old-age poverty.

3. Valdés-Prieto (2002c) has also suggested introducing age-related contributions.

4. As argued earlier and in chapter 9, the poverty prevention objective is best served through a separate, PAYG-financed pillar.

5. The floor for mandatory contributions to the savings pillar would depend on the poverty alleviation target of the first pillar. This is usually set in relation to the minimum or average wage.

6. The experience with occupationally defined benefit plans in Brazil—the country with the largest occupational system in the region—has hardly been a success. Despite their relative maturity (some have existed for more than 40 years), these plans suffer from chronic underfunding and offer little protection to beneficiaries in terms of vesting and portability rules. The Brazilian government has been trying to revamp the regulatory and supervisory system over the last few years and some improvements are starting to be seen. Much work remains to be done, however, before the Brazilian system can be a reference model for other Latin American countries.

7. The voluntary defined contribution occupational plan system in the United States is also worthy of analysis, although possibly as an example not to be followed. The 401(k) plan in the United States may have been heralded as a success and an international model to be commended in Latin America, except for the lack of limits on investment in plan sponsor assets. The risks arising from investment in shares of the sponsoring employer to the extent observed in some U.S. companies may be bearable for relatively wealthier American workers, but are certainly not advisable for plans that substitute for a public social security system, or indeed for the poorer Latin American population.

8. In fact, governments sometimes do the opposite. In Chile, for example, the pension contributions of self-employed workers are not tax deductible.

9. The range of choice available in Sweden (more than 600 mutual funds) may not be suitable for Latin America, given the perceived need for ongoing, expensive supervision and the level of financial literacy of the population. A choice between three or five types of funds, as in Chile, may be more appropriate.

10. It should be noted, however, that despite the extent of centralization of administrative functions, Swedish workers have much more investment freedom than Latin American ones during the accumulation stage. Hence it may be argued that the Swedish system is more protected against political risk than the Latin American one, where investments are decided by investment regulations and the pension funds' portfolios resemble one another.

11. The three-fund classification matches that of mutual funds in Chile. The Mexican pension legislation also permits multiple funds, but this has not been put into practice yet.

12. To be precise, the Latin American pension funds resemble open-ended mutual funds, which stand ready to redeem shares or units of the fund at its net asset value at any time.

13. An expenditure tax enables individuals to receive investment income gross of tax and is therefore neutral to the choice between consumption now and in the future. It can be of two forms: EET (exempt contributions and investment income but tax benefits), or TEE (tax contributions but exempt investment income and benefits). Individuals typically prefer EET because tax rates are lower in old age and because there is a risk in a TEE environment that a new government would

decide to impose taxes on benefits. In most Latin American countries, except Mexico and Peru, voluntary retirement savings in the pension funds are subject to the EET taxation system, but savings in other financial products are subject to a less attractive tax treatment. Moreover, voluntary pension fund savings are illiquid and must be kept until retirement. In Peru voluntary savings in the pension funds are subject to a TEE system (as are mandatory retirement savings), whereas in Mexico there is double taxation. In both countries voluntary savings can be withdrawn before retirement.

14. A similar subsidy is offered to contributing low-income workers in the Czech Republic (Vittas 2002) and in Germany's *Riester* pensions.

15. However, some of the mandatory savings have passed through to the mutual fund sector because pension funds can invest up to a certain ceiling in mutual funds (the ceiling varies between 0 and 15 percent depending on the country). As of December 2001, however, only Argentina (3.3 percent of total assets), Chile (2.6 percent), and Peru (0.5 percent) recorded any pension fund investment in mutual funds.

16. As mentioned already, Chile was the first country to liberalize the voluntary savings market (March 2002), thereby eliminating the restriction on withdrawals (although these withdrawals are now penalized) and permitting workers to place their voluntary savings in a variety of financial instruments (including mutual funds).

17. Pension fund commissions are set on contributions, not assets. A 0.7 percent commission on assets is approximately equivalent to a 15 percent charge of contributions during a worker's career, which is the current level of commissions in Chile.

18. Mexico is the only country in Latin America that permits different commission structures in the mandatory pension pillar.

11

The Way Forward

THE ISSUE OF PRIVATIZATION FIGURES prominently in the quest for a new development paradigm triggered by economic failures in the developing world. Privatization of government-produced goods and services was, for example, one of the 10 key measures in the erstwhile "Washington Consensus" (see Williamson 1999). In the Latin American region, for which this consensus of policy prescriptions was believed to best apply, structural reforms to social security may well have been the most important wave of privatization of government services. The region has the longest and richest history of experience in privatization of social security, starting with the reform pioneered by Chile in 1981. Some variant of the Chilean model of social security has been adopted by many of Chile's neighbors in the region, and it has been a serious contender as a reform model in other developing countries and even in some industrial countries. Today it is even considered by some as an alternative to the current U.S. social security system, despite the latter being perhaps one of the best-managed traditional public pension systems in the world.

Why This Survey Now?

Disappointing economic growth rates, persistently high macroeconomic volatility, and increasing concerns regarding income distribution have led to a reevaluation of the Washington Consensus model in Latin America since the late 1990s. There is growing sentiment that although the policies that composed the original consensus are sound, they are insufficient to address institutional shortcomings in the region. In particular, critics of the Consensus have called for stronger competition policy and financial market regulation to improve the outcomes of privatization and for more targeted efforts at poverty reduction to improve equity. The assessment of regional pension reforms presented in this volume takes place in the context of this larger debate on the course of Latin America's development.

It should not come as a surprise then that the Latin American model of pension reform is being scrutinized—even reconsidered—in countries within the region. The principal concern is the alleged failure of the reforms to increase the coverage of people by social security systems, which was considered an important selling point of reforms when they were initiated. But there are other concerns as well, some of which may reflect a lack of appreciation of the aspects in which the reforms have paid dividends. This book was commissioned by the chief economist of the World Bank's Latin America and the Caribbean Region to provide a balanced assessment of social security reform as a contribution to the debate about the region.[1]

There is a concern that it is premature to conduct an assessment of pension reform because the experience in most countries is not long enough to permit a reliable investigation. But while economists and pension specialists wait for the reforms to bear riper fruit, these reforms may well be uprooted in some countries. Consider the following developments:

• In Peru in late 2002, during the process of rewriting the constitution, articles that would allow affiliates of the private funded system to return to the public PAYG system and to lower the retirement age from 65 to 60 were narrowly defeated.

• In Bolivia in late 2002, the government approved measures that would integrate the fund that finances the noncontributory pension benefit with the contributory pension funds, a measure that would lead to less than transparent cross-subsidization and could cut the return earned by affiliates on their retirement savings.

• In Argentina in 2002, a draft law that would allow workers to switch between the public and the private branches of the pension system was passed in the Lower House—with only one vote against and one abstention. By late 2003 the government was working on a reform that would allow workers to return to the old PAYG system. Among the alternatives being weighed are a mixed public–private system with universal coverage to protect the indigent and replacement of the current largely private pension system with a single regimen in which workers would see their contributions apportioned between a state-managed pension agency and a private pension system.

Similar discontent has emerged in some of the other countries that have adopted the multipillar model with its emphasis on privately managed individual accounts. Even in Chile where reforms have been implemented with the most vigor—and the new pension model has been in place for the longest period—there are concerns that low participation in funded pensions will keep effective replacement rates low, and thus put mounting pressures on the minimum-income guarantee for affiliates who have completed the minimum required period of contribution to the system. This book aims to provide a balanced and reliable assessment of country experience with the multipillar model to date, so that any further reform measures are contemplated in an informed manner.

What Have Been the Main Benefits of Reform?

In light of the concerns above, it is important that the benefits of reforms be made widely known. And, as documented in this volume, the benefits are considerable.

First, the reforms are based on a more sustainable social contract where the consumption-smoothing goal is "individualized." The reforms rely on the implementation of individual accounts in which benefits are based on workers' contributions. The costs of financing increased life expectancy are therefore passed on to each generation rather than pooled in a discretionary way, as tends to be the case in defined benefit plans. All countries surveyed in this book have introduced such accounts.

Second, the aggregate liabilities of governments have fallen. Work commissioned for this volume reveals that the implicit pension debt has been significantly reduced in most countries that reformed their pension systems. Compared with the hypothetical, counterfactual scenario of no reform, projections show that implicit pension debt (IPD) as a share of GDP in 2001 was lower in the reformed systems by 100 percentage points in Chile, 50 points in Bolivia, and about 25 points in El Salvador, Peru, and Uruguay. The reductions in IPD as a share of GDP are much higher further out in the future: by 2030, for example, the difference between the reform and no-reform scenarios becomes 200 percent of GDP in Bolivia and Chile and 100 percent in El Salvador and Peru (figure 3.1; Zviniene and Packard 2002).

Third, there have been important distributional benefits. Besides allowing countries of the region to spend more on public education, health, and social assistance, in all the reforming countries the regressivity of public pension expenditures has been markedly reduced for those who are covered, when measured using (gross of commission and fee) rates of return obtained by wealthier and poorer workers. In some countries, such as Argentina and Chile, reforms helped regressive systems become progressive (figure 5.1, and Zviniene and Packard 2002).

Fourth, at least initially reforms led to some improvements in coverage. That is, even though casual analysis shows a fall in contribution rates (see figure 5.5), more careful estimations in two background papers for this book indicate that coverage rates might have been even lower without the reforms (Packard 2001; Valdés-Prieto 2002a).

Fifth, the shift to multipillar systems can be credited with setting up a new financial industry that has been a role model for other industries in the region in terms of regulatory oversight. As a paper commissioned for this book argued, the new systems have achieved high standards in asset valuation, risk rating, and disclosure (Yermo 2002a). So whereas the direct role of pension reform in increasing national saving is debatable, the indirect effect on saving of improved financial sector functioning is likely to have been positive.

Finally, another financial benefit of the reforms has been the rapid growth of a new form of saving in the region. Between 1998 and 2002 the ratio of pension fund assets to GDP rose from 40 percent to 56 percent in Chile, from 2.7 percent to 5.3 percent in Mexico, from 3.3 percent to 11.3 percent in Argentina, from 2.7 percent to 7.7 percent in Colombia, from 2.5 percent to 8.1 percent in Peru, from 1.3 percent to 5.7 percent in Uruguay, from 0.4 percent to 7.4 percent in El Salvador, and from 3.9 percent to 15.5 percent of GDP in Bolivia (see table 4.3). Furthermore, insurance companies have flourished in their auxiliary role as providers of disability, survivor, and longevity insurance in the new systems. Although it is not obvious how much of this growth in pension fund assets has taken place at the expense of other institutional investors such as mutual funds (which operate on the basis of financial principles similar to those of the pension funds), there should be little doubt that the importance placed on mandatory individual savings accounts has helped financial sector development. It should be noted, however, that financial sector development can take place effectively in the absence of pension privatization. After all, pension fund assets have also risen impressively in Brazil, a country that has *not* introduced mandatory private retirement accounts, from US$33 billion in 1994 to $75 billion in 1998 before falling to $53 billion in 2001, and mutual fund assets have grown from slightly over 15 percent of GDP in 1998 to nearly 30 percent in 2001 (see figure 10.2).

What Are the Principal Concerns about Reforms?

Why is there growing discontent with reforms to social security in Latin America? Some of this discontent may be transitory (arising from sharply lower rates of return on private savings accounts in the past few years compared with rates during much of the 1990s), and some perhaps unwarranted. But it is hard to dismiss *all* such complaints as baseless. This section considers some potentially valid concerns.

First, fiscal concerns are prominent for many policymakers. Although there is no doubt about the long-term fiscal benefits of reform, the short- to medium-term fiscal effects depend greatly on initial fiscal conditions, the extent to which reforms reduce contingent liabilities, and the quality of the reform's implementation. Not all countries have the luxury of embarking on structural reform from a strong fiscal position, but those that take steps to (a) reduce contingent liabilities before making implicit pension debt explicit, and (b) curb fraud and mismanagement in reform implementation can limit transition costs to manageable levels. Finalizing the "first generation" of pension reforms should be a priority for policymakers.

Second, there are concerns over the new structure of the multipillar pension systems. Some countries in the region maintain large, defined benefit PAYG programs that offer earnings-related pensions. In Costa Rica and Uruguay the PAYG plan is mandatory—whereas in Argentina, Colombia, and Peru workers can choose between the defined-benefit PAYG plan and an individual account in the funded defined contribution pillar. These earnings-related, defined benefit PAYG plans will become increasingly costly to finance as life expectancy increases unless policymakers are able to enact increases in retirement ages or introduce longevity factors into their benefit formulas.

At the same time, many countries have not implemented poverty prevention pillars for the uncovered population, whereas others have not even done so for the covered population. In Peru, a country that ostensibly adopted the multipillar model of old-age income security in 1992, there are understandable concerns that although the system of private mandatory savings accounts was vigorously implemented, the government did not institute the minimum pension guarantee (see box 8.2). And beginning in early 2002, when the guarantee component was finally installed, only affiliates who were 55 or older who had contributed for at least 20 years were eligible in the private pillar. It is important to point out that the Peruvian authorities have included the extension of the minimum pension guarantee to all the affiliates of the AFP system who complete the minimum years of contribution as part of the reform agenda. But it is worth noting that it will have taken more than a decade for the component designed to alleviate old-age poverty to be instituted. No concrete moves have yet been taken toward extending the minimum guarantee. It may well be that the administrative and political demands associated with installation of the private second pillar—which generally has powerful champions in bankers and financiers—actually divert attention from efforts to set up the arguably more important poverty prevention pillar, whose main beneficiaries are the largely unchampioned poor people.

Similar concerns have surfaced over Bolivia's universal pension benefit, the BONOSOL. Only workers who were 21 years old or older in 1995 are eligible for this benefit, leaving later generations without resort to any mechanism for pooling poverty risk. Nevertheless, as in Peru, a strong political constituency could build over the next few years to demand the extension of the benefit to future generations. Programs such as BONOSOL should always be modest; but in Bolivia's current circumstance of debt and high fiscal deficits, restraint is a necessity not an option.

Another serious structural concern is the potential inconsistency of reformed systems that aim to pursue poverty prevention and consumption-smoothing objectives through the savings component (i.e., conditioning eligibility for poverty prevention benefits on contribution to second-pillar individual savings accounts). Workers in Chile who earn close to the minimum wage are now expected to choose among five different funds with various levels of investment in equities. A rational worker would choose the highest risk portfolio in the knowledge that the government guarantees them a minimum pension if they meet the minimum contribution period. In this book we have argued that the instruments for poverty prevention and consumption smoothing are different and should be kept separate from each other. In particular, access to instruments that pool the risk of poverty should not be conditioned on participation in the savings component. Individual choice over investment is an essential ingredient of the latter, but efficient pooling of poverty risk requires the transfer of investment choice to the underwriter of the risk—the state in this case.

Third, there are concerns over the operation of the savings component. Poor and young people may face other pressing demands on their consumption and may have limited disposable income for retirement saving. High mandatory contribution rates may, therefore, dissuade these groups from participating in the pension system. Individuals may also find other forms of investment, such as housing or education, equally or even more attractive than the pension funds—especially because of the high ceilings on earnings that are subject to mandatory contributions. It fact, in Peru there is no ceiling and the mandatory contribution rate is levied on affiliates' full earnings. High ceilings on workers' earnings that are subject to the mandate to save restrict voluntary savings in alternative instruments by even richer workers. If due to a large mandate workers are forced to borrow to meet important demands (such as housing, education, or healthcare), workers can face a further cost represented by the spread between the cost of consumer credit and the return earned on mandatory savings.

Policy risk also remains omnipresent in the private funded systems. In Argentina the value of pension fund assets fell sharply when the government forced pension funds to hold its increasingly risky debt and then defaulted on that debt. The experience of Argentina has brought into clear relief what has always been acknowledged by balanced observers, namely, that "there is little reason to believe that a government that administered a public system poorly would regulate a private system well" (de Ferranti, Leipziger, and Srinivas 2002, p. 42). Argentina's experience shows that even privately administered pension systems are not immune to public policy mistakes.

Even in countries such as Chile that have proved over time to be competent regulators of mandatory pension funds, there are worrisome equity-related findings. Three are especially noteworthy:

1. About half of the cumulative net (of insurance premium) contributions of the average worker who retired in 2000 after contributing to the system since its inception in the early 1980s went toward administrative and insurance fees (see figure 7.7), which raises questions of fairness. The high fees charged for administering the funds have prompted critical commentary.

As administrative costs have fallen, later cohorts of workers may do better, but even this positive development raises concerns of intergenerational equity in nascent privately managed mandatory saving systems. Whereas the former PAYG systems transferred wealth from future generations to current ones, these systems have a reverse bias as current generations are forced to pay the set-up costs of financial structures from which future generations would benefit. At least in the Chilean case, earlier cohorts benefited from higher gross returns, but this has not been the case in all Latin American countries. Besides, the experience in Peru indicates that falling operational costs do not necessarily mean lower fees for contributors, and may indeed simply translate into higher profit margins for the fund administrators (see Lasaga and Pollner 2003).

2. The commission structures in countries such as Chile imply that poor people may end up paying a higher share of their salaries in commissions than do wealthy people. Thus the management fees act like a regressive tax. In Chile the commission rate differential between rich and poor people has narrowed during the last decade, but only because the effective commission for richer workers has increased (see figure 7.8).

3. Some random intergenerational inequity is inherent in a system of defined contributions even when it matures because of the uncertainty associated with annuitization. Chileans retiring between 1988 and 2001 with identical accumulated balances could end up with annual pension differentials of more than 20 percent (figure 7.9). Such volatility is naturally a legitimate concern in a publicly sponsored system designed to reduce uncertainty during retirement.

Risk management considerations are also a cause of concern in the new Latin American systems. International diversification of pension fund portfolios is heavily constrained or even prohibited, whereas exposure to public debt is excessive, given the extent of default risk in much of Latin America. Workers outside Chile cannot choose their investment portfolio and are thus unable to adjust the asset allocation of their individual accounts to their risk and time preferences. The retirement stage is also subject to some possibly unnecessary constraints. Annuities are mandatory at retirement in some countries and in others they cannot be combined simultaneously with scheduled withdrawals. Deferred and variable annuities markets are also insufficiently developed.

Finally, and perhaps most importantly, in many of the reform countries the coverage of social security systems has stagnated at levels that seem unacceptable to many Latin Americans (see chapter 5). Although structural pension reform is not the only factor influencing participation, stagnant coverage ratios are a major concern for reforms that were expected to extend access to formal protection to a wider segment of the population. A large portion of affiliates (more than 30 percent in Chile according to our estimates) may not even qualify for the minimum pension guarantee of

PAYG or funded systems. Many more affiliates may only qualify for the minimum guaranteed benefit. Those who do not qualify for the minimum pension, together with those who are not affiliated with any system, have generally only rationed social assistance benefits to look forward to in old age. The mass of uncovered informal workers is less likely to take to the streets in protest than are formal sector beneficiaries whose benefits are cut, but people without coverage nonetheless form a large constituency of dissatisfaction with pension reform. Because increased coverage was one of the objectives of the multipillar reforms, it is understandable that lack of progress in this area has raised discontent.

It is reasonable to ask whether this preoccupation is legitimate. It can be argued on the basis of cross-country evidence (such as that presented in figure 11.1) that coverage is greater in higher-income countries. The only sustainable way for countries in Latin America to increase coverage is to focus on policies that increase economic growth rather than social security coverage. But two caveats should give us pause:

1. There is considerable variation in coverage rates within reasonably narrow income groups. Thus, for example, countries with per capita

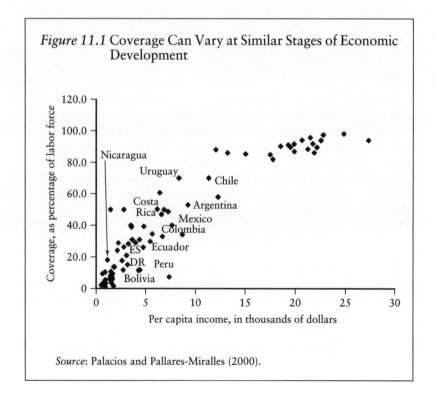

Figure 11.1 Coverage Can Vary at Similar Stages of Economic Development

Source: Palacios and Pallares-Miralles (2000).

incomes between US$2,000 and $3,000 have coverage ratios ranging from almost 0 to about 50 percent of the labor force. Again, countries with income levels of about $7,000 to $8,000 have coverage rates ranging from less than 10 percent to more than 60 percent. Although part of this variation results from the socialist pasts of some countries, institutional variation cannot be ignored. Such variation exists within Latin America, as well. Witness coverage rates of 62 percent in Chile versus 22 percent in Costa Rica (both upper-middle-income countries), or 25 percent in El Salvador versus 11 percent in Peru (both lower-middle-income countries).[3]

2. There may be reason to believe that access to social security—unemployment benefits, antipoverty programs, and retirement income programs—can promote openness and other growth-oriented economic policies, since they help in dealing with the higher volatility that accompanies these economic reforms. In Latin America there are especially good reasons to believe this (de Ferranti et al. 2000).

In opinion polls income insecurity among workers and retirees is usually one of the top concerns of the electorate. Democratic governments legitimately consider it a policy priority.

What Is the Way Forward?

The analysis in this book—a blend of the economics of insurance, detailed review of the experience in Latin America, simulations based on administrative data, and econometric analysis of individual and household surveys—leads to several conclusions.

First, and most important, the *poverty prevention* pillar should get a lot more attention than it has in Latin America during the past decade. This role of government may be even more important than that of providing a safe savings instrument at a reasonable price; the behavior of Chilean contributors reported in chapter 8 appears to reveal a preference for the minimum pension guarantee over the mandatory savings instrument. The poverty prevention role of government only *increases* in importance with economic development—as the likelihood of poverty in old age declines, the fundamentals of insurance make pooling of this risk across individuals more, not less, appropriate (see chapter 6). A government mandate is necessary for this type of defined benefit system because private insurance markets are unlikely to cover the risk of poverty. When funded from general revenues (in contrast with earmarked payroll taxes) and not conditioned on contributions, such a plan is sometimes called a zero pillar. Regardless of what it is called, such a system can permit governments to play a less ubiquitous role in other forms of old-age income security. Although most countries have some form of minimum pension benefit, some countries (Chile, Colombia, El Salvador, Mexico, and Peru when it is implemented) have tied eligibility to the contribution record in the savings component. These countries should consider reopening the debate on the need for a poverty prevention pillar offering benefits that keep households out of poverty and that is based on pure pooling principles (a PAYG defined-benefit plan). Also needed is further analysis of whether universal, subsistence-level pension benefits are more suitable than targeted benefits for low- and middle-income countries with high levels of informality and weak public governance. If contributory systems are retained they should be complemented with means-tested social assistance, which is not yet the case in four of the countries surveyed.

Second, it should be emphasized that although first-pillar programs will provide a minimum pension to those people who are unfortunate or unwise, the mainstay for *earnings replacement* during old age—that is, mechanisms to help households smooth consumption and cover the loss of earnings capacity while living—should be saving. For most workers it should consist of plans that closely link benefits to contributions and life expectancy and involve no redistribution of benefits or pooling of longevity risk across generations. The design of defined contribution plans is better suited for the earnings replacement function because those plans uncouple the contributions of individuals in one generation from the benefits obtained by previous generations. It should be noted also that defined contribution plans can be as effective at pooling longevity risk within the same generation as are defined benefit plans. In all Latin American countries one option at retirement is to purchase an annuity that offers such protection. The move from pure defined-benefit PAYG systems to defined contribution individual accounts as the mainstay of retirement income security is therefore clearly an improvement that conforms to the simplest principles of the economics of insurance because it leads to a better matching of instrument to covered risk, thereby increasing the role of saving at the expense of pooling. For this reason alone the reforms in Latin America are worth preserving and strengthening. But one should also acknowledge the progress made in countries such as Brazil that have moved from pure defined benefits to a hybrid that results in a tighter link between how much workers contribute and how much they receive as pensions. Countries such as Colombia, Costa Rica, Peru, and Uruguay that have retained PAYG systems that provide generous earnings-related pensions should also carefully consider reforms—such as introducing longevity factors in benefit formulas that will improve the actuarial fairness and solvency of their remaining public plans.

Third, more attention should be paid to the size of the mandatory savings pillar relative to country-specific circumstances. High contribution rates and similarly high ceilings on earnings subject to the mandate can discourage workers from participating and may leave little space for the growth of the third pillar. This is most likely in developing countries for poorer and younger workers who have other urgent competing demands on their disposable income. As long as a broad and fiscally sustainable poverty prevention pillar is in place, one option is to lift the obligation to save for workers below a certain income level. Contribution rates could also be made age-related so that workers contribute more into the savings system as they approach retirement, although the work incentives of older workers should be considered. Participation by richer workers could also be encouraged by lowering earnings ceilings. These measures would allow greater flexibility in mandatory saving for old age and could foster the development of the voluntary pensions market.

Fourth, the usefulness of second-pillar pensions in making a transition from overly generous PAYG systems and, even more so, in providing an initial boost to capital and insurance markets should be put into context. Some countries do not have such needs, which makes mandatory saving plans redundant (see box 11.1). Countries such as Brazil that have reasonably well-developed capital markets may choose to change the parameters of their public PAYG pension systems rather than switch to a mandatory funded program. Moving to a system of notional defined contributions is also an option. Conversely, countries such as Paraguay that have not reformed their PAYG pensions and wish to rejuvenate or develop their financial sector could seriously consider mandatory saving plans. But although workers are likely to respond to improved incentives to contribute at the margin, such countries should be warned not to expect a second pillar to increase coverage on its own, and should be advised to institute a robust poverty prevention pension program, however modest. In general, to the extent that governments have limited resources to administer or supervise pension systems, the priority should be the poverty prevention pillar rather than mandatory saving plans.

Fifth, the twin goals in countries that already have well-regulated private second pillars should be to institute equally well-run and fiscally sustainable public poverty prevention programs and to lower the costs of mandatory saving plans. Although there have been several attempts to reduce the commissions in second-pillar pensions through regulatory measures and to offer a wider array of savings instruments that differ in their risk and return features, commission rates are still not as low as they could be. In Bolivia commission rates are between two-thirds and one-half of those in other Latin American countries, despite the relative immaturity and small size of the system. Countries can benefit from evaluating this and other experiences in cost management that range from fully centralized models to fully contestable markets where competition is the time-tested ingredient for efficiency. Between these two extremes there are arrangements such as occupational plans in which employers act as intermediaries between workers and pension providers (a practice well extended in OECD countries), and systems with centralized account management and record keeping but open competition in asset management, as in Sweden. Policymakers in the region have also balked at increasing

Box 11.1 The Role of the Second Pillar

Despite the clear message in *Averting the Old Age Crisis* (World Bank 1994) that all three pillars—the "mandatory tax-financed public pillar that has primary responsibility for redistribution," the "mandatory funded private pillar (of personal saving or occupational plans) that has primary responsibility for saving," and the "voluntary pillar that provides supplementary protection" (p. 48)—are necessary to ensure against life's risks and uncertainties, it would not be an exaggeration to say that the component that has received most attention in countries of Latin America during the last decade is the second pillar. Because this was the novel component (most countries in the region already had some social assistance pensions and voluntary retirement savings), the preoccupation with mandatory saving plans is understandable. There are two other possible rationales for this intense attention to mandatory saving schemes:

1. *Shifting from unsustainable defined benefit plans.* Most reforming countries started from a situation of fiscally unsustainable PAYG systems. Politically it may have been difficult to renege on these generous promises. The second pillar may have changed the basis of old-age income security from overly generous defined benefit programs to defined contribution plans, which are by definition fiscally balanced. Of course, privately managed individual accounts are not the only way to change the basis of earnings replacement from defined benefits to defined contributions: *notional* defined contribution programs are an obvious option (see Fox and Palmer 2001).

2. *Fostering capital market development.* Most of these countries had underdeveloped private financial markets, so the second pillar was seen as an instrument for jump-starting financial sector development. Although there are alternative ways to encourage private financial markets to begin offering financial instruments for long-term savings, it may well be that second-pillar pension plans are an effective instrument for doing so.

In either case, the role of a mandatory, privately managed individual savings accounts appears to be more transitory in nature than suggested in *Averting the Old Age Crisis.* The most important reasons for a permanent privately administered second pillar are in fact a general distrust of the ability of governments to manage such accounts and the belief that people are generally irrational or ill-informed about their retirement needs. Based on Latin America's experience in the last decade—which provides little in the way of assurance that the three central dilemmas posed in *Averting the Old Age Crisis* (see box 1.1) are not serious contradictions—mandating private savings is seen as a transitional device in this volume. The simplest way to highlight the differences between *Averting the Old Age Crisis* and this book is to consider what each would recommend for countries such as the United States. Whereas *Averting*

Box 11.1 (continued)

would recommend a sizable system of privately managed mandatory savings accounts for the United States, the reasoning in this report would not lead to that conclusion.

Of course this does not mean that countries should *never* institute a second pillar even when conditions warrant. But it would be equally unwise to advocate a second pillar in *every* country that wishes to move the mainstay of old-age income security from pooling (i.e., defined-benefit PAYG systems) to saving (e.g., defined contribution plans), even if the capacity to effectively regulate such a system existed. Other instruments such as notional defined contribution accounts may serve the purpose equally well or better. In fact, where the obligations of the PAYG system are exceptionally high, mandatory savings accounts may be eschewed because of macroeconomic concerns.

---

competition between mandatory and voluntary pension providers. But all governments must squarely face the question: At what stage of financial sector development is it safe to stop cradling this infant industry created by structural pension reform? It is difficult to translate this into elapsed time. Chile appears to have arrived at this point after two decades of successful implementation of the second pillar: preferential tax treatment of retirement saving is being extended to voluntary contributions to approved (non-AFP) providers, which has led to a sharp increase in the number of contributors. In countries such as Argentina it may be necessary to increase competition to restore faith in the system. At the same time it should be noted that increased competition is only effective in lowering costs and improving performance to the extent that it is accompanied by measures to improve the disclosure of fees and performance, as well as the financial education of workers.

Sixth, some risk management aspects of the second pillar are also in dire need of a second generation of reforms. Investment regulations are generally overly prescriptive. In some countries there is still a dangerous inclination to divert pension funds toward government securities of low credit rating and a lack of consideration of the virtues of international diversification. The consumption-smoothing objective that underpins the savings pillar also requires individual portfolio choice. Although considerations over the financial literacy of the population may delay this reform in the second pillar, it would be wise to permit it at least for voluntary pensions, in which mainly better informed individuals participate. Greater flexibility may also be needed in the retirement stage so that workers may better hedge, diversify, and insure investment and longevity risk.

Conclusion

Given the importance of reducing the risk of poverty in old age, in this volume we call for greater attention to the poverty-prevention pillar. While individual savings should be a mainstay of consumption smoothing, we also call for a reassessment of the relative size of pillars two and three. But we do not argue that there is *never* a role for a mandatory savings component within a comprehensive old-age income security system. Almost anything that helps the move from pooling to saving would improve programs designed to replace earnings given rising longevity. But the arguments for large mandatory savings pillars appear to be mainly *transitional* in nature. This reasoning assumes that countries such as Chile, Colombia, El Salvador, Mexico, and Peru follow the advice offered in this book and introduce separate poverty prevention pillars based exclusively on pooling principles. The reality is that most countries in the region started from a situation of high and unsustainable rates of replacement promised by PAYG systems; politically the second pillar may be a convenient tool for ratcheting down these expectations. Reforms have been a step in the right direction but can go further in reducing remaining liabilities of the earlier PAYG system—and thereby create fiscal space for a poverty prevention pillar and reduce the size of the second pillar, to make room for the third.

To see the second pillar as a large permanent part of the pension system is to assume individuals are irrational—or, not to have faith in the ability of people to plan their own futures—*and* to assume that governments have the capacity to vigorously regulate these growing pools of money—that is, to have a lot of faith in governments to behave in an even-handed manner. There is little evidence that either assumption is justified; the coincidence of both in a single country is likely to be rare. Even assuming widespread improvidence in the population (systematic underestimation of consumption needs in old age until it is too late) rather than irrationality implies a much smaller and perhaps less permanent second pillar.

As longevity increases and poverty decreases in the region, the consequent need for individualization of pension systems becomes clearer, and the proper role of government becomes of paramount concern. As we have argued in this book, the desirable principles of a pension system—fiscal sustainability, access, equity, incentives to participate, choice, and poverty prevention—do not map into universal policy packages, just as Rodrik (2003) has noted with regard to economic policies in general. The need to reform the region's old single-pillar PAYG pension systems is clear. But just as fiscal, financial, social, and political conditions differ greatly across countries in the region, successful approaches to securing income and preventing poverty in old age will differ too.

Notes

1. The 16 background papers commissioned for this study are available online at www.worldbank.org/keepingthepromise.

2. The rationale behind this regulation was to eliminate disincentives for older workers who were still contributing to the public earnings-related plan to move into the private system of individual accounts.

3. Data on coverage ratios are calculated from recent household surveys and reported in figure 1.1, rather than those from Palacios and Pallares-Miralles (2000) reported in figure 11.1, which uses data from the mid-1990s.

Technical Annex. Assumptions of PROST Simulations

The PROST (*Pension Reform Options Simulation Toolkit*, developed by the World Bank) simulations presented in chapter 3 impose a uniform set of macroeconomic and certain systemic assumptions, in addition to country-specific assumptions based on each case, to isolate the impact of structural reforms. Although the use of a uniform set of macroeconomic assumptions would seem a strange choice when simulating reforms in a group of countries as diverse as El Salvador, Mexico, and Uruguay, it is not without precedent in cross-country simulation analysis (see Holzmann, Palacios, and Zviniene 2001). The assumptions that are common to all country cases are presented in table TA.1. Details particular to each country case are presented in table TA.2.

In addition to the parameter assumptions documented in table TA.1 (and those listed in table TA.2), there are assumptions behind the simulated pension outcomes used in the equity analysis that have to be kept in mind when analyzing our results.

Calculations of Internal Rates of Return

Zviniene and Packard (2002) calculated internal rates of return from representative affiliates' "investments" in the formal retirement security system—

Table TA.1 Assumptions Common to All Country Cases

GDP growth = 3 percent.

Inflation = 0 percent.

Market interest, discount rate = 5 percent.

Interest in "deaccumulation" or "payout" phase = 4 percent.

Interest on PAYG investments = 3 percent.

Wage bill is set at a constant portion of GDP.

Full compliance with retirement age increase: everyone contributes if not allowed to retire.

Collection rate of contribution revenue = 100 percent.

For sustainable benefit we assume that all benefits (old age, disability, survivors, and so forth) are reduced by the same percentage.

All demographic data are taken from World Bank population database (see Bos et al. 1994).

No coverage expansion or contraction.

Recognition bonds are not included in implicit pension debt calculations.

Minimum pension guarantees are modeled where applicable.

PAYG-pillar benefits, income thresholds, contribution ceilings, and minimum pensions are indexed to nominal wage growth.

Fees are paid by affiliates to funded second pillars, as in Devesa-Carpio and Vidal-Meliá (2002).

Table TA.2 Country-Specific Details, Assumptions, and Sources of Data

Country case	Reforms modeled	Assumptions	Data sources
Chile	Introduction of a funded second pillar	Administrative costs of PAYG pillar as a percentage of contributions are assumed to be 5 percent (reliable data were not available). Average length of service will continue to be 23/38 (women/men).	Wage distribution, pension distribution, beneficiary numbers, current spending, current average length of service data from the Pension Normalization Institute (*Instituto de Normalización Previsional*) and the Superintendency of Pension Fund Administrators (*Superintendencia de Administradoras de Fondos de Pensiones*)
Peru	Introduction of a funded second pillar. Increase in contribution rate from 9 percent to 13 percent in PAYG second pillar and 12.4 percent in funded second pillar	Average length of service stays constant at 23.8 years. Administrative costs of PAYG pillar as a percentage of contributions are assumed to be 5 percent (reliable data were not available).	Wage distribution, pension distribution, beneficiary numbers, current spending data from the Pension Normalization Office (*Oficina de Normalización Previsional*) and the Banking and Insurance Superintendency (*Superintendencia de Banca y Seguros*)

Colombia	Introduction of a funded second pillar Increase in retirement age from 55/60 to 62/57 (men/women) in year 2014	Average length of service is 20 years (mandated minimum). Only the Institute of Social Security (*Instituto de Seguro Social*) is modeled (33 percent of all pension liabilities); other special regimens for civil servants make up the rest.	Beneficiary numbers, current spending, administrative costs of PAYG data from local sources Wage distribution, switching patterns data from Kleinjans (2001)
Argentina	Introduction of a funded second pillar Decrease in contribution rate for employers from 16 percent to 7 percent in PAYG second pillar	Administrative costs of PAYG pillar as a percentage of contributions are assumed to be 5 percent (reliable data were not available). Average length of service since 2008 is assumed to be 30 years for those who retire at ages younger than 70 and 15 years for those who retire later (mandated minimum).	Wage distribution, pension distribution, beneficiary numbers, current spending data from the National Social Security Administration (*Administración Nacional de la Seguridad Social*) and the Superintendency of Retirement and Pension Fund Administrators (*Superintendencia de Administradoras de Fondos de Jubiliación y Pensiones*)

(Table continues on the following page.)

Table TA.2 (continued)

Country case	Reforms modeled	Assumptions	Data sources
Uruguay	Introduction of a funded second pillar (more appropriately characterized as a "tier" because participation is determined by income) Equalization of retirement ages for both genders at age 60	Average length of service is assumed to be 35 years for those who retire at ages younger than 70 and 15 years for those who retire later (mandated minimum).	Wage distribution, pension distribution, beneficiary numbers, current spending, administrative costs of PAYG pillar, switching patterns data from local sources
Mexico	Introduction of a funded second pillar	Average length of service is expected to grow from current 22 years to 25 years by 2012 and then stay constant (mandated minimum). Male/female ratios in contributor and beneficiary populations are taken from Argentina, which has a labor force gender structure that is very similar to Mexico (Mexico 1980: 27 percent female; 1996: 31 percent female. Argentina 1980: 28 percent female; 1996: 31 percent female [WBI data]). For working-age disabled people we used contributor ratios and for elderly disabled people we used old-age pensioner ratios. INFONAVIT and social quota programs are included.	Wage distribution, pension distribution, beneficiary numbers, current spending, administration costs of PAYG pillar data from the National Retirement Savings Commission (*Comisión Nacional del Sistema de Ahorra para el Retiro*) and the Mexican Social Security Institute (*Instituto Mexicano del Seguro Social*) Gender differences in wages data taken from ENEU (1998)

Bolivia	Introduction of a funded second pillar	Administrative costs of PAYG pillar as a percentage of contributions are assumed to be 5 percent (reliable data were not available). Average length of service is 25 years (mandated minimum). BONOSOL program is modeled.	Wage distribution, pension distribution, beneficiary numbers, current spending data from local sources. Gender differences in wages data from CEPAL (1999)
El Salvador	Introduction of a funded pillar	Average length will continue to be 25/27 years (men/women).	Wage distribution, pension distribution, beneficiary numbers, current spending, administrative costs, current average length of service data from local sources

an indicator that can/be used to assess the likely impact of reforms to the formal pension systems on income equity. When an individual participates in a pension system, he or she contributes during the working years and receives benefits after retirement. This can be seen as an investment process where the individual invests the contribution amount into a financial instrument and receives returns. The internal rate of return (IRR) evaluates this particular investment in the pension system and gives an idea of how much an individual gets for the contributions he or she made. It can be compared with the market rate of interest to evaluate participation in the system relative to other alternatives.

In PROST the profiles of different types of individuals are entered. These profiles vary in terms of gender, starting wage as a percentage of average economy wage, starting age of work, retirement age, and life expectancy. PROST then calculates the IRR for each individual based on the individual's cash flows. When comparing different profiles, the IRR statistic acts as a very good indicator of the redistributional properties of a pension system. For example, it can answer the following question: Who gets more out of the pension system—low-income worker or high-income worker, male or female, young or old?

By definition, the internal rate of return is the discount rate for which the net present value of the contributions made and the future benefit payments for the individual until death becomes zero. PROST calculates IRR in the following way:

1. The first step is to calculate the cash flows of the individual for each year. The cash flows consist of the contributions from the individual during the working years and the benefits received after retirement. Contributions are taken as negative because they are cash outflows from the individual, and benefits are taken as positive. The cash flows are then converted into real terms by discounting for inflation.

2. PROST then uses the following formula to equate the net present value of the real cash flows at the starting year to zero and solve for the internal rate of return.

$$balance_t = \begin{cases} - flow_t^r, & \text{if } t = \text{start year} \\ balance_{t-1} \left[1 + irr \right] - flow_t^r & \text{if } t > \text{start year} \end{cases}$$

where $flow_t^r$ is real cash flows at time t

Equating $balance_t$ to zero at the end of the individual's life gives the irr.[1]

Affiliate Profiles and Other Assumptions

Details on the affiliate profiles used in this analysis are shown in table TA.3. We used gender-specific average retirement ages and average years of contributions from PROST output tables. The average retirement age for men and women was applied to each of the three affiliate profiles that we constructed for each gender (poorer affiliates, average affiliates, richer affiliates). When including years out of the formal labor market (particularly when calculating the internal rate of return for representative affiliated women), we assumed that these years were evenly spread throughout the affiliate's adult pre-retirement life. Survivor benefits were not included in the internal-rate-of-return calculations.

Finally, in most of the country cases shown structural reforms are more than several years old (see table 2.1). In most cases pension system data for the years prior to structural reforms are scarce and when available rarely can be found in the level of disaggregation required for our simulation model. In those cases (Argentina, Chile, Colombia, and Peru) the simulations presented were based on current data.

To project a "no-reform scenario"—the counterfactual to structural reforms—the current number of beneficiaries, wage distribution of contributors, and so forth were used and the parameters of the old single-pillar PAYG system were applied. To simulate structural reforms—particularly the introduction of individual retirement accounts—we assumed that reforms were introduced in the base year (the year to which the data actually correspond). However, the switching pattern (i.e., the distribution by gender and age of workers moving from single-pillar to multipillar arrangements) was set to reflect the actual distribution of contributors between the old PAYG and new multipillar systems.

To take account of workers' savings in individual accounts from the actual date of reforms to the base year we simulated a one-off transfer of

Table TA.3 Assumed Profiles of Representative Affiliated Men and Women

Profile	Entry age	Years of contributions	Starting wage	Productivity growth	Mortality
Poorer affiliate	16	Average + 3	50 percent of average	50 percent of average	Dies two years earlier than average
Average affiliate	19	Average	100 percent of average	100 percent of average	100 percent of average
Richer affiliate	22	Average − 3	150 percent of average	150 percent of average	Lives two years longer than average

Note: Average affiliate of each gender is considered representative.

Source: Contribution data from each country's social security and pension agencies, as in table TA.2

funds into the new private pillar. We did this by setting the contribution rate (as a percentage of wages) to the new individual accounts in the base year equal to the actual statutory contribution plus a percentage of wages that reflected average accumulated assets in each country. In this way we simulated a one-off contribution into individual accounts equal to the average accumulation of savings, divided by average wages. The value of recognition bonds was also adjusted for the actual date of reforms. Although this technique is admittedly second-best, past applications have rendered simulation results very similar to those of other authors.

Note

1. PROST calculates the life expectancy of the individual using the individual's mortality multiplier indicated in the input file and the mortality tables of the general population.

Appendix. Background Papers for *Keeping the Promise*

Author	Title	Focus area
Oliver Azuara	The Mexican Defined Contribution System: Perspective for Low Income Workers	Country case
Abigail Barr and Truman Packard	Preferences, Constraints, and Alternatives under Peru's Pension System	Labor, coverage
Abigail Barr and Truman Packard	Revealed Preferences and Self Insurance: Can We Learn from the Self-Employed in Chile?	Labor, coverage
Federico Escobar	Pension Reform in Bolivia: A Review of Approach and Experience	Country case
Norbert Fiess	Pension Reform or Pension Default? A Note on Pension Reform and Country Risk	Macroeconomics
Truman Packard	Is There a Positive Incentive Effect from Privatizing Social Security? Evidence from Pension Reforms in Latin America	Labor, coverage
Truman Packard	Pooling, Savings, and Prevention: Mitigating the Risk of Old Age Poverty in Chile	Labor, coverage
Truman Packard, Naoko Shinkai, and Ricardo Fuentes	The Reach of Social Security in Latin America and the Caribbean	Labor, coverage
Rafael Rofman	The Pension System and the Crisis in Argentina: Learning the Lessons	Country case
Salvador Valdés-Prieto	Improving Programs That Mandate Savings for Old Age	Labor, coverage

Author	Title	Focus area
Salvador Valdés-Prieto	Justifying Mandated Savings for Old Age	Labor, coverage
Salvador Valdés-Prieto	Social Security Coverage in Chile, 1990–2001	Labor, coverage
Juan Yermo	Pension Reform and Capital Market Development	Financial sector
Juan Yermo	Delivering Promises in the Chilean Funded Pension System	Labor, coverage, financial sector
Juan Yermo	Pension Reform and Capital Market Development	Financial sector
Asta Zviniene and Truman Packard	A Simulation of Social Security Reforms in Latin America: What Has Been Gained?	Fiscal, equity

Note: All papers are available online at the following World Bank Web site: www.worldbank.org/keepingthepromise.

Bibliography

The word "processed" refers to informally produced works that may not be commonly available through libraries.

Acuna, R., and A. Iglesias. 2001. Chile's Pension Reform after 20 Years. Social Protection Discussion Paper 0129, World Bank, Washington, D.C.

Agulnik, Phil. 2000. Maintaining Incomes after Work: Do Compulsory Earnings Related Pensions Make Sense? *Oxford Review of Economic Policy* 16 (1): 45–56.

AIOS (International Association of Pension Funds Supervisory Organisms; *Asociación Internacional de Organismos de Supervisión de Fondos de Pensiones*). 2002. *Boletín Estadístico Número 8* (December).

Alderman, H., and C. Paxson. 1992. Do the Poor Insure? A Synthesis of the Literature on Risk and Consumption in Developing Countries. Policy Research Working Paper 1008, World Bank, Washington, D.C.

Alessie, Rob, and Arie Kapteyn. 2001. New Data for Understanding Saving. *Oxford Review of Economic Policy* 17 (1): 55–69.

Amadeo, Eduardo, Indermit Gill, and Marcelo Neri. 1998. Do Labor Laws Matter? The Pressure Points in Brazilian Labor Legislation. In *Crafting Labor Policy: Techniques and Lessons from Latin America*, eds. I. Gill, C. Montenegro, and D. Domeland. London: Oxford University Press.

ANSES (National Social Security Administration [Argentina]; *Administración Nacional de la Seguridad Social*). 1995. *Series Financieras del Sistema Nacional de Previsión Social. Período 1962–1994*. Buenos Aires.

Appelbaum, E., and E. Katz. 1991. The Demand for Children in the Absence of Capital and Risk Markets: A Portfolio Approach. *Oxford Economic Papers* 43: 292–304.

Arango, Carlos, and William F. Maloney. 2000. Employment, Informality and Poverty in the Argentine Labor Market. In *Poor People in a*

Rich Country: A Poverty Report for Argentina. Report 19992-AR, World Bank, Washington, D.C.

Arenas de Mesa, Alberto. 2000. *Cobertura Previsional en Chile: Lecciones y Desafios del Sistema de Pensiones Administrado por El Sector Privado.* Santiago, Chile: Economic Commission for Latin America and the Caribbean.

Arenas de Mesa , Alberto, and Hector Hernández Sánchez. 2001. Cobertura del Sistema de Pensiones de Capitalización Individual Chileno: Diagnostico y Propuestas. *SOCIALIS: Revista Latinoamericana de Política Social* 4 (April): 93–124.

Arenas de Mesa, Alberto, and Mario Marcel. 1999. Fiscal Effects of Social Security Reform in Chile: The Case of the Minimum Pension. Paper presented at the APEC Second Regional Forum on Pension Fund Reforms, Vina del Mar, Chile.

Aroca Gonzalez, Patricio, and William F. Maloney. 1999. Logit Analysis in a Rotating Panel Context and an Application of Self Employment Decisions. Policy Research Working Paper 2069, World Bank, Washington, D.C.

Arrau, P., and S. Valdés-Prieto. 2001. *Para Desconcentrar los Fondos de Pensiones y Aumentar la Competencia en su Administración.* Capital Markets Reform Project Proposal. http://www.cepchile.cl.

Arriagada, Ana Maria, and Gillette Hall. 2000. Managing Social Risks in Argentina. Human Development Network, World Bank, Washington, D.C. Processed.

Atkinson, Antony B. 1987. Income Maintenance and Social Insurance. In *Handbook of Public Economics,* eds. A. Auerbach and M. Feldstein. Amsterdam: North-Holland.

Atkinson, Antony B., and John Hills. 1989. Social Security in Developed Countries: Are There Lessons for Developing Countries? Discussion Paper WSP/38, London School of Economics.

Atkinson, Antony B., and Joseph Stiglitz. 1980. *Lectures in Public Economics.* New York: McGraw-Hill.

Attanasio, Orazio P., and James Banks. 2001. The Assessment: Household Saving—Issues in Theory and Policy. *Oxford Review of Economic Policy* 17 (1): 1–19.

Auerbach, Alan J., and Laurence J. Kotlikoff. 1987. *Dynamic Fiscal Policy.* Cambridge, U.K.: Cambridge University Press.

Azuara, Oliver. 2003. The Mexican Defined Contribution Pension System: Perspective for Low Income Workers. Background Paper for the Regional Study on Social Security Reform, LAC Region, World Bank, Washington, D.C.

Baker, Dean, and Debayani Kar. 2002. Defined Contributions from Workers, Guaranteed Benefits for Bankers: The World Bank's Approach to Social Security Reform. Centre for Economic Policy Research, London. Processed.

Baker, D., and M. Weisbrot. 2002. *The Role of Social Security Privatization in Argentina's Economic Crisis.* Washington, D.C.: Center for Economic and Policy Research.

Barnes, K., and W. Cline. 1997. Spreads and Risks in Emerging Markets Lending. Working Paper 97-1. Institute of International Finance, Washington, D.C.

Barr, Abigail, and Truman Packard. 2000a. Revealed and Concealed Preferences and Self Insurance: Can We Learn from the Self Employed in Chile? Discussion Paper 53, Department of Economics, Oxford University, London.

———. 2000b. A Tool for Measuring Risk Aversion and Time Preferences in the Field. World Bank, Washington, D.C. Processed.

———. 2002a. Revealed Preferences and Self Insurance: Can We Learn from the Self-Employed in Chile? Policy Research Working Paper 2754, World Bank, Washington, D.C.

———. 2003. Preferences, Constraints, and Alternatives to Coverage Under Peru's Pension System. Background Paper for the Regional Study on Social Security Reform, World Bank, Washington, D.C.

Barr, Nicholas.1992. Economic Theory and the Welfare State: A Survey and Interpretation. *Journal of Economic Literature* 30 (2): 741–803.

———. 1998. *The Economics of the Welfare State*, 3d ed. London: Oxford University Press.

———. 2000. Reforming Pensions: Myths, Truths, and Policy Choices. Working Paper WP/00/139, Development Issues Division, International Monetary Fund, Washington, D.C.

———. 2001. *The Welfare State as Piggy Bank*. London: Oxford University Press.

Barrientos, Armando. 1996. Pension Reform and Pension Coverage in Chile: Lessons for Other Countries. *World Development* 15 (3): 309–22.

———. 1997. Pension Reform and the Individual Capitalization Pension Scheme Stampede in Latin America, Working Paper 17, University of Hertfordshire Business School, U.K.

———. 1998a. Pension Reform, Personal Pensions, and Gender Differences in Pension Coverage. *World Development* 26 (1): 125–37.

———. 1998b. *Pension Reform in Latin America*. Aldershot, U.K.: Ashgate.

——. 1999a. Retirement, Household Income, and Economic Vulnerability of Older Groups. Working Paper 20, University of Hertfordshire Business School, U.K.

——. 1999b. Economic Risks, the Labor Market and Older Workers in Latin America. Working Paper 21, University of Hertfordshire Business School, U.K.

Beck, T., A. Demirgüç-Kunt, and R. Levine. 1999. A New Database on Financial Development Structure. Policy Research Working Paper 2146, World Bank, Washington, D.C.

Beck, T., and R. Levine. 2001. *Stock Markets, Banks, and Growth: Correlation or Causality*. Policy Research Working Paper 2670, World Bank, Washington, D.C.

Becker, Gary S., and Casey B. Mulligan. 1997. The Endogenous Determination of Time Preference. *Quarterly Journal of Economics* 112 (3): 729–58.

Becker, Gary S., and Kevin M. Murphy. 1988. A Theory of Rational Addiction. *Journal of Political Economy* 96 (4): 675–700.

Becker, Gary, and N. Tomes. 1976. Child Endowments and the Quality and Quantity of Children. *Journal of Political Economy* 84 (4): 143–62.

Beltrão, Kaizô Iwakami, Sonoê Sugahara Pinheiro, and Francisco Eduardo Barreto de Oliveira. 1999. *A População Rural E A Previdência Social No Brasil: Uma Análise Com Ênfase Nas Mudanças Constitucionais*. Institute of Applied Economic Research (*Instituto de Pesquisa Econômica Aplicada*), Brasilia, Brazil. Processed.

Bernheim, Douglas, B. 1993. *Is the Baby-Boom Generation Preparing Adequately for Retirement?* New York: Merrill Lynch.

Bertranou, Fabio, and Rafael Rofman. 2002. Providing Social Security in a Context of Change: Experience and Challenges in Latin America. *International Social Security Review* 55 (1): 67–82.

Bertranou, Fabio, C. Solorio, and W. Van Ginneken, eds. 2002. *Pensiones No-Contributivas y Asistenciales: Argentina, Brazil, Chile, Costa Rica y Uruguay*. Santiago, Chile: International Labour Organization.

Blanchflower, D., and Andrew J. Oswald. 1991. Self Employment and Mrs. Thatcher's Enterprise Culture. Discussion Paper 30, Centre for Economic Performance, London School of Economics.

——. 1998. What Makes an Entrepreneur? *Journal of Labor Economics* 16 (1): 26–60.

Blau, David M. 1985. Self-Employment and Self-Selection in Developing Country Labor Markets. *Southern Economic Journal* 51 (2): 351–63.

——. 1987. A Time-Series Analysis of Self-Employment in the United States. *Journal of Political Economy* 95: 445–67.

Blommestein, H. J. 1998. Impact of Institutional Investors on Financial Markets. In *Institutional Investors in the New Financial Landscape.* Paris: OECD.

————. 1997. Institutional Investors, Pension Reform, and Emerging Securities Markets. Working Paper 359, Inter-American Development Bank, Washington, D.C.

Bodie, Z. 1989. Pension Funds and Financial Innovation. Working Paper 3101, National Bureau of Economic Research, Cambridge, Mass.

Bos, E., M. T. Vu, E. Massiah, and R.A. Bulatao. 1994. *World Population Projections 1994.* Estimates and Projections with Related Demographic Statistics, Washington, D.C.: World Bank and Johns Hopkins University Press.

Bourguignon, François, Martin Cicowiez, Jean-Jacques Dethier, Leonardo Gasparini, and Pierre Pestieau. What Impact Would a Minimum Pension Have on Old Age Poverty? Evidence from Latin America. Paper Presented at the Keeping the Promise of Old Age Security Conference, Bogotá, Colombia, June 22–23, 2004.

Brooks, Sarah, and Estelle James. 2001. The Political Economy of Pension Reform. In *New Ideas About Old Age Security: Toward Sustainable Pension Systems in the 21st Century,* eds. Robert Holzmann and Joseph Stiglitz. Washington, D.C.: World Bank.

Burchardt, Tania, and John Hills. 1997. *Private Welfare Insurance and Social Security: Pushing the Boundaries.* New York: Joseph Rowntree Foundation.

Butelmann, Andrea, and Francisco Gallego. 1999. *Household Savings in Chile.* Santiago: Division of Economic Research, Central Bank of Chile.

Campbell, J. Y., J. F. Cocco, F. J. Gomes, and P. J. Maenhout. 1999. Investing Retirement Wealth: A Life Cycle Model. Working Paper 7029, National Bureau of Economic Research, Cambridge, Mass.

Carranza, Eliana, and Eduardo Morón. 2003. *Diez Años del Sistema Privado de Pensiones (1993–2003): Avances, Retos y Reformas.* Lima, Peru: Universidad del Pacífico.

Carroll, Christopher D. 1992. The Buffer Stock Theory of Saving: Some Macroeconomic Evidence. *Brookings Papers on Economic Activity* 2: 61–135.

Case, Karl, John Quigley, and Robert Shiller. 2001. Comparing Wealth Effects: The Stockmarket Versus the Housing Market. Working Paper 8606, National Bureau of Economic Research, Cambridge, Mass.

CASEN (National Socioeconomic Characterization Survey; *Caracterización socioeconómica nacional*). 2000. MIDEPLAN, Santiago, Chile.

Catalán, M. 2003. Pension Funds and Corporate Governance in Developing Countries: What Do We Know and What Do We Need to Know? Pension Primer Paper, World Bank, Washington, D.C.

Catalán, M., G. Impavido, and A. B. Musalem. 2000. Contractual Savings or Stock Market Development: Which Leads? Policy Research Working Paper 2421, World Bank, Washington, D.C.

CEPAL (Economic Commission for Latin America and the Caribbean; Comisión Económica para América Latina y el Caribe). 1995. La Medicion de los Ingresos en la Perspectiva de los Estudios de Pobreza: El caso de la Encuesta CASEN de Chile: 1987–1994. Working Paper LC/R. 1604, Santiago, Chile.

Cerda, Luis, and Gloria Grandolini. 1998. The 1997 Pension Reform in Mexico. Policy Research Working Paper 1933, World Bank, Washington, D.C.

Chaloupka, Frank. 1991. Rational Addictive Behaviour and Cigarette Smoking. *Journal of Political Economy* 99 (4): 722–42.

Chamorro, Claudio. 1992. La Cobertura del Sistema de Pensiones Chileno. Thesis 107, Economics Institute, Catholic Pontificate University of Chile.

Cheyre, H. 1991. La Prevision en Chile Ayer y Hoy. Center for Public Studies, Santiago, Chile.

Coate, Stephen. 1995. Altruism, the Samaritan's Dilemma, and Government Transfer Policy. *American Economic Review* 85: 46–57.

Cohen, Wilbur J., and Milton Friedman. 1972. *Social Security: Universal or Selective*. Washington, D.C.: American Enterprise Institute.

Cole, William E., and Richard D. Sanders. 1985. Internal Migration and Urban Employment in the Third World. *American Economic Review* 75: 481–94.

Corbo, Vittorio, and K. Schmidt-Hebbel. 2003. Efectos macroeconómicos de la reforma de pensiones en Chile. Study prepared for the Pension Fund Administrators' Industrial Association, Santiago, Chile. Processed.

Corsetti, G. 1994. An Endogenous Growth Model of Social Security and the Size of the Informal Sector. *Journal of Economic Analysis* 9 (1): 57–76.

Corsetti, G., and K. Schmidt-Hebbel. 1997. Pension Reform and Growth. In *The Economics of Pensions: Principles, Policies, and International Experience*, eds. S. Valdés-Prieto. Cambridge, U.K.: Cambridge University Press.

Cortazar, R. 1997. Chile: The Evolution and Reform of the Labor Market. In *Labor Markets in Latin America: Combining Social Protection with Market Flexibility*, eds. S. Edwards and N. Lustig. Washington, D.C.: Brookings Institution Press.

Cowell, F. D. 1985. Tax Evasion with Labor Income. *Journal of Public Economics* 26 (1): 19–34.

Cox, Donald, Zekeriy Eser, and Emmanuel Jimenez. 1998. Motives for Private Transfers over the Life Cycle: An Analytical Framework and Evidence from Peru. *Journal of Development Economics* 55:57–80.

Cox-Edwards, Alejandra. 2000. Pension Projections for Chilean Men and Women: Estimates from Social Security Contributions. California State University, Long Beach. Processed.

Cuesta, Jose A. 2000. Social Transfers, the Household, and the Distribution of Incomes in Chile. PhD diss., University of Oxford.

Cuesta, J., R. Holzmann, and T. Packard. 1999. Extending Coverage in Multi-Pillar Pension Systems: Constraints and Hypothesis, Preliminary Evidence and Future Research Agenda. Paper prepared for World Bank New Ideas about Old-Age Security Conference, Washington, D.C.

Cunningham, Wendy, and William F. Maloney. 2002. Re-examining the Informal Sector. In *Brazil Jobs Report 24408-BR*, 40–60. Washington, D.C.: World Bank.

Davis, E. P. 2001. Institutional Investors, Corporate Governance, and the Performance of the Corporate Sector. *Economic Systems* 26 (3): 203–29.

———. 1998. Regulation of Pension Fund Assets. In *Institutional Investors in the New Financial Landscape*. Paris: OECD.

Deaton, Angus. 1989. Savings in Developing Countries. *World Bank Economic Review* 3 (Suppl): 61–96.

———. 1991. Saving and Liquidity Constraints. *Econometrica* 59 (5): 1221–248.

———. 1997. *The Analysis of Household Surveys: A Microeconomic Approach to Development Policy*. Washington, D.C.: World Bank and Johns Hopkins University Press.

de Ferranti, David, Danny Leipziger, and P. S. Srinivas. 2002. The Future of Pension Reform in Latin America. *Finance and Development* (39)3.

de Ferranti, David, Guillermo Perry, Indermit Gill, and Luis Servén. 2000. *Securing Our Future in a Global Economy*. Latin American and Caribbean Flagship Regional Study, World Bank, Washington, D.C.

Demarco, Gustavo, and Rafael Rofman. 1998. Supervising Mandatory Funded Pension Systems: Issues and Challenges. Social Protection Discussion Paper 9817, World Bank, Washington, D.C.

Demirgüç-Kunt, Asli, and D. Levine. 1999. Bank-Based and Market-Based Financial Systems: Cross-Country Comparisons. Policy Research Working Paper 2143, World Bank, Washington, D.C.

Devesa-Carpio, José E., and Carlos Vidal-Meliá. 2002. The Reformed Pension Systems in Latin America. Social Protection Discussion Paper 0209, Human Development Network, World Bank, Washington, D.C.

Devesa, J. E., M. Martinez, and C. Vidal. 2000. Análisis y valoración de los sistemas de pensiones reformados en Latinoamérica. WIP-EC-11-2000, Instituto Valenciano de Investigaciones Economicas, Valencia, Spain.

Diamond, Peter A. 1993. Privatization of Social Security: Lessons from Chile. Working Paper 4510, National Bureau of Economic Research, Cambridge, Mass.

———. 1998. The Economics of Social Security Reform. Working Paper 6719, National Bureau of Economic Research, Cambridge, Mass.

Diamond, Peter A., and James A. Mirrlees. 1978. A Model of Social Insurance with Variable Retirement. *Journal of Public Economics* 10: 295–336.

———. 1982. Social Insurance with Variable Retirement and Private Savings, Working Paper 296, Massachusetts Institute of Technology, Cambridge, Mass.

———. 1986a. Payroll-Tax Financed Social Insurance with Variable Retirement. *Scandinavian Journal of Economics* 88 (1): 25–50.

———. 1986b. Insurance Aspects of Pensions. In *Pensions, Labor and Individual Choice,* eds. David A. Wise. Cambridge, Mass: National Bureau of Economic Research and University of Chicago Press.

Disney, Richard, Robert Palacios, and Edward Whitehouse. 1999. Individual Choice of Pension Arrangement as a Pension Reform Strategy. Working Paper W99/18, Institute for Fiscal Studies, London.

Disney, Richard, and Edward Whitehouse. 1999. Pension Plans and Retirement Incentives. Social Protection Discussion Paper 9924, Human Development Network, World Bank, Washington, D.C.

Disney, Richard F., and Edward Whitehouse. 2002. The Economic Well-Being of Older People in International Perspective: A Critical Review. Luxembourg Income Study Working Paper 306.

Dolton, P. J., and G. H. Makepeace. 1987. Interpreting Sample Selection Effects. *Economics Letters* 24: 373–79.

Donkers, Bas, and Arthur van Soest. 1999. Subjective Measures of Household Preferences and Financial Decisions. *Journal of Economic Psychology* 20: 613–42.

Dulitzky, Daniel. 1998. Social Security Reforms, Retirement Plans, and Saving Under Labor Income Uncertainty. PhD diss., Massachusetts Institute of Technology, Cambridge, Mass.

Easterly, William. 2001. *The Elusive Quest for Growth.* Cambridge, Mass.: MIT Press.

ECH (Longitudinal Household Survey; *Encuesta Continua de Hogares*). 1999. La Paz, Bolivia.

ECH (Longitudinal Household Survey; *Encuesta Continua de Hogares*). 2000. La Paz, Bolivia.

ECLAC/CELADE (Economic Commission for Latin America and the Caribbean/Demography Center for Latin America and the Caribbean (*Centro Latinoamericano y Caribeño de Demografía*). 1998. Latin America Population Projections 1970–2050. Demographic Bulletin 62 Santiago, Chile: ECLAC/CELADE.

Edwards, Sebastian. 1986. Are Devaluations Contractionary? *Review of Economics and Statistics* 68 (3): 501–08.

Edwards, Sebastian, and Alejandra Cox-Edwards. 2000a. Economic Reforms and Labor Markets: Policy Issues and Lessons from Chile. Working Paper 7646, National Bureau of Economic Research, Cambridge, Mass.

————. 2000b. Economic Reforms and Labor Markets: Policy Issues and Lessons from Chile. *Economic Policy* 30: 183–229.

Edwards, Sebastian, and Nora Lustig. 1997. *Labor Markets in Latin America: Combining Social Protection with Market Flexibility*. Washington, D.C.: Brookings Institution Press.

EHM (Household Sampling Survey; *Encuesta de hogares por muestreo*). 2000. Caracas, Venezuela.

EHPM (Multipurpose Household Survey; *Encuesta de hogares de propósitos múltiples*). 1998. San Salvador, El Salvador.

EHPM (Multipurpose Household Survey; *Encuesta de hogares de propósitos múltiples*). 2000. San Salvador, El Salvador.

Ehrlich, Isaac, and Gary Becker. 1972. Market Insurance, Self-Insurance and Self-Protection. *Journal of Political Economy* 80: 623–48.

————. 2000. Market Insurance, Self-Insurance, and Self-Protection. In *Foundations of Insurance Economics: Readings in Economics and Finance*, eds. G. Dionne and S. Harrington. Boston: Kluwer Academic Publishers.

Ehrlich, Isaac, and Hiroyuki Chuma. 1990. A Model of the Demand for Longevity and the Value of Life Extension. *Journal of Political Economy* 98 (4): 761–82.

Eichengreen, Barry, and Ashoka Mody. 1998. What Explains Changing Spreads on Emerging-Market Debt: Fundamentals or Market Sentiment? Working Paper w6408, National Bureau of Economic Research, Cambridge, Mass.

Elter, Doris. 1999. *Sistema de AFP Chileno: Injusticia de un Modelo*. Santiago, Chile: LOM Publishing.

ENAHO (National Household Survey; *Encuesta Nacional de Hogares*). 2000. Lima, Peru.

ENEU (National Urban Employment Survey; *Encuesta nacional de empleo urbano*). 1998. Mexico City, Mexico.

ENEU (National Urban Employment Survey; *Encuesta nacional de empleo urbano*). 2001. Mexico City, Mexico.

ENFT (National Laborforce Survey; *Encuesta Nacional de la Fuerza de Trabajo*). 2000. Santo Domingo, Dominican Republic.

ENH (National Household Survey; *Encuesta nacional de hogares*). 1999. Bogotá Colombia.

ENMV (National Living Standards Measurement Survey; *Encuesta Nacional sobre Medición de Niveles de Vida*). 1999. Managua, Nicaragua.

EPH (Permanent Household Survey; *Encuesta Permanente de Hogares*). 2002. Buenos Aires, Argentina.

Epps, T. W., and K. Singleton. 1986. An Omnibus Test for the Two-Sample Problem Using the Empirical Characteristic Function. *Journal of Statistical Computation and Simulation* 26: 177–203.

Escobar, Federico. 2003. Pension Reform in Bolivia: A Review of Approach and Experience. Background Paper for the Regional Study on Social Security Reform, LAC Region, World Bank, Washington, D.C.

Evans, D., and L. Leighton. 1989. Some Empirical Aspects of Entrepreneurship. *American Economic Review* 79: 519–35.

Eyzaguirre, N., and F. Lefort.1999. Capital Markets in Chile: A Case of Successful International Financial Integration. In *Chile: Recent Policy Lessons and Emerging Challenges*, eds. G. Perry and D. M. Leipziger. Washington, D.C.: World Bank Institute.

Faccio, M., and M. A. Lasfer. 2001. *Institutional Shareholders and Corporate Governance: The Case of UK Pension Funds*. Working Paper 11/01, Center for Research on Pensions and Welfare Policies, Torino, Italy.

Fafchamps, Marcel, and S. Lund. 2000. Risk-Sharing Networks in Rural Philippines. Oxford University. Processed.

Feldstein, M. 1985. The Optimal Level of Social Security Benefits. *Quarterly Journal of Economics* 100: 303–19.

Feldstein, Martin, and Stephanie Seligman. 1981. Pension Funding, Share Prices, and National Savings. *Journal of Finance* 36 (4): 801–24.

FIAP (International Federation of Pension Fund Administrators). 2002. Boletin No. 12. Santiago, Chile.

Fields, Gary. 1974. Rural–Urban Migration, Urban Unemployment and Under-employment, and Job Search Activities in LDCs. *Journal of Development Economics* 2: 165–88.

———. 1990. Labor Market Modeling and the Urban Informal Sector: Theory and Evidence. In *The Informal Sector Revisited*. Paris: OECD.

Fiess, Norbert. 2003. Pension Reform or Pension Default? A Note on Pension Reform and Country Risk. Background Paper for the Regional Study on Social Security Reform, LAC Region, World Bank, Washington, D.C.

Fiess, Norbert, William F. Maloney, and Rashmi Shankar. 2000. The Informal Sector, Wage Rigidities, and Real Exchange Rates. Poverty Reduction and Economic Management Department, World Bank, Washington, D.C. Processed.

Fiorito, Riccardo, and Flavio Padrini. 2001. Distortionary Taxation and Labor Market Performance. *Oxford Bulletin of Economics and Statistics* 63 (2): 173–96.

Fischer, B. 1998. The Role of Contractual Savings Institutions in Emerging Markets. In *Institutional Investors in the New Financial Landscape.* Paris: OECD.

Fox, Louise, and Edward Palmer. 2001. New Approaches to Multipillar Pension Systems: What in the World Is Going On? In *New Ideas about Old Age Security: Toward Sustainable Pension Systems in the 21st Century*, eds. Robert Holzmann and Joseph Stiglitz. Washington, D.C.: World Bank.

Fuchs, Victor R. 1986. *The Health Economy.* Cambridge, Mass.: Harvard University Press.

Gallego, F., and N. Loayza. 2000. Financial Structure in Chile: Macroeconomic Developments and Microeconomic Effects. Paper presented at the World Bank Financial Structures and Economic Development Conference, Washington, D.C.

Genicot, G., and D. Ray. 2000. Endogenous Group Formation in Risk Sharing Arrangements. Department of Economics Working Paper, New York University. Processed.

Getler, Paul. 2000. Insuring the Economic Costs of Illness. In *Shielding the Poor: Social Protection in the Developing World*, ed. Nora Lustig. Washington, D.C.: Brookings Institution Press and the Inter-American Development Bank.

Gill, Indermit, and Nadeem Ilahi. 2000. Economic Insecurity, Individual Behavior, and Social Policy. Office of the Chief Economist, Latin America and the Caribbean Region, World Bank, Washington, D.C.

Gill, Indermit, and Claudio Montenegro. 2001. Is Chile's Labor Market Serving the Poor as Well as It Does the Rich? In *Crafting Labor Policy: Techniques and Lessons from Latin America*, eds. I. Gill, C. Montenegro, and D. Domeland. London: Oxford University Press and the World Bank.

Gill, Indermit, Truman Packard, Anita Schwarz, and Juan Yermo. 2001. Brazil: Critical Issues in Social Security. Country Study, World Bank, Washington, D.C.

Grandolini, Gloria, and Luis Cerda. 1998. The 1997 Pension Reform in Mexico. Policy Research Working Paper 1933, World Bank, Washington, D.C.

Gruber, Jonathan. 1995. The Incidence of Payroll Taxation: Evidence from Chile. Working Paper 5053, National Bureau of Economic Research, Cambridge, Mass.

Gruber, Jonathan, and James M. Poterba. 1993. Tax Incentives and the Decision to Purchase Health Insurance: Evidence from the Self Employed. Working Paper 4435, National Bureau of Economic Research, Cambridge, Mass.

Guiso, L., and M. Paiella. 2000. Risk Aversion, Wealth, and Financial Markets Imperfections. Working Paper, Ente Luigi Einaudi for Monetary, Banking, and Financial Studies and the Bank of Italy Research Department, Rome.

Haque, Nadeem Ul, Manmohan S. Kumar, Mark Nelson, and Donald J. Mathieson, 1996. The Economic Context of Indicators of Developing Country Creditworthiness. Working Paper 9619, International Monetary Fund, Washington, D.C.

Harris, John R., and Michael P. Todaro. 1970. Migration, Unemployment and Development: A Two-Sector Analysis. *American Economic Review* 60 (March): 126–42.

Hayashi, Fumio, Joseph Altonji, and Laurence Kotlikoff. 1996. Risk-Sharing Between and Within Families. *Econometrica* 64 (2): 261–94.

Hemmer, Hans R., and C. Mannel. 1989. On the Economic Analysis of the Urban Informal Sector. *World Development* 17 (10): 1543–552.

Hernández, L., and E. Walker. 1993. Estructuras de financiamiento corporativo en Chile (1978–1990). Public Studies 51, Center for Public Studies, Santiago, Chile.

Hirshleifer, John, and John Riley. 1979. The Analytics of Uncertainty and Information—An Expository Survey. *Journal of Economic Literature* 17: 1375–421.

Hoddinott, John. 1992. Rotten Kids or Manipulative Parents: Are Children Old Age Security in Western Kenya? *Economic Development and Cultural Change* 40 (3): 545–66.

Hogan, John J. 1987. Pensions and the Self Employed. *Irish Banking Review* Summer: 18–26.

Holzmann, Robert. 1997. Pension Reform, Financial Market Development, and Economic Growth: Preliminary Evidence from Chile. Working Paper WP/96/34, International Monetary Fund, Washington, D.C.

———. 1998. Financing the Transition to the Multi-Pillar. Social Protection Discussion Paper 9809, World Bank, Washington D.C.

Holzmann, Robert, and Steen Jorgensen. 1999. Social Protection as Social Risk Management: Conceptual Underpinnings for the Social Protection Strategy Paper. Social Protection Discussion Paper 9904, Human Development Network, World Bank, Washington, D.C.

Holzmann, Robert, Robert Palacios, and Asta Zviniene. 2001. Implicit Pension Debt: Issues, Measurement and Scope in International Perspective. Pension Primer Paper, World Bank, Washington, D.C.

Holzmann, Robert, Truman Packard, and Jose Cuesta. 2000. Extending Coverage in Multi-Pillar Pension Systems: Constraints and Hypotheses, Preliminary Evidence and Future Research Agenda. In *New Ideas About Old Age Security*, eds. R. Holzmann and J. Stiglitz. Washington, D.C.: World Bank.

Holzmann, Robert, and Joseph Stiglitz, eds. 2001. *New Ideas about Old Age Security: Toward Sustainable Pension Systems in the 21st Century*. Washington, D.C.: World Bank.

Hubbard, R. G., J. Skinner, and S. P. Zeldes. 1993. The Importance of Precautionary Motives in Explaining Individual and Aggregate Savings. Working Paper 4516, National Bureau of Economic Research, Cambridge, Mass.

———. 1994. Expanding the Life-Cycle Model: Precautionary Savings and Public Policy. *American Economics Association Papers and Proceedings* 84 (2): 174–79.

Hurd, Michael. 1990. Research on the Elderly: Economic Status, Retirement, Consumption and Saving. *Journal of Economic Literature* 28 (2): 565–637.

Hurd, Michael, Daniel McFadden, and Li Gan. 1998. Subjective Survival Curves and Life Cycle Behavior. In *Inquiries in the Economics of Aging*, ed. David Wise. Chicago: University of Chicago Press and National Bureau of Economic Research.

Hurd, Michael D., and Kathleen McGarry. 1997. The Predictive Validity of Subjective Probabilities of Survival. Working Paper 6193, National Bureau of Economic Research, Cambridge, Mass.

IADB (Inter-American Development Bank). 2000. *Social Protection for Equity and Growth*. Washington, D.C.: Poverty and Inequality Advisory Unit, Sustainable Development Department, Inter-American Development Bank.

Iglesias, A. 1998. The Impact of Pension Reform on Capital Markets: The Chilean Experience. Paper presented at the Conference on Capital Market Development in Emerging and Transition Economies: Trends and Challenges, Washington, D.C.

———. 2000. Pension Reform and Corporate Governance: Impact in Chile. *Revista ABANTE* 3 (1): 109–41.

ILO (International Labour Organization). 1993. Resolution II Concerning Statistics of Employment in the Informal Sector. Presented at the 15th International Conference of Labour Statisticians, Geneva. www.ilo.org/public/english/120/res/infsec.htm.

———. 1996. *Labor Overview: Latin America and the Caribbean, No. 3.* Geneva: ILO.

———. 1998. *Labor Overview: Latin America and the Caribbean, No. 5.* Geneva: ILO.

———. 1999. *Labor Overview: Latin America and the Caribbean, No. 6.* Geneva: ILO.

———. 2000. *World Labor Report.* Geneva: ILO.

Impavido, Gregorio, Alberto R. Musalem, and Thierry Tressel. 2001a. Contractual Savings, Capital Markets, and Firms' Financing Choices. World Bank Financial Sector Development Department, Washington, D.C. Processed.

———. 2001b. Contractual Savings Institutions and Banks' Stability and Efficiency. Policy Research Working Paper 2751, World Bank, Washington, D.C.

Impavido, G., A. Musalem, and D. Vittas. 2002. Contractual Savings in Countries with a Small Financial Sector. In *Globalization and Financial Systems in Small Developing Countries,* eds. James Hanson, Patrick Honohan, and Giovanni Majnoni. Washington D.C.: World Bank.

Insinga, Ralph. 1998. The Retirement Outlook for Chile's Independently Employed Workers: A Case Study of Attitudes and Saving Behavior. LC/R 1840, Economic Commission for Latin America and the Caribbean, Santiago, Chile.

International Insurance Council. 1998. *Latin America: An Insurance Reference Guide.* Washington, D.C.: International Insurance Council.

International Monetary Fund (IMF). 2003. *International Financial Statistics.* Washington, D.C.

James, E. 1996. Protecting the Old and Promoting Growth: A Defense of *Averting the Old Age Crisis.* Policy Research Working Paper 1570, World Bank, Washington, D.C.

———. 1997. Pension Reform: Is There a Tradeoff Between Efficiency and Equity? Policy Research Working Paper 1767, World Bank, Washington, D.C.

———. 1999. Coverage Under Old Age Security Systems and Protection for the Uninsured: What Are the Issues? Paper presented at the Inter-American Development Bank Conference on Social Protection, Washington, D.C.

James, E., A. Cox-Edwards, and R. Wong. 2003. The Gender Impact of Pension Reform: A Cross-Country Analysis. Policy Research Working Paper 3074, World Bank, Washington, D.C.

James, E., G. Ferrier, J. Smalhout, and D. Vittas. 1998. Mutual Funds and Institutional Investments: What Is the Most Efficient Way to Set Up Individual Accounts in a Social Security System? Paper presented at the NBER Conference on Social Security, Bordeaux, France.

James, E., J. Smalhout, and D. Vittas. 2001. Administrative Costs and the Organisation of Individual Account Systems: A Comparative Perspective. In *Private Pension Systems: Administrative Costs and Reforms*. Private Pension Series. Paris: OECD.

Kamin, Steven B., and Karsten von Kleist. 1999. The Evolution and Determinants of Emerging Market Credit Spreads in the 1990s. International Finance Discussion Paper 653, Federal Reserve Board of Governors, Washington, D.C.

Karpoff, J. M., P. H. Malatesta, and R. A. Walkling. 1996. Corporate Governance and Shareholder Initiatives: Empirical Evidence. *Journal of Financial Economics* 42: 365–95.

Kleinjans, Kristin J. 2001. The Colombian Pension System After the Reform of 1994: An Evaluation. Department of Economics, University of Pittsburgh. Processed.

Knight, F. 1921. *Risk, Uncertainty, and Profit*. New York: Houghton-Mifflin.

Kotlikoff, Laurence J., William Samuelson, and Stephen Johnson. 1988. Consumption, Computation Mistakes and Fiscal Policy. AEA Papers and Proceedings. *American Economic Review* 78 (2): 408–12.

Krebs, Tom, and William F. Maloney. 1999. Quitting and Labor Turnover: Microeconomic Evidence and Macroeconomic Consequences. Policy Research Working Paper 2068, World Bank, Washington, D.C.

Laboul, A. 1998. Private Pension Systems: Regulatory Policies. Ageing Working Paper 2.2, OECD, Paris.

Laffont, Jean-Jacques. 1979. *Aggregation and Revelation of Preferences*. Amsterdam: North-Holland.

Laibson, David I., Andrea Repetto, and Jeremy Tobacman. 1998. Self-Control and Saving for Retirement. *Brookings Papers on Economic Activity* 1: 91–196.

La Porta, R., F. Lopez-de-Silanes, A. Shleifer, and R. W. Vishny. 1998. Law and Finance. *Journal of Political Economy* 106 (6): 1113–155.

Lasaga, Manuel, and John Pollner. 2003. Peru's Private Pension System: An Analysis of Its Evolution, Current Market Structure and Recommendations for Reform. Background Paper for Analytical and Advisory

Assistance to the Government of Peru, Social Protection Sector Unit, Latin America and the Caribbean Regional Office, World Bank, Washington, D.C.

Lawrence, Emily C. 1991. Poverty and the Rate of Time Preference: Evidence from Panel Data. *Journal of Political Economy* 99 (1): 54–77.

Lazear, Edward P. 1986. Incentive Effects of Pensions. In *Pensions, Labor and Individual Choice*, ed. David A. Wise. Chicago: University of Chicago Press and National Bureau of Economic Research.

Lefort, F., and E. Walker. 2000a. Pension Reform and Capital Markets: Are There Any (Hard) Links? Working Paper, Catholic University of Chile, Santiago.

———. 2000b. The Effects of Economic and Political Shocks on Corporate Governance Systems in Chile. *Revista ABANTE* 2 (2): 183–206.

Levenson, Alec R., and William F. Maloney. 1998. The Informal Sector, Firm Dynamics and Institutional Participation. Policy Research Working Paper 1988, World Bank, Washington, D.C.

Levine, R. 1997. Financial Development and Economic Growth: Views and Agenda. *Journal of Economic Literature* 32 (2): 688–726.

Levine, Ross, Norman Loayza, and Thorsten Beck. 2000. Financial Intermediation and Growth: Causality and Causes. *Journal of Monetary Economics* 46(1):31–77 (August).

Levine, R., and S. Zervos. 1998. Stock Markets, Banks, and Economic Growth. *American Economic Review* 88 (June): 537–58.

Lewis, W. 1954. Economic Development with Unlimited Supply of Labor. *Manchester School of Economics and Social Studies* 22: 139–91.

Lindbeck, Assar, and Mats Persson. 2003. The Gains from Pension Reform. *Journal of Economic Literature* 41 (March): 74–112.

Litchfield, Julie. 2001. Updated Income Distribution and Poverty Measures for Chile: 1987–1998. Background Paper 1. In *Poverty and Income Distribution in a High Growth Economy: The Case of Chile 1987-1998*. Washington, D.C.: World Bank.

Lucas, Robert E. B., and Oded Stark. 1985. Motivations to Remit: Evidence from Botswana. *Journal of Political Economy* 93 (5): 901–17.

Macias, Osvaldo, and Jorge Tarzijan. 1994. Origen y Magnitud de la Evasion en el Sistema de Pensiones Chileno Derivado de la Capitalizacion Individual. Fiscal Policy Series Economic Commission for Latin America and the Caribbean/United Nations Development Programme, Santiago, Chile.

Maloney, William F. 1998a. The Structure of the Labor Market in Developing Countries: Time Series Evidence and Competing Views. Policy Research Working Paper 1940, World Bank, Washington, D.C.

————. 1998b. Are Labor Markets in Developing Countries Dualistic? Policy Research Working Paper 1941, World Bank, Washington, D.C.

————. 1999. Does Informality Imply Segmentation in Urban Labor Markets? Evidence from Sectoral Transitions in Mexico. *World Bank Economic Review* 13 (2): 275–302.

————. 2000. Minimum Wages in Latin America: A Note. Poverty Reduction and Economic Management Department, World Bank, Washington, D.C. Processed.

————. 2003. Informality Revisited. Policy Research Working Paper 2965, World Bank, Washington, D.C.

Maloney, William F. and Jairo Nuñez. 2001. Measuring the Impact of Minimum Wages: Evidence from Latin America. Policy Research Working Paper 2597, World Bank, Washington, D.C.

Manski, C. 1989. Anatomy of the Selection Problem. *Journal of Human Resources* 24 (3): 343–60.

Marcouiller, D.,V. Ruiz de Castilla, and C. Woodruff. 1997. Formal Measures of the Informal Sector Wage Gap in Mexico, El Salvador, and Peru. *Economic Development and Cultural Change* 45 (2): 367–92.

Marquez, Gustavo, and Carmen Pages. 1998. The Ties That Bind: Protecting Employment and Labor Trends in Latin America. Paper presented at the annual meeting of the Board of Governors, Inter-American Development Bank, Cartagena, Colombia.

Marshall, John R. 1976. Moral Hazard. *American Economic Review* 66: 880–90.

Mastrángelo, Jorge. 1999. Políticas Para la Reducción de Costos en los Sistemas de Pensiones: El Caso de Chile. Financing Development Series. Santiago, Chile: CEPAL/ECLAC.

Maturana, G., and E. Walker. 1999. Rentabilidades, Comisiones, y Desempeño en la Industria Chilena de Fondos Mutuos. *Estudios Públicos* 73 (Summer): 293–334.

Mesa-Lago, Carmelo. 1991. Social Security and Prospects for Equity in Latin America. Discussion Paper 140, World Bank, Washington, D.C.

————. 2000. Social Assistance, Pensions and Health Care for the Poor in Latin America and the Caribbean. In *Shielding the Poor: Social Protection in the Developing World,* ed. Nora Lustig. Washington, D.C.: Brookings Institution Press and Inter-American Development Bank.

————. 2001. La Cobertura de Pensiones de Seguridad Social en America Latina Antes y Después de la Reforma Previsional. *Socialis: Revista Latinoamiricana de Política Social* 4 (April): 17–27.

Min, Hong G., and Jung-goo Park. 2000. How the Republic of Korea's Financial Structure Affects the Volatility of Four Asset Prices. Policy Research Working Paper 2327, World Bank, Washington, D.C.

Mincer, Jacob A. 1974. *Schooling, Experience and Earnings.* New York: Columbia University Press.

Ministerio de Economía. 2000. Caracterización y Evolución del Gasto Público Social. Dirección de Gastos Sociales Consolidados, Secretaría de Política Económica, Ministerio de Economía, Buenos Aires.

———. 2002. Series de Gasto Público Consolidado por Finalidad-función (1980–2001). Dirección de Gastos Sociales Consolidados, Secretaría de Política Económica, Buenos Aires.

Mitchell, Olivia S. 1998. Building an Environment for Pension Reform in Developing Countries. Social Protection Discussion Paper 9803, Human Development Network, World Bank, Washington, D.C.

Montenegro, Claudio. 2001. *Wage Distribution in Chile: Does Gender Matter? A Quantile Regression Approach.* Washington, D.C.: World Bank Development Research Group. Processed.

Moody's Investor Service. 1998. *Moody's Approach to Analyzing Pension Obligations of Corporations.* Moody's Investor Service, New York, N.Y.

Morande, Felipe G. 1992. Dynamics of Real Asset Prices, the Real Exchange Rate, Trade Reforms and Foreign Capital Inflows: Chile, 1976–1989. *Journal of Development Economics* 39 (1): 111–39

Morande, Felipe, and Raimundo Soto. 1992. Una Nota sobre la Construcción de Series de Precios de Activos Reales: Tierra y Cases en Chile (1976–1989). *Revista de Analisis Economico (Chile)* 7: 169–77.

Murgai, R., P. Winters, E. Sadoulet, and A. de Janvry. 2000. Localized and Incomplete Mutual Insurance. University of New England Working Paper Series in Agricultural and Resource Economics 2000-5. New South Wales, Australia. Processed.

Nesbitt, S. L. 1994. Long-Term Rewards from Shareholder Activism: A Study of the CalPERS Effect. *Journal of Applied Corporate Finance* 6: 75–80.

OECD (Organisation for Economic Co-operation and Development). 1997. *Insurance Guidelines for Economies in Transition.* Paris: OECD Centre for Co-operation with the Economies in Transition.

———. 1998. *Maintaining Prosperity in an Ageing Society.* Paris.

———. 1999. *Institutional Investors' Statistical Yearbook 1998.* Paris.

———. 2001. *Insurance Regulation and Supervision in Asia and Latin America.* Paris.

Orszag, Peter, and Joseph Stiglitz. 2001. Rethinking Pension Reform: Ten Myths About Social Security Systems. In *New Ideas About Old Age Security: Toward Sustainable Pension Systems in the 21st Century*, eds. R. Holzmann and J. Stiglitz. Washington, D.C.: World Bank.

Packard, Truman. 1997. Adjustment, Migration and Economic Informality in Latin America. M.Sc. Economics for Development, Extended Essay, Queen Elizabeth House, University of Oxford, U.K.

———. 2001. Is There a Positive Incentive Effect from Privatizing Social Security? Evidence from Pension Reforms in Latin America. Policy Research Working Paper 2719, World Bank, Washington, D.C.

———. 2002. Pooling, Savings and Prevention: Mitigating the Risk of Old Age Poverty in Chile. Background Paper for the Regional Study on Social Security Reform, LAC Region, World Bank, Washington, D.C.

Packard, Truman, Naoko Shinkai, and Ricardo Fuentes. 2002. The Reach of Social Security in Latin America and the Caribbean. Background Paper for the Regional Study on Social Security Reform, LAC Region, World Bank, Washington, D.C.

Pages, Carmen, and Claudio Montenegro. 1999. *Job Security and the Age Composition of Employment: Evidence from Chile*. Washington, D.C.: Inter-American Development Bank.

Palacios, Robert J. 1996. *Averting the Old Age Crisis:* Technical Annex. Policy Research Working Paper 1572, World Bank, Washington, D.C.

Palacios, Robert J., and Montserrat Pallares-Miralles 2000. International Patterns of Pension Provision. Social Protection Discussion Paper 0009, Human Development Network, World Bank, Washington, D.C.

Paredes, Ricardo, and Jorge Nino. 2001. Proyecto Contra la Evasión, Rebajas de Impuestos y Compensaciones. *Economy and Administration* 140 (April/May).

Pemberton, James. 1997. Protecting the People from Themselves: Switching from Universal to Means-Tested Pensions When Some People Are Myopic. Discussion Papers in Economics and Management 387, University of Reading, U.K.

———. 1999. Pension Reform, Latin American Style: A National Free Lunch? Discussion Papers in Economics and Management 414, University of Reading, U.K.

Perry, Guillermo, and Luis Servén. 2003. The Anatomy of a Multiple Crisis: Why Was Argentina Special and What Can We Learn From It? Policy Research Working Paper 3081, World Bank, Washington, D.C.

Pinera, Jose E. 1991a. *El Cascabel al Gato: La Batalla por la Reforma Previsional*. Santiago, Chile: Zig Zag.

———.1991b. Principios y Fundamentos del Sistema Privado de Pensiones en Chile. In *Análisis del Sistema Privado de Pensiones en Chile,* ed. Rosario Cruz Ovalle. Santiago, Chile: Ibero-American Congress of the Association of Pension Fund Adminsitrators.

———. 1995. Empowering Workers: The Privatization of Social Security in Chile. *Cato Journal* 15: 155–66.

Poterba, James M. 1988. Are Consumers Forward Looking? Evidence from Fiscal Experiments. AEA Papers and Proceedings. *American Economic Review* 78 (2): 413–18.

Poterba, James M., Steven F. Venti, and David A. Wise. 1994. Targeted Saving and Net Worth of Elderly Americans. *American Economics Review Papers and Proceedings* 84 (2): 180–85.

Pradhan, Menno. 1995. Sector Participation Decisions in Labor Supply Models. Living Standards Measurement Study Working Paper 113, World Bank, Washington, D.C.

PRIESO (*Encuestas de Previsión de Riesgos Sociales*). 2000. *Social Risk Management Survey*. Washington, D.C.: World Bank.

———. 2002. Social Risk Management Survey. Washington, D.C.: World Bank.

Pritchett, Lant, and Lawrence H. Summers. 1993. Wealthier Is Healthier. Policy Research Working Paper 1150, World Bank, Washington, D.C.

Queisser, M. 1998a. Pension Reform: Lessons from Latin America. Policy Brief 15, OECD Development Centre, Paris.

———. 1998b. The Role of Pension Funds in the Stabilization of the Domestic Financial Sector. Washington, D.C.: World Bank. Processed.

———. 1998c. *The Second Generation Pension Reforms in Latin America*. Paris: OECD Development Centre.

Rabin, Matthew, and Richard Thaler. 2001. Anomalies: Risk Aversion. *Journal of Economic Perspectives* 15 (1): 219–32.

Ramos, J. 1999. La Experiencia de las Administradoras de Fondos de Pensiones en el Financiamiento de las Empresas a través del Mercado de Capitales en el Perú. AFP Integra, Lima. Processed.

Rees, H., and A. Shah. 1986. An Empirical Analysis of Self-Employment in the U.K. *Journal of Applied Econometrics* 1: 95–108.

Reisen, H. 1997. Liberalising Foreign Investments by Pensions Funds: Positive and Normative Aspects. Technical Paper 120, OECD Development Centre, Paris.

Reisen, Helmut, and J. Bailliu. 2000. Do Funded Pensions Contribute to Higher Aggregate Savings? A Cross-Country Analysis. In *Pensions, Savings and Capital Flows,* ed. Helmut Reisen. Paris: OECD.

Revilla, Ernesto. 2002. The Cost of Social Security Reform in Bolivia. IADB, Washington, D.C. Processed.

Robson, Martin T., and Colin Wren. 1999. Marginal and Average Tax Rates and the Incentive for Self Employment. *Southern Journal* 65 (4): 757–73.

Rodriguez, L. Jacobo. 1999. In Praise and Criticism of Mexico's Pension Reform. Policy Analysis 340, Cato Institute, Washington, D.C.

Rodrik, Dani. 2003. Growth Strategies. Kennedy School of Government, Harvard University, Cambridge, Mass. Processed.

Rofman, Rafael. 1999. El Costo Laboral como Explicación del Desempleo en la Argentina: Un Análisis de los Efectos de las Reducciones en las Contribuciones Patronales sobre el Desempleo entre 1994 y 1999. *Jornadas Argentinas de Población.*

———. 2000. The Pension System in Argentina: Six Years After the Reform. In *Pension Reform Primer,* eds. R. J. Palacios and E. Whitehouse. Washington, D.C.: World Bank.

———. 2002. The Pension System in Argentina: Learning the Lessons. Background Paper for the Regional Study on Social Security Reform, LAC Region, World Bank, Washington, D.C.

Rofman, Rafael, and Gustavo Demarco. 1999. Collecting and Transferring Pension Contributions, Social Protection Discussion Working Paper 9907, World Bank, Washington, D.C.

Rofman, Rafael, Gustavo Stirparo, and Pablo Lattes. 1997. Proyecciones del Sistema Integrado de Jubilaciones y Pensiones. Special Studies 12, Superintendency of Retirement and Pension Fund Administrators, Buenos Aires.

Rojas, E. 1999. *The Long Road to Housing Reform. Lessons from the Chilean Experience.* Sustainable Development Department Best Practices Series. Washington, D.C.: Inter-American Development Bank.

Rosenzweig, M. R. 1988. Labor Markets in Low-Income Countries. In *Handbook of Development Economics,* Vol. 1, eds. H. Chenery and T. N. Srinvasan. Amsterdam: North-Holland.

———. 2001. Savings Behavior in Low Income Countries. *Oxford Review of Economic Policy* 17 (1): 40–54.

Rubalcava, L., and O. Gutierrez. 2000. *Políticas para canalizar mayores recursos de los fondos de pensiones hacia la inversion real en México.* Financing Development Series. New York: United Nations.

SAFJP (*Superintendencia de AFJP*). 2002. *Memoria Trimestral 31.* Buenos Aires.

SAFP (Chilean Pension Fund Administrators' Superintendency; *Superintendencia de Administradoras de Fondos de Pensiones de Chile*). 1998. Santiago, Chile.

———. 1999. *El Sistema Chileno de Pensiones.* Santiago, Chile: SAFP.

————. 2000. *Buletin Estadistico del Sistema Chileno de Pensiones.* Santiago, Chile.

Salomon Smith Barney. 1998. *Private Pension Funds in Latin America.* Salomon Smith Barney Latin America Equity Research. New York.

Samwick, A. 1997. Discount Rate Heterogeneity and Social Security Reform. Working Paper 6219, National Bureau of Economic Research, Cambridge, Mass.

Schmidt-Hebbel, K. 1997. Pension Reform, Informal Markets and Long-Term Income and Welfare, Working Paper 04, Central Bank of Santiago, Chile.

Schmidt-Hebbel, K. 1998a. Does Pension Reform Really Spur Productivity, Saving, and Growth? Working Paper 33, Central Bank of Chile, Santiago, Chile.

————. 1998b. Pension Reform and Labor Market Adjustment. Processed.

Schmidt-Hebbel, Klaus. 1999. Chile's Pension Revolution Coming of Age. (English version) In *Gesetzliche Alterssicherung, Reformerfahrungen im Ausland: Ein systematischer Vergleich aus sechs Landern (Reforming the Pension System: What Germany Can Learn from Other Countries).* Cologne: Deutsches Institut für Altersvorsorge.

Schmidt-Hebbel, K., and Luis Servén. 1996. Hacia una Menor Inflacion en Chile: Contraccion Monetaria Bajo Expectativas Racionales. In *Analisis Empirico de la Inflacion en Chile,* eds. F. Morande and F. Rosende. Santiago, Chile: Latin American Institute of Doctrine and Social Studies and Pontifica Universidad Catolica de Chile.

Schreiber, Sven. 2001. Estimating the Fiscal Cost of the Minimum Pension Guarantee in Chile. Paper presented at the International Institute of Public Finance meeting, August 27–30, 2001, Linz, Austria.

Schubert, R., M. Brown, M. Gysler, and H. W. Branchinger. 1999. Financial Decision-Making: Are Women Really More Risk-Averse? *American Economic Review* 89 (2): 381–85.

Schwarz, A. 1998. Comment to the Shift to a Funded Social Security System in Argentina. In *Privatizing Social Security,* ed. Martin Feldstein. Chicago: University of Chicago Press.

Serrano, Carlos. 1999. Social Security Reform, Income Distribution, Fiscal Policy and Capital Accumulation. Policy Research Working Paper 2055, World Bank, Washington, D.C.

Shah, Hemant. 1997. Towards Better Regulation of Private Pension Funds. Policy Research Working Paper 1791, World Bank, Washington, D.C.

Skully, M., and D. Vittas. 1991. Overview of Contractual Savings Institutions, Working Paper 605, World Bank, Washington, D.C.

Smith, M. P. 1996. Shareholder Activism by Institutional Investors: Evidence from CalPERS. *Journal of Finance* 51: 227–52.

Snyder, James M., Jr., and Irene Yackovlev. 2000. Political and Economic Determinants of Government Spending on Social Protection Programs. Background Paper, World Bank Latin America and Caribbean Studies, Washington, D.C.

Srinivas, P. S., and J. Yermo. 1999. *Do Investment Regulations Compromise Pension Fund Performance? Evidence from Latin America.* Latin America and Caribbean Region Viewpoint Series. Washington, D.C.: World Bank.

————. 2000. *Risk Management Through International Diversification: The Case of Latin American Pension Funds.* Philadelphia: Wharton School, University of Pennsylvania.

————. 2002. Risk Management Through International Diversification: The Case of Latin American Pension Funds. In *Innovations in Retirement Financing*, eds. O. S. Mitchell, Z. Bodie, P. B. Hammond, and S. Zeldes. Philadelphia: University of Pennsylvania Press for the Pension Research Council.

Srinivas, P. S., Edward Whitehouse, and Juan Yermo. 2000. Regulating Private Pension Funds' Structure, Performance and Investments: Cross-country Evidence. Social Protection Discussion Paper 0113, World Bank, Washington, D.C.

Stark, Oded. 1990. A Relative Deprivation Approach to Performance Incentives in Career Games and Other Contests. *Kyklos* 43: 211–27.

Stark, Oded. 1995. *Altruism and Beyond: An Economic Analysis of Transfers and Exchanges within Families and Groups.* Cambridge, U.K.: Cambridge University Press.

St. John, Susan, and Larry Willmore. 2001. Two Legs Are Better Than Three: New Zealand as a Model for Old Age Pensions. *World Development* 29 (8): 1291–305.

Summers, Lawrence H. 1989. Some Simple Economics of Mandated Benefits. *American Economic Review Papers and Proceedings* 79 (2): 177–83.

Taubman, Paul, and Michael L. Wachter. 1986. Segmented Labor Markets. In *Handbook of Labor Economics, Vol. 2*, eds. O. Ashenfelter and R. Layard. Amsterdam: North-Holland.

Taylor, Mark, P. 1996. Earnings, Independence or Unemployment: Why Become Self Employed? *Oxford Bulletin of Economics and Statistics* 58 (2): 253–65.

Thaler, Richard H. 1994. Psychology and Savings Policies. *American Economic Review Papers and Proceedings* 84 (2): 186–92.

Thoenissen, Christoph. 1998. Pensions, Longevity and the Pursuit of Leisure: An Analysis of Pension Reform and Ageing in an Overlapping Generations Model with Endogenous Labor Supply. Discussion Paper in Economics and Management 385, University of Reading, U.K.

Thomas, J. 1996. The New Economic Model and Labor Markets in Latin America. In *The New Economic Model in Latin America and Its Impact on Income Distribution and Poverty*, ed. Victor Bulmer-Thomas. London: Institute of Latin American Studies, University of London.

Thompson, Lawrence H. 1998. *Older and Wiser: The Economics of Public Pensions*. Washington, D.C.: Urban Institute Press.

Titelman, Daniel. 2000. Reformas al Sistema de Salud en Chile: Desafios Pendientes. Economic Commission for Latin America, Financing Development Series, 104, Santiago, Chile.

Tokman, V., ed. 1992. *Beyond Regulation: The Informal Economy in Latin America*. Geneva: World Employment Program, International Labour Organization.

Tokman, Victor, and Daniel Martinez. 1999. Costo Laboral y Competitividad en el Sector Manufacturero de America Lanita, 1990–1998. *Revista de la CEPAL* 69 (December): 53–70.

Torche, Aristides, and Gert Wagner. 1997. Prevision Social: Valoración Individual de un Beneficio Mandatado. *Cuadernos de Economia* 103: 363–90.

Truglia, V. 2000. Can Industrialized Countries Afford Their Pension System? *Washington Quarterly* (Summer): 201–11.

———. 2002. Sovereign Ratings and Aging Societies. Paper presented at Rosenberg Institute of Global Finance Conference on Financing Global Aging, Waltham, Mass. http://www.brandeis.edu/global/rosenberg_papers/truglia_paper.pdf.

Uthoff, Andras. 1997. Baja Cobertura de la Seguridad Social en America Latina: Un Problema de Incentivos o de Exclusion Social? Paper presented at the Social Security, Micro-enterprise and Self Employment in Latin America seminar organized by World Bank, ILO, CEPAL, and International Association of Social Security, San Jose, Costa Rica.

———. 1998. *Pension Funds, the Financing of Transition Costs and Financial Markets Development: Lessons from the Chilean Privatization Reform*. Santiago, Chile: CEPAL/ECLAC.

———. 2001. La Reforma del Sistema de Pensiones en Chile: Desafios Pendientes. Economic Commission for Latin America, Financing Development Series, 112, Santiago, Chile.

Uusitalo, Roope. 1999. Homo Entreprenaurus? Working Paper 205, Government Institute for Economic Research, Helsinki.

Valdés-Prieto, Salvador, ed. 1997. *The Economics of Pensions: Principles, Policies and International Experience*. Cambridge, U.K.: Cambridge University Press.

————. 1998. Administrative Costs in a Privatized Pension System. Paper presented at the Pensions Systems Reform in Central America Conference, Cambridge, Mass.

————. 2002a. Improving Programs That Mandate Savings for Old Age. Background Paper for the Regional Study on Social Security Reform, World Bank, Washington, D.C.

————. 2002b. Justifying Mandated Savings for Old Age. Background Paper for the Regional Study on Social Security Reform, World Bank, Washington, D.C.

————. 2002c. Social Security Coverage in Chile, 1990–2001. Background Paper for the Regional Study on Social Security Reform, World Bank, Washington, D.C.

Van De Ven, Wynand P.M.M., and Bernard M. S. Van Praag. 1981. The Demand for Deductibles in Private Health Insurance. *Journal of Econometrics* 17: 229–52.

Vittas, Dimitri. 1996. Pension Funds and Capital Markets. Financial Sector Development Note 71, World Bank, Washington, D.C.

————. 1998a. Regulatory Controversies of Private Pension Funds, Policy Research Working Paper 1893, World Bank, Washington, D.C.

————. 1998b. Institutional Investors and Securities Markets: Which Comes First? Paper presented at the World Bank Conference on Development in Latin America and the Caribbean, San Salvador, El Salvador.

————. 1999. Pension Reform and Financial Markets. Discussion Paper 7, Harvard Institute for International Development, Cambridge, Mass.

————. 2002. Policies to Promote Saving for Retirement: A Synthetic Overview. Policy Research Working Paper 2801, World Bank, Washington D.C.

Von Gersdorff, Hermann. 1997. Pension Reform in Bolivia: Innovative Solutions to Common Problems. Policy Research Working Paper 1832, World Bank, Washington, D.C.

Wahal, S. 1996. Pension Fund Activism and Firm Performance. *Journal of Financial and Quantitative Analysis* 31: 1–23.

Walker, E. 1998. The Chilean Experience Regarding Completing Markets with Financial Indexation. Working Paper 29, Central Bank of Chile, Santiago.

Walker, Eduardo, and Fernando Lefort. 2001. Pension Reform and Capital Markets: Are There Any (Hard) Links? In *Pension Reform Primer*, eds. R. J Palacios and E.Whitehouse. Washington, D.C.: World Bank.

————. 2002. Pension Reform and Capital Markets: Are There Any (0) Links? Social Protection Discussion Paper. 0201, World Bank, Washington, D.C.

Whitehouse, Edward. 2000. How Poor Are the Old? A Survey of Evidence from 44 Countries Social Protection Discussion Paper 0017, Human Development Network, World Bank, Washington, D.C.

———. 2001. Administrative Charges for Funded Pensions: Comparison and Assessment of 13 Countries. In *Private Pensions Systems: Administrative Costs and Reforms*. Private Pensions Series. Paris: OECD.

Williamson, John. 1999. What Should the Bank Think about the Washington Consensus? Paper prepared as a background to the *World Development Report 2000*. World Bank, Washington, D.C.

Willmore, Larry. 2001a. Three Pillars of Pensions: Is There Really a Need for Mandatory Contributions? In *OECD Private Pensions Conference*, 385–97. Private Pension Series. Paris: OECD.

———. 2001b, Universal Pensions in Low-Income Countries. Paper prepared for a meeting of International Association of Pension Fund Supervisory Organisms, San Jose, Costa Rica. Processed.

Wodon, Quentin. 2000. Poverty and Policy in Latin America and the Caribbean. Technical Paper 467, World Bank, Washington, D.C.

Woidtke, T. 2001. Agents Watching Agents? Evidence from Pension Fund Ownership and Firm Value. *Journal of Financial Economics* 63: 99–31.

World Bank. 1994. *Averting the Old Age Crisis: Policies to Protect the Old and Promote Growth*. Washington, D.C.: World Bank and Oxford University Press.

———. 1996a. Argentina: Provincial Pension Reform Adjustment Loan Project. President's Report P6967, Loan 4116, Washington, D.C.

———. 1996b. Mexico: Contractual Savings Development Program Project. President's Report P7018, Loan 4123. Washington, D.C.

———. 1998. Mexico: Second Contractual Savings Development Program (CSDP II) Adjustment Loan Project. President's Report P7239, Loan 4343. Washington, D.C.

———. 2000. Nicaragua: Pension and Financial Market Reform Technical Assistance Credit Project. Project Appraisal Document, Report 19680, Credit 3344. Washington, D.C.

———. 2001. Poverty and Income Distribution in a High Growth Economy: The Case of Chile 1987–1998. Report 22037-CH, Poverty Reduction and Economic Management Sector Unit, Latin America and the Caribbean Regional Office, Washington, D.C.

———. 2002. Brazil: The New Growth Agenda. Volume I: Policy Briefing. Report 22950-BR, Brazil Country Management Unit, Latin America and the Caribbean Region, Washington, D.C.

Yamada, G. 1996. Urban Informal Employment and Self-Employment in Developing Countries: Theory and Evidence. *Economic Development and Cultural Change* 44: 289–314.

Yermo, Juan. 2001. Simulation of Minimum Pension Distributions Based on PRIESO Survey Data. Background Note for the Regional Study on Social Security Reform, World Bank, Washington, D.C.

———. 2002a. Pension Reform and Capital Market Development. Background Paper for the Regional Study on Social Security Reform, LAC Region, World Bank, Washington, D.C.

———. 2002b. The Performance of Funded Pension Systems in Latin America. Background Paper for the Regional Study on Social Security Reform, LAC Region, World Bank, Washington, D.C.

———. 2002c. Delivering Promises in the Chilean Funded Pension System. Background Paper for the Regional Study on Social Security Reform, LAC Region, World Bank, Washington, D.C.

Zurita, Salvador. 1994. Minimum Pension Insurance in the Chilean Pension System. *Revista de Analisis Economico* 9 (1): 105–26.

Zviniene, Asta, and Truman Packard. 2002. A Simulation of Social Security Reforms in Latin America: What Has Been Gained? Background Paper for the Regional Study on Social Security Reform, LAC Region, World Bank, Washington, D.C.

Index

Note: *f* indicates figures, *n* indicates notes (*nn* more than one note), and *t* indicates tables.

A

accumulation stage
  defined contribution formula
    for, 31
  and life insurance industry, 246,
    257
  and return rates, 130–43
administrative costs, 32–33,
    272–73
  commissions to cover, 144
  funded systems, 130
  intergenerational impact of, 148,
    162*n*16
  Peru, 234*f*10.1
  reforms to decrease, 232–39,
    264*nn*7–10
  see also commissions and
    commission rates
*admistradora de fondos de
  pensiones. see* pension
    fund administrators (AFPs)
ADRs. *see* American depository
    receipts (ADRs)
adverse selection, and annuities
    market, 152, 163*n*21
AFORE system, 208*b*9.1
AFPs. *see* pension fund
    administrators (AFPs)
age, 187
  and accumulated wealth, 201,
    204*f*9.2

and contribution rates, 194*n*11,
    232, 264*n*3
and investment choices, 157,
    159–60, 159*f*7.12
  see also elderly; old age
agency risk, 127*b*7.1, 129, 237,
    261–62
American depository receipts
    (ADRs), 60, 72, 87*n*6
annuities
  inflation-indexed, 245–46
  and life insurance industry,
    256
  and longevity risk, 199, 224*n*1,
    245
  and personal pension plans,
    250–51*b*10.2
  scheduled withdrawal, 150, 151,
    151*f*7.4
Argentina, 70, 82, 103, 105*n*7, 214
  and bond market, 76, 83
  Capital Markets Law, 65*b*4.1
  commission structure, 162*n*10
  and coverage rates, 99, 100
  features of reforms in,
    23–25*t*2.1
  and fiscal issues, 5, 44,
    47–48*b*3.2, 262
  funds portfolio, 38*n*12
  inflation-indexed securities,
    74–75*b*4.2

Argentina (*continued*)
  investments
    choices of, 160
    in government bonds, 87*n*3
    in pension funds, 59–60, 80
    returns on, 140
    and risk, 132, 155
  and IPDs, 40*f*3.1, 41
  mandatory savings plans,
    31–32
  pensions
    AFPs, 33, 239
    choices, 4, 5
    deficits, 41, 42*t*3.1, 43–44,
      43*f*3.2, 54*n*3
    guarantees, 33, 211
    noncontributory poverty
      prevention, 216*t*9.3
  and policy risk, 133–35*b*7.3,
    272
  portfolios, 137–38*b*7.4, 138–39
  ratio of variable commission
    rates to contributions, 146,
    147*f*7.6
  reforms
    reversal of regressive nature
      of, 90–91
    to social security, 20–21
    taxonomy of, 22, 28, 37*n*7
    women and reform gains,
      91
  switch to PAGY systems, 15*n*6
  transition debt, 69–70
  venture capital and real estate
    investment, 84
  voluntary savings plans, 35*t*2.4
Arrau, P., 237
assets and asset classes
  data on, 175
  and investment of pension
    funds, 59–60, 61*t*4.1
  management of, 70–71
Averting the Old Age Crisis, 1, 2, 3
  and coverage rates, 97–98*b*5.2
  and economic growth, 46, 49
  pillars of, 278*b*11.1
  and reliance on tax base, 223

B
Banco Hipotecario, 87*n*10
banking sector
  investment of pension funds in,
    67
  pension funds impact on
    efficiency and stability of,
    78–80
  reforms to, 66*b*4.1, 76–80,
    87*nn*9–11
  return on deposits, 136, 138,
    140*f*7.4
bankruptcies, insurance companies,
  257, 258*f*10.6
Barr, Nicholas, 11, 49, 99, 121
  and contribution density, 101
  and economic growth, 46
  on macroeconomics of pensions,
    110–11*b*6.1
  and tier vs. pillar plans, 15*n*1
Barrientos, Armando, 167, 170
Becker, Gary, 109, 113*b*6.2, 114,
  123*n*1
benefits
  forms of, 150, 151*t*7.4, 151–53,
    154*f*7.9, 163*n*21
  link to contributions, 22, 98–99
  relationship to participation
    rates, 103, 104*t*5.2
  relationship to wages, 164*n*22
Bertranou, Fabio, 225*n*7
Bismarkian PAYG systems, 225*n*3
Bolivia, 8, 30, 76, 83, 145
  BONOSOL program,
    210–11*b*9.2, 271
  cash-flow gap, 45*f*3B1
  commission structure, 144,
    162*n*11
  coverage rates, 99
  distribution choices, 152, 153
  fiscal abuse by government, 5
  impact of reforms on women,
    92
  interest rate spreads, 79, 79*f*4.2
  investment of pension funds,
    59–60
  and IPDs, 40*f*3.1, 41

pension assets, 62, 62t4.3
pension deficits, 41, 42t3.1,
    43f3.2
pension fund managers, 33, 68
portfolios, 62t4.2, 137–38b7.4,
    138–39
poverty prevention, 207
reforms to social security in,
    20–21, 22, 23–25t2.1, 28
returns on investments, 131
transition costs, 44, 45–46b3.1
transition debt, 69, 70
and transparency, 87n3
voluntary savings plans, 35t2.4
BOLIVIDA, 211b9.2
bond market, 73
dollar-linked, 141
interest rate volatility of, 257
see also government bonds
bond swaps, 134b7.3
BONOSOL program, 210–11b9.2,
    271
Brazil
capital market development, 246
inflation-indexed securities,
    74–75b4.2
investment choices, 249–50,
    250–51b10.2
mutual fund industry, 251–52,
    254
noncontributory poverty
    prevention pensions, 216t9.3
reforms to retirement system,
    37n5
role of financial systems in
    savings plans, 250–51b10.2
and stock market liquidity, 81,
    82

C
capital accounts, liberalization of,
    82
capital inflows, 132
capitalization, limits on, 71
capital markets
development of, 85, 246,
    278b11.1

international, 137–38b7.4
links to mandatory savings, 119
Capital Markets Law, 60, 65b4.1
capital reserves, 58
Caribbean, and pension funds, 71
Carranza, Eliana, 233
cash-flow gap, Bolivia, 45f3B1
centralization in pension
    administration, 238
charge ratio, 143–44, 145, 146
cumulative, 149, 162n18
relationship to wages, 149,
    149f7.8, 150
at retirement, 146–47, 148f7.7,
    162nn12–15
children
child care, 176–77b8.1, 183
influence on contribution rates,
    174–75
as substitute for investment in
    pension systems, 188, 194n13
Chile, 54, 69, 70, 83, 143
banking sector, 76
bond market, 73, 75, 79–80
and charge ratio, 145
commissions
    ratio of variable rates to
        contributions, 146,
        147f7.6
    structure of, 8, 144, 149,
        162n11
contribution density, 101,
    180–81f8.1
and corporate governance role
    of AFPs, 71, 72
and cost of universal pensions,
    222
coverage rates, 99–101
distribution choices, 151,
    152–53, 154f7.9, 164nn22
household surveys, 175
increase in savings, 119
inflation-indexed securities,
    74–75b4.2
insurance sector, 246, 257
intercohort differences in
    returns, 135–36, 139f7.3

Chile (*continued*)
  interest rate spreads, 79, 79*f*4.2,
    80
  investments
    choices of, 213
    in corporate bonds, 87*n*7
    pension funds, 59, 60, 131
    returns, 131, 140
    risk management, 155–60,
      242, 243–44*t*10.3
  and IPDs, 40*f*3.1, 41
  life insurance industry, 259–60
  and management fees, 146, 147,
    148*f*7.7
  multiple fund system in, 242,
    264*n*11
  mutual fund industry, 254,
    255*f*10.4, 259–60, 261
  new funds in, 157–58, 157*t*7.5,
    163*n*24
  participation choice, 177
  participation rates, 15*n*5
  PASIS benefits, 225*n*7
  pensions
    and AFPs, 5–6, 33, 58
    assets, 60, 62, 62*t*4.3
    choices, 4, 5
    comparison of reformed
      pension systems with
      Peru, 175, 178*t*8.2
    deficits, 41, 42*t*3.1, 43,
      43*f*3.2
    impact on stock market, 80
    minimum pension guarantees,
      53, 207, 211, 219
    noncontributory poverty
      prevention, 216*t*9.3
    occupational pension plans,
      237
    and real returns, 136, 138,
      140*f*7.4
    value of annuitizing pension
      fund balances, 245
  portfolios, 137–38*b*7.4, 138–39
  and private sector securities
    markets, 63
  private sector workers, 30

reforms
  features of, 22, 23–25*t*2.1,
    28, 38*n*8
  fiscal impact of, 44,
    47–48*b*3.2
  gains for women, 91
  impact on economic growth,
    49
  reversal of regressive nature
    of, 90–91
  tax reform, 66*b*4.1
  returns on deposits, 140*f*7.4
  and risk, 8, 181–83, 194*n*12
  shareholders' rights, 65*b*4.1
  Social Risk Management Survey,
    175, 176–77*b*8.1
  and stock market liquidity, 82
  switch to PAGY systems, 15*n*6
  venture capital and real estate
    investment, 84
  voluntary savings plans, 34,
    35*t*2.4, 161*n*1, 248,
    248*b*10.1, 249, 258–60
Chilean Association of Pension
  Funds, 71
Cia. de Minas Buenaventura, 82
civil servants, 29
clearing and settlement systems,
  64*b*4.1
Cobb-Douglas production function,
  49
Colombia, 29, 70, 99
  commission structure, 144
  corporate bond market, 83
  and cost of universal pensions,
    222
  creditors' rights, 65*b*4.1
  distribution choices, 152–53
  gains in rates of return, 91
  government debt markets, 72
  inflation-indexed securities, 73,
    74–75*b*4.2
  interest rate spreads, 79, 79*f*4.2
  and investment of pension
    funds, 59–60
  and IPDs, 40*f*3.1, 41
  mandatory savings plans, 31

minimum pension guarantees,
211, 219
and mortgage bond market, 78
pension choices, 4, 5
pension deficits, 41, 42*t*3.1, 43,
43*f*3.2
pension fund managers, 33
and portfolio risk, 137–38*b*7.4
poverty prevention, 207
reforms to social security in,
20–21, 23–25*t*2.1, 28
voluntary savings plans, 34,
35*t*2.4
commissions and commission rates,
8, 32–33, 273
caps on, 233–34, 239,
240–41*t*10.2
as cost to retirement accounts,
143, 162*n*9
flat, 149
insurance products, 260
mutual funds, 254, 255*f*10.4,
265*n*17
ratio of to total contributions,
144, 145*t*7.3, 145–46,
146*f*7.6
reductions in, 12
reforms to decrease, 232–39,
240–41*t*10.2, 264*nn*7–10
regressive nature of structure,
149–50, 149*f*7.8
regulation of, 144, 162*n*10
relationship to pension fund
performance, 150
transparency in structure of, 260
variable, 144, 145, 145*t*7.3
competition, 239, 253
compliance, with reform, 43, 55*n*4
comprehensive insurance, 15*n*9, 112,
113*b*6.2, 115, 123, 123*n*1
consumer price index, and pension
subsidies, 31
consumption
and contributions to pension
funds, 168
of elderly, 219
inter-temporal, 247, 264–65*n*13

life-cycle consumption and
savings theory, 194*n*12
consumption smoothing, 15*n*9,
229, 271–72
goal of, 269
and minimum pension
guarantee, 212, 213
and risk management of
mandated savings, 239,
242–47, 264*n*11–12
contribution density, 177,
193*nn*7–9
Peru, 184–85*f*8.4, 185–86
relationship to gender, 179–81,
193–94*nn*10–11
threshold for, 179, 180
contribution rates, 12, 13, 277
in accumulation stage, 31
age-related, 232, 264*n*3
coverage gap, 186
earnings-linked, 32*t*2.3, 232,
264*n*3
and eligibility threshold,
190–91, 194*n*15
employer, 43, 55*n*4
gender-related, 193*n*8
link to benefits, 22, 96, 98–99
Peru, 6
of poorer workers, 211–12
ratio of variable commissions to
total contributions, 144,
145–46, 145*t*7.3, 146*f*7.6
relationship of participation
level to, 101, 103, 105*nn*7–8
requirements of, 22, 183–84,
190
and risk aversion, 191,
194–95*n*16
Corbo, Vittorio, 49, 54
corporate bond market,
development of, 81–82
corporate governance, 58, 65*b*4.1,
119
Corsetti, G., 99
Costa Rica
commission structure, 144
corporate bond market, 84

Costa Rica (*continued*)
  investments
    choices of, 160
    investment risk, 155
    of pension funds, 59–60, 60
    in private sector, 67
    mandatory individual retirement
      accounts, 237
    noncontributory poverty
      prevention pensions, 216t9.3
    and pension guarantees, 33
    portfolio floors, 62t4.2
    reforms in, 4, 20–21, 26–27t2.2,
      29
    taxonomy of reform, 22, 28,
      37n7
    voluntary savings plans, 34,
      35t2.4
country risk, 53
coverage ratios, 5–7
Cox-Edward, Alejandra, 91, 101,
  193n8
creditors' rights, 65b4.1
credit-to-GDP ratio, 76
cross-country comparisons, 54n1
Cuenta 2 plan, 249, 249f10.2, 259
Cuesta, Jose, 167, 170
Cuota Social, 149, 208–09b9.1
custodian services, 64b4.1
Czech Republic, 265n14

D
DB. *see* defined-benefit (DB) system
DC. *see* defined contribution (DC)
  system
death, insurance against risk of,
  38n13
debt markets, 246
default risk, 7, 131, 140, 262
defined-benefit (DB) system, 4, 9,
  12, 15n6, 31
  and life expectancy, 129, 161n4
defined contribution (DC) system,
  4, 21, 129
demand-side measures, to reduce
  costs, 234, 240–41t10.2
Demirgüç-Kunt, Asli, 81

demographics
  changes in, 19–20
  and contribution behavior,
    170–75, 193nn5–6
disability insurance, 31, 38n11,
  38n13, 105n4
distribution stage
  and performance of new funded
    pillar, 150–53, 154f7.9,
    162–63nn19–22
  and risk management, 245–47
diversification, 135, 138
  of assets, 7
  in domestic equities, 139–40,
    142t7.2
  in foreign equities, 140, 142t7.2
  international, 159–60
  and risk, 9, 242, 243–44t10.3
dollar-indexed bonds, 78
Dominican Republic
  mandatory savings plans, 31–33
  minimum pension guarantees, 211
  private sector workers, 30
  reforms to social security in,
    20–21, 26–27t2.2, 28
  self-employed workers in, 238
  subsidies for savings, 247

E
EAP. *see* economically active
  population (EAP)
earnings
  and contribution rates, 32t2.3,
    232, 264n3
  loss of capacity for, 110b6.1,
    111, 189
  maximum taxable, 12, 15n10
  relationship to pension income,
    94f5.3
  replacement of, 11–12, 276
Easterly, William, 49
Eastern Europe, multipillar reforms
  in, 2
economically active population (EAP)
  and participation rates, 99, l,
    100f5.4, 105nn4–5
  pension system coverage, 6f1.1

economic development
    effects of pension reform on, 46,
        49–50, 51
    and variation in coverage, 274,
        274*f*11.1, 275
economies of scale, and mutual
    fund management, 254,
        256*f*10.5
Ecuador, reforms in, 20–22,
    26–27*t*2.2, 28, 29, 37*n*3,
    37*n*7
education, 183
Edwards, Sebastian, 101
Ehrlich, Isaac, 109, 113*b*6.2, 114,
    123*n*1
elderly
    accumulated wealth of, 201,
        204*f*9.2
    consumption of, 219
    and the *Cuota Social*,
        208–09*b*9.1
    growth in share of, 20, 20–21*f*2.1
    impact of population increase on
        pension systems, 200*f*9.1
    instruments of income security,
        10*t*1.1
    pension coverage, 7*f*1.2, 103
    poverty prevention among,
        206–11
        role of government in,
            199–205, 224–25*nn*1–3
    poverty rate when measured by
        current income, 200–01,
        202–03*t*9.1, 224*n*2
    social insurance coverage of,
        95–96*b*5.1
    see also old age
Electronic Stock Exchange, 70
eligibility threshold, 188, 190–91
El Salvador, 4, 29, 99, 222
    bond market, 75
    commission structure, 144
    corporate bond market, 84
    demographics, 19
    distribution choices, 151, 152,
        153, 164*n*22
    government debt markets, 72

investment in private sector,
    67
and IPDs, 40*f*3.1, 41, 52
mandatory savings plans,
    31, 33
minimum pension guarantees,
    211
pension deficits, 41, 42*t*3.1, 43,
    43*f*3.2
pension fund managers, 33
and portfolio risk, 137–38*b*7.4
poverty prevention, 207
reforms, 20–22, 23–25*t*2.1, 28,
    30
    impact on women, 92
transition debt, 69
voluntary savings plans, 34,
    36*t*2.4
Emerging Market Bond Index, 51,
    52, 52*f*3.3
employers
    contributions to pension plans,
        43, 55*n*4
    employer-sponsored retirement
        programs, 251
    and pension plans, 234, 237–38,
        264*nn*6–8
employment, and contribution
    behavior, 170–75, 193*nn*5–6
enforcement, of contribution
    mandates, 99
Escobar, Federico, 44
Estonia, 238
explicit debts, 51, 55*n*7, 132
    converted from IPDs, 44, 47*b*3.2
    and NDCs, 128*b*7.2
extended family, and old-age
    security, 168–69, 192–93*nn*3

F
fee structure, 247
    Mexico, 260–61, 265*n*18
    mutual funds, 254, 255*f*10.4,
        265*n*17
fertility rate, 20*f*2, 1
Fiess, Norbert, 44, 51
financial literacy, 247, 260

financial sector
  and decisionmaking in
      oligopolistic industry,
      68–69
  importance of reforms in,
      64–66*b*4.1
  investments in, 63, 63*f*4.1, 67,
      67*t*4.4, 131, 132*f*7.1
  modernization of, 64*b*4.1, 85
  and policy risk protection,
      133–35*b*7.3
  role in savings plans,
      250–51*b*10.2
  and transparency of costs and
      benefits of, 247
first-pillar pensions
  argument for, 121, 122
  objective of, 9, 37*n*4
  vs. pillar zero, 205–06
  see also defined benefit (DB)
      system; poverty prevention
fiscal impact of reform, 40–44,
      58*nn*2–3, 59*n*4
  Argentina, 44, 47–48*b*3.2
  Chile, 44, 47–48*b*3.2
  simulations of, 44–46, 47*b*3.2
flat pensions, 206–07, 209–11
Fondo 1, 156–58
Fondo 2, 156–58
foreign assets, 140
foreign currencies, 59–60
foreign debt, 72
foreign investments, 59–60,
      138–39, 242
foreign investors, 81–82, 87*n*12
formal sector, 96, 98, 99, 174,
      193*n*6
fraud, rise in fraudulent claims,
      45–46*b*3.1
Fuentes, Ricardo, 170, 193*n*5
fund management industry, 22

G
GDP. *see* gross domestic product
      (GDP)
gender
  and contribution density,
      179–81, 193–94*nn*10–11
  and contribution histories,
      184–86, 193*n*8
  and disparities in rates of return,
      92*f*5.2, 93–95
  impact of reforms on, 92, 92*f*5.2
  and investment choices, 157
Germany, 265*n*14
global factors, and reforms in Latin
      America, 53, 55*n*11
government
  and BONOSOL program,
      210–11*b*9.2
  credibility of, 169
  and the *Cuota Social*, 208–09*b*9.1
  fiscal issues, 5, 7–8, 262–63
  and fund withdrawals, 231
  and investment risk, 245
  and macroeconomic arguments
      for mandatory savings,
      116–21
  management of centralized
      pension systems, 238–39,
      264*n*10
  and market insurance, 113*b*6.2
  pension deficits financed by, 41,
      42*t*3.1, 43
  regulation of mutual funds, 253
  role in investment choices, 260
  role in pillars, 9, 10*t*1.1, 15*n*8
  role in poverty prevention,
      110–11*b*6.1, 199–205,
      224–25*nn*1–3
government bonds, 139
  AFPs as purchasers of, 119,
      121
  dollar-linked, 141
  effects of pension funds on
      market for, 75–76
  inflation-indexed, 76, 155
  investment in, 59–60, 131,
      132*f*7.1, 263
  and NDC, 127, 128*b*7.2, 129
  and policy risk, 132
  wage-indexed, 128*b*7.2
government debt
  default risk, 140
  investment in, 63, 63*f*4.1, 67,
      67*t*4.4, 134*b*7.3

and leasing bonds, 77
rating of, 141, 162*n*8
weakness of markets for, 72–75
gross domestic product (GDP)
credit as share of, 76
IPDs as share of, 40*f*3.1, 41, 269
mutual fund assets as share of, 252
pension assets as share of, 60, 62, 62*t*4.3, 71, 270
pension debt as share of, 4, 44, 48, 48*f*3B.2b
pension-related deficits as share of, 45*f*3B.1
relationship to *Cuota Social*, 208–9*b*9.1
stock market capitalization as share of, 80
guarantees, 22
eligibility threshold for, 188
and insurance company offerings, 246, 257
see also minimum pension guarantees

H
Harrod-Domar growth models, 49
Holzmann, Robert, 41, 44, 80, 167, 170
households
and contribution behavior, 170–75, 193*nn*5–6
income, 168
housing, 129
financing of, 77–78, 87*n*9
as investment choice, 188, 194*n*13, 230–31
human capital, 231

I
Iglesias-Palau, A., 71, 80
Impavido, Gregorio, 78
implicit pension debts (IPDs), 40, 40*f*3.1, 41, 50, 269
converted to explicit debt, 44, 47*b*3.2
defaulting on, 132, 135

Mexico, 52
and NDCs, 129
relationship with country risk, 51, 55*n*7
implicit-to-explicit debt conversion, 51
improvidence arguments, 116, 152, 162–63*n*19
incentives, 12
improvement of, 189, 194*n*14
and participation rates, 101, 102*t*5.1, 103
and pension guarantees, 207
and voluntary savings plans, 34, 249–50
income
and disparities in rates of return, 92*f*5.2, 93–95
household, 168
and investment choices, 159–60, 159*f*7.12
per capita, 105, 105*n*6
poverty rate among elderly when measured by income, 200–01, 202–03*t*9.1, 224*n*2
replacement of, 201, 204, 225*n*3
retirement, 126–30
risks to old-age income security, 126–30, 161*nn*2–4
see also wages
indexation unit, 71–75
individual behavior
as argument for mandatory savings, 115–16
characteristics relative to contribution behavior, 170–75, 193*nn*5–6
conclusions about, 166
implications of income security preferences made by, 189–91, 194–95*nn*14–16
and low participation rates, 166–70, 192–93*nn*3–4
individualization of social security, 4, 11, 114
individual retirement accounts, 89, 90, 128*b*7.2, 129, 208*b*9.1, 237

industries, and contribution
behavior, 170–75, 193nn5–6
inflation, 128b7.2, 129, 135b7.3
inflation-indexed government
bonds, 76, 155, 257
and NDC, 127, 128b7.2, 129
inflation-indexed liabilities, 153
inflation-indexed securities, 60, 73,
74–75b4.2
Argentina, 134b7.3
and investment risk, 242, 245
private annuities, 245–46
INFONAVIT, 31
informal sector
employment in, 193n6
equity implications of, 93–96
and social insurance coverage,
96b5.1, 97–98b5.2, 98,
105n2
infrastructure bonds, 83
institutional investors, 63, 67, 78
institutional structures, and
coverage, 99, 105n3
insurance industry, 66b4.1
comprehensive insurance,
15n9
and pension assets, 62–63
and personal pension plans,
250–51b10.2
rates of return, 246
interest-bearing assets, 131
interest rate spreads, 79, 79f4.2
intergenerational issues, 162n16,
273
administrative costs, 148,
162n16
commission rates, 8
intermediation, 230, 238
internal rates of return, 92, 92f5.2
International Labour Organization,
214, 215, 215t9.2
investment floors, 60
investment risk, 126, 127b7.1, 129
management of, 154–60, 242,
243–44t10.3
and occupational savings plans,
264n7

investments and investment choices,
272
Brazil, 249–50, 250–51b10.2
caveats to, 85–86
and centralized pension
administration, 238,
264nn9–10
and corporate bond markets,
81–82
and financial literacy, 247
government bonds, 59–60, 131,
132f7.1
government debt and financial
institutions, 67, 67t4.4
government role in, 260
and guarantees, 8
home ownership, 188, 194n13,
230–31
human capital, 231
and longevity risk management,
154–60, 163n24
and moral hazard, 213–14
restrictions on, 59–60, 87nn3–6
returns from, 130–43
and risk management, 242, 245
and stock market liquidity,
80–83, 87n12
and transition debt, 70, 87n7
IPDs. *see* implicit pension debts
(IPDs)
Ireland, 239

J
James, E., 91, 99, 167

L
labor force
and choice of pension systems,
187
and contribution density, 180
and coverage issues, 96–103,
105nn2–8
and the *Cuota Social*, 208–09b9.1
decreases in, 19, 20f2.1
and improved incentives, 49
new entrants into, 28–29, 30,
38n9

participation in pension systems, 125, 177
and perceived benefits and contribution link, 98–99
and Peru's reformed pension system, 177, 179b8.2
relationship of participation rates to mandated contributions, 101, 103, 105nn7–8
see also workers
La Porta, R., 65b4.1
Lasaga, Manuel, 233
leasing bonds, 83
Lefort, F., 70, 71, 80
legislation
and coverage rates, 99
and participation rates, 103
letras hipotecarias, 77–78
Levine, R., 78, 81
licensing process, insurance companies, 257
life-cycle consumption and savings theory, 194n12
life cycle needs, meeting of, 229–32, 263–64nn1–4
life expectancy, 12, 92–93, 128b7.2
and choices at distribution stage, 150–52, 163n20
cost of increases in, 129, 161n4
impact of increase in on pooling pension systems, 200f9.1
information on, 246
rise in, 20–21f2.1
life insurance industry, 31, 246, 256–57, 258f10.6
Lima, Peru, PRIESO survey, 184–85f8.4, 185–86
Lindbeck, Assar, 114
longevity risk, 12, 38n15, 92–93
and annuities, 199, 224n1
and investments, 154–60, 163n24
management of, 129, 243–44t10.3, 245
overview, 127b7.1
protection against, 128b7.2

long-term government bonds, 128b7.2
loyalty discounts, 144
lump-sum distributions, 150, 162–63n19

M
macroeconomics
and arguments for mandating savings, 116–21
of pensions, 110–11b6.1
and portfolio performance, 141
and structural pension reform, 50–54, 55nn6–7, 55nn9–11
management fees, 7, 8, 146, 147, 148f7.7
mandatory individual retirement accounts, Costa Rica, 237
mandatory pension systems
administrative costs of, 232–39
burden of, 125–26
destination of contributions, 29f2.2
mandatory private savings, 5, 14, 22
mandatory savings plans, 1, 8, 13, 272
contribution rates and earnings ceilings, 32t2.3
individual welfare argument for, 115–16
and life cycle needs, 229–32, 263–64nn1–4
macroeconomic argument for, 116–21
and mutual funds, 265n15
regulation of, 57–60, 86n1, 87nn3–6
role of, 277, 278–79b11.1
size of, 12, 227–28, 276–77
structure and implementation of, 30–33, 38nn10–13
market concentration, and pension fund managers, 68t4.5
marketing, 143
market insurance, 113b6.2, 114
market value of assets, 33, 38n12

Mastrángelo, Jorge, 143, 150
Maturana, G., 254
maximum taxable earnings, 12,
    15n10
means testing, 207, 209
Mesa–Lago, Carmelo, 44
Mexican Stock Exchange, 65b4.1
Mexico, 59, 72, 83, 99
    bond market, 75–76
    calculation of fees, 260–61,
        265n18
    capital market development, 246
    civil servants pension plan, 29
    commission structure, 144, 149,
        162n11
    creditors' rights, 65b4.1
    Cuota Social, 208–09b9.1
    distribution choices, 153
    financial market infrastructure,
        64b4.1
    fiscal burden of pensions, 5
    housing loans, 87n10
    increase in country risk, 51–52,
        52f33.3
    inflation-indexed securities, 73,
        74–75b4.2
    investments
        in mutual funds, 84
        of pension funds, 60
        returns on, 131, 140
    and IPDs, 40f3.1, 41
    life insurance policyholders, 257
    mandatory savings plans, 31–32,
        33
    pension deficits, 41, 42t3.1, 43,
        43f3.2
    pension guarantees, 33, 87n5
    portfolios, 62t4.2, 137–38b7.4,
        138–39, 162n7
    poverty prevention, 207
    private sector workers, 30
    reforms in, 20–22, 23–25t2.1, 28
        impact on women, 91, 92
        taxonomy of, 22
    and stock market liquidity, 81,
        82, 82–83
    subsidies for savings, 247
    tax structure, 66b4.1

    traditional security systems of,
        174
    transition debt, 69, 70
    valuation mechanisms, 59, 87n4
    voluntary savings plans, 34,
        36t2.4, 161n1
microeconomics, and contribution
    density, 180
military personnel, 29
minimum pension guarantees, 8, 53,
    194n15, 211–14, 225nn4–5
    Chile, 53, 207, 211, 219
    and contribution density
        threshold, 179, 193–94n10
    contributory, 211–14, 225nn4–5
    and high-risk portfolios, 59,
        87n5
    mandatory funding protection
        by, 33
    Peru, 271
    and risk pooling, 224
Moody's, 50, 55n6
moral hazard
    and benefit guarantees vs.
        individual choice, 8
    and distribution choices, 152
    and fund withdrawals, 231
    and investment choices, 213–14
    of overly generous social
        assistance, 207
    Peru, 160
    relationship to years of
        contribution, 190
Morgan Stanley Capital
    International Europe,
    Australia, Far East index, 140
Morón, Eduardo, 233
mortality rates, 92–93, 168
mortgage bonds and securities, 60,
    77–78
multipillar systems, equity of,
    90–91, 91f5.1
Musalem, Alberto R., 78
mutual fund administrators, 253
mutual fund industry, 66b4.1, 85,
    238, 261
    experience in Chile, 259–60
    investment in, 84

as retirement savings, 246,
264*n*12
and voluntary savings plans,
251–56, 265*nn*15–17

N
National Housing Fund for
Workers Institute, 87*n*10
National Retirement Savings
Commission, Mexico, 87*n*4
NDC. *see* notional defined
contribution (NDC) systems
net interest margins, 78, 87*n*11
net investment returns, 131
net-present-value calculations, 50
New Zealand, 211, 222
Nicaragua
and coverage rates, 99
reforms to social security in,
20–21, 26–27*t*2.2, 37*n*3
noncontributory pension programs,
213–18, 225*nn*6–7
notional defined contribution
(NDC) systems, 127,
128*b*7.2, 129, 194*n*14

O
occupational pension plans, 237,
250, 250–51*b*10.2, 264*nn*6–7
OECD. *see* Organisation for
Economic Co-operation and
Development (OECD)
old age
losses associated with,
110–11*b*6.1
macroeconomic argument for
mandatory savings for,
116–21
mandatory savings and
individual welfare, 115–16
pooling risk to insure against
poverty, 114–15
risks to income security during,
126–30, 161*nn*2–4
savings as income security,
112–14
traditional strategies for income
security, 168–69, 192–93*n*3

see also elderly
operating costs
of banks, 79–80
Chile, 254
ratio to management fees, 8
reduction of, 233–34,
235–36*t*10.1
Organisation for Economic
Co-operation and
Development (OECD), 69
Orszag, Peter, 99
oversight, 85

P
Packard, Truman, 54, 101, 105*n*8,
167
and fiscal impact of reforms,
39–40
on minimum pension guarantee,
194
on pension contributions, 89
risk preferences in Chile, 183
worker's contribution behavior,
170, 193*n*5
Palacios, Robert J., 41, 44, 99,
101, 105*n*6
Pallares-Miralles, Montserrat, 99,
101, 105*n*6
participation rates, 5–6, 273–74
Chile, 15*n*5
and education of participants,
156–57, 156*f*7.10
and extent of private provision,
101, 105*n*7
impact of pension reform on,
189–90, 194*n*14
and incidence of benefits, 103,
104*t*5.2
as indicator of coverage,
99–101, 105*nn*4–5
mandatory vs. voluntary, 9–10,
10*t*1.1
overview, 175–77
for poorer workers, 149*f*7.8
as reflection of demand, 175–77
as social inclusion or individual
choice, 166–70, 192–93*nn*3–4
PASIS benefits, 225*n*7

pay-as-you-go (PAYG) systems, 4
  Bismarkian PAYG systems,
    225n3
  and retirees, 30
  and rising life expectancy,
    20–21f2.1
pension debt
  accumulated after 2001, 42,
    43f3.2
  debt-to-GDP ratios, 4
  financed by government
    transfers, 41, 42t3.1, 43,
    43f3.2
  and fiscal sustainability, 44, 48,
    48f3B.2b
pensiones graciables, 225n6
pension fund administration,
    centralization of, 238
pension fund administrators
    (AFPs), 68, 70, 85, 175
  Argentina, 239
  Bolivia, 238
  Chile, 33
  collective action by, 58
  and commission structure, 144
  competition among, 233
  and corporate governance, 71
  and Cuenta 2 plan, 249,
    249f10.2
  fees and commissions charges,
    32–33, 233
  as financial risk managers, 53
  providing advice on choices, 158
  as purchasers of government
    bonds, 119, 121
  and rate of return, 137–38b7.4
  recordkeeping of funds
    collected, 31–33
  regulation of, 57–59, 86n1,
    87n2
  and voluntary savings plans,
    248b10.1
  workers use of AFP accounts,
    5–6
pension fund investments. see
    investments and investment
    choices

pension income, relationship to
    earned income, 94f5.3
Pension Reform Options
    Simulation Toolkit (PROST),
    39–40, 54n1, 225n8
pensions and pension funds, 5, 19,
    119
  approach to study of, 2–4
  Barr's list of myths about,
    110–11b6.1
  BONOSOL program,
    210–11b9.2
  Brazil, 250, 250–51b10.2
  choice of by younger workers,
    187
  costs of, 218–23
  coverage in EAP, 6f1.1
  and the Cuota Social,
    208–9b9.1
  default option, 158, 158f7.11
  deficits, 41, 42t3.1, 43f3.2
  equity limits, 157, 157t7.5
  growth in, 60, 62–67
  impact on bank efficiency and
    stability, 78–80
  impact on government bonds
    market, 75–76
  investment in venture capital
    and real estate funds, 84
  as investors in government debt,
    63, 63f4.1
  and new entrants into labor
    force, 28–29, 30, 38n9
  noncontributory compared to
    contributory, 217, 217f9.4
  operations of industry, 67–72,
    87nn7–8
  participation rates as social
    exclusion or individual
    choice, 166–70,
    192–93nn3–4
  pillar zero vs. pillar one,
    205–06
  populations receiving, 7f1.2
  private management of, 126,
    161n2
  ratio of assets to GDP, 270

role in development of bank
  securities markets, 77–78,
  87nn9–10
setting minimum benefits at
  minimum wage, 218–19
survey of contribution behavior,
  170–75, 193nn5–6
three-fund systems, 242, 245,
  264n11
top-up, 206
see also poverty prevention
per capita income, 105, 105n6
Persson, Mats, 114
Peru, 6, 58, 70, 91, 146
  administrative costs, 234f10.1
  bond market, 75, 78
  civil servants pension plan, 29
  commission structure, 162n10
  contribution density, 101,
    184–85f8.4, 185–86
  corporate bond market, 83
  creditors' rights, 65b4.1
  distribution choices, 152–53,
    163nn22
  and distribution of returns, 91
  household surveys, 175
  interest rate spreads, 79, 79f4.2
  investments
    choices, 160
    of pension funds, 60, 80
  and IPDs, 40f3.1, 41
  management fees, 8
  mandatory savings plans, 31
  measures of risk preference,
    186–87, 187f8.5, 188f8.6
  participation choice, 177
  pensions
    choices, 4, 5
    deficits, 41, 42t3.1, 43, 43f3.2
    and guarantees, 33, 271
    pension fund management, 33
  and portfolios, 137–38b7.4,
    138–39
  profits for fund managers, 233
  ratio of variable commission
    rates to contributions, 146,
    147f7.6
reforms, 20–21, 23–25t2.1, 28,
  38n8, 177, 179b8.2
  comparison of reformed
    pension systems with
    Chile, 175, 178t8.2
return rates, 131, 138, 140
securities
  housing-related securities, 77
  inflation-indexed securities,
    73, 74–75b4.2
  limits on private sector
    securities, 59–60
  and private sector securities
    markets, 63
shareholders' rights, 65b4.1
social insurance coverage gap,
  96b5.1
Social Risk Management Survey,
  175, 176–77b8.1
and stock market liquidity, 82,
  87n12
switch to PAGY systems, 15n6
value of annuitizing pension
  fund balances, 245
venture capital and real estate
  investment, 84
voluntary savings plans, 36t2.4
peso devaluation, 134b7.3
pillar zero, vs. pillar one, 205–06
policy risk, 127b7.1, 129, 131,
  261–62, 272
  Argentina, 133–35b7.3
  and investment in government
    bonds, 132
political risk, 264n10
  and government credibility, 169
politics, and BONOSOL program,
  211b9.2
Pollner, John, 233
pooling arrangements
  forecasting cost of, 218–23,
    225n8
  vs. savings, 9–10, 10t1.1, 11
pooling risk, 112–14
  to insure against old-age
    poverty, 114–15
  and market failures, 113b6.2

pooling risk (*continued*)
  and minimum required
    contributions, 190
  risks that justify pooling,
    121–22
portfolios
  asset allocation and portfolio
    limits, 142t7.2
  investment in corporate bonds,
    83
  leasing bonds in, 77
  limits on, 53, 55n10, 59, 60
  maturities of, 76
  and minimum pension
    guarantees, 59, 87n5
  regulation of, 62t4.2
  and risk, 137–38b7.4
  see also pensions and pension
    funds
poverty, among elderly when
    measured by current income,
    200–01, 202–03t9.1, 224n2
poverty prevention, 11, 14, 152,
    161n3, 271–72
  assessment conclusions, 275–76
  and BONOSOL program,
    210–11b9.2
  and contributory minimum
    pension guarantees, 211–14,
    225nn4–5
  and the *Cuota Social*,
    208–09b9.1
  focus on, 201, 204
  forecasting cost of pooling
    arrangements for, 218–23,
    225n8
  and funding of benefits, 230
  generosity and cost to taxpayers,
    209, 212f9.3
  institution of programs for, 277,
    279
  noncontributory programs,
    213–18, 225nn6–7
  options for elderly, 206–11
  Peru's reformed pension system,
    177, 179b8.2
  pillar zero vs. pillar one, 205–06

relationship of mandatory
    contributions to age and
    income, 232
  role of government in, 110b6.1,
    199–205, 224–25nn1–3
  Uruguay, 264n2
price elasticity, 143, 150
price indexation, 77
PRIESO survey, 175, 176–77b8.1,
    179–86
private sector bonds and securities,
    63, 67, 77–78, 80–84, 87n12
private sector workers, 30
privatization, 267
  of pensions, 3b1.1, 28
  and use of income from for
    pensions, 210–11b9.2
PROST. *see Pension Reform
    Options Simulation Toolkit*
    (PROST)
provident funds, 161n2
publicly managed individual
    retirement systems, 127,
    128b7.2, 129
public pension systems, changes to,
    29
public sector, bond market, 75
public sector debt, market for,
    72–75

R
rates of return, 131
  and AFPs, 58
  Chile intercohort differences in,
    135–36, 139f7.3
  December 1994 to December
    2002, 130, 130t7.1, 131
  by insurance companies, 246
  ratio of return to standard
    deviation, 135, 136f7.2,
    137–38b7.4
  risk-adjusted, 140
  value placed on, 191,
    194–95n16
  volatility of, 136
real estate, investment in, 84, 188,
    194n13, 230

record-keeping functions, 239
reforms
    assessment conclusions, 275–80
    assessment overview, 268–69
    on banking sector, 76–80,
        87nn9–11
    benefits of, 34, 36–37, 126,
        269–70
    comparison of system in Chile
        and Peru, 175, 178t8.2
    concerns about, 270–75
    and coverage issues, 96–103,
        105nn2–8
    to decrease costs and
        commissions, 232–39,
        240–41t10.2, 264nn7–10
    features of
        1980s and 1990s, 23–25t2.1
        1990s and 2000s, 26–27t2.2
    in financial sector, 64–66b4.1
    and fiscal positions of
        governments, 7–8
    impact of risks and
        macroeconomic concerns on,
        50–54, 55nn6–7, 55nn9–11
    impact on economic growth, 46,
        49–50, 51
    impact on other benefits, 37n1
    impact on private sector
        securities, 80–84, 87n12
    improvement of equity of,
        91f5.1
    incentive effects, 101, 102t5.1,
        103
    and increase in coverage,
        97–98b5.2
    and individualization of social
        security, 11, 114
    inequitable effects of social
        security and reform progress,
        89–93
    and longevity risk management
        of, 129, 243–44t10.3, 245
    multipillar approach to, 1, 4,
        15n1
    options to reduce operational
        costs, 235–36t10.1

progress in Latin America, 4–9,
    15nn4–6
and risk management, 239,
    242–47, 264n11–12
simulated fiscal impact of,
    40–44, 58nn2–3, 59n4
success of, 4–5
taxonomy of, 20–30, 37n7,
    37nn2–5, 38n8
voluntary savings plans, 258–61,
    265n18
regulations
    asset management practices,
        70–71
    insurance companies, 257,
        258f10.6
    investment strategies, 53, 59–60,
        82, 83, 87nn3–6, 131–32,
        161–62n6
    of mutual funds, 253, 253–54
    of pension fund administrators,
        57–59, 68, 86n1, 87n2
    portfolio floors, 62t4.2
retirement
    charge ratio at, 146–47,
        148f7.7, 162nn12–15
    choices at distribution stage,
        150–53, 154f7.9,
        162–63nn19–22
    and management fees, 146, 147,
        148f7.7, 162nn18
    withdrawal of funds prior to,
        259–60
retirement systems, investment in
    housing as substitute for,
    188, 194n13
Riester pensions, 265n14
risk-adjusted returns, 140
risk and risk management, 12, 126,
    130, 273, 279
    and choices at distribution stage,
        150–51
    comparison of, 137–38b7.4
    diversification of, 9
    faced by poorer households, 168
    government vs. households, 169,
        193n4

risk and risk management (*continued*)

of mandated retirement savings, 239, 242–47, 264*n*11–12

and measures of preference in Peru, 186–87, 187*f*8.5, 188*f*8.6

Mexico's pension reform, 51–52, 52*f*33.3

to old-age income security, 126–30, 161*nn*2–4

restrictions on, 155

and retirement income security systems, 126, 127*b*7.1

strategies for, 110*b*6.1

and structural pension reform, 50–54, 55*nn*6–7, 55*nn*9–11

see also pooling risk

risk aversion, 129

and choice of pension system, 191

measure of, 181–83, 184, 194*n*12

self-employed in Peru, 188*f*8.6

risk pooling

as mechanism to mitigate poverty in old age, 201

and minimum pension guarantees, 212–13, 224, 225*n*4

public options for, 209

risk ratings, 50, 51, 59

Rofman, Rafael, 103, 105*n*7, 150

S

Samaritan's dilemma, 95*b*5.1

Santiago, Chile, 176–77*b*8.1

Santiago Stock Exchange, 64*b*4.1, 70, 80

savings

costs to affiliates of, 143–50, 162*nn*9–18

as mainstay for earnings replacement, 11–12

vs. pooling, 9–10, 10*t*1.1, 11

see also mandatory savings plans

Schmidt-Hebbel, K., 49, 53, 54, 119

second-pillar pensions, 122, 277, 278–79*b*11.1

accounts funded with defined contributions, 21

costs for poorer workers, 149*f*7.8

objective of, 9, 15*n*8, 37*n*4

reform options to reduce operational costs of, 235–36*t*10.1

see also consumption smoothing; contribution rates; mandatory savings plans

securities markets, reforms in, 65*b*4.1

self-employed workers, 193*n*6

and contributions, 105*n*3

and mandatory pension plans, 237–38

and participation choices, 175

and risk preferences, 181–83, 187*f*8.5, 188*f*8.6, 194*n*12

self-insurance, 113*b*6.2

self-protection, 113*b*6.2

set-up costs, 143

shareholders, 71

and AFPs, 58

of companies traded in stock market, 119

rights of, 65*b*4.1, 81

Shinkai, Naoko, 170, 193*n*5

simulations

of fiscal impact of reform, 40–44, 58*nn*2–3, 59*n*4

interpretations of results, 44–46, 47*b*3.2

social exclusion, and participation rates, 166–70, 192–93*nn*3–4

social insurance system, coverage problems, 95–96*b*5.1, 96

Social Risk Management Survey, 175, 176–77*b*8.1

social security reform. *see* reforms

Specialized Retirement Fund Investment Societies, 76

Srinivas, P.S., 140

Standard & Poor's index, 140
Stiglitz, Joseph E., 99
stock market
    capitalization of, 80
    liquidity of and pension fund
        investment, 80–83, 87n12
subordinated bonds, 83
subsidies
    flat contribution, 208b9.1
    and funded systems, 31
    for home purchase, 87n9
    and savings plans, 247–48,
        265n14
supply-side measures, to reduce
        costs, 233–34
survivor insurance, 31, 38n11,
        38n13, 105n4
swap of bonds, 134b7.3
Sweden, 238, 239, 264n10

T
targeted benefits, 219, 222
targeted pensions, 206–07, 209–11
taxation
    after-tax returns, 66b4.1
    Cuenta 2 plan, 259
    expenditure tax, 247,
        264–65n13
    and mandatory savings,
        31–32
    and mutual fund savings, 253
    and perceived benefits and
        contribution link, 98–99
    reforms in, 66b4.1
    tax liability and retirement
        savings, 247
    and voluntary savings plans,
        248, 249–50
tax-preferred voluntary retirement
        savings, 34
Telmex, 82–83
third-pillar pensions, 122
    and defining incentives, 21
    objective of, 9, 37n4
    see also consumption
        smoothing; incentives;
        voluntary savings plans

three-fund systems, 242, 245,
        264n11
thrift savings plans (TSPs), 242
time preference rate, 168, 183
transaction costs, in securities
        markets, 80
transition costs, 132, 262
    Bolivia, 44, 45–46b3.1
    financing of, 53, 55n9
transition debt, 69–70, 87n7
transparency, 71, 85
    Bolivia, 87n3
    commission structure, 260
    and company pension plans,
        234
    of costs and benefits of financial
        products, 247
    of fees, 239
    and mutual funds, 253
treasury bonds, 73
Tressel, Thierry, 78
Truglia, V., 50
TSPs. *see* thrift savings plans (TSPs)
turnover ratios, 80–81, 81f4.3

U
unidad de fomento (UF), 71–75, 77
unisex mortality tables, 93
United Kingdom, 239
United States, 242, 264n7
universal benefits, 206–07, 209–11,
        219, 222
Uruguay, 4, 72, 99
    commission structure, 144
    corporate bond market, 84
    demographics, 19
    distribution choices, 152–53
    investments
        choices, 160
        investment risk, 155
        in mutual funds, 84
        of pension funds, 59–60, 60
        in private sector, 67
    and IPDs, 40f3.1, 41
    mandatory savings plans, 31
    noncontributory poverty
        prevention pensions, 216t9.3

Uruguay (*continued*)
  pension deficits, 41, 42*t*3.1, 43, 43*f*3.2
  pension fund managers, 33
  and pension guarantees, 33
  portfolios, 62*t*4.2, 137–38*b*7.4
  and poverty prevention, 264*n*2
  reforms to social security in, 20–22, 23–25*t*2.1, 28, 29, 37*n*7
  transition debt, 69, 70
  voluntary savings plans, 36*t*2.4
Uthoff, Andras, 66*b*4.1

V
VAC. *see valor adquisitivo constante* (VAC)
Valdés-Prieto, Salvador, 103, 141, 163*n*21, 194–95*n*16
  age-related contributions, 264*n*3
  and mandated savings, 116, 237
valor adquisitivo constante (VAC), 77–78
valuation mechanisms, 59, 87*n*4
Venezuela, life insurance policyholders, 257
venture capital, 84
voluntary savings plans, 8, 13, 125, 161*n*1, 228, 237
  Brazil, 250–51*b*10.2
  improving of, 247–51, 258–61, 264–65*nn*13–14, 265*n*18
  and life insurance industry, 256–57, 258*f*10.6
  and mutual funds, 251–56, 265*nn*15–17
  structure and implementation of, 34, 35–36*t*2.4
  taxation of, 248

W
wage employees. *see* workers
wage-indexed government bonds, 128*b*7.2
wages, 162*n*13
  and cost of providing pension equal to minimum wage, 220–21*t*9.5
  and costs of pension fund administration, 148–49, 162*n*17
  and mandatory savings plans, 31
  maximum taxable, 232
  minimum wages as share of average wages, 218–19, 218*t*9.4
  relationship to benefits, 164*n*22
  setting minimum pension benefits at minimum wage, 218–19
Walker, E., 70, 71, 80, 254
Washington Consensus model, 267
wealth, accumulated, 201, 204*f*9.2
Whitehouse, Edward, 143, 201
Willmore, Larry, 209, 211
withdrawals, restrictions on, 265*n*16
women
  contribution histories, 193*n*8
  losses in rates of return, 92–95
Wong, R., 91
workers
  commissions on pension funds, 144, 145*t*7.3
  contribution behavior, 170–75, 193*nn*5–6, 211–12
  contribution histories, 183–85
  costs of participation in second pillar, 149*f*7.8
  disposable income of, 253
  and distribution choices, 150–53
  and foreign investors, 82, 87*n*12
  impact of mandatory savings on life cycle needs, 229–32, 263–64*nn*1–4
  improvident, 230, 232
  inequitable impact of pension benefits on, 93–96
  and management fees, 146, 147, 148*f*7.7
  participation rates as social exclusion or individual choice, 166–70, 192–93*nn*3–4
  and policy risk protection, 133–35*b*7.3